THE EUROPEAN ECONOMY
1914–1990

Economically, at least, the start of the 1990s has been less than auspicious. Amid growing fears of a slump to match the 1930s, for many, the feeling must be one of deja-vu. Yet despite the vicissitudes of the twentieth century, the European economy has proved remarkably resilient, and history does not suggest that current problems will prove insoluble.

As with the earlier edition, *The European Economy 1914–1980*, in this new updated and revised volume, Professor Aldcroft presents a succinct and lucid summary of this past. He examines the economic development of Europe between 1914 and 1990 and provides a broad survey of the main economic trends and forces which have been at work this century. The text divides into clearly defined periods: from the depression of the 1920s and 1930s; the upset of two world wars; the post-war boom; through the oil crises and recurrent inflation and unemployment. This new edition of *The European Economy 1914–1980* has been modified to take account of the decade 1980–90, and as such covers some of the most dramatic and profound economic events of the twentieth century. The work includes two additional chapters, one dealing with the western European economies, and in particular, the fight against inflation and unemployment, which have largely dominated the period. The author also considers the impact of growing economic convergence. Chapter 9 assesses the astounding events in eastern Europe and the initial movements towards the establishment of market economies. Ultimately, *The European Economy 1914–1990* presents an invaluable guide to the major economic developments of the twentieth century.

Derek Aldcroft is professor of economic history at the University of Leicester. He is also editor of the *Routledge European Economies* series.

THE EUROPEAN ECONOMY 1914–1990

3rd Edition

Derek H. Aldcroft

London and New York

First published 1978 by Croom Helm Ltd
Reprinted 1980, 1981, 1982, 1986 and 1987
Reprinted by Routledge 1989

This third edition first published 1993
by Routledge
11 New Fetter Lane, London EC4P 4EE

Simultaneously published in the USA and Canada
by Routledge
29 West 35th Street, New York, NY 10001

Typeset in Baskerville
by Pat and Anne Murphy, Highcliffe-on-Sea, Dorset
Printed and bound in Great Britain by
by Mackays of Chatham PLC, Chatham, Kent

British Library Cataloguing in Publication Data
A catalogue record for this book is available from
the British Library.
ISBN 0–415–09587–5
ISBN 0–415–09160–8 Pbk

Library of Congress Cataloging-in-Publication Data
Aldcroft, Derek Howard.
The European economy, 1914–1990/Derek H. Aldcroft. –
3rd ed., updated and rev.
p.   cm.
Rev. ed. of: The European economy, 1914–1980.
2nd ed., c1980.
Includes bibliographical references and index.
ISBN 0–415–09587–5. – ISBN 0–415–09160–8 (pbk.)
1. Europe – Economic conditions – 20th century.
I. Aldcroft, Derek Howard. European economy, 1914–1980.
II. Title.
HC240.A6657   1993   330.94′05–dc20
92-38193 CIP

CONTENTS

LIST OF FIGURES AND TABLES

FIGURE

TABLES

INTRODUCTION

Both politically and economically the twentieth century has been, to date, far more turbulent than the nineteenth. Two world wars and a great depression are sufficient to substantiate this claim. And if the 1950s and 1960s seem by comparison relatively stable, more recent events suggest that this may not necessarily be the natural order of things.

The liberal and fairly stable order of the first decade or so of the present century was rudely shattered by the outbreak of the First World War. Up to that time international development and political relations, though subject to strains of a minor nature from time to time, had never been seriously exposed to an external shock of such violent magnitude. Unfortunately at the time few people realized what a lengthy war it was going to be, and even fewer appreciated what an enormous impact it was going to have on economic and social relationships. Moreover, there was a general feeling, accepted readily in establishment circles, that after the period of hostilities it would be possible to resume where one had left off – in other words to recreate the *belle époque* of the Edwardian era.

This was not to be, however, though for nearly a decade statesmen strove to get back to what they regarded as 'normalcy'. In itself this was one of the profound mistakes of the first post-war decade, since it should have been clear that the war and post-war clearing-up operations had shattered Europe's former equipoise and had sapped her strength to a point where the economic system had become vulnerable to external shocks. Moreover, it was not only in the economic field that her strength had been eroded; both politically and socially Europe was weakened and many countries in the early post-war years were on the verge of social upheaval.

For the most part Europe's economic and political fragility was ignored in the 1920s, out of ignorance rather than intent. In trying to resurrect the pre-war system statesmen believed they were providing a solution, and the fact that Europe shared in the prosperity of the later 1920s seemed to indicate that their judgement had not been misplaced. But as soon as the bubble of prosperity burst in 1929 the vulnerability of the European economy became apparent. The structural supports were too weak to withstand violent shock and so the edifice came tumbling down.

1

It is not surprising therefore that the years 1929–32 saw one of the worst depressions in history. Nor given the state of economic science at the time is it surprising that governments adopted policies which only served to worsen the crisis. Moreover, the policies adopted tended to be of a protective nature designed to insulate domestic economies from the influence of external events. When recovery came in 1933 it owed relatively little to policy considerations, though subsequently some governments did attempt more ambitious programmes of stimulation. But recovery, at least in terms of employment generation, was slow and patchy so that even by 1937 many countries were still operating well below their resource capacity. The gap was subsequently closed by rearmament and the outbreak of war.

Europe entered the Second World War in a relatively weaker state than in 1914, and she subsequently emerged from it in 1945 in a more prostrate condition than in 1918. Certainly in terms of the loss of life, physical destruction and decline in living standards Europe's position was much worse than after the First World War. On the other hand, both during the war and in the post-war reconstruction phase of the late 1940s some of the mistakes and blunders of the earlier experience were avoided. Inflation was contained much more readily between 1939 and 1945 and the violent inflations of the early 1920s were not for the most part perpetuated in the aftermath of the Second World War. The map of Europe was divided much more clearly and neatly (with the exception of Berlin) than had been the case after 1918, even though it resulted in two power blocs, the east and the west. The vanquished were not burdened by unreasonable exactions which had been the cause of so much bitterness and squabbling in the 1920s. Finally, governments no longer looked backwards to the halcyon pre-war days; this time it was planning for the future which occupied their attention. This line of thought was reflected in the commitment to maintain full employment and all that this entailed in terms of growth and stability. On a wider plane it also found positive expression in the readiness to co-operate internationally to further reconstruction, and the liberal American aid programme of the later 1940s was a concrete manifestation of the new approach.

Thus by the early 1950s Europe had recovered sufficiently to be in a position to look to the future with confidence. During the next two decades her record of economic advancement was better than anything previously recorded, and this is true of both western and eastern Europe. The latter forged ahead under a planned regime, while the western democracies achieved their successes under a mixed enterprise system with varying degrees of market freedom. In both cases, however, the state played a much more important role than hitherto, and neither system was free of problems. The planning mechanism in eastern Europe functioned less smoothly than its proponents anticipated with the result that it had to be modified in due course. The market system of the west also seemingly failed to register the right results on occasions so that governments were forced to interfere to an increasing extent.

2

The biggest problem was trying to achieve a series of objectives – full employment, price stability, growth and stability and external equilibrium – simultaneously. In practice it proved impossible given the policy weapons available to governments.

Despite what seemed to be incompatible objectives there was little cause for serious alarm throughout the period. It is true that there were minor lapses from full employment; fluctuations still occurred but these were very moderate and took the form of growth cycles; some countries experienced balance of payments problems, while prices rose continuously though at moderate annual rates. But such lapses could be accommodated within an economic system that was growing rapidly. By the late 1960s it seemed that Europe had entered a phase of perpetual prosperity akin to what the Americans had conceived in the 1920s. It was not very long before that particular illusion was shattered. By 1973–4 the growth trend had been reversed, the business cycle had reappeared and most western governments were experiencing inflation at a rate higher than at any time in the last half century.

The chapters which follow examine Europe's development since 1914 along the lines indicated above. They are designed to show the main trends in that development and the forces which have determined it. Since the study is designed primarily as an introductory overview it will of necessity deal in fairly broad aggregates. Readers who wish to enquire further into specific areas or topics are referred to the chapter reading lists at the end of the book.

1

THE END OF THE OLD REGIME,
1914–1921

INTRODUCTION

During the nineteenth century the European continent – taken here to include Britain at one extreme in the west to Russia in the east – had experienced substantial economic development. Few countries had failed to be affected in some way by the forces of modern economic growth which had had their origins in the northwest corner of the continent. As Pollard rightly points out, the development process may be seen as a general European phenomenon transcending national frontiers rather than as something confined to the geographic boundaries of a few states. On the other hand, economic growth was very uneven in its incidence, while in comparison with more recent times rates of economic growth were quite modest. The centre of progress was undoubtedly in northwest Europe – Britain, France, Germany, Belgium, Holland – whence it spread south and east through the rest of the continent getting weaker the further it moved from the point of origin. It is true that in the later nineteenth century and through to 1914 the pace of economic change was quite rapid in some of the lesser developed countries, notably Italy, Austria and Russia. Even so, by the eve of the First World War most of the countries of east and southeast Europe remained very backward in comparison with the northwest. Incomes per head on average in southern and eastern Europe were one half or less those in the northwest and in some cases, for example Bulgaria, Romania, Spain and Greece, they were but a fraction of those prevailing in the most developed sector of the continent. In fact, an income contour map for Europe would show (with minor exceptions) income contour lines of steadily diminishing strength as one moved south and east from the 'high pressure' zone of advanced development.

Though eastern and southern Europe undoubtedly benefited from the transmission of growth forces from the point of origin, modern capitalism found more fertile ground in some overseas territories, particularly in North America and Oceania, than it did elsewhere in Europe. The former areas were more receptive to the flows of European capital, labour and technology, so much so that by 1913 incomes per head were already above those in northwest

Europe. What is more, these three areas – northwest Europe, North America and Oceania, more especially the first two – monopolized modern economic development. They accounted for the bulk of the world's manufacturing production and though containing only 18 per cent of the world's population they accounted for nearly 62 per cent of global income.

To a certain extent Europe's position was already being challenged by developments overseas, more especially by the rapid rise in the economic strength of the United States. But the threat to European supremacy was not at this stage serious, since in many respects developments in both continents were partly complementary. Moreover, the world order of the pre-war period was such as to ensure the survival of both parties. The strength of pre-war capitalist development rested on the freedom with which resources could be transferred between nations, the ease with which the industrial nations of the centre, especially northwest Europe, could draw upon the primary resources (food and raw materials) of the periphery – mainly but not exclusively the less developed nations – and the fact that there was no serious disparity in the rate of economic progress among the major industrial countries. The latter point is important since it was this rather than the commonly alleged virtues of the international gold standard which gave the pre-war system a measure of stability, a stability which was regarded with some nostalgia in the years of disequilibrium following the First World War.

What would have happened to this set-up had the 1914–18 war not intervened is a debatable counterfactual proposition which will no doubt be put to the test in the course of time. One can say with certainty, however, that the war affected Europe's economic position adversely. Europe emerged from the war in a seriously weakened state and with a residue of problems that were to plague it and the international economy for much of the inter-war period. But whether the war can be blamed for all the difficulties of that period or whether it can be regarded as a direct cause of the slump of 1929–32 are matters which will be taken up at a later point in this study. Some of the more immediate consequences of the war must be considered first.

Given the scale of the European war it is hardly surprising that the consequences were far-reaching. Resource mobilization exceeded anything previously known. Altogether more than 60 million men were drafted into the armed services during the four years or so of hostilities and in all belligerent countries there was extensive control of economic activity especially in the latter half of the period. The details of wartime operations and resource mobilization need not concern us here since the primary interest is to determine the main consequences of war, and more especially those which have a bearing on subsequent events in the 1920s and early 1930s.

It is important, however, to distinguish between the direct economic consequences of war and the policy actions of the Allied governments in the immediate aftermath. The war itself gave rise to manpower losses, physical destruction, financial disorganization, a contraction in output and unstable

5

social and political conditions. Given the weakened state of many countries, especially in central and eastern Europe, the process of reconstruction and recovery required the assistance of the Allied powers, the United States in particular. In fact, as we shall see, not only was the amount of direct assistance forthcoming minimal, but the process of reconstruction was hindered by the peace treaty settlements and the policies adopted to deal with the boom of 1919–20.

POPULATION LOSSES

It is difficult to make an exact count of the population losses arising from the war. This is partly because the data for the period are far from perfect but also because military casualties were but a small proportion of the total number of deaths recorded in the period. Many more people died of starvation and disease, or as a result of civil war, than on the battlefield. In addition, some estimate must be made of the population deficit caused by the shortfall in births as a result of wartime conditions. The Russian statistics are notoriously difficult to interpret.

Military casualties were quite small in relative terms. During the period of hostilities some 8.5 million men (including tentative guesses for Russia) lost their lives in active service, that is, about 15 per cent of those mobilized for duty. This was equivalent to less than 2 per cent of the total European population and about 8 per cent of all male workers. In addition, some 7 million men were permanently disabled and a further 15 million more or less seriously wounded.

The incidence of fatalities varied considerably although obviously the belligerents were the main sufferers. The largest absolute losses were in Germany and Russia with 2 and 1.7 million respectively; France lost 1.4 million, Austria-Hungary 1.2 million and the UK and Italy almost three-quarters of a million each. Some of the smaller countries such as Romania (250,000) and Serbia and Montenegro (325,000) also suffered badly. In most cases, however, the proportionate impact in terms of population was quite small. Of the major powers France was the chief loser with 3.3 per cent of the population decapitated through military action; Germany was not far behind with 3 per cent; in most other cases the proportion was 2 per cent or less. In fact in relative terms the smaller countries came off worst generally; Serbia and Montenegro, for example, lost 10 per cent of their population.

The impact of course was greater than the absolute figures indicate since most of the persons killed were in the prime of their life and therefore constituted the most productive part of the labour force. In the case of Germany, 40 per cent of the casualties fell within the age group 20–24 and 63 per cent were between 20 and 30 years old. Both France and Germany lost about 10 per cent of their male workers, Italy 6 per cent and Britain 5 per cent. On the other hand, callous as it may sound, the losses may have been something of a blessing in disguise given the limited employment opportunities which were to eventuate in the inter-war period.

Civilian losses are more difficult to determine; these arose from several causes including disease, famine, privation as well as military conflict, the assumption being that they would not have occurred but for the war. War-induced deaths of civilians probably amounted to about 5 million in Europe excluding Russia, with Austria-Hungary, Germany and Italy bearing the brunt of the burden in absolute terms, though once again Serbia and Montenegro experienced the greatest relative impact.

Adding together military and civilian deaths gives a combined death toll for Europe excluding Russia in the region of 12 million, of which just over 6.5 million were due to military causes. This amounted to some 3.5 per cent of Europe's pre-war population. Germany and Austria-Hungary had the largest absolute losses, while in relative terms mortality ranged from about 1 per cent in Scandinavia to as much as 20 per cent in Serbia. France, Italy, Germany and Austria-Hungary lost about 4 per cent of their population, and the UK and Belgium under 2.5 per cent.

Account must also be taken of the birth deficits or numbers of unborn arising from wartime conditions. Some of the belligerents recorded very high birth deficits: Austria-Hungary 3.6 million, Germany 3 million. France and Italy had deficits of about 1.5 million, Britain 700,000 and Romania just over 500,000. Altogether the population loss from this cause was similar to the combined figure for military and civilian deaths.

The combined tally of the European population deficit therefore amounts to between 22 and 24 million people. This was equivalent to 7 per cent of Europe's pre-war population, or the whole of her natural increase between 1914 and 1919. Thus at the beginning of 1920 Europe's population was about the same as it was at the start of the war. The largest absolute losses were incurred by Germany and Austria-Hungary with over 5 million apiece, but in relative terms Serbia and Montenegro were by far the worst sufferers with deficits approaching one-third of their pre-war population. The neutral powers fared best with losses of 2 per cent or less. Of the Allied powers, France and Italy bore the brunt of the burden. France's population deficit amounted to just over 3 million, or 7.7 per cent of her pre-war population. This includes a shortfall of some 1.4 million in births as a result of a dramatic decline in her birth rate. The net result was that by the middle of 1919 France's population, at 38.7 million, was some 1.1 million lower than in 1914 even with the inclusion of Alsace-Lorraine which she had recovered from Germany.

The figures for Russia are much less reliable though it is probable that losses in this country exceeded the combined total for the rest of Europe. Military casualties in the Great War itself were relatively small but millions died in the subsequent revolution and civil war. The total toll was not far short of 16 million. Add to this some 10 million for birth deficits and one gets a figure of 26 million, and even this takes no account of the losses in the territories ceded by Russia as a result of the peace treaty concluded with Germany in 1918.

Europe therefore suffered a serious depletion and deterioration in quality of population during the war period. Moreover, the figures cited are not strictly complete since further losses, arising from causes associated with the war, occurred in the post-armistice period. The influenza epidemic of 1918–19 claimed many victims, while substantial numbers of people died in eastern Europe and the Balkans as a result of famine. Post-war border conflicts and massacres between 1919 and 1921, especially in southeastern Europe, added further to the toll.

In sum, therefore, the final casualty list for the whole war period, 1914–21, runs into many millions. An approximate figure would be between 50 and 60 million with Russia accounting for around one-half. Direct military deaths in the war proper formed only a small proportion of the total population loss in this period.

In human terms the disaster can be regarded as nothing short of tragic. But it is doubtful whether the loss had a severe or lasting impact on the countries concerned. Most countries of course lost some of their best manpower, often highly skilled, but few, apart from France, suffered from labour shortages in the decade following the war. Indeed, as it turned out, the post-war period was marked by high unemployment in many European countries and so it could be argued that the check to population growth was something of a mixed blessing.

PHYSICAL DESTRUCTION AND CAPITAL LOSSES

Capital losses are even less easy to estimate with accuracy than those of population. The value of Europe's capital stock undoubtedly deteriorated during the war as a result of physical damage, the sale of foreign assets, the check to investment and the neglect of maintenance. Stamp calculated that the war destroyed some three to four years' normal growth of income-yielding property in Europe (excluding Russia), or one part in thirty of its original value, and to this must be added an unknown quantity for the deterioration of the existing capital stock due to neglect or lack of maintenance. Europe also lost about one-thirtieth of her fixed assets as a result of destruction and physical damage, while some countries, notably France and Germany, relinquished most of their foreign investments. In addition, of course, some countries sacrificed territory and property under the peace treaty settlements. This aspect is discussed separately in a later section.

The incidence of the destructive impact varied considerably from country to country. The neutral countries – Scandinavia, the Netherlands, Switzerland and Spain – escaped unscathed and in some cases were in better physical shape in 1919 than at the beginning of the war. Most of the belligerent countries, on the other hand, experienced substantial cuts in investment with the result that their capital stocks were lower at the end of hostilities. Physical damage was greatest in the main theatres of war, especially in France and Belgium, though Italy, Russia and some eastern European countries also fared badly. By comparison Britain, Austria and Germany, though major belligerents, got off fairly lightly. Bulgaria too did much better than her neighbours on the Balkan peninsula since the country never became a war zone and so avoided severe destruction or despoliation of property.

The occupied territories undoubtedly fared the worst since they shared the privations of the central empires while at the same time they were exploited to the utmost for the good of their temporary masters. It was inevitable that Belgium and France should bear the main burden given that much of the fighting occurred on their land. Destruction of farms, factories and houses was widespread and substantial in both cases, though in France most of the physical damage tended to be concentrated in the north of the country. Belgium was less fortunate. Practically the whole of the country was invaded and the list of damage makes dismal reading. About 6 per cent of the housing stock, half the steel mills and three-quarters of the railway rolling stock were destroyed or smashed beyond repair, thousands of acres of land were rendered unfit for cultivation, while the animal population was decimated. Though geographically concentrated, France's losses were severe and they occurred in the richest and most advanced part of the country.

In absolute terms these two countries accounted for the bulk of the wartime property losses. Yet in relative terms some of the smaller countries further east probably emerged from the war in an even more devastated condition. The value of property lost by Poland was only a little less than that of Germany but the impact was very much greater. The occupying powers literally devastated the country by destruction and looting. Large tracts of good agricultural land were laid waste, 60 per cent of the cattle stock disappeared, much of the railway rolling stock was taken, many factories were either destroyed or denuded of equipment, and 1.8 million buildings were lost by fire. The same story could be told of Serbia, parts of Austria and also of Russia, though in the latter case much of the damage occurred as a result of the civil war. In fact, in some areas the scale of destruction was so great that the question of repair could scarcely be considered; rather it was a matter of clearing the land and rebuilding from scratch.

Elsewhere the physical damage was far lighter, though most countries had a substantial backlog of investment to work off. Germany lost few domestic assets but most of her foreign assets were either sold or seized and she was to pay a heavy price in reparations for her transgression. Most of Britain's physical losses consisted of shipping though she did sell a small portion of her overseas investments to pay for the war. France lost about two-thirds of her pre-war foreign assets by sale, default, as in the case of Russian investments, or through inflation.

The task of reconstruction was certainly a substantial one and in some countries it could only be accomplished by a resort to inflationary financing.

However, the process of European recovery as a whole was made more difficult by the fact that the peace treaty settlements imposed heavy penalties on the vanquished and proceeded to carve up the map of Europe in a manner detrimental to the economic well-being of that continent.

FINANCIAL LEGACIES OF WAR

The financial implications of the First World War were more serious than those of the Second. Essentially this was because the method of financial control was much laxer in the first case, and not because the scale of military operations was greater – in fact it was the reverse. The total direct cost was of course large – some 260 billion dollars if all the belligerents are included – though the absolute figures do not have a great deal of meaning. The largest expenditures were incurred by Britain, the United States, Germany, France, Austria-Hungary and Italy in that order. An idea of the magnitude of the total outlay can be gained from the fact that it represented about six and a half times the sum of all the national debt accumulated in the world from the end of the eighteenth century up to the eve of the First World War.

The size of the war-expenditure programme is not particularly significant though one could naturally point to the more fruitful and constructive ways in which the money might have been spent. What matters is the way the spending was financed. Almost overnight governments hastily abandoned the sound financial orthodoxy of the nineteenth century which meant abandonment of the discipline of the gold standard and a resort to deficit financing. Credit operations of one sort or another rather than taxation were the main source of war finance. Germany and France, for example, relied almost entirely on borrowing, while even in the United States only just over 23 per cent of war expenditures was derived from revenue sources. On average, some 80 per cent or more of the total war expenditure of the belligerents was financed by borrowing. This method of financing the war need not have been unduly inflationary had the loans been derived from genuine savings, but in fact much of the finance was raised through bank credit. Banks either granted loans to governments by the creation of new money or else received 'promises to pay' from the governments and then proceeded to increase the supply of money using the promises as reserves. The details of the mechanism varied from one country to another but the end result was much the same. Public debts rose rapidly with the proportion of short-term debt rising as time went on, the money supply was increased considerably, and the banks' metallic reserves in relation to liabilities fell sharply. By the end of 1918 the German money supply had risen ninefold, the budget deficit six times, while the ratio of metallic reserves to bank notes and deposits had declined from 57 to 10 per cent. The situation was even worse in the case of the Austro-Hungarian Empire, while France and Belgium also fared badly. In general, the deterioration in financial conditions was most acute in central European countries, least acute in the neutral countries and of moderate extent else-where.

Such conditions automatically gave rise to price inflation and currency depreciation, since nearly all countries abandoned the fixed parities of the gold standard either during the war or shortly thereafter. Inflation was much more rapid than during the tighter financial regime of the Second World War. Most countries experienced a doubling or trebling of prices, and in some cases much more, depending upon the degree of monetary inflation. For example, whole-sale prices in Germany at the end of hostilities were five times the pre-war level, while the mark had declined to 50 per cent of its former value. Austria and Hungary experienced even greater inflation with currency values falling to between 30 and 40 per cent of the original parity. Other countries whose currencies had begun to depreciate significantly were Finland, France, Italy, Belgium and Portugal. Most of the neutrals, on the other hand, managed to retain or improve the value of their currencies despite significant degrees of inflation.

The implications of the wartime financial arrangements are important and will be taken up in greater detail later. At the end of the war the inflationary problems were not for the most part unmanageable, with the possible exceptions of those of Germany and Austria-Hungary. However, they were made worse in the first year or so of peace by continued lax monetary and fiscal policies. The policy turning-point came in 1920 when several countries, the United States, Britain and Sweden in particular, imposed savage retrench-ment policies which adversely affected their domestic economies and made recovery in the rest of Europe that much more difficult. Most European coun-tries, however, continued to inflate, with disastrous consequences for some, notably Germany, Austria, Poland and Hungary. Second, currency insta-bility hindered the process of recovery, while the failure of governments to accept the decline in currency values and the abandonment of gold as anything but temporary eventually led to a disorganized attempt to try to restore the pre-war monetary system in quite different conditions. Third, reference may be made to the complex series of inter-governmental debts contracted among the Allies and the reparations burdens imposed on the vanquished, which not only proved a source of international friction throughout the 1920s but also hampered the process of financial reconstruction.

EUROPE'S ECONOMIC DECLINE

Perhaps more serious than war losses and destruction from the long-term point of view was the severe check to European income and output growth during the war, and the fact that from this point in time Europe's position in the world economy began to decline. Nearly all countries experienced a decline in output despite the exertions on the war front and at the end of hostilities the stock of productive assets was in poor shape. At the same time many European countries became dependent on external sources of supply and finance, while some were forced to sell both domestic and foreign assets. In a global context the United States of course was the main beneficiary of war, and she in turn helped to finance the Allied cause and later became a source for European loans. However, the United States was not the only country to gain from the ordeal. Many countries on the periphery of the international economy received a stimulus from wartime demand for food and raw materials, while the shortage of manufactured goods in Europe accelerated the process of industrial development in overseas countries.

By the end of the war the world as a whole was certainly worse off than in 1913–14 even though some countries, such as the United States and Japan, had considerably surpassed their pre-war levels of production. But in terms of output and income the brunt of the burden fell on Europe. Svennilson has calculated that if there had been no war and the 1881–1913 European rate of industrial output growth had been maintained (3.25 per cent per annum) then the 1929 level of production would have been achieved in 1921. Thus, on a crude basis, it can be said that the war caused an eight-year setback to the growth of production.

Most countries suffered a reversal in the level of economic activity especially during the latter part of the war, and given the run-down condition of fixed assets together with the dislocation following the war, levels of economic activity in 1919 and 1920 were still some way below those of 1913. The extent of the shortfall varied from country to country. By far the worst performance was recorded by Russia where industrial output in 1920 was down to about 13 per cent of the 1913 figure. Here there were special circumstances to account for the disastrous performance, in particular the continuing border conflicts, the repercussions of the civil war through 1920, and the general chaos and mismanagement of the new Soviet regime. Indeed, the economy was in a state of complete collapse in 1920, and with justification Nove has referred to this period as one of 'nightmare conditions'.

No other country could match this record but many did experience a severe check to growth in the later years of war. Even by 1920 industrial output in Germany, France, Belgium, Bulgaria, Poland, Czechoslovakia, Austria, Hungary, Romania and Latvia was at least 30 per cent lower than in 1913. Yet even this was an improvement from the position prevailing immediately after the war, when in central and eastern Europe industrial production was about 50 to 60 per cent less than pre-war. Agricultural activity held up somewhat better though even here there was a serious shortfall. Production was about one-third below normal in continental Europe, though in some of the devastated regions in France, Belgium and eastern Europe the decline was considerably greater.

Most of the neutrals and one or two other countries fared somewhat better. Both Britain and Italy managed to regain their 1913 levels of output in 1920. Sweden, Norway and Switzerland did much better, however, and easily surpassed their previous peak levels of activity. The neutral countries, and Sweden in particular, benefited considerably from wartime demands, which caused a rapid expansion in heavy manufacturing and which gave rise to a number of innovations and new methods of production. For example, the metal shortage gave a boost to new methods of ore prospecting, the kerosene shortage accelerated the process of electrification, while the rapid break-through in lightweight metals can be attributed to the same cause. However, there were losses as well as gains in the neutral countries. Apparent prosperity was purchased at the expense of a sharp rise in the cost of living, a shortage of essential commodities and a stagnation or decline of certain trades and classes of exports.

Europe's output loss would not have mattered so much had not countries overseas gained at her expense. The two chief beneficiaries were the United States and Japan. American production was boosted sharply by Allied requirements and demand from countries formerly supplied by Europe. America therefore ended the war with a large excess balance in commodity trade. Furthermore, largely as a result of loans floated on behalf of the Euro-pean Allies and the liquidation of foreign holdings in the United States, America was transformed from net debtor status and became a large-scale creditor, a position which she strengthened during the course of the 1920s. Japan also emerged from the war in a much stronger position. Her participa-tion in the war was only marginal and she was therefore able to benefit from the opportunities opened up by the indisposition of the major belligerents. She became far more industrialized and technically mature, and, with a large increase in output to her credit, a creditor instead of a debtor nation. As a result Japan became a serious competitor in many markets formerly supplied by European countries.

Japanese competition was not the only source of worry for European indus-trial countries. In many lesser developed countries wartime shortages and suspension of competition had provided the opportunity to expand the industrial sector. Wherever one looks the story is the same: in the Far East, in Asia, in Latin America, in the White Dominions and even in parts of Africa, especially South Africa, acceleration in industrial activity can be discerned. Some of it of course was little more than hot-house growth which withered away when trading conditions returned to normal and foreign supply was resumed. Even so, there is little doubt that many formerly dependent countries had become industrially more self-sufficient by the end of the war to the detriment of the European exporting nations. To add to Europe's difficul-ties, at least later in the 1920s when agricultural output recovered, the war gave a big stimulus to primary production, both food and raw materials, in overseas countries. The expansion of cereal output in particular was to pose a serious problem for high-cost European producers later in the 1920s when overcapacity became endemic.

Thus the overall effect of the wartime check to activity was a shift in the

13

balance of economic power away from Europe towards the Americas and to a lesser extent the Pacific. In the inter-war years Europe never recovered her former economic power status. Much of the gain accrued to North America and Japan, though the war fostered sufficient interest in industrial activity in the lesser developed areas to ensure that import substitution and subsequently export competition would increase rather than diminish in the decades following, to the detriment of Europe. The extent of the shift in power can be appreciated from the figures for the distribution of world trade: by 1920 the Americas accounted for 32.1 per cent of world trade as against 22.4 per cent in 1913, while Asia's share rose from 12.1 to 13.4 per cent. By contrast the share of Europe and the USSR fell from 58.4 to 49.2 per cent over the same period.

STRUCTURAL PROBLEMS

Svennilson has suggested that the European economy suffered a prolonged structural transformation crisis during the inter-war period; growth was slowed down because of formidable structural problems which the war had thrown into relief. Only countries which adapted rapidly to new conditions could hope to achieve a satisfactory performance; Sweden might be cited as one of the few examples. But even these countries were not wholly immune to the more pervasive maladjustments arising out of the war, maladjustments in the international economic mechanism rather than simply problems of industrial structure with which Svennilson was most concerned.

In fact it could be argued that the dislocation of economic relationships caused by the war was far more serious than actual physical destruction. It disrupted former economic systems and partially destroyed the elaborate and often delicate trading connections of the nineteenth century. For example, the whole system of banking, credit and organization of money markets was suspended, controlled or modified during the war and had to be re-established or adjusted to new conditions. The delicate mechanism of the gold standard was abandoned and most currencies lost much of their former value and stability; indeed the problem of currency stabilization became one of the crucial issues in the post-war years. New problems in the form of large internal debts, war debts among the Allied powers and massive reparations imposed on the vanquished made the problem of currency stabilization an even more difficult one. Severe capital shortages in central and eastern Europe hampered the process of reconstruction which in turn accentuated the problem of currency stabilization. Furthermore, as we shall see, the redrawing of many boundaries in Europe entailed the recasting of trading connections and lines of transport, the adoption of new currencies and, in some cases, the entire replanning of economic systems.

During the war the productive effort of belligerent countries, and to a certain extent that of the neutrals, was directed to new purposes, new trading links were often hastily improvised and relations with former customers had to be severed. Many of the former trading links were lost for ever; others had to be painfully rekindled during the course of the 1920s at a time when import substitution and increasing protection made the going more difficult. Thus the trading operations of the Baltic ports, Riga, Revel and Narva, as suppliers of products to the Russian Empire and as entrepôt centres in the trade between Russia and western Europe were shattered beyond repair by 1918. Russia herself, the main source of some materials and an important supplier of timber and wheat, was cut off from the west after the civil war, only to re-emerge again late in the 1920s as an exporter at a time when her products were least required. The break-up of the Austro-Hungarian Empire dealt a serious blow to the economic relationships established within central Europe during the latter half of the nineteenth century and necessitated the creation of altogether new patterns of trade and exchange among the successor countries. Similar problems, as noted earlier, were encountered by European countries in their trading connections overseas.

One of the most serious and intractable problems of the inter-war period was that of excess capacity. Even before 1914 there were signs that some industrial countries in Europe were beginning to experience excess capacity in certain sectors, and that a process of structural transformation associated with new technologies was imminent. The war accelerated this process and at the same time brought several new factors into play. In the process of servicing the war machine certain sectors of activity became seriously over-expanded in relation to peacetime requirements, and unfortunately they were often the very sectors whose long-term growth potential was limited. Thus shipbuilding, iron and steel, some branches of engineering and coal were considerably expanded in the war with the result that excess capacity developed in the 1920s. World shipbuilding capacity, for example, almost doubled during the war and by the time the post-war boom was complete there was enough shipping space in existence to last a decade or more without further building. Iron and steel capacity of continental Europe and Britain was some 50 per cent higher by the mid-1920s than before the war, yet for much of the inter-war period output remained below the pre-war level. The coal industry was also affected adversely by a sharp deceleration in the growth of demand and the opening up of new seams on the continent. Moreover, the problem was by no means confined to Europe. Many countries overseas expanded their primary and industrial base in response to war demands and inevitably this posed a threat to European producers once production recovered. The situation was perhaps most serious with respect to primary products. The vast expansion of wheat production in North America and Australia and sugar in Cuba would have spelt ruin for high-cost European producers but for tariff protection.

The problem was aggravated of course by the fact that the war stimulated import substitution and economic nationalism. One of the most notable sufferers in this respect was the Lancashire cotton industry, but it was only one of many. The major industrial nations faced the same process over a wide range of manufactured commodities, and they were also participants in the game. The manufacture of dyestuffs provides a good illustration of this point. Before the war Germany produced over 80 per cent of the world output of dyes. When this source of supply was cut off during hostilities several countries, including Britain, France, Italy and Japan, were forced to increase their own output. Important dye industries were created and subsequently protected with the result that Germany's share of world production had fallen to 46 per cent by 1924.

Finally, new technical developments and the speeding up of the application of existing ones added to the structural problem and inevitably gave rise to redundant capacity in competing industries. The boost given to electricity and oil, the internal combustion engine and rayon are some of the more obvious examples, all of which had serious implications for the future prosperity of older staple industries. In the longer-term context aviation might also be mentioned, the feasibility of which became clearly apparent as a result of war-time aerial activities, but which did not present a real threat to surface and ocean transport until after the Second World War. The way in which the simultaneous emergence of a series of innovations and new methods together with a more rapid application of existing methods created tensions between new and old sectors of activity, thereby forcing a rapid and painful liquidation of the latter, is well illustrated by the Swedish case. Fortunately, Sweden accomplished the transformation process fairly quickly and hence avoided some of the more severe structural problems which were to confront the older capitalist countries during the inter-war period.

POLITICAL AND SOCIAL CHANGES

Though the immediate concern of this book is with economic matters it is important to stress that the war had important political and social consequences which were subsequently to influence, if not determine, the course of development in many European countries. Indeed it could scarcely be expected that political and social life would remain immune after a war of such magnitude. The great mixing of the social classes within the military ranks, the influx of women into industrial occupations, the strengthening of trade unionism and workers' participation in industry and the levelling effect of high taxation could hardly fail to have some impact on society.

In particular these changes found expression in the demand for more democratic government and greater equality. Inevitably the response fell short of the ideal but there can be little doubt that heightened social consciousness paved the way for improvements in the conditions of the less fortunate classes of society. Progress may at times have seemed slow but the lower classes stood to benefit in the long term from the increasing participation of the state in economic and social affairs. In turn this participation can be ascribed in part to the influence of war. It gave governments considerable experience in the management of economic affairs, and though most of the wartime control apparatus was hastily abandoned, the precedent for greater state participation had been set and partially accepted. Second, the war itself exposed some of the inequalities and social injustices present in most societies. Third, and perhaps most important, it raised the tolerance level of taxation. Although the high levels of wartime taxation were reduced, taxation rates never returned to their former peacetime levels; the displacement effect worked in favour of permanently higher levels of taxation. This gave governments much greater leverage in economic matters and provided a base for more extensive social reform than could have been achieved under pre-war fiscal systems.

In this respect, therefore, the war might be regarded as beneficial to society. However, in a wider context it can be argued that it had an adverse effect in that it seriously weakened the stability of existing social structures. For some people, of course, this was undoubtedly a gain since it accorded greater power to the lower orders, whose long-standing discontent was expressed forcibly once their position was strengthened. This paved the way for much upheaval and turmoil in society as the lower classes clashed with the once entrenched ruling establishment. Russia provides the best example in the sense that the political *coup* was a complete success, though economically it was disastrous in the short term. In this case the seeds of change had been sown long before 1914 though whether they would have born fruit so early, if at all, had it not been for the war is a debatable point. Elsewhere events were much less dramatic though some countries were close to social revolution in the immediate post-war period. The degree of success was generally limited and short-lived. Hungary spawned a communist dictatorship in 1919, while the existing regimes in Germany, Austria, Bulgaria and Turkey were deposed, though the replacements could scarcely be regarded as revolutionary. In Italy there was a wave of strikes, with workers occupying factories and farm estates, but again little was gained from the exercise. Strikes of course were commonplace within the western world and beyond in the aftermath of war. The growth in the size and importance of labour organizations during the war strengthened the power of the workers and gave rise to severe industrial unrest in most countries. France, Britain and the United States in particular were hit by massive strikes, some of them inspired by political motives, but for the most part the concrete achievements were either very limited or lost in the subsequent depression.

At the same time as new regimes emerged in central and eastern Europe there were widespread demands for land reform which envisaged the break-up of large estates and the redistribution of land to small impoverished farmers – the possible exception being Russia since the ultimate aim here was to liquidate the independent farmer. Altogether twelve European countries carried out agrarian reform and some 60 million acres or 11 per cent of the total territory was redistributed. More than half the acreage was allotted to former tenants, landless labourers and owners of small plots, one-quarter was acquired by the state and the remainder was retained by the former landlords. The area redistributed was greatest in Latvia and Romania, approximately 42 per cent and 30 per cent respectively, and least in Finland and Bulgaria, about 2 per cent.

Few countries escaped social and political disturbance in these years. The important point is not the degree of success achieved, which was generally fairly small, but the fact that the social fabric of society was weakened by such events. It gave rise to weak governments and inevitably to policies which impeded reconstruction and economic progress. For example, the movement against the forces of reaction in Germany led to a series of weak governments under the Weimar Republic which were powerless to stem the tide of inflation. Similarly, the political upheavals in Bulgaria resulted in policies – notably victimization of owners of wealth and capital – which penalized economic initiative and thereby paralysed the forces of economic recovery. Nor did the land ownership reforms in the east bring immediate economic benefits. Indeed, because of the fragmentation of holdings, the marketable surpluses of agricultural products often fell after the completion of reform. Thus, however desirable in practice, it would probably be true to say that on balance the move towards greater political and social equality was not in the best interests of the immediate task of recovery.

POST-WAR POLICY REVERSALS

There can be little doubt that the war left Europe in a seriously weakened state. Few countries escaped unscathed from its influence and for many countries the task of reconstruction and recovery was substantial. At the time of the armistice few statesmen of the world appreciated fully the enormity of the economic problems which the war had left behind. It was generally believed, moreover, that such problems as there were would soon disappear once things got back to normal, and getting back to normal meant recreating the world that had been lost. Thus in contrast to the position after 1945, when economic conditions were far worse, governments vainly sought to move back into the past without realizing that there could be no return given the substantially changed conditions. Only by the time it was too late, when a new set of problems emerged in the form of a world slump, was it realized that the past held no special attractions. Some may say that this judgement is too harsh. It could be argued that statesmen were overtaken by a series of events as a result of which they had little time and energy to spare for more fundamental problems. Certainly in the early years after the war there was much to occupy the policy-makers, though some of their decisions suggest that the previous comments are not far wide of the mark. The immediate post-war years especially were not marked by wise decisions.

Initially it is true that there were signs that governments were about to plan a better future. Grandiose reconstruction schemes were being planned in the later stages of the war, the relief of Europe was under consideration, and it seemed possible that the beneficial experience of international co-operation in wartime might bear fruit in peacetime. President Wilson's Fourteen Points and the launching of the League of Nations seemed to herald a new spirit of international harmony and goodwill. Yet within less than three years little was left of these high ideals. By a series of policy reversals the Allied powers left Europe in a more precarious state than at the time of the armistice. In particular, the provisions of the peace treaties, the abandonment of European relief and the measures taken to control the boom of 1919–20 adversely affected the recovery of Europe.

THE PEACE TREATY SETTLEMENTS

Separate peace treaties were made with each of the enemy powers, the most important of which were those with Germany, Austria and Hungary. They not only imposed heavy penalties on the enemies but also made provision for extensive territorial changes in central and eastern Europe. In fact the post-war geographic changes constituted the biggest exercise in reshaping the boundaries of Europe ever undertaken. The process involved the greater part of the continent and the only countries not affected were Holland, Luxembourg, Switzerland, Spain and Portugal. The number of separate customs units in Europe was increased from 20 to 27, while political frontiers were lengthened by 12,500 miles. The newly created independent states comprised Poland, Czechoslovakia, Yugoslavia, Finland, Estonia, Latvia and Lithuania. These states were created out of the ruins of the German, Austrian and Russian Empires.

The German losses were considerable. Under the terms of the Treaty of Versailles she lost all her colonies, Alsace-Lorraine and the Saar which went to France,[1] North Schleswig to Denmark, West Prussia and Upper Silesia to Poland, Eupen and Malmédy to Belgium, as well as a number of smaller territories. In total she was deprived of about 13.5 per cent of her pre-war territory and 10 per cent of the population of 1910. These figures tend to underestimate the extent of the damage, however, since the areas ceded contained some of the richest agricultural and industrial resources. In addition, the Allies confiscated nearly the entire German mercantile marine, almost all her foreign investments, while payments in kind were demanded in the transitional period before the heavy reparations bill was presented in 1921. The Treaty also provided for the disarmament of Germany; she was forbidden to have an air-force, the army and navy were reduced to insignificant proportions and conscription was abolished, while provision was also made for an Allied occupation force in the Rhineland.

The loss of resources was bad enough but perhaps even worse was the dislocation caused by the partition of industrial regions which had once formed single integrated units, such as Upper Silesia, and the breaking of the link

19

between Ruhr coal and the iron of Lorraine. But this sort of partitioning was not confined to Germany since the peace-makers were to repeat the exercise again and again in the course of treaty formulation for the European continent.

An even worse fate awaited the Austro-Hungarian Empire which was already on the point of disintegration in the latter stages of the war. The old Empire was literally decimated with the result that in territorial terms Austria and Hungary were but a quarter of their former size and only a little larger in terms of population. Economic criteria were scarcely taken into account when the partitioning took place. Hungary was dismembered largely on the grounds of racial diversity, yet the resulting territorial formations proved no more racially homogeneous and made even less economic sense. Slabs of the Empire were distributed among no less than seven states, including the remnants of the old regime, Austria and Hungary. Romania alone secured an area larger than that left to Hungary herself. Austria did little better. She ceded major territories to Italy, Romania, Yugoslavia and Czechoslovakia including some of her best industrial areas. In effect, therefore, both Austria and Hungary became land-locked areas no larger than some of their surrounding neighbours.

Other countries to suffer territorial losses were Bulgaria, Turkey and Russia. In the case of the first two the concessions were relatively small but Russia gave up much. She lost Bessarabia to Romania, four peripheral territories which became the independent states of Finland, Estonia, Latvia and Lithuania, and subsequently a large slice of her western frontier after the Polish defeat of the drive on Warsaw in 1920.

The main beneficiaries from the carve-up of Europe were Poland, Yugoslavia, Czechoslovakia and Romania. Poland, back on the map after more than a century, secured substantial chunks of territory from Germany, Austria and Russia, the original partitioning powers in the late eighteenth century. The newly created states of Czechoslovakia and Yugoslavia also did well from the break-up of the Habsburg Empire, while Romania more than doubled its former size as a result of gains from neighbouring countries.

The territorial realignments cannot be regarded as satisfactory from any point of view, and least of all from an economic one. In truth they created more problems than they solved. The reorganization brought into being several new states with a consequent increase in the number of separate tariff units, it left many national minorities under alien rule and it created enormous problems of economic integration. Possibly these difficulties were the inevitable outcome of an attempt to satisfy several objectives simultaneously, namely ethnic delineation, national self-determination, the reconstruction of historic frontiers and economic requirements, since to satisfy one often meant the modification of another.

If economic factors were not completely ignored it is clear that they were given very short shrift when defining the boundaries of the newly created and reconstituted states. Each country received whatever resources and equipment happened to be located in the territory assigned to it. This often meant the complete break-up of former trading patterns and lines of communication and the separation of mutually dependent branches of industry. Such problems were particularly acute in central and eastern Europe. Yugoslavia, for example, inherited five railway systems with four different gauges; each of the systems served different centres so that they were practically unconnected with each other, and the task of unifying these disparate parts took most of a decade. The textile industry of Austria was split apart; the spindles were located in Bohemia and Moravia, which became part of Czechoslovakia, while the weaving looms were mainly in and around Vienna. Hungary, a country which before 1914 had been making reasonable industrial progress, was shorn of some important raw materials needed to service her developing industries. She retained about half her industrial undertakings but lost the bulk of her timber, iron ore, salt, copper and other non-ferrous metals and water power. Such changes were bound to hinder economic recovery and in the long term they created resentment and frustration which was partly reflected in the growing tide of nationalism throughout the inter-war period.

Apart from the normal job of reconstruction, therefore, the new states had the additional task of building new economic organizations out of the multiple segments of territories they inherited. This usually involved the creation of new administrative units, new currencies, new lines of communication and the forging of fresh economic and trading links to replace those that had been destroyed. Inevitably it led to the increased role of the state in economic affairs and a drive towards greater self-sufficiency. The gainers as well as the losers faced equally difficult problems. Romania and Yugoslavia, with their domains greatly enlarged, had the task of integrating the diverse parts, with their ethnic contrasts, into unified states. In terms of industrial equipment Czechoslovakia did very well, but she was left with a host of racial minorities to consolidate. Poland faced the most difficult task, that of welding together three separate segments of territory formerly under different alien rule, with no natural frontiers and little in the way of developed industry. The three parts did not constitute a single economic unit since they had different systems of civil, commercial and fiscal legislation, they belonged to different customs units and they had different money and credit systems.

In contrast, Austria and Hungary had the reverse problem of creating viable economic units out of remnants of the old Empire. Not that the former monarchy had been a very efficient economic organization but at least it had a greater degree of economic coherence than what was to follow. The best portions of the Empire were sliced off and Austria and Hungary were left with the rump. Austria ended up with a head larger than is body in that Vienna, the once glittering capital city of Europe, which now harboured an overgrown bureaucracy, tended to dwarf the rest of the country. With a population of under 6.5 million, nearly one-third of whom lived in Vienna, Austria had become a top-heavy and economically precarious state. Hungary secured a somewhat larger population but since she lost many valuable resources to neighbouring countries her economic system was considerably weakened and disrupted.

Apart from the dislocation caused by geographic changes in Europe, a second impediment to recovery arose out of the failure to devise a satisfactory solution to the problem of war debts and reparations. Except in the case of Hungary and Bulgaria the peace treaties did not deal with these matters specifically. Allied war debts were negotiated among the interested parties, while the burden imposed on Germany was fixed by the Reparations Commission in 1921. The sums were large and initially no attempt was made to scale them down, or to link the two. The reasons for this were simple: the United States insisted on recouping the loans it had made to the Allies, while the latter, France in particular, maintained that these could only be paid so long as reparations from the enemy were forthcoming – hence the large reparations bill of $33 billion imposed on Germany in 1921. Since France and Britain were the largest debtors of the United States and at the same time the chief recipients of reparations from Germany, their debts and credits could have been offset with Germany settling direct with the United States. America, however, opposed the mixing of claims on the grounds that there was a much greater likelihood of Germany defaulting on her obligations than the Allies, in which case America would have been left with a much larger balance of bad debts than if one of the Allies had ceased payment.

The post-war debt problem created a great deal of bitter feeling among the nations concerned; it involved complex difficulties with respect to the transfer of payments and imposed severe burdens on the debtor countries. Subsequent events in Germany, in particular the great inflation of 1922–3, were not unrelated to this issue. Eventually some scaling down of debts was achieved in the 1920s but not before damage had been done.

THE FAILURE OF RELIEF

In the immediate aftermath of the war Europe's chief problem was one of relief. The greater part of the continent was impoverished in nearly every conceivable respect. Output was low, famine was imminent, capital and raw materials were in desperately short supply, transport systems were completely disorganized and currency and financial mechanisms were running out of control. Social and political ferment led to weak governments with limited capacity to deal with the situation. Conditions were worst in central and eastern Europe; indeed the position in some countries was little short of chaotic with economic and social systems bordering on collapse. Russian society had already disintegrated and economic activity there was virtually at a standstill. Prospects of recovery were slim indeed without external assistance since inexperienced governments battled against almost insuperable odds.

The failure to organize a comprehensive programme of reconstruction and assistance was partly responsible for the collapse of some economic systems.

In one respect the Allied governments were forced to take action, namely the relief of poverty and hunger. By the end of 1918 the spectre of famine prevailed over a wide area of central and eastern Europe. Food was in very short supply since output of agricultural products was one-third or more below pre-war levels, while countries in this region had limited means of paying for imports of food.

The bulk of the relief provided was effected by or through American organizations, principally the American Relief Administration created early in 1919 as the executive agency of the Allied Supreme Council responsible for relief. Under arrangements made by this body a steady stream of food deliveries began to take place and by August 1919 food to the value of $1,250 million had been delivered to Europe. Most of it was provided on a cash or credit basis, and less than 10 per cent consisted of outright gifts. The Allied and liberated countries generally got their provisions on credit, most of which was never repaid, while enemy countries had to pay in cash.

After the middle of 1919 official relief programmes were sharply curtailed, and subsequently relief activities were confined mainly to private and semi-official organizations. These managed to distribute some $500 million worth of foodstuffs over a period of two to three years, mostly in the form of gifts. Basically, however, the task of providing sufficient food for the people of Europe was left to the respective governments.

Useful though the relief programme was it fell short of real needs. Except for deliveries to Belgium and northern France, supplies on any scale never really got under way until the beginning of February 1919, and then they came to an abrupt halt in the summer of that year, long before the problem of hunger and poverty had been solved. On average every child in central and eastern Europe was fed for one month only by US relief organizations. Child poverty alone, therefore, remained critical in many countries; a League of Nations medical inquiry carried out in Czechoslovakia in March 1921 showed that 60 per cent of the country's children remained undernourished or lacking in vitality. The real extent of the problem was never adequately surveyed; the whole exercise of relief was hastily improvised and there were innumerable difficulties encountered in co-ordinating the relief efforts of the United States and the Allies. Though the United States was the main participant it should be borne in mind that she had large food stocks at the end of the war and this was obviously an important consideration in drawing up the relief programme. Furthermore, the fact that the enemy states were expected to pay their way where possible only made the task of reconstruction that much more difficult.

Relief of famine was of course only the first step in the process of reconstruction. Europe was short of raw materials, capital and consumer goods, and supplies of the first two were especially important for purposes of recovery. But no overall plan of reconstruction relief was ever conceived and international efforts outside that of meeting food requirements were very limited indeed. Consequently Europe had to fend as best she could and in the scramble for materials in the boom of 1919–20 many central and eastern countries were left with a minimal supply. Raw material and capital equipment imports were only a fraction of pre-war levels and food imports fell off sharply later in 1919 when the relief programme expired. High prices were paid for what was imported and the large deficit in the trade accounts which resulted had to be covered by borrowings. In monetary terms the total import surplus of continental Europe on trade account in 1919 and 1920 was $12.5 billion of which less than one-half was covered by invisible receipts and the export of gold, leaving $6.7 billion to be financed by the import of capital.

Clearly, then, international efforts to promote reconstruction in Europe were woefully inadequate after the First World War, a lesson which was appreciated by the planners responsible for the same task after 1945. A coordinated plan for the relief and reconstruction of Europe was never conceived at any stage, let alone implemented, and the relief that was handed out was very inadequate. Moreover, it tended to be regarded more as a form of charity which should be extended to some countries but not to others. Political considerations rather than need or capacity to pay determined the type and amount of relief given, which is why western countries did better than their counterparts in central and eastern Europe.

The consequences of inadequate action had a direct bearing on later events. Since many countries were unable to obtain sufficient supplies recovery was delayed, factories remained idle and unemployment high. As a result unemployment benefits, relief programmes and continued military spending kept government expenditure at a high level which, coupled with the low taxable capacity of the population, meant that balanced budgets were out of the question. Furthermore, inadequate foreign credits to finance imports meant pressure on the demand for foreign exchange with a consequent depreciation of currency values. It is true that for a time each depreciation of the exchange helped to promote exports and create employment. But the final consequences were disastrous. The price paid for temporary relief was increasing inflation, declining real incomes, loss of confidence and eventually the flight of capital from productive activity. Ultimately it led to the disintegration of several economies. For several years the whole economic and social organization of many countries was allowed to rot away and 'when it was finally faced, it had ceased to be a general problem of transition and reconstruction and had become a problem of cutting the gangrene out of the most affected areas'. Ironically this observation was made by the League of Nations, an organization of which so much had been expected but from which so little transpired.

Thus the breakdown in several European countries in the early 1920s can be attributed partly to the failure to take effective action to check the disease before it got too severe. This required adequate provision for the most stricken

24

areas to permit rehabilitation and hence obviate the need for exchange depreciation; the immediate support of currencies weakened by inflationary policies rather than waiting until the collapse was under way. And, finally, if the boom of 1919–20 had been controlled more sensibly the European burden would have been eased. It is to this aspect we now turn.

THE POST-WAR BOOM AND SLUMP, 1919–21

While much of Europe was struggling to cope with famine, poverty and reconstruction the western Allies and not a few other countries were enjoying one of the most spectacular booms in history, only to be followed by an equally spectacular slump. The causes of the boom and of the subsequent collapse are important, and even more so are the consequences in terms of European recovery.

Initially it was expected that the war would be followed by a recession as military orders were cancelled, soldiers were demobilized and the process of converting to peacetime operations took place. For a few months after the armistice there was a mild recession but this soon gave way in the spring of 1919 to 'a boom of astonishing dimensions'. It was one of the shortest and sharpest upswings on record. It lasted for about a year with the peak occurring in the spring and summer of 1920. One of its most notable features was the very sharp rise in prices as pent-up demand for commodities was unleashed at a time when production was still recovering from the effects of war. Factories were swamped with orders and the consequent demand for labour assisted the process of demobilization. Within just over a year from the armistice Britain had demobilized some 4 million men and had abandoned most wartime controls. The process of conversion was even more rapid in the United States.

The boom was most marked in the United States, Britain and Japan and in some of the neutral countries since their economies were in better shape to meet the sudden upsurge in demand. Much of continental Europe and Russia were in no fit state to participate properly though inflationary conditions continued unchecked in many European countries. Primary producers also benefited from the sharp rise in commodity prices, while everywhere there was a great deal of speculative activity.

One of the main forces behind the boom was undoubtedly that of war. A large pent-up demand for goods had been created which was backed by financial assets accumulated during the period of hostilities. This demand was released at a time when stocks were low and productive capacity was still recovering so that initially it was simply translated into soaring prices. The price inflation was aggravated by several other factors. Shortages of shipping space and dislocation of internal transport systems in the immediate post-war period tended to create artificial shortages since in some cases there were considerable accumulations of primary commodities overseas waiting to be moved. There was also a considerable amount of speculative stock buying in anticipation of rapid upward price movements, since the gains to be made from cornering markets were large.

Government policies must also share part of the blame. Controls over economic activity were abandoned very rapidly after the war as businessmen pressed for a return to 'normalcy' as soon as possible. Thus despite the fact that commodities were in short supply many wartime controls were dismantled during the first half of 1919. Relaxation of control was followed in nearly every instance by a sharp price increase, and had control been retained somewhat longer it is almost certain that the severity of the price rise would have been lessened. In addition, lax fiscal and monetary policies pumped funds into the economy and expanded credit. For much of 1919 government spending continued at a high level and credit conditions remained easy. In fact all over the world, partly by force of circumstances, governments tended to pursue fiscal and monetary policies which accentuated the upswing. The inflationary process went further in central and eastern Europe where financial and currency conditions were already in a chaotic state before the end of the war. The needs of reconstruction, limited tax potential and weak administrations meant a continuation of inflationary fiscal and monetary policies. Here little attempt was made to check the process. Indeed in most cases it was aggravated by policy measures with the result that the inflationary spiral got worse and eventually ended in disaster.

Elsewhere the boom ended almost as dramatically as it had begun. The first sign of a break came early in 1920 when business activity began to slacken in the United States. During the spring of that year a number of countries including Britain recorded turning-points in economic activity and by the autumn there was little doubt that the bubble had burst. During the remainder of the year production, exports and prices fell far and fast, while unemployment rose sharply. As a result the year 1921 proved to be one of the worst on record.

Few countries escaped the severe check to activity between 1920 and 1921 (and in some cases it ran on until 1922) except those in central and eastern Europe whose currencies had so depreciated that they were enjoying a temporary boost to exports. Thus Germany, Austria, Czechoslovakia and Poland actually recorded increases in industrial production in 1921. Here inflation gave an artificial stimulus to activity, though still well down on pre-war levels, but the consequences were soon to follow. Elsewhere the picture was grim and for some the downturn proved to be more severe, though of shorter duration, than that of 1929–32. Production and incomes in Sweden and Britain fell much more sharply in 1920–1 than they were to do in the downswing following 1929. On a monthly basis the decline was also more severe in the United States. The main blessing was that the post-war depression was shorter than the later one, and by 1922 most countries began to show signs of revival.

Several reasons can be put forward to explain this sudden and sharp contraction. One simple and commonly quoted reason is that it was the inevitable reaction to the violent boom; as output began to catch up with demand and supplies of commodities began to arrive from overseas the basis of the boom disintegrated. A second possibility is that price inflation produced its own cure in that rapidly rising prices and lagging wages checked the growth of real incomes and led to consumer resistance. There is certainly evidence to suggest that consumer demand began to tail off in the first few months of 1920 in Britain. Furthermore, the rapid rise in industrial costs produced business uncertainty, while in some cases, notably the United States, supply inelasticities became operative in the winter of 1919–20. These aggravated the pace of inflation and thereby increased consumer resistance, though supply restraints were probably not the chief cause of the turning-point.

Many writers place considerable emphasis on the role of government policy in checking the boom. Restrictive fiscal and monetary policies, especially in the United States and Britain, served to check expansion and reduce the flow of credits abroad, which in turn curtailed the demand for exports. Certainly the timing of policy measures in the United States is not inconsistent with the belief that the downswing was induced by government action. Government spending declined after the middle of 1919; tax revenues rose while monetary policy was tightened severely late in the year. Severe retrenchment measures were also implemented in other countries, notably Britain, Sweden and Japan, at roughly the same point in time. Though it is not always easy to determine just how crucial government policy was in breaking the boom, there can be little doubt that the sharp monetary contraction and fiscal retrenchment of this period exacerbated the downswing once it was under way. Such action certainly put paid to inflation but, given the magnitude of the subsequent slump, it must be condemned for being too severe and too late.

In the circumstances it is not surprising that severe corrective action was taken to control the boom. It did appear to be getting somewhat out of hand during the course of 1919 and the rapid rise in prices in particular was bound to give grounds for alarm given the prevailing conditions in much of Europe, where lax financial policies were seen as being a powerful force in the inflationary spiral. If the boom did not break through natural forces then the danger of continuing inflation was real, given no change in government policy. In any case, there was almost bound to be a reaction against wartime financial practices since belief in the virtue of sound finance was still widely held in some countries. This along with other adjustments in policy, including abandonment of controls, reductions in government spending and taxes, removal of trade barriers and a speedy return to gold as the basis for national currencies, were regarded as vital prerequisites for a return to 'normalcy' in economic affairs. Thus it is not so much that the policies were wrong in the conditions then obtaining, but rather that they were pursued too vigorously and for too long. Unfortunately the lessons of this episode went unheeded in 1929.

The consequences were not as disastrous, however, as those which followed from the great inflations in central and eastern Europe. Nevertheless they should not be minimized. The prospects of a smooth and speedy transition to peacetime conditions were shattered. In 1921 many factories lay idle, millions of men and women were without work, and industrial unrest was widespread as wages were forced down sharply under sliding-scale agreements. Inevitably this delayed the process of reconstruction. Moreover, the boom itself was not an unmixed blessing. In many respects it was an artificial one created by paper shortages and supply bottlenecks arising out of the dislocation caused by war. Though production expanded it could not in the short term keep pace with rising demand and hence inflationary conditions dominated the upswing. Under these conditions it developed into a speculative ramp. In fact the outstanding feature of the boom was the extent of speculative buying in commodities, securities and real estate and the very large number of industrial transactions at inflated prices. The financial orgy was made possible by the extremely liquid state of firms as a result of high wartime profits, the relatively easy money conditions and the large-scale creation of bank credit. Activity in the new issue market reached phenomenal proportions. New issues on the London market increased by a factor of more than six between 1918 and 1920 to reach a total of £384 million, a level which was not surpassed until the 1960s. Most of the increase in new issues represented flotations for domestic purposes.

The worst excesses occurred in some of the older industries – coal, cotton, shipbuilding and steel – whose future growth prospects were limited. The flotation of new companies, the sale of old ones and the issue of new shares became almost a daily event in 1919. Expectations of high profits attracted speculators and a large number of companies were bought up and refloated at inflated capital values, often with the assistance of the banks. Such transactions had disastrous consequences for the industries concerned. Their wartime profits were dissipated in a frivolous manner and once the bottom fell out of the market they were left with virtually worthless assets together with a heavy burden of debt as a result of increased interest liabilities, the issue of bonus shares and the watering of capital stock. The cost of over-capitalization in the boom was to remain a heavy burden to some industries throughout the inter-war period. Finally, the boom fostered the growth of capacity often in sectors in which future prospects were least promising. The most notable example is in the maritime trades where enough capacity came on stream to last a decade or more.

The boom and slump of the western hemisphere had important implications for European debtor countries, comprising most of central and eastern Europe. It impeded their reconstruction and forced them to adopt dangerous expedients. During the boom these countries found difficulty in securing essential supplies and for what they did obtain they were forced to pay high prices, thereby incurring further debt. Moreover, when commodity prices collapsed in the latter half of 1920 the burden of debt increased, especially in eastern countries with heavy dependence on primary exports. Second, retrenchment in the United States had serious repercussions for Europe as a whole. The drop of more than 40 per cent in the general level of dollar prices imposed a heavy burden on all European countries which had contracted debt at inflated prices. The transfer problem was aggravated since it was difficult to service debt at lower prices, and the result was that European primary producers strove to increase their output which only made matters worse. The price decline in the United States also accentuated the deflationary difficulties of countries attempting to restore their currencies to pre-war parity. This is particularly true of Britain since sterling prices had risen more than dollar prices during the war.

Furthermore, the downturn in the United States led to a sharp curtailment of imports into that country and a check to overseas lending with the result that the volume of dollars supplied to foreigners was reduced by no less than 50 per cent between 1919 and 1921. By late 1920 the dollar shortage in Europe had become so acute as to require an increasingly large outflow of gold. In the face of their difficulties, therefore, the European debtors abandoned any attempt at financial reform and currency stabilization; instead they allowed their exchanges to slide further, thus aggravating the problem of inflation.

In short, therefore, American economic policy in the post-war period exacerbated Europe's problems. The United States failed to take account fully of its changed status during the war – to a large creditor nation with a strategic role in the international economy. Adjustment to a positive trade balance required that it continue to enlarge its imports and lend abroad. The cutback in both respects in 1920–1 was a vital blow to European countries struggling to recover from the war. Had the American authorities stimulated demand in the spring of 1920 instead of deflating, the process of European reconstruction would have been eased and some of the worst excesses of inflationary policies might have been avoided. The sad thing is that America repeated the exercise again in the years 1928–30.

CONCLUSION

The decade of the 1920s did not open on a very auspicious note. Several major economies were sliding into recession, others were continuing on an inflationary course. Reconstruction and recovery from the war were far from complete and the policies of the Allied governments in the post-armistice period had done as much to hinder as to promote the economic revival of Europe. In particular, the failure to organize a satisfactory programme of international assistance to enable war-stricken countries to get on their feet again may be regarded as one of the chief mistakes of this period. It contrasts sharply with the position after the Second World War when both America and the United Nations came to the rescue of Europe in a big way. The failure in the earlier instance can be readily explained. The League of Nations was a relatively weak and ineffective organization which for the most part only took action to assist individual countries when they were on the verge of collapse. The weakness of the League partly reflected the fact that the spirit of international co-operation was still in its infancy; hence some member countries accorded the League only token support while the United States refused even that. The United States of course was the one country which was in a position to render assistance to Europe but since she was anxious to disengage herself from this area as rapidly as possible it is not surprising that the relief programme was short-lived.

In the event, therefore, Europe was forced to work out her own salvation. The process of recovery for some countries proved a long and painful one, punctuated by crises and reversals. In certain cases, notably Austria, Poland, Bulgaria and even Germany, complete recovery had scarcely been achieved before the slump of 1929–32 struck a further blow to their prospects. For others, however, the decade of the 1920s was one of significant economic progress although, as the next chapter shows, it was a period of unstable equilibrium which eventually terminated with the severest depression on record.

NOTE

1 The Saar coalmines went to France but the Saar itself was put under League trusteeship.

2

RECOVERY AND INSTABILITY PROBLEMS IN THE 1920s

Although in terms of economic growth the 1920s were far from being an unrespectable decade, any broad generalization about the performance and achievements of Europe as a whole during this decade is not particularly illuminating given the widely varying experience between countries within the region. It is true that nearly all countries experienced some economic progress and that most managed to regain or surpass their pre-war income and production levels by the end of the decade. But there was a world of difference between the rapid growth achieved by countries such as the Netherlands, Norway, Czechoslovakia and Switzerland and the near stagnation recorded by Austria, Russia and Bulgaria. Any comparison of relative performance of this kind depends very much on the time-span chosen. Countries like Austria, which only just about regained their 1913 output levels by the end of the 1920s, managed to record rapid growth over the period 1920–9 simply because recovery took place from a very low base. Moreover, for this period it seems sensible to make some distinction between the first and second halves of the 1920s. During the former period, that is, up to about 1925, most countries were in the process of recovering from the war; growth rates were often high and yet even so a number of countries, especially in central and eastern Europe, had still not fully regained their pre-war output levels by the middle of the decade. On the other hand, the latter half of the period was one of consolidation and further growth, with boom conditions in some cases, though against a basically unstable international economic background with obvious implications for the cyclical downturn that began in 1929. In these later years eastern Europe probably performed somewhat better than the west though the area still remained extremely backward in comparison with the major industrial countries.

Whatever the record of individual countries it should be stressed that European development of the 1920s took place against an unstable political and economic background. Even by the middle of the decade, by which time a greater degree of political and economic stability and a substantial measure of recovery had been achieved, the international economy was still in a fragile state and it continued to remain vulnerable to shocks throughout the later

31

1920s despite the semblance of equilibrium achieved in that period. Perhaps this is not so surprising, since the war had given rise to many problems most of which were only partially solved, if at all, during the course of the decade. Apart from the question of physical reconstruction, some of the most important included war debts and reparations, currency disorganization, inflation, and structural problems reflected in excess capacity and higher unemployment compared with the pre-war period. Furthermore, the fact that Europe, and especially central and eastern Europe, emerged from the war in a weakened state meant that the area as a whole became more dependent on outside assistance which again served to expose the vulnerability of the European economy.

Given the magnitude of the problems what is perhaps surprising is that Europe's performance in the 1920s was as good as it was. No doubt but for these overall performance would have been better, though quite by how much it is impossible to tell. But clearly also, despite the complications, there were forces making for growth, notably war-induced recovery forces, new technological opportunities and even, especially in eastern Europe, a greater degree of autarchy with respect to economic matters. However, possibly of greater relevance than the growth-retarding effects of such problems is the way in which their existence and the solutions adopted served to limit the achievement of a stable equilibrium, which meant that the European economy was less able to withstand the pressure of external events as they developed from 1928 onwards.

THE RECONSTRUCTION PHASE

Seven years elapsed before Europe as a whole gained her former levels of activity and even by 1925 the process of recovery was not really complete. Some countries had still not managed to reach their pre-war output levels, while many of those which did continued to suffer from excess capacity and heavy unemployment; at the end of 1925 there were over 2.5 million unemployed workers in Britain, Germany, Belgium, Italy and Poland, not to mention the large number of under-employed workers especially in agriculture. Second, Europe's trade still fell somewhat short of the pre-war volume. Third, the fact that production had barely surpassed the 1913 level at a time when population was rising suggests that income per head was still below the pre-war peak.

The rate of recovery was very uneven not only between regions but also between countries in the same area. Central and eastern Europe, which had suffered the most from the war and its aftermath, lagged seriously behind the west. The fact that some countries in this region escaped the post-war slump because of inflation was little consolation since once it got out of hand economic activity was checked more sharply than in countries which had adopted deflationary policies. The result was that by 1925 industrial production in this area was still 13 per cent below that of 1913 whereas the western Allies and neutral countries were recording gains of a similar magnitude. Within these major groupings some countries did very much better than others. Italy, for example, far surpassed the performance of any of her allies; Denmark and the Netherlands did better than the other neutrals, while Finland outpaced the Scandinavian countries. France and Belgium, though subject to similar amounts of destruction, registered somewhat different rates of recovery, while France did better on balance than Britain. As far as central and eastern Europe is concerned it is a case of selecting the best out of a bad lot, though Czechoslovakia stands out with an increase in manufacturing output of more than one-third above the pre-war level.

Most countries of course had special problems to contend with in this period, but several general factors can be presented to explain the relatively slow rate of European recovery.

For one thing the task of reconstruction was a large one. Nor was it simply a question of restoring physical damage although this in itself was a considerable item in some cases. The absolute amount of physical destruction of land and property may not in total seem large but for some countries it constituted a severe burden at a time when resources were in short supply. In addition, for many countries in central and eastern Europe there was the problem of literally creating viable economic systems out of territories which had been sliced up and reformulated by the peace treaty provisions.

At the same time economic and political conditions were scarcely conducive to rapid recovery in the first few years after the war. Hardly a year passed without some event or crisis occurring which served to hamper progress. Between 1919 and 1922 strikes, political upheavals and border hostilities abounded throughout Europe. The sharp contraction in economic activity in 1920–1 in most west European countries abruptly cut short recovery, and for some it spelt the beginning of an intermittent policy of deflation in preparation for the return to the gold standard. Meanwhile inflationary pressures were building up in the rest of Europe and 1922–3 saw the unleashing of these forces on a grand scale in Austria, Hungary, Poland and Germany, accompanied in the latter case by the abortive occupation of the Ruhr by France and Belgium. After 1923 things quietened down somewhat and by the middle of 1924 the outlook was generally more favourable to sustained progress than at any time since the armistice. Even so there were still events which gave cause for alarm; Germany and Poland in 1924 experienced partial stabilization crises, while in the following year the French and Belgian currencies weakened seriously at a time when other countries, notably Britain, Switzerland and Norway, were experiencing deflationary pressures in connection with the return to gold. Finally, in 1926 Britain experienced the worst strike in history.

Some of these events affected particular countries more than others though by no means all the problems were of a local nature. Currency difficulties were widespread throughout this period and currency instability was certainly an important impediment to general recovery even though some countries gained, at least initially, from depreciated currencies and inflationary financing of reconstruction. But against this have to be set certain adverse effects. Several countries failed to bring inflation under control and their currencies eventually collapsed under the strain, which left them in a much weaker state than at any time since the end of the war. Second, the uncertainty created by extremely volatile exchanges hindered the revival of foreign trade and made it difficult to plan for the future. Much energy was spent in speculative currency deals rather than in cultivating real trade transactions, and the very slow recovery in European trade must in part be attributed to the uncertainty engendered by currency instability. Third, while certain countries, notably France, did derive benefit from inflation and depreciated exchanges, many in central and eastern Europe did not. For these countries a depreciated currency often brought little real gain since supply inelasticities precluded them from taking advantage of their more competitive position, while imports of equipment on which their future development depended were made more expensive. Furthermore, the artificial protection which currency depreciation provided tended to lead to the establishment of inefficient enterprises or industries which subsequently had to be given state assistance to keep them in business.

A further important barrier to recovery was shortage of resources. This was certainly a major problem in central and eastern Europe in the immediate post-war years and even beyond. Nor was it simply a question of a physical shortage of equipment and raw materials, though this was certainly an acute problem in the early years after the armistice. There was the added problem, however, of a serious shortage of capital, both long and short term. Central and eastern European countries were incapable of raising sufficient capital internally, nor were they able to earn sufficient foreign exchange to pay for imports of materials and equipment essential for the development of their economies. The only solution to this problem was recourse to foreign borrowing but this failed to materialize on anywhere near the scale required. Once the post-armistice assistance for famine and relief dried up the import of capital into continental Europe was very limited. Unsettled political and economic conditions made investors extremely reluctant to grant long-term loans to these countries, and hence they had to struggle on as best they could, relying on short-term credits and limited assistance from the League of Nations under its *ad hoc* rescue operations. Not until the middle of the 1920s when economic conditions became more stable did the flow of lending increase markedly, but by this time the damage had already been done.

Undoubtedly the task of reconstruction and recovery in the territories of central and eastern Europe was on a scale quite different from that of the west. Virtually all the countries of this region[1] were faced with a whole series of almost insuperable problems, and with resources very much inferior to those

34

of the west European powers. The list of problems makes depressing reading: physical devastation; territorial adjustments and all that this entailed in terms of economic reorganization; financial chaos, including unbalanced budgets, inflation and currency instability; balance of payments problems, unemployment, rapidly rising population and agrarian reform; political instability and weak administrative organizations; lack of a balanced economic structure and shortages of almost everything. Not every country suffered from all these problems simultaneously though it is difficult to find any which did not face at least a large proportion of them. Thus for the most part it was scarcely a case of getting back to normal as quickly as possible; rather it was a question of trying to avoid economic disintegration. Indeed, many of these countries barely managed to regain pre-war levels of activity by the middle of the decade, and some failed to do even that.

The region as a whole had of course been economically backward before the war. The extent of industrial development, even in the Czech lands and Russia, was relatively limited and the population was still heavily dependent on agriculture; in Bulgaria, Romania and Yugoslavia up to 80 per cent of the population earned a livelihood from the land. Productivity and income per capita were low which meant limited savings for purposes of investment outside the primary sector. Yet though economically very backward there was a degree of economic cohesion and stability within the region prior to the outbreak of the war. However, the impact of war and its aftermath shattered any semblance of unity and stability which eastern Europe might once have had. The economic, political and social life of virtually all the countries in the region was left in complete chaos. Famine was rife, destruction and pillage by invading armies had damaged much of the productive facilities, trade was almost non-existent, while financial and currency systems were in ruins. The peace treaty settlements made things worse since the new territorial arrangements, by splitting up viable economic units and destroying former patterns of communication and trading links, merely served to impede economic development. The new states, moreover, inherited various fragments of territory which required welding into viable and cohesive political and economic units. In other words, not only had these countries to tackle the ordinary problem of physical reconstruction but they literally had to create new administrations and national economies out of the motley collection of territories they inherited. Moreover, they were left to accomplish these tasks almost unaided at a time when resources were desperately short, and with financial and administrative systems far from commensurate with the needs at hand.

Population pressures added to these problems. In many countries population was rising very much faster than in the west and at a time when the traditional safety-valve of emigration was closing up. This meant even further pressure on already densely populated farmlands and the attempt to solve this problem by extensive land reforms led to a fragmentation of holdings and a significant increase in small-scale subsistence farming. The effect of the land reforms is difficult to assess precisely since the extent of reform and its impact varied a great deal from one country to another. But initially it probably had a perverse effect on production and yields by reducing the scope for mechanization and improved efficiency and by perpetuating all the defects of individualistic farming. In Romania, for example, where large estates were confiscated and some 30 per cent of the land redistributed, the reforms had a harmful effect and delayed recovery. The cultivated area declined sharply and the output of cereals fell likewise. But land reform was only one of many factors which retarded the recovery of the primary sector. Others included the widespread wartime devastation, increased tax burdens, shortage of capital, the fall in primary product prices in the early 1920s and the closing of west European markets to the agricultural produce of the east.

In any case, recovery of agricultural production could not really offer a viable long-term solution to the basic problem, namely increasing pressure on land resources. The obvious alternative was industrial development but conditions were far from conducive. Shortages of plant, raw materials and capital were widespread, while currency depreciation and financial instability of the new states left little prospect of much assistance from abroad. Moreover, several countries, e.g. Hungary and Austria, had lost parts of their industrial sectors as a result of the peace treaty terms. The disorganization of the infrastructure, particularly communications, the generally chaotic economic conditions after the war and the poverty of the mass of the people were hardly conducive to rapid industrialization. Export outlets were also limited because of the loss of many markets and the inefficient nature of production. Futhermore, the state could provide little direct assistance, at least initially, given the inefficient tax systems and the large burden of public debt.

Under such circumstances the only solution lay in short-term expedients. Thus inflation, currency depreciation and tariff protection became the means by which these countries sought to adjust their economies by fostering industrial development. The first two are normally regarded as detrimental to economic systems and so they are once they get out of control. On the other hand, both inflation and exchange depreciation did initially provide a stimulus to investment and exports. Nearly all the countries concerned solved their low capacity problem temporarily by inflationary financing of investment. Thus in Austria there was a big expansion of capacity between 1919 and 1923 with the result that industrial equipment was some 20 per cent greater than pre-war. The same was true in Hungary where virtually every industry except clothing recorded additions to industrial capacity. Physical reconstruction also proceeded quite rapidly in Poland, while currency depreciation allowed the country to exploit the markets of countries with more stable currencies. At the same time currency depreciation and liberal tariff protection helped to protect the domestic market from competing imports. Most of the countries in the region had higher tariffs than before the war, a reflection of what was to become a more sustained drive towards economic autarchy in later years.

36

When completed in 1925–6 the Czech tariff structure was almost double that of the old Austro-Hungarian tariff, representing 36.4 per cent of the total value of imports.

It is doubtful whether the expedients employed offered a real and lasting solution to the problems of this area. Certainly inflation and currency depreciation did for a time serve to boost activity in these countries, but once it got out of control, as in the case of Austria, Hungary and Poland, it probably did more harm than good. The German example is instructive in this respect as we shall see later. Once stabilization and financial control were effected there was a temporary setback to industrial growth. Forced industrialization gave rise to inefficient undertakings and much excess capacity. In fact development was reflected more in the expansion of capacity than in output. For example, though Austria and Hungary expanded their industrial capacity considerably in the early 1920s, by the middle of the decade industrial output was running at about 75–80 per cent of pre-war, or about two-thirds the capacity available. Over the region as a whole capacity was probably expanded in excess of requirements, once the artificial conditions of inflation and currency depreciation had ceased to exist.

In other words, the measures resorted to in the early 1920s gave an artificial boost to the economies but they produced few real and lasting benefits. For the region as a whole industrial and agricultural output by 1925 still fell short of the 1913 level. There were one or two notable bright spots. Czechoslovakia, which inherited important industrial interests from Austro-Hungary and had reformed her financial and currency systems at an early date, experienced rapid growth, with an increase in manufacturing output of 36 per cent above the 1913 level. But for the majority it was a struggle for survival with little hope at this stage of working off the 'gigantic backlog of backwardness'. Inflation and currency depreciation could provide only temporary alleviation of the fundamental problems of this region, and they in turn became problems which ultimately necessitated remedial action. Once some sort of financial stability was restored capital imports provided a source of relief, but again these proved to be transient since at the crucial moment, in the late 1920s, they were hastily curtailed.

Russia presents something of a different case and therefore merits a few separate comments. Under the new regime the country was virtually cut off from the west, and in the years 1919 to 1921 the economy ground almost to a halt under the impact of civil war and external border hostilities, inflation and communization. The process of recovery from this chaos was long and arduous but the groundwork was laid in the years 1922–4, with a partial return to private enterprise under the New Economic Policy (NEP), the stabilization of the currency, the restoration of budgetary equilibrium and the end of civil violence and external conflict. In the first year of what might be regarded as normality (1922–3), output of large-scale industry rose by 50 per cent but this still left it some 60 per cent down on the 1913 level. Not until 1926 did industrial and agricultural output exceed the pre-war base and then only by a small margin. A multiplicity of factors impeded recovery including the famous price 'scissors' crisis, the destruction and neglect of basic capital equipment, shortages of skilled labour, fuel, materials and spare parts, a disorganized transport system and the lack of competent managerial personnel.

By comparison with the east the problems facing western Europe were much less severe, though one or two countries, notably France and Belgium, were in a poor state at the end of the war. France emerged almost bankrupt with large debts and some 10 per cent of her territory devastated. Industrial and agricultural output was some 40 per cent down on 1913 with exports a fraction of their pre-war level. In fact France's industry and agriculture were probably more severely crippled than those of her neighbours with the possible exception of Belgium. The franc had lost 50 per cent of its former purchasing power and worse was still to follow in this respect.

Despite these setbacks France made a fairly rapid recovery. By the middle of the 1920s most major indices had regained or surpassed pre-war levels, though agriculture lagged behind somewhat. Several factors were responsible for the success. Physical reconstruction went ahead very rapidly, assisted by generous governmental aid on the assumption that the Germans would foot the bill through reparations. In the process France gained a more modernized industrial structure, with heavy investment in new equipment and modern technology which made French industry more competitive than previously. The sharp decline in the value of the franc encouraged industrialists to borrow for investment purposes, while the same factor also boosted the tourist trade and exports. The latter increased rapidly after 1922, and by 1926 they had risen by 56 per cent, at which point they were over one-third greater than in 1913. The economy still suffered from weak spots and France nearly paid the price of inflationary financing in a collapse of the currency, but she was probably one of the few countries to gain on balance from inflation and currency depreciation. Belgium had a somewhat similar experience, though here the recovery effort was not so impressive.

Of the belligerent powers Italy's post-war performance was probably the most spectacular. This country was less severely affected by the war and post-war slump than either France or Belgium, although according to some accounts Italy's economic machinery was badly disorganized, almost to the point of breakdown in the post-armistice period. If this is correct then Italy certainly staged a remarkable recovery since by 1922 industrial production and domestic output had regained their pre-war levels. From 1922 onwards Mussolini's industrialization and efficiency drive did much to hasten expansion. Aided by generous government assistance and a liberal credit policy Italy enjoyed continuous industrial expansion through to 1926. By that date industrial output was 42 per cent above that in 1913, with domestic output over a fifth greater. Exports too received a considerable boost from currency depreciation and the occupation of the Ruhr, which allowed Italy to re-enter eastern markets, so that by 1925 they were one-third above the 1913 level. Good harvests in 1923 and 1925 and a flow of surplus labour to neighbouring countries assisted the process of development. But then the expansion came almost to a halt as the favourable factors disappeared one by one. Credit facilities were tightened, emigration outlets declined, and bad harvests followed good. Above all, Mussolini's promise to defend the lira resulted in an overvalued currency after stabilization in 1927.

The country least affected by wartime dislocation, Britain, had a rather chequered performance in the first half of the 1920s. A fairly sharp recovery to 1920 was followed by one of the most severe depressions in history, when all indices of activity fell sharply. Recovery set in during late 1921 and 1922 and was sustained through to 1925 when income and production levels had cleared those of 1920 or 1913 by a reasonable margin. However, the recovery was by no means complete. Exports were still 25 per cent down on 1913 while unemployment, even at its lowest, was still around 1 million, or 9.2 per cent of the insured labour force. The intermittent policy of deflation in connection with the return to the gold standard in April 1925 helped to depress activity below potential though the main problem was a structural one. A large proportion of resources was tied up in the old basic industries of textiles, shipbuilding and coal, the demand for whose produces, both at home and abroad, was declining rapidly.

Though the main neutral countries (Norway, Sweden, Denmark and the Netherlands) were not directly involved in the war effort their economies did not escape unscathed. One of the biggest setbacks was the loss of export markets, especially in Europe, so that by 1920 export volumes were some 30–50 per cent lower than pre-war. These countries also made the effort to return to the gold standard at pre-war parity which meant they experienced a bout of deflation during the course of the 1920s. Following the post-war boom they experienced a sharp contraction in activity (with the exception of the Netherlands), which was partly occasioned by severe retrenchment policies. Nevertheless, compared with Britain the neutrals recorded a far better performance in the first half of the 1920s.

Initially recovery from the wartime setback in activity was rapid so that by 1920 levels of output were already above the pre-war base. The collapse of the boom coupled with deflationary policies brought a violent contraction in 1921 in all countries apart from the Netherlands. It was most severe and prolonged in Sweden largely as a result of the government's severe retrenchment policy in anticipation of the return to gold in 1924 after which renewed progress set in. Norway and Denmark on the other hand recovered much more rapidly from the 1921 depression since deflationary policies were not forced to such extremes as in Sweden. Both achieved rapid rates of expansion through to 1925 when levels of activity were far higher than in 1913. The Netherlands avoided the severe post-war deflationary crisis and experienced sustained growth throughout the decade, assisted by a strong upswing in exports.

THE BOOM OF THE LATER 1920s

By the middle of the 1920s economic and political conditions in Europe were somewhat more stable than they had been in the early 1920s. The Locarno Pact of 1925, the revised reparations settlement of the previous year and the negotiated agreements relating to Allied war debts did much to boost international confidence and reduce political tensions and suspicions of war. Most of the great inflations had run their course and Britain's return to the gold standard in 1925 paved the way for the completion of currency stabilization elsewhere. Primary commodity prices had firmed considerably after the disastrous drop following the post-war boom. Above all, the European reconstruction process was almost complete and it seemed that Europe could look forward to a period of real and sustained progress. The tensions and underlying weaknesses of the international economic system were all but forgotten in the boom of the later 1920s.

The expansion in activity was a fairly worldwide phenomenon although the most dramatic manifestations of the boom occurred in America where excessive stock market speculation attracted much attention. However, the upswing of the later 1920s differed in several respects from those of the past. For one thing there was no significant pressure on real resources at the peak of the cycle; indeed, if anything there was still a considerable amount of slack to be taken up in most economies. Unemployment rates remained high and there was still a margin of under-utilized capacity. Prices were trending downward slowly while wages were only subject to marginal upward adjustments. The main point of similarity was the significant rise in output, together with the upsurge in business profits in industrial countries. But these were by no means spectacular in comparison with those occurring in similar phases of past cycles. What marked the boom out from previous ones was the intense stock market speculation which occurred in the United States, and to a lesser extent in some European countries, and for this reason, together with the dramatic collapse which followed, the boom has attracted more interest than it would otherwise deserve.

Europe as a whole progressed more rapidly than most of the major regions of the world in this period. Industrial production kept pace with the average while the output of crude products advanced at a considerably faster rate. Hence by 1929 Europe had recovered part of the ground lost earlier, though the League of Nation's comment to the effect that the pre-war equilibrium between Europe and the rest of the world had largely been restored now seems somewhat wide of the mark. If there was an equilibrium it was more apparent than real. Below the surface there were plenty of signs of maladjustment, notably large areas of underemployed resources in certain sectors, the rise in primary inventories, the dependence of some countries on foreign capital and the rather patched-up nature of the international currency system. But despite these difficulties, Europe enjoyed some real progress and by 1929 income per capita was greater on average than in 1925 or 1913 even though it still remained somewhat unevenly distributed.

Though most countries experienced an increase in economic activity in the years 1925–1929 the pace of expansion varied considerably from country to country and it was rarely free from interruptions. It ranged from the dramatic, with Russia surging ahead in the last year or two under the impetus of the first Five Year Plan, to partial stagnation in the case of Denmark and Norway, both of which were suffering from gold parity deflation. Italy, the UK and Austria performed modestly, and in the west the best achievements were recorded by Sweden, Germany, Belgium, France and Luxembourg. On balance eastern Europe probably did better than the west – Hungary, Romania and Czechoslovakia in particular had quite impressive rates of industrial growth together with a good recovery in primary production – though one should bear in mind that the east was only recovering most of the ground lost during the war and through to 1925. Cyclical experience also varied a great deal especially at the upper turning-point. Several countries experienced minor interruptions to growth – for example Britain in 1926 and again in 1928, Germany in 1926, France, Italy and Denmark in 1927 – while the spread at the turning-point was quite wide. Poland hit the peak as early as February 1929, followed by Belgium in March and Germany in April. The Swedish downturn came in the second quarter of the year, then the British in July 1929, but France hung on until March 1930. This suggests some evidence of independent recessionary tendencies within Europe before the US downturn in the summer of 1929, though in some cases these could have been prompted by the prior decline in American lending.

Several countries suffered the adverse effects of currency policy in this period. The classic case frequently cited is that of Britain where the return to the gold standard at the pre-war parity in 1925 is estimated to have overvalued sterling by some 10 per cent. This certainly made exporting more difficult for Britain but the dampened nature of the boom in Britain during this period cannot be attributed solely to the lag in exports, while it is debatable whether a lower parity for the pound would have made that much difference to exports. The main problem with the export trade was a structural one, namely specialization in a range of products for which the demand was declining, which could not readily be cured by an undervaluation of the currency. Unfortunately the domestic market did not compensate for the weakness of exports. In the United States, for example, the boom of the 1920s was powered by domestically based industries, construction, services, transport and the new consumer durable trades, some of which experienced rapid technical progress leading to a sharp fall in unit costs. These sectors were much less buoyant in Britain. The rise in investment was very modest, especially after 1927, while many of the potential growth industries exerted only a moderate impact on the economy. Building, for example, collapsed in 1927–8 following the cutback in subsidies and over the years 1926–9 there was a negative rate of growth in

41

construction. Most of the service industries recorded modest rates of expansion, while the rates of growth in some of the newer industries, electricity, electrical engineering and vehicles in particular, was no greater than the average for all industry and considerably lower than in the first half of the 1920s.

Currency policy had a far more drastic impact in the case of Italy. The deliberate appreciation of the lira by Mussolini in 1927 was clearly a mistake since it involved severe domestic deflation and high unemployment. Unemployment nearly tripled between 1926 and 1929, industrial production stagnated and the growth of exports was checked. The Italian economy made very limited headway compared with the first half of the 1920s, though some slowing down was probably inevitable given the over-vigorous expansion through to 1926 and the fact that many factors favourable to growth were beginning to disappear by the middle of the decade. Norway and Denmark also had a similar experience though it was less severe in its effects than in the case of Italy. Here the objective of monetary policy was to increase the exchange value of their currencies prior to stabilization (1927–8) at the pre-war parities. The example of Finland, a country which achieved rapid economic progress throughout the 1920s, suggests that Denmark and Norway could have avoided severe compression and disequilibrium had they allowed their currencies to depreciate. Sweden went through a similar experience somewhat earlier but managed to adjust more rapidly partly thanks to sustained industrial transformation and a buoyant demand for exports. Thus in the later 1920s Sweden's economy was expanding vigorously despite a return to parity in 1924, though one should bear in mind that much of the domestic adjustment required to carry through the stabilization had been accomplished in the violent contraction of 1920–2.

Two countries which did rather better in the later 1920s were France and Belgium, partly by dint of different policies from those followed by the countries previously discussed. Both countries had faced a big reconstruction task at the end of the war but they had made the most of government reconstruction payments, inflationary financing and disrupted exchanges to recoup lost ground. Nor did currency stabilization in the mid-1920s halt the process of expansion since neither country made the mistake of restoring the former parity, much though it was desired. In fact both currencies were somewhat undervalued in the later 1920s, though the gains on this account were probably less marked than in the first half of the decade. France's achievements were quite impressive. Industrial production rose by a quarter between 1925 and 1929, while income per head increased by nearly 17 per cent. By the end of the decade industrial production was some 35–40 per cent greater than pre-war, income per head was higher by one-quarter or more, while the volume of exports was nearly 50 per cent larger. Such gains were partly the result of a considerable increase in industrial capacity, especially in sectors such as chemicals, engineering and metallurgy, and fairly rapid technical advances in new industries such as rayon, electricity and motor-car manufacturing. France did much to modernize her industrial structure in these years.

While both France and Belgium were consolidating on the reconstruction gains of the early 1920s, Germany by contrast had to start the reconstruction phase again since the explosive inflation of 1923 wreaked havoc with the economy. True it did not destroy fixed assets – indeed it brought into being much new plant and equipment albeit that a considerable part of the new capacity was not entirely suitable for future needs – but it did severely check the expansion of the early 1920s, so much so that the level of activity was little better than it had been at the end of the war. Most fixed debts were wiped out but this was offset by a severe loss of working capital. For a short time stabilization itself exerted a deflationary impact and led to the collapse of a number of cumbersome industrial empires which had been formed during the inflationary period. Doubts about whether stabilization would hold led to a minor crisis in 1926 with further deflationary implications.

The tasks ahead were formidable. Apart from the critical liquidity problem much industrial plant and equipment required renovating to make it more efficient. Productivity had sunk to a low level in 1923 and the large amount of capacity brought on stream did little to improve the situation. Moreover, given the reparations bill, Germany needed a large boost to exports and this could only be attained by improving her competitive position.

Despite the difficult situation Germany achieved a remarkable rejuvenation of her economy in the later 1920s. Heavy reliance was placed on foreign borrowing, the consequences of which are discussed elsewhere. It is doubtful whether much of this found its way directly into 'productive' or foreign-exchange-earning enterprises, but the inflow of funds certainly eased the capital shortage and released domestic resources for internal development. Whatever the precise direction of the capital flow the record is impressive. Progress was especially marked in the heavy capital goods sector and the newer science-based industries but much less apparent in the consumer goods trades. Large additions to capacity were accompanied by extensive programmes of mechanization and rationalization in many of the key sectors such as coal, iron and steel, chemical and electrical industries. The loss of hard coal reserves in Silesia and the Saar was offset by rapid exploitation of lignite, the production of which doubled. Mining operations in general were extensively mechanized and, by 1928, 75 per cent of the Ruhr coal output was cut mechanically.

By dint of these efforts German industry was placed on a more secure footing by the end of the decade. But though considerable expansion was achieved between 1925 and 1929 much of it only made up for ground lost earlier. It was only in the last couple of years that levels of economic activity and real income regained or surpassed pre-war dimensions, and by then there were signs that the economic prosperity was coming to an end as the inflow of foreign capital diminished. There were, too, several weak spots. Certain sectors remained depressed, notably agriculture despite substantial protection, and unemployment was still far too high. Exports barely managed to regain their pre-war level, a performance hardly in keeping with Germany's heavy external commitments. Indeed, given the weaknesses in the latter respects one cannot but conclude that Germany's prosperity was very precariously based and that the economy was literally kept in motion by the influx of foreign funds.

It is more difficult to make firm generalizations about the rest of Europe and the Baltic countries owing to the paucity of information on some of the countries. But it does appear that eastern Europe as a whole did slightly better than the west in terms of absolute growth in the later 1920s. Certainly primary production increased more rapidly and there were some impressive gains in industrial production, particularly in Hungary, Romania, Latvia, Czechoslovakia and Poland. As noted earlier, Russia also experienced a sharp burst of expansion under the first Five Year Plan. After the lean years of reconstruction the whole area registered an expansion of capital formation and a diversification of output with notable gains in coal, iron and steel, cement and oil production. The process of adaptation was assisted by the influx of foreign capital and systematic encouragement of industry by state subsidies, tax reliefs, import controls and high tariffs. The drive towards greater self-sufficiency was also accompanied by an extension of state enterprise. Even so, the gains in per capita income were often very modest, partly because of rapid population growth in some of the countries, notably Romania, Bulgaria and Poland. In the case of the last two countries income per head at the end of the decade was still below that of pre-war. Income levels generally were much lower than those of western Europe.

For virtually all the countries in what may be termed the agrarian sector of Europe – the population dependent on agriculture was 50 per cent or more in all central and eastern European countries apart from Austria and Czechoslovakia – the 1920s as a whole was a period of reconstruction and fundamental adjustment to new conditions both internally and outwith these countries. New economic systems had to be established, new markets sought, new products developed, agricultural methods were in urgent need of improvement, while expansion in the industrial sector was required to cater for the growing population and the resources released from the land. Most countries managed to make some progress in all respects albeit slowly. Given the high agricultural content of their economies and their dependence on imported supplies to further the process of industrial diversification probably the first and most essential step was to reform agriculture and improve its efficiency so as to permit an increase in exports to provide much-needed foreign exchange. This in itself was no easy task in this period since the outlets for primary products, especially in western Europe which had been the traditional market, were drying up. Moreover, some of the land reforms of the post-war period

44

only served to impede progress in this respect since they led to a greater fragmentation of holdings which was inimical to innovation and enhanced efficiency. Nevertheless, several countries did make considerable progress which
helped to strengthen their economic position. An enlightened agricultural
policy in Czechoslovakia did much to support the prosperity of industry. Land
reform was accompanied by technical and financial assistance to farmers
which enabled them to improve their methods of production and concentrate
on the more profitable crops such as sugar beet. The break-up of large estates
in Lithuania was replaced by a progressive co-operative movement, the
leaders of which recognized that unless old practices were changed the
peasantry would be condemned to subsistence farming. Within the matter of a
decade Lithuania, like Denmark, had shifted from cereals to dairy and
livestock products which fetched good prices abroad. The other Baltic states
also proved highly successful in adapting their primary sectors by exploiting
their forest resources and, in the case of Estonia and Latvia, developing
foreign markets for butter and bacon.

Evidence of progress is not difficult to find but it hardly amounted to a
revolution. By the end of the 1920s eastern Europe for the most part still
remained a backward and economically vulnerable area. Standards of living
were low and both agriculture and industry were highly inefficient by comparison with western standards. A policy of economic nationalism, while it
had visible effects, tended to foster inefficiency and high-cost enterprises. The
area remained very sensitive to tendencies in the outside world because of its
heavy dependence on the export of primary products, especially agricultural
commodities, at favourable prices and reliance on imported capital. Only so
long as these conditions held could this shaky equilibrium be maintained.

On balance therefore the economic performance of Europe during the 1920s
as a whole was quite respectable. After a rather shaky start in the immediate
reconstruction period many countries managed to achieve quite high rates of
growth, though inevitably the rates are inflated somewhat by the very low base
prevailing at the end of the war. However, even considering the period
1913–29 the average rate of growth of domestic output for western Europe was
about 2 per cent per annum and slightly less for eastern Europe. This compares favourably with the period following (1929–38) when average growth
rates were about half this figure. The most successful countries were the
Netherlands, Norway, Sweden, Switzerland and Denmark with growth above
average, whereas Austria, Germany and the UK had a below-average performance. In eastern Europe Czechoslovakia and Yugoslavia did somewhat
better than the average for this area.

Despite the creditable growth performance the foundations of prosperity, at
least in Europe and probably elsewhere, remained 'fragile and precarious'.
There were certainly signs of underlying weaknesses within particular
countries and with the working of the international economy as a whole.
These of course became all too apparent once the basis of prosperity was

45

undermined. But for the time being the expansion of these years was sufficient to conceal the sources of instability which in turn reduced the urgency for making the necessary adjustments. We must now turn to examine some of the major international problems which affected European stability.

WAR DEBTS AND REPARATIONS

War debts and reparations proved to be one of the most controversial issues of the post-war decade. Negotiations as to the amounts involved and methods of payment dragged on endlessly and to little avail since ultimately most of them were never paid. Apart from causing considerable international bitterness the process of debt collection impeded the smooth functioning of the international economy and seriously weakened Germany, the main debtor.

Altogether some twenty-eight countries were involved in one way or another with war debts and reparations. But for many countries the amounts involved were quite small; by far the most important participants were Germany, the United States, Britain, France, Italy and Belgium. Germany was of course the chief debtor with eleven creditors to her name, while the United States had sixteen debtors, Britain seventeen and France ten. The sums involved were enormous; inter-Allied debts alone amounted to $26.5 billion, most of which was due to the United States and Britain, with France the principal debtor. The burden imposed on Germany, as eventually fixed by the Reparations Commission in 1921, was $33 billion, the greater part of which was to be paid to France and Britain. These amounts were in fact scaled down during the course of the 1920s though the sums, together with accrued interest, still remained large: too large in fact to be met in full with the inevitable result that they were declared moribund in the depression of the early 1930s.

Whether sums on this scale should have been imposed and whether in practice they could have been paid are still matters of debate. What is certain is that in the political context of the time there was little prospect of them either being cancelled altogether or of the two being linked together. France insisted on exactions from the enemy while the United States expected payment for services rendered to the Allies. Allied payment of war debts was dependent upon reparations flowing from Germany. The possibility of offsetting reparations and inter-Allied claims so that Germany could have settled directly with the United States was thwarted by America's opposition to the mixing of claims, partly no doubt on the grounds that there was a much greater likelihood of Germany defaulting on her obligations than the Allied powers.

Most of the reparations bill fell to Germany. Interim payments had been made before the final bill of $33 billion was presented which provided for fixed payments on a quarterly basis beginning in January 1922. The Germans, while accepting the imposition with reluctance, regarded the claims as excessive, and argued that on both budgetary and exchange transfer grounds it was not within the country's capacity to pay. Certainly there was some justification for these views at the time since Germany's financial and economic situation deteriorated markedly during the course of 1922 as inflation and currency depreciation rapidly accelerated. Repeated requests for a moratorium were met with refusal. By the end of 1922 Germany's capacity to meet its obligations was virtually exhausted and the prospects of further payments looked bleak. Fearing the worst French and Belgian troops were marched into the Ruhr on 11 January 1923.

The invasion completed the collapse of Germany's financial system. The objective was to enforce payment by direct control of the Ruhr industrial system, but passive German resistance thwarted French efforts, the financing of which sent the mark up to 'stellar magnitudes'.[2] Neither side gained but the struggle continued until the mark was rendered worthless. Whether the German government deliberately provoked the inflationary crisis to prove to the world she could not pay reparations is a moot point, but the effect was certainly spectacular. By September 1923 the currency was in such a state that Germany called off the resistance and proposed the introduction of a new currency, the *Rentenmark*.

The upshot of this debacle was a reconsideration of the reparations issue by the Reparations Commission. A Committee under General Dawes proposed an extension of the payment period and a reduction in annual payments to more manageable proportions, though no reduction in the total reparations debt was contemplated. The Dawes Plan came into force in September 1924 and on the surface it worked well. Annuities were paid regularly and transferred without much apparent difficulty. But the underlying weaknesses in Germany's payments situation were masked by an entirely new factor, namely massive foreign borrowing. Because of budgetary and balance of payments difficulties Germany borrowed 28 billion marks abroad in the period 1924–30 out of which she paid reparations amounting to 10.3 billion. In other words, her reparation payments were covered at least two and a half times by the import of capital. So long as foreign capital poured into the country the settlement of reparations ran smoothly, but once funds dried up then the basic weakness of the position was exposed. The crunch came in the late 1920s when American lending was sharply curtailed; this set off a chain reaction among foreign banks demanding the withdrawal of loans from Germany. The position was extremely tricky since not only had Germany piled up large foreign liabilities, but many of these were in the form of short-term debts liable to immediate recall.

Recognition of Germany's precarious financial position led to one last attempt to solve the reparations issue. A committee of experts set up in 1929 under Owen D. Young proposed a reduction in the capital sum and a scaling down of the annuities. By the time the new arrangements came into effect, in April 1930, the impact of depression was making it difficult to comply with even these modified terms. Within a year Germany was engulfed in financial crisis and in June 1931 President Hoover proposed a moratorium on reparations.

Altogether Germany paid only a fraction of the original reparations bill of $33 billion; estimates vary but the highest suggest no more than one-quarter. Clearly it was a futile exercise to attempt to recover such large debts. Whether Germany could have discharged her obligations more satisfactorily had she made the effort is a debatable point, though most writers have tended to argue that they were beyond her means. Whatever the true position the fact remains that the reparations burden had unfortunate consequences for Germany, especially in 1923 and again in 1929–31, and, in turn, for the economic and financial tranquillity of Europe.

The first mistake of the Allied powers when dealing with the problem was not so much that they accepted an unrealistically large reparations bill but that initially the annuities were set at too high a level. These could easily have been set at a more reasonable level in the early years when Germany was in the process of recovery from the shock of 1923, and then adjusted in time in accordance with improvements in her economic position. By fixing them as they did they left Germany with what seemed an impossible task and hence little real effort was made to try and meet either the budgetary or transfer objectives. The second mistake was for the Allies to continue to bale out Germany with loans. Foreign borrowing on the scale indulged in during the later 1920s had several adverse consequences. For one thing large capital imports tended to aggravate the transfer problems in so far as they raised Germany's propensity to import, and at the same time reduced the buying power of lending countries and hence their import of German products. In addition, the rise in German purchasing power occasioned by capital inflows meant a diversion of resources towards production for the home market rather than for exports. Capital imports all too frequently were channelled into non-export-earning activities. In a wider context massive foreign borrowing simply stored up trouble for the future: Germany simply incurred one debt to pay another and the real problem of redemption was never squarely faced. As it was, Germany was able to meet her payments without great hardship to herself and with the minimum of disturbance to creditor nations in the form of unwanted German goods. Borrowing simply concealed the payments problem for a time but it could not do so indefinitely. Once foreign lending dried up Germany, and other European countries with large external debts, were unable to stand the strain and financial collapse was therefore inevitable.

The settlement of debts among the Allied powers proved no more satisfactory. The final tally amounted to $23 billion (excluding Russian debts). The United States was the largest creditor, accounting for about one-half of the total, most of it having been lent to Britain, France and Italy. Britain was the next largest creditor with claims on other countries far exceeding her debts to America. The main net debtors were France, Italy and Belgium.

Several early attempts to find a workable solution to the war debts issue all ran foul of the United States who insisted on being paid in full. This meant that the other Allied powers had no alternative but to insist on collecting their own debts including reparations. Subsequently, the United States relaxed its hard attitude and concluded agreements with countries individually, by which the terms of payment were liberalized and the capital sums scaled down considerably. Even these concessions did not solve the problem. As with reparations, the payment of war debts raised budgetary and transfer difficulties. Easily transferable commodities were in short supply and creditors were reluctant to accept payment in competing goods. Clearing claims with the United States proved the most difficult task since increasing protection in that country and her demand for payment in gold and dollars made it difficult for the debtors to raise the requisite funds, especially since nearly all of them had unfavourable payments balances with the United States. In fact payments were made but the process was a somewhat farcical one and indirectly it involved a link with reparations which the Americans were never prepared to accept in practice. The United States, and to a lesser extent other creditors, made capital loans to Germany who then paid her creditors, while the latter in turn passed on the money to the United States in settlement of their own debts. This process went on until the flow of funds from America dried up, and when, in the early 1930s, the Allies were forced to relinquish their claims on Germany war debts very soon died a natural death. The final accounting shows that America received $2.6 billion from the European Allies, a small amount compared with the original $12 billion and less than half that under the revised settlements of the 1920s. Four countries, Britain, France, Italy and Belgium, were responsible for the bulk of the payments to America and collected most of the reparations, which more than covered their combined indebtedness.

Thus after a decade of political wrangling little was paid, either in reparations or war debts, against the original claims presented. The process of negotiation involved much valuable time and energy, and the continued existence of the problems served as a source of international friction throughout the 1920s. The manner in which the payments were eventually effected concealed the real issues and gave rise to basic disequilibrium in the international payments mechanism which was bound to be exposed sooner or later.

INFLATION AND CURRENCY STABILIZATION

Few countries emerged from the war with their monetary and currency systems unscathed. Nearly all currencies lost their stability and depreciated in value once the tie with gold was broken or the artificial pegging practised in wartime was released. By the end of 1920 most European currencies were well below their pre-war par values in relation to the dollar and in some cases the depreciation had much further to go. The loss in value was not surprising since the war had seriously weakened the productive mechanism of economies;

it had also created balance of payments problems, and inflationary methods of financing had been widespread.

The restoration of monetary stability was regarded as a matter of some urgency after the war. It was considered highly desirable that each nation should return to a fixed gold parity as soon as possible. But the stabilization process proved to be a long drawn-out affair which lasted most of the decade. No systematic plan was drawn up to deal with the problem although the United States, which had little difficulty in readopting the full gold standard in 1919, served as a rough benchmark for the realignment of all other currencies. Each country stabilized and returned to the gold standard as soon as conditions were deemed to be suitable, and this depended very much on how quickly countries got their financial affairs under control.

The manner in which stabilization was carried out and the characteristics of the new standard varied considerably. At one extreme there was a select band of countries that managed to regain their pre-war parities: these were Britain, Switzerland, the Netherlands, Denmark, Sweden and Norway. Rigorous retrenchment at an early stage enabled these countries to avoid the inflationary problems of much of Europe. At the other extreme there were five countries – Austria, Hungary, Poland, Germany and Russia – who were forced to introduce new monetary units since violent bouts of inflation wrecked their currencies completely. The remaining countries stabilized between these two extremes at values well below pre-war, as for example France at 20.0 per cent of the former dollar value, Belgium (14.3 per cent), Italy (25.0 per cent), Romania (3.7 per cent), Bulgaria (3.7 per cent), Yugoslavia (9.1 per cent), Czechoslovakia (14.3 per cent) and Finland (12.5 per cent).

The full gold standard, or specie standard, in which gold coins circulate internally and all other money is readily convertible into gold, was abandoned almost universally. Instead a watered-down version of the gold standard was generally adopted which meant that restrictions were placed on the convertibility of non-commodity money into gold and on the export of gold. In the case of the few countries which went onto the gold bullion standard (e.g. Britain, Denmark, Norway) notes could not readily be converted into gold on demand except for export purposes and then only at a fixed price and in large minimum amounts. The majority of countries, however, opted for a gold exchange standard whereby the monetary authority of a country tied its currency to gold indirectly by maintaining a fixed exchange rate with a foreign currency that was on either a gold coin or gold bullion standard. In other words, the central bank had the obligation to maintain the value of a national currency at par with other gold currency countries by buying and selling foreign exchange at the gold parity.

For most European countries currency stabilization could only be achieved when inflation had been brought under control. Much of Europe suffered from inflationary forces of varying degrees of intensity in the early 1920s.

The methods of financing the war had started the inflationary process and the fiscal demands of governments after 1918 ensured that it would continue. The burden of reconstruction was heavy in many parts of Europe and this was one of the main factors making for large budgetary deficits. Government expenditures were also boosted by continued heavy military outlays, rising social security spending, and in the case of Germany reparation payments which accounted for one-half of the budgetary deficit in the early 1920s. The pressures came at a time when savings were low and the administration of tax systems was inefficient and inadequate for the tasks in hand. In any case, a squeeze on consumption through increased taxation would probably have been politically unacceptable at the time given the fact that consumption levels were already low in many countries. The easiest way out was therefore to resort to inflationary spending which imposed the sacrifices in a roundabout way. This form of enforced taxation was relatively easy to administer and therefore held attractions for governments which were weak, inexperienced and disorganized. The whole process was ultimately dependent on one factor, namely ignorance about inflation and what it implied, since Europe had not experienced severe inflation for more than a century.

But in several cases it moved into the runaway stage of hyperinflation. The process by which this develops is complex and dependent partly on the psychological reaction of the people. Once they realize what is happening they begin to take steps to protect themselves against inflation and by so doing complicate the fiscal process and throw the monetary mechanism into disorder. First, the lag between money incomes and prices is eliminated by adopting systems of indexation for wages and salaries. Second, the savings propensity drops rapidly as money loses its value and ultimately dissaving takes place which forces up the velocity of circulation of money. Finally, capital flight occurs as the market loses confidence and anticipates further currency depreciation, which in turn speeds up exchange depreciation and the rise in prices. As a result the fiscal needs of government are in jeopardy, because of the fall in the real value of tax receipts, and reaction to this aggravates the inflationary conditions. This process played an important part in all cases of hyperinflation in the early 1920s. By 1923 the depreciation of tax revenues in Germany had reached a point at which taxes cost more to collect than they brought in.

It has been argued that hyperinflation could never have occurred but for the continued increase in the money supply and that the process could have been checked at any time had the authorities tapered off the issue of new money, which finally they did. This argument, while not incorrect, tends to overlook the *raison d'être* behind the growth of the money supply, namely fiscal needs. That the money supply was pumped up so vigorously can be explained by the fact that printing money provided a convenient way of providing governments with real resources, and, second, that the effectiveness of the process declined over time as ever larger issues were required. The size of the problem was compounded in the case of Germany because of the financing of passive

resistance to the Ruhr invasion in 1923. The issue of money provided governments with a means of revenue by a special kind of tax on cash balances held
by people, and the rate of tax was equivalent to the depreciation of the value of
money. Not until tax rates exploded (that is, prices) causing wholesale disruption to the economic system did the authorities substitute a traditional tax
programme for a policy of printing money.

The consequences of inflation are difficult to assess precisely. The first
phase of relatively moderate inflation probably did make an effective contribution to the resources needed for reconstruction. Countries which experienced
inflation escaped the worst effects of the depression of 1921 – in Germany output actually rose quite strongly – and benefited from the encouragement given
to capital investment. France and Belgium, who managed to contain inflation
within reasonable bounds, probably did quite well out of it. But once inflation
was allowed to run out of control the story was rather different. Germany, for
example, gained initially from inflation in that production and employment
were higher than in countries which followed a policy of retrenchment. But she
reaped the costs in 1923 when activity rates fell sharply. By the end of that year
real income was barely one-half of that in 1913 and industrial production was
even below the level of 1920. Unemployment rose to very high levels towards
the end of 1923. In fact it took some time for Germany to recover from the
shock and it was not until the later 1920s that production and real incomes
were restored to pre-war levels. Moreover, since most liquid capital and
savings were destroyed in the inflation the propensity to save was low after
1923; this meant that capital was short and interest rates high, forcing
Germany to borrow heavily with unfortunate consequences from the point of
view of economic stability.

The way in which inflation was brought under control and stabilization was
effected varied a great deal from one country to another, though usually severe
financial and monetary measures were required to ensure success. One of the
first countries to achieve success was Latvia who, without foreign aid, put a
definite stop to inflation in the summer of 1921. State recourse to the printing
press for budgetary purposes ceased in July 1921 and the national currency
was abandoned for fiscal accounting purposes with taxes being 'valorized' in
terms of gold, a practice adopted by Germany in 1923. Czechoslovakia also
dealt with the inflationary problem promptly by instituting severe fiscal
measures. All the countries which experienced hyperinflation were forced to
bring in new currency units. In the case of Austria and Hungary, both of
which secured League assistance, the currency was stabilized by means other
than fiscal policy so as to achieve a monetary unit on the basis of which fiscal
policy could be made effective. Though attempts were made to increase taxes
in both cases there was no systematic effort to adjust them to the depreciation
of the currency through tax 'valorization' schemes. The initial stabilization
was achieved by a return of confidence as a result of the League's financial
reconstruction schemes. The League arranged international loans for Austria

in 1922 and Hungary in 1924 and the League's staff took over the supervision of the finances of both countries until 1926. Once confidence in the new currencies was secured fiscal policy rapidly became effective and budgetary equilibrium was achieved in a very short time.

Germany, on the other hand, managed her preliminary stabilization without external assistance though subsequently an international loan was arranged to ensure its success. Two important measures preceded the stabilization of the mark in November 1923. The passive resistance expenditure in the Ruhr was stopped in September and taxes were assessed in terms of gold. Almost simultaneously with preparations for restoring budgetary equilibrium it was announced that a new currency, the *Rentenmark*, would be introduced to replace the worthless currency then in existence. It success was ensured by two factors: the issue was strictly limited and it was backed by the security of an internal loan on the basis of real assets (land and buildings). In the final analysis much depended on the public's confidence in the experiment. Once there appeared to be a reasonable prospect that the *Rentenmark* would retain its value the public's demand for cash recovered quickly, though it is doubtful whether the new currency would have lasted long had the government failed to complete its fiscal reforms quickly.

Attempts at currency reform were sometimes quite prolonged and often involved an initial stabilization of the currency and then a return to the gold standard. This was true in the case of France, Belgium and Italy as well as a number of other countries. Though inflation was not excessive in these cases the early and somewhat half-hearted attempts at reform ensured its continuation. The French franc, for example, was almost on the point of collapse before firm action was taken. Fortunately the right-wing Poincaré government of July 1926 restored confidence quickly by a series of rigorous measures, including increased taxes, reduced public spending and the funding of a large part of the floating debt. By the end of the year *de facto* stabilization of the franc was achieved and in June 1928 France completed her currency reform by returning to the gold standard at the existing exchange rate which effectively undervalued the franc. Being closely tied to the French currency the Belgian reform followed a rather similar pattern, but Italy provides something of a contrast in that political authority assumed a greater role. Mussolini, intent on demonstrating his absolute authority and enhancing his prestige, pledged support for the currency 'to the last drop of blood'. He pushed through a hefty deflationary package of measures and then proceeded to stabilize the lira (December 1927) at an overvalued rate which adversely affected the Italian economy in the later 1920s.

By the end of the decade nearly all European countries had brought inflation under control, stabilized their currencies and adopted some form of the gold standard. In fact the dominant force in economic policy throughout the period was the currency question: first the effort involved in stabilizing exchange rates and returning to gold, and then the struggle to maintain the new standard. The monetary ideal took predominance over all other matters of economic policy simply because the authorities believed that by restoring the pre-war monetary mechanism the post-war economic maladjustments would be corrected. These illusions were soon shattered, however. Far from correcting the underlying maladjustments the restored gold standard itself was subject to serious strains from the start, and it disintegrated soon after it had been re-established. To understand why it was that the system failed to function in the expected manner it is important to examine some of the weaknesses of the post-war gold standard.

THE GOLD STANDARD UNDER PRESSURE

The gold standard of the 1920s differed considerably from what might be termed the classical system of the pre-war period. It was not a full gold standard since gold coins disappeared from circulation almost everywhere; nor could it be regarded as a proper bullion standard by which currencies were directly convertible into gold since few countries adopted this form. Most countries, through lack of gold reserves and other factors, were forced onto a gold exchange standard under which they held their legally required reserves partly or wholly in the form of foreign exchange. This system was not unknown before 1914 but it became much more widespread during the 1920s. The effect was to increase considerably the foreign exchange component of central bank reserves; by 1927 foreign exchange accounted for 42 per cent of the total reserves (gold and foreign exchange) of twenty-four European central banks compared with about 12 per cent in 1913.

The gold exchange standard may have eased the pressure on gold supplies but it only transferred the problem by one remove. Indeed, it was a source of weakness rather than one of strength. It led to a 'pyramiding' of claims on gold centres so that in the event of a crisis in one country a whole series of currencies might be affected with serious consequences for the reserve currency. Gold exchange standard countries built up their exchange reserve holdings by short-term claims on key currencies, chiefly sterling and the dollar, the accommodation of which put severe strain on the central money markets since the funds proved highly volatile and moved from centre to centre in response to shifts in interest rates and changes in confidence. The fact that there was now more than one international financial market of importance (New York as well as London, and later Paris) provided ample opportunity for fund switching, whereas before the war sterling's unchallenged supremacy and strength provided much less incentive for such activity. And there was always the possibility that such funds might be withdrawn in the form of gold at short notice. Nor was the danger of conversion contingent solely upon a crisis of confidence. The gold exchange standard was regarded by many as a temporary expedient or transitional phase prior to the adoption of the real thing. France in particular was very loath to sacrifice national prestige by remaining on an exchange standard. After the *de facto* stabilization of the franc in 1926 the Bank of France acquired the largest stock of foreign exchange (mainly in sterling and dollars) in the world. This was partly to prevent unnecessary appreciation of the French currency but at the same time there was the ever-present threat, which in the later 1920s became a reality, that these holdings would be liquidated and converted into gold in order to realize French dreams. Germany also followed a similar policy soon after the stabilization of the mark.

Inevitably therefore the gold exchange standard put greater pressure on the key centres, London and New York. This meant that they needed to hold larger gold stocks than those required to meet normal trading transactions in order to guard against the possibility of the sudden conversion of foreign claims into gold. In this respect New York, with its large gold stocks, faced no real problem. It was London that was the weak link since this centre had large claims against it but little with which to meet them since gold stocks were low. Had sterling been a strong currency with no competitors as before the war there would probably have been little difficulty in operating with a low gold reserve. But in fact sterling was continually under strain in the 1920s and the gold exchange standard merely served to increase the pressure. Indeed, Britain's inability to exercise control over the international monetary system in the way she had formerly done was an important factor contributing to the collapse of the gold standard in the early 1930s.

A further source of weakness arose out of the stabilization process itself. The piecemeal and unco-ordinated manner in which it was accomplished meant that little attention was paid to the crucial question of correct parity values. The haphazard choice of exchange rates, often under the influence of speculation and political motives, invariably meant that countries ended up with the wrong parities. Some were overvalued, others undervalued, and it was a stroke of luck if a country made the right selection. Thus the system started off from a point of disequilibrium and once the pattern was set there was little chance of adjustment. The rates chosen came to be regarded as sacrosanct so that the authorities were reluctant to adjust them even when they were seen to be incorrect. Countries which had undervalued their currencies were unwilling to forgo the benefits derived from a depreciated exchange; France in particular did her best to neutralize the impact of the flow of funds into the country immediately following stabilization by acquiring large amounts of foreign exchange. Those countries with overvalued currencies faced a more difficult problem. To devalue soon after stabilization was out of the question since this would have involved a serious loss of prestige. In any case, the currency most out of alignment was the British and a devaluation of sterling might well have set off a chain reaction and undermined the whole process of stabilization. The alternative was therefore to adjust the domestic economy to accord with the exchange rate, which involved compressing domestic cost and price levels. One or two countries, notably Sweden, managed to do this fairly well but Britain was unable to deflate to the necessary extent given the already high unemployment. Sterling could not therefore regain its former strength.

Given the initial disequilibrium in exchange rates it is not surprising that the gold standard functioned less smoothly than before 1914. The choice of the wrong exchange rates magnified balance of payments problems and consequently the system was called upon to make adjustments on a scale far greater than previously and for which it was never designed, and at a time when the adjustment mechanism was less easy to operate. Few countries were prepared to sacrifice the stability of their domestic economies completely for the sake of external equilibrium. Thus countries with overvalued exchanges were reluctant to carry through the necessary adjustment to their domestic economies, while surplus countries were equally unwilling to meet the former half-way. This is shown clearly by the frequency with which central banks neutralized the domestic monetary effects of gold flows which had formerly been the traditional mechanism for dealing with balance of payments disequilibrium. Gold surplus countries in particular were active in this respect, the United States throughout the 1920s and France in the later 1920s when she experienced a 'golden avalanche'.

Such stabilization procedures may have been justified in terms of insulating domestic economies from monetary movements but they were not compatible with the maintenance of the gold standard. In particular, neutralization of gold flows by the major surplus countries placed a severe strain on the system and threw much of the burden of adjustment onto those countries experiencing gold outflows. This was an especially serious problem for Britain with her persistent tendency to lose gold, and one she was not fully prepared to accept given the state of her domestic economy. The Bank of England therefore attempted to minimize the impact of gold losses as far as possible.

The failure of surplus and deficit countries to meet each other half-way meant that the pre-war adjustment mechanism was rendered largely inoperative, a situation all the more serious given the initial disequilibrium arising from the fixing of exchange rates. Inevitably this accentuated the maldistribution of the world's monetary reserves which had been in process since 1914. The United States, France and the European neutrals absorbed an increasing share of the world's gold reserves so that by the end of the 1920s they accounted for nearly 65 per cent of the total as against 54 per cent in 1913. For the most part gold went to those countries which did not need it, either because their currencies were not used for reserve purposes (e.g. those of the neutrals) or because they had more than enough gold in relation to current liabilities. American gold stocks for example amounted to over $4 billion in the later 1920s against dollar liabilities (central bank holdings of dollar exchange) of only $0.6 billion. By contrast Britain's sterling liabilities to central banks were nearly four times the Bank of England's gold reserves. It is true that Britain had short-term assets on which she could theoretically call in an emergency, but even allowing for these her liabilities still amounted to some three times the Bank's free reserve. In practice, however, short-term assets became 'locked-in' during a crisis, as in 1931. Clearly then Britain was the weak link in the system. She had the largest liabilities and the smallest gold reserves of any major country, while her balance of payments was far from strong. Any deterioration in the latter or loss of confidence in sterling was bound to bring pressure to bear on the reserves which could not be met. It is true that Britain operated with a very small gold reserve before the war but then her liabilities were smaller, her quick assets could easily be recalled, the balance of payments was stronger and confidence in sterling remained firm.

Given the manner in which it was restored and the way in which it was subsequently operated, it was inconceivable that the gold standard of the 1920s could have provided any solution to the fundamental problems of the period. Indeed, it was only a matter of time before the new system itself disintegrated since once exposed to pressures countries were not prepared to sacrifice their domestic economies on the altar of the exchanges. While the depression of 1929–32 cannot be attributed directly to the defects of the gold standard, the latter did make it more difficult for adjustment to take place between creditor and debtor nations and, as we shall see, the existence of a system of fixed exchange rates tended to exacerbate the downswing once it got under way.

It is possible that the new system might have been able to hobble along for several years in the absence of severe strains and as long as American lending continued to paper over the fundamental maladjustment between creditor and debtor countries. Once the United States relinquished its stabilization role then the pressures on the system were too great to withstand. To complete the story therefore we must look briefly at the position of the debtor countries and the role of foreign lending in this period.

INTERNATIONAL LENDING AND THE DEBTOR NATIONS

The war had a dramatic effect on the pattern and character of international debts and international lending. For one thing it created a whole series of new international debts in the form of reparations and war loans. Second, western Europe's status as a creditor changed substantially. Most European countries were forced to relinquish sizeable portions of their foreign assets either to help pay for the war or because of default on the part of debtors. Germany lost most of her overseas holdings, France over one-half and Britain about 15 per cent. At the same time these countries contracted heavy debts as a result of the war. By contrast the United States emerged as a strong net creditor; excluding inter-governmental debts America's net position on long-term account was $3.3 billion compared with a net debtor status of a similar amount before the war.

During the 1920s international lending was resumed on a scale comparable with that before 1914 and by 1929 the total volume of foreign-owned assets was considerably larger than in 1913. The United States replaced Europe as the major investor. Between 1919 and 1929 her long-term investments abroad rose by nearly $9 billion, accounting for two-thirds of the world total increase and raising her stake to nearly one-third the world total. No other country came anywhere near to matching the scale of America's lending. Britain resumed lending on a diminished scale, while France failed to recoup all her wartime losses. These three countries accounted for over three-quarters of all foreign investments in 1929.

Though the volume of foreign lending was substantial after the war it by no means follows that it was utilized or disbursed in an optimal way. Indeed it can be argued that the manner in which it was invested did more to destabilize the international economy than to maintain equilibrium. Low-income under-developed countries came off badly since the bulk of long-term lending went to developed or semi-developed countries not all of which were equally deserving. In the first instance funds tended to flow to the richer creditworthy countries rather than to areas most in need of assistance. This reflected a lack of coherent policy on the part of the creditor nations as to what factors should determine the flow of funds to particular areas and the continued dominance of the profit motive in selecting areas for investment. Even so, extravagant and imprudent lending was common in the 1920s, no doubt a product of uncertain conditions and speculation. The United States, with her lack of experience in this matter, failed to exercise a discriminating policy with the result that unwise investments were often made, particularly in European and Latin American countries. Loans were often used unproductively in the sense that they failed to guarantee sufficient exchange proceeds to service the debt. In effect borrowers were allowed to over-extend themselves, the debt burden mounted and the only way out was to keep on borrowing.

The flow of funds was far from steady from year to year and such instability gave rise to difficulties in the borrowing countries. Large swings in the volume of investment were quite common partly as a consequence of changes in domestic conditions in the creditor countries. Thus in 1921, 1923 and again in 1926 the net capital outflow from the main creditors fell sharply only to rise equally sharply in subsequent years. The contraction in the immediate post-war period was particularly serious since it delayed the European recovery effort. The really critical period came in the years 1928–30 when overseas lending collapsed at a time when many borrowers were showing signs of strain. The position was made worse by the increasing pressure on short-term funds, many of which had been employed unwisely in central Europe. After 1925 especially there was a growing volume of short-term lending, part of which was used to finance long-term projects. In addition, short-term capital movements in and out of the major financial centres added a further destabilizing influence.

Most countries in central and eastern Europe depended heavily on foreign capital throughout the 1920s, first for reconstruction and stabilization purposes and second for furthering the diversification of their economies.

After the war all these countries were desperately short of resources, especially capital. The immediate problems were the financing of relief and reconstruction and the stabilization of currency and financial systems which had been severely weakened by current economic conditions. Since conditions were not propitious for large-scale private lending in the immediate post-war years it was left to governmental agencies to fill the gap. Unfortunately the US government aid programme for relief and reconstruction in Europe was curtailed sharply in 1920–1 and by 1923 the supply of overseas finance generally had dwindled to insignificant proportions. Moreover, the amounts involved were generally insufficient and much of the aid went to countries who needed it least. First-aid loans, organized under the aegis of the League of Nations, provided a second source of assistance. These were designed to provide borrowers with exchange reserves, to establish central banks and supply them with capital, and to fund short-term debts at home and abroad. For the most part imported capital in this reconstruction phase did not go directly into productive enterprise, though it would be a mistake to level too much criticism on this score. Stabilization and relief loans were necessary and foreign capital played a positive role in stabilizing monetary systems and preventing total collapse of economic systems. That they were not represented by income-producing assets should not be allowed to obscure the fact that they were an essential condition of obtaining further capital which could be invested in self-liquidating assets. On the other hand, it is clear that the relief offered by foreign capital in this period was insufficient for the task in hand.

Foreign lending on a large scale was resumed again in 1924. The improvement in economic and political conditions generally, and particularly the progress achieved in currency stabilization in central and eastern Europe, encouraged the movement of private capital. But it was borrowing in the post-stabilization phase which was the primary cause of the subsequent difficulties in many European countries. The need for imported capital was not in dispute, yet reliance on foreign investment served to create more problems than it solved. One of the main problems was that insufficient attention was given to ensure that the increase in debts was self-liquidating. Only a small proportion of government loans – between 30 and 50 per cent – was used for increasing the productive capacity of the borrowing countries. Nor was private capital always in the best interests of the debtors. Its flow was unstable and it did not always find its way into foreign-exchange-earning activities. Moreover, in so far as capital imports were employed as safeguards to plug up balance of payments disequilibria they simply served to increase the service burden without contributing to the process of development in a way which would have rectified fundamental imbalances. Also part of the capital receipts was used to stimulate agricultural development in an effort to boost exports, a process which led to a deterioration in agricultural prices which provided the basis for foreign exchange earnings.

For most of the period the cost of borrowing was fairly high and inflexible.

Most of the foreign capital absorbed by central and eastern Europe went into fixed interest securities at nominal interest rates of between 6 and 9 per cent, and often much more when allowance is made for the discount price of many issues. This meant that a large proportion of the debt service burden remained fixed when incomes and activity declined. An additional complication was that high interest rates tended to attract short-term capital which, up to 1929 at least, often served to offset temporary declines in long-term capital inflows, and the internal credit systems tended to convert external short-term loans into long-term domestic ones. This proved a serious source of weakness once the going got sticky, as in 1930–1, since then it was impossible to attract short-term accommodation to offset the decline in long-term borrowing. Hungary was particularly affected in this respect although in most central and east European countries foreign liabilities constituted between 20 and 40 per cent of commercial bank deposits.

Thus by the end of the 1920s the debt burdens of central and east European countries had reached alarming proportions. Throughout the years 1924–9 all countries, with the exception of Czechoslovakia, borrowed heavily and on average foreign capital equalled or exceeded the rate of domestic accumulation. Since much of foreign capital was not self-liquidating in terms of foreign exchange earnings the servicing of former debts could only be done by raising new loans. In most countries the sums required for amortization purposes annually were larger than the amount of new loans; for example, in the case of Hungary the total interest and amortization due in 1929 exceeded the amount of new loans by 16 per cent, and half of the new credits were used to pay off old debts. In many cases debt service payments constituted one-quarter or more of the value of current exports, though given the fact that servicing of the foreign loans called for 'strong currencies' obtainable from a limited range of exports, the actual strain on the balance of payments was much heavier than these figures would suggest. In view of the initial strain it could be argued that the insolvency of these countries was simply aggravated rather than created by the depression of the 1930s. The weight of the burden was of course very much increased by the large decline in capital inflows and primary product prices after 1928, and, with limited reserves, the burden of adjustment was bound to fall with a vengeance on the domestic economic structure.

Germany's problem was somewhat different in that the magnitudes involved were much greater and her position was complicated by reparations. Furthermore, she was not dependent on primary products for exchange earnings as was the case with her eastern neighbours. Nevertheless, she too resorted to borrowing on a massive scale to patch up a temporary stability at the expense of the future. Large-scale borrowing began effectively with currency stabilization and the floating of the Dawes Loan in 1924. The main attraction for investors was the high rates of interest consequent upon the scarcity of capital and the degree of risk. Lenders poured capital into Germany without much thought as to how the loans were to be serviced. At the peak of indebtedness in the summer of 1930, Germany's external liabilities were of the order of 28 billion marks, some 16 billion of which were in the form of short-term credits. The bulk of this sum came from the United States, Britain and the Netherlands.

It would be a mistake to infer that most of this capital was squandered on frivolous activities such as pleasure gardens and planetaria, so much lamented by Dr Schacht in 1927. Some of it was, but even so capital imports did assist German recovery after the great inflation when two-fifths of Germany's investment came from abroad. Nearly three-quarters of the total capital imports found their way into private industry and this facilitated re-equipment and expansion. Nevertheless borrowing did seriously increase the vulnerability of the German economy. Most of the foreign investment proved unproductive in that it did relatively little to boost exchange earnings, while part of it financed an import surplus which raised the standard of living. More serious was the use to which short-term funds were put. A large part of these consisted of loans to German banks by foreign bankers which were invested in long-term projects. Since such funds were liable to sudden withdrawal this left the German banking system in a potentially vulnerable state. The first indication of what lay in store came in the spring of 1929 when pressure on Germany's foreign exchange position resulting from reparation payments caused a temporary financial crisis. Foreign banks withdrew their support and called in some of their short-term loans, and the difficulties were aggravated by the decline in American short-term lending as a result of the stock market boom. This crisis was soon overcome but it was merely the tip of the iceberg. Far greater disasters were to hit the German banking system in the liquidity crisis of 1931.

In effect, therefore, Germany, like her neighbours, was living on borrowed time in the later 1920s. Foreign debts were allowed to pile up to an extent which could never be justified by reference to her actual or potential export earnings. How Germany was supposed to meet her obligations once capital imports ceased was something her creditors never seem to have considered seriously. Even had there been no economic crisis or check to lending at the end of the decade it was inconceivable that Germany could have gone on absorbing capital imports on such a scale for very much longer. The alternatives were no doubt limited since any attempt to secure an improved external balance would have required severe domestic deflation. It is possible that the Germans shrank from more positive action in an attempt to demonstrate their aversion to the obligations imposed by the Allies. Be that as it may, that the latter should have attempted to conceal the impossibility of the burden, at least in the short term, by pouring capital into Germany speaks volumes for their lack of economic wisdom.

In short, therefore, the international lending of the 1920s created an illusion of soundness and stability that did not in fact exist. So long as the flow of capital to debtor countries continued the cracks in the international economic structure remained concealed. Yet at the same time the process of lending served to widen the cracks so that once the flow was cut off the superficial stability of the system was undermined completely.

NOTES

1 The countries included in the following discussion are Austria, Czechoslovakia, Bulgaria, Hungary, Poland, Romania, Yugoslavia and Russia. Germany is dealt with separately since her position is somewhat different from the countries listed.
2 The German inflation is covered in more detail below.

3

ECONOMIC CRISIS
AND RECOVERY, 1929–1939

EUROPE IN DEPRESSION

Throughout 1929 and even some way into 1930 few people appreciated that the world was on the point of experiencing one of the worst depressions in history. Even after the dramatic collapse of the American stock market in October 1929 and the sharp check to economic activity in the latter half of that year there were still many people, especially in the United States, who were prepared to believe that these events represented merely a temporary and moderate hiccup in the rate of expansion, a view that gathered some force in the first half of 1930 when the US economy showed some signs of revival. By the middle of 1932, however, all such illusions had been shattered completely. After nearly three years of precipitous decline and a severe financial crisis in Europe and America no one could be in any doubt about the gravity of the situation. At that point in time the burning question was when was recovery going to take place? It was not long before this question was answered.

An idea of the magnitude of the depression can be gained from the first two columns of Table 3.1 which show the fall in industrial production and gross domestic product between 1929 and 1932 for all European countries for which data are available. The figures are best used for indicating broad dimensions of the collapse since not all the estimates are equally reliable. Virtually all countries suffered substantial declines in both industrial production and domestic output, the major exception being Russia which was by that time insulated from the ravages of the modern capitalist system. There output moved forward rapidly under the impetus of the first Five Year Plan and provided a sharp contrast with what was happening elsewhere in Europe and the rest of the free world. Outside the United States the most severe declines in economic activity occurred in Austria, Germany, France, Italy, Luxembourg, Czechoslovakia and Poland. Scandinavian countries, the Netherlands, Britain, Spain and Romania were less severely affected, at least as far as industrial production was concerned, though even in these countries the fall in economic activity was by no means modest. Denmark was something of an exception in that she managed to record a rise in domestic output over the course of the depression; so too did Bulgaria and on a rather larger scale, though a decline came later. Barring the latter exception eastern Europe on balance probably suffered a sharper decline than Europe as a whole where the fall in GDP averaged about 10 per cent.

Table 3.1 Percentage changes in industrial production and output (GDP), 1929–38

| | 1929–32 | | 1932/33–1937/8 | | 1929–1937/8 | |
| | Industrial | | Industrial | | Industrial | |
Country	production	GDP	production	GDP	production	GDP
Austria	– 34.3	– 22.5	53.8	18.6	1.0	– 4.8
Belgium	– 27.1	– 7.1	42.3	9.8	3.7	2.0
Denmark	– 5.6	4.0	47.1	15.1	38.9	19.7
Finland	– 20.0	– 5.9	96.2	48.7	56.9	39.9
France	– 25.6	– 11.0	20.0	7.9	– 11.8	– 4.0
Germany	– 40.8	– 15.7	122.2	67.5	31.6	41.1
Italy	– 22.7	– 6.1	48.5	20.8	14.8	13.5
Luxembourg	– 32.0	n.a.	40.2	n.a.	4.7	n.a.
Netherlands	– 9.8	– 8.2	35.1	12.2	22.0	3.1
Norway	– 7.9	– 0.9	40.8	29.2	29.9	28.0
Spain	– 11.6	– 8.0	3.0[a]	9.0[a]	– 13.1[b]	0.4[c]
Sweden	– 11.8	– 8.9	72.4	38.3	53.8	26.0
UK	– 11.4	– 5.8	52.9	25.7	35.4	18.4
Bulgaria	n.a.	26.8	n.a.	17.7	n.a.	49.2
Czechoslovakia	– 26.5	– 18.2[c]	51.5	20.3[d]	– 3.9	– 1.6
Hungary	– 19.2	– 11.5	58.7	24.5	29.9	10.2
Poland	– 37.0	n.a.	86.2	n.a.	17.4	n.a.
Romania	– 11.8	n.a.	49.3	n.a.	31.6	n.a.
Yugoslavia	n.a.	– 11.9	n.a.	28.0	n.a.	12.8
USSR	66.7	6.9	146.7	59.3	311.1	70.2
United States	– 44.7	– 28.0	86.8	46.6	3.3	5.6

Sources: Organization for European Economic Co-operation, *Industrial Statistics, 1900–1959*, 1960, p. 9; United Nations, *Statistical Yearbook 1948*, 1949, Table 36; League of Nations, *Statistical Yearbook, 1935/36*, 1936, Table 107; A. Maddison, *Economic Policy and Performance in Europe, 1913–1970*, London: Collins/Fontana, 1973, Table 22

Notes: [a] 1933–5.
 [b] 1929–35.
 [c] 1929–35.
 [d] 1935–7.

Other indicators of economic activity tell a similar story; commodity prices, share prices, exports and imports fell sharply while unemployment rose to alarming levels. Wholesale prices and share values fell by one-half or more, while the value of European trade declined from $58 billion in 1928 to $20.8 billion in 1935 and even by 1938 it had only recovered to 41.5 per cent of its former peak. Socially perhaps the worst aspect of the depression was the high levels of unemployment experienced in most countries since for those in work there was some compensation in so far as prices tended to fall faster than wages and salaries. In this respect Germany had one of the worst records; between 1929 and the end of 1930 unemployment more than doubled to reach a figure of 4.5 million; two years later it had crept up to 6 million. Britain's worst figure was just over 3 million, which though bad appears modest in comparison with Germany's total. For Europe as a whole it has been estimated that unemployment totalled 15 million at the trough of the depression though it was probably rather greater than this because of statistical under-recording. During the course of the downswing many firms, banks and financial institutions went out of business altogether. In one year alone, 1931, about 17,000 enterprises closed down in Germany.

Bald statistics fail to do justice to the dramatic events of the depression but they do show clearly the scale of the cataclysm. In any case, as Landes has observed, it is difficult to give a coherent analysis of the crisis 'that does justice to the rush of disasters, tumbling one upon another; or to give a narrative account that illuminates the confusion of events'. It is doubtful moreover whether a detailed blow-by-blow account of the crisis would serve a useful purpose in a volume of this sort when there are many more pressing questions to be posed. In particular, therefore, we should attempt first to determine the origins of the downturn, and explain why the depression was so long and so intense.

ORIGINS OF THE 1929 DOWNTURN

It has been argued that apart from its unusual severity the depression of 1929–32 was no exception to the long-run historical sequence of cyclical activity and hence requires nothing more in the way of explanation than a general theory of the cycle. While perhaps a little overdrawn this point of view merits consideration. The depression did occur at a logical sequence in time on the basis of past business-cycle history and some of its characteristics had been reflected in previous downturns. The war did not break the pre-war pattern of business-cycle periodicity. In 1914 most industrial countries were about to move into recession but the outbreak of hostilities postponed the working-out of normal forces and in effect produced a distorted or muted continuation of the upswing which eventually peaked in 1919–20. The reaction came in the sharp slump of 1920–1 which was then followed, with minor interruptions, by another major upswing to a peak at the end of the decade. Thus the nineteenth-century Juglar pattern of cycles of about seven to ten years' duration was preserved and a depression could have been expected in 1929–30. Moreover, the amplitude of the 1929–32 slump was no greater in some countries than that of the immediate post-war depression, while its duration had been matched in crises of the nineteenth century though not simultaneously with the same intensity. Even the worldwide scope of the depression was not especially unique; the immediate post-war depression fell not far short in this respect, while international recessions were not unknown in the nineteenth century. The question is therefore whether we should simply regard it as another contraction in the business-cycle sequence or whether it was unique in itself and needs to be explained in terms of special circumstances, for example by the maladjustments in the economic system arising from the shock administered by the war.

On balance, given the combination of duration, intensity and worldwide scope the crisis of 1929–32 may be regarded as a rather special case worthy of particular attention. It may also be regarded, if we ignore the rather minor recession of 1937–8, as marking the grand culmination to trade-cycle history for, soon after the Second World War, the growth cycle became the established norm. This does not mean, however, that the downturn of 1929 can be explained specifically in terms of unique circumstances. It would be difficult, for instance, to argue that the First World War and its aftermath was the prime causal factor of the crisis that began at the end of the 1920s. Certainly the repercussions of war created maladjustments and elements of instability within the world economy which thereby made it more vulnerable to shocks of one sort or another, but the turning-point of the cycle cannot be attributed directly to the war itself. Indeed, though the war imparted a severe shock to the economic mechanism it did not, as we have noted, upset the former cyclical pattern. It distorted the economic system in several ways and made it more unstable, while it also probably aggravated the amplitude of subsequent cyclical movements, but it did little, if anything, to destroy the traditional periodicity of cyclical activity.

The real origins of the slump must be located in the United States. This is not to say that there were not cyclical weaknesses elsewhere; indeed it is quite possible that several European countries would have experienced at least a moderate recession in the early 1930s even had conditions not deteriorated in America. But events in the United States, together with that country's influence over the world economy, determined to a large extent the timing, the severity and the duration of the depression. In brief, the United States administered two severe shocks to the world economic system at a time when it was most vulnerable and therefore least able to withstand them. The initial shock came with the curtailment of foreign lending in 1928–9 and the second with the peaking of the American boom in the summer of 1929.

The first of these had serious implications for debtor countries. There can be little doubt that many debtor countries, both in central and eastern Europe and elsewhere, Latin America especially, were in a precarious financial position in the latter half of the 1920s. They had borrowed freely and accumulated massive obligations which for the most part were not self-liquidating. Consequently they depended on continued capital imports to maintain external equilibrium. These fulfilled the purpose in the short term but inevitably they aggravated the debt burden and served to conceal the basic disequilibrium between creditors and debtors. This process could not continue indefinitely and any reaction on the part of the creditors was bound to throw the burden of adjustment onto the debtors. Unfortunately, the creditors reacted rather too sharply in applying the brake to foreign lending.

The United States and France were largely responsible for the initial check to foreign lending since total British lending held up fairly well until 1930. French lending was in fact the first to decline (1927–8), though in sheer magnitude it was swamped by the American cutback in the following year. French capital exports were halved in 1928 and wiped out altogether in 1929. A good part of this movement represented the withdrawal of French short-term balances abroad (especially from Britain and Germany) and the import of gold following on the legal stabilization of the franc in June 1928. Since the French investor could not be persuaded to place his funds abroad on a long-term basis it was inevitable that a large part of them should have been repatriated since, apart from increasing fears as to their safety, especially in the case of Germany, the balances could not be attracted to any great extent by short-term rates in London, or, after the autumn of 1929, by those in New York. French action put strain on the major centres of credit and also on Germany, but for the most part it left the debtors on the periphery unscathed.

The major destabilizing influence came with the collapse in American lending. This began in the summer of 1928 and was prompted by the domestic boom and the action of the Federal Reserve to check it by raising interest rates, both of which had the effect of attracting funds into the home market. US capital issues on foreign account fell by over 50 per cent between the first and second halves of 1928; there was then a slight revival in the first half of 1929 followed by a further sharp fall in the second part of that year, giving a total for 1929 of $790 million as against $1,250 million in 1928 and $1,336 million in 1927. Altogether the net outward capital flow (both long term and short term) from the major creditors fell from $2,214 million in 1928 to $1,414 million in 1929, while an even greater fall to $363 million occurred in the following year.

This dramatic curtailment of lending exercised a powerful deflationary impact on the world economy. It did not of course affect all countries simultaneously but it was sufficiently widespread to undermine the fragile stability of the international economy. The position of the debtor countries deteriorated sharply between 1928 and 1929 as they experienced a hefty drop in their net capital inflow. Net capital imports into Germany, the largest borrower, fell from $967 million in 1928 to $482 million in 1929 and to $129 million in 1930. Other European borrowers, Hungary, Poland, Yugoslavia, Finland and Italy, suffered similar sharp reversals to their capital inflows. The cessation in the flow of capital affected these countries directly in that it led to a tailing off in domestic investment and economic activity. It also in turn reduced Europe's import demand for products outside the region. However, it was through the balance of payments that the impact was first felt since most debtor countries depended on capital imports to close the gap in their balance of payments. Hence once capital imports declined the only way of adjusting their external accounts was to draw upon their limited reserves of gold and foreign exchange to cushion the impact. When these were exhausted more drastic measures became necessary, involving domestic deflation and protective restrictions.

The initial shock to the system might have been overcome had it not been for subsequent adverse events. For a time debtor countries could meet temporary difficulties by drawing on their reserves and by taking measures to ease the strain on their external accounts. But this process of adjustment could not cope indefinitely with a prolonged strain following from reduced lending at a time when primary product prices were giving way. Nor could it cope with further pressures. The second shock came in the summer of 1929 when the Amerian boom petered out. The reasons for the reversal in US activity are still the subject of debate though it seems very likely that it was partly a reaction to the over-hectic expansion of the 1920s. Certainly there were signs of a temporary exhaustion of investment opportunities especially in those sectors, construction and consumer durable products, which had led the upswing, and this, together with a restraint on the growth of incomes and consumer expenditure towards the end of the decade, led to a deterioration in business confidence. A tightening in monetary policy at this time may also have contributed, though monetary factors probably played a relatively minor part in the initial breaking of the boom. Once the downswing was under way, however, it was aggravated and prolonged by the severe monetary contraction initiated by the Federal Reserve System. The rapidity of the American slide into depression was assisted by the complete collapse of business confidence after the stock market crash in October 1929.

The American downturn in economic activity was accompanied by a further reduction in foreign lending and a sharp contraction in import demand, the consequences of which were a severely reduced flow of dollars to Europe and the rest of the world. Given America's preponderating influence in the world economy the impact on the rest of the world was bound to be severe. The process of attrition in debtor primary producing countries was completed as commodity prices fell dramatically. These countries faced a severe deterioration in their trade balances as export values fell faster than import values, while external interest obligations, which were fixed in terms of gold, rose sharply as a proportion of export receipts. Attempts to make up the deficiency by releasing stocks of commodities, which were costly to maintain, onto the market only made matters worse since it aggravated the fall in prices. Thus with dwindling reserves and an inability to borrow further, debtor countries in Europe and overseas were forced to take drastic measures to staunch the outflow of funds. The way out of the impasse was sought through deflation, devaluation, restrictive measures and default on debts. The initial deflation was quickly transmitted through the links forged by the fixed exchange rates of the gold standard, but deflation could never be more than a temporary expedient since to meet external obligations would have required politically intolerable doses of deflation. Consequently the easiest solution was to break the links by abandoning the gold standard. This was done by several Latin American countries and Australia and New Zealand late in 1929 and early in 1930. Inevitably this imposed a greater burden on the countries still on gold and hence intensified the deflationary spiral either automatically or through deliberate government action. Industrialized countries in Europe felt the impact directly from America and indirectly via the periphery as demand for industrial imports declined, and in turn declining demand for raw materials and foodstuffs on the part of the industrial powers fed back to the periphery. Once started therefore the deflationary process became cumulative and eventually it led to the general collapse of the gold standard and the adoption of restrictive policies to protect domestic economies. These events are taken up in the next section.

Though the role of the United States is seen as crucial in determining the worldwide slide into severe recession it should be stressed that the sequence of events in that country came at a weak point in time as far as the international economy was concerned. For one thing, cyclical forces were reaching their peak in a number of countries, for example, Britain, Germany and Poland, in the later 1920s, and in some cases independently of the United States. Britain for instance experienced sagging demand for her exports to primary producing countries a year or so before the peak in economic activity in the United States. At the same time the incomes of the primary producers in eastern Europe and elsewhere were being squeezed as a result of the weakness of world commodity prices stemming from oversupply problems in some cases. Second, the cyclical developments of the period must be set against the background of an unstable international economy arising partly from the legacies left by the war. Thus the cyclical downturn came at a time when many countries were still struggling with post-war distortions to their economies which left them inherently unstable. Structural or sectoral deflationary tendencies were common and these were reflected in excess capacity problems, in both industrialized and primary producing countries, and in external account imbalances, arising from reparations and war debts, tariff policies, and the distortions produced by the ill-conceived currency stabilization process among other things. The position was also aggravated by the transformation of economic power relationships due to the war and the lack of strong and enlightened economic leadership on the part of the new creditor powers which might have helped to stabilize the international economic system. These disequilibrating forces were not crucial to the initial downturn, but they were sufficient to ensure that the system exploded once the initial shocks had been imparted, thereby producing a depression of unusual severity.

That the depression was so intense and widespread and of long duration is not altogether surprising. Given the severity of the American depression and the repercussions this had on foreign lending and US import demand the multiplier effects were bound to be large. Moreover, the fact that the cyclical downturn occurred against a backdrop of structural deflation and international disequilibrium was bound to intensify the process. Misguided government policies also helped to aggravate the deflationary spiral. Monetary and fiscal retrenchment, tariffs and other protective measures simply made things worse. The spread of depression was also encouraged by the fairly close economic relationships between nations; in particular, the complex but precarious monetary relationships and the fixed exchange rates of the gold standard system facilitated the transmission of recessionary forces from one country to another.

Finally we should ask what could have been done to avert or alleviate the crisis. With the benefit of hindsight it is easy to argue that enlightened government policies applied rapidly by the major powers might have eased the situation. But in the conditions then prevailing it is difficult to conceive that this could or would have been done, and even less likely that the depression could have been avoided altogether. At the very minimum it would have required appropriate policy action to have been taken a few months before the peak in economic activity because of the lag effects involved. This of course is assuming that governments had the foresight, skill and aptitude to do so, which clearly they did not at that time. In fact it is doubtful even today whether they are any better at forecasting turning points in the cycle and timing their policy actions correctly. However, the question of expertise apart, it is doubtful in the conditions then obtaining whether such action would have been forthcoming. Initially the main burden of adjustment lay with the United States since the other two major creditors, France and Britain, were unable and also unwilling to stabilize the system. Two courses of action would have been required of the United States: first, reversing the contraction in foreign lending and, second, taking measures to refuel the boom. Neither of these courses would have appeared very logical to the US authorities at the time in question. By the late 1920s it was quite apparent that debtor countries had borrowed far too much and that their capacity to repay was being severely strained. To have kept up the rate of lending, let alone to have increased it, would have made things worse and at best would only have postponed the date at which adjustment had to be made. The mistake in the 1920s was that creditor nations had been too generous with their funds: debtors had been allowed to over-borrow and as a consequence they had made little attempt to adjust their economies so that they developed within their means. That the crunch came in 1928–9 as a result of the US boom was unfortunate, but it was bound to occur sooner or later since creditors were hardly likely to maintain lending indefinitely to insolvent borrowers. The difficulties of European debtors could have been alleviated by the scrapping of reparations and a more liberal commercial policy on the part of the United States but such adjustments would have by no means solved the fundamental problem. But the United States was in no mood anyway to alleviate world problems as evidenced by her more restrictive commercial policy in the Hawley–Smoot tariff of 1930.

As to the second course of action, the last thing the authorities were likely to do in 1929 was to take action to revitalize the boom. After all, with memories of the one of 1919–20 and the subsequent European inflations still close at hand, the authorities were more concerned with bringing it under control, and more particularly with curbing the excessive stock market speculation. In any case, heavy government spending would not have gone down well with the American public because of the tax implications that it would have entailed. Moreover, for most of 1929 many Americans were still convinced that the country had entered a period of perpetual prosperity and there seemed little indication to them of the dire events which were soon to follow. In these circumstances, therefore, it is very unlikely that any government would have acted differently. It was not until after the stock market crash in October that Americans began to realize that the halcyon days were over, and by then it was too late. Economic activity and business confidence drained away so rapidly, both in America and elsewhere, that it is unlikely that any policy action could have done much to save the situation in the short term. This should not be construed as an apology for inaction on the part of the government. Clearly had they made a concerted effort to combat the depression in 1929 and early in 1930 the duration and severity of the downswing and the accompanying financial crisis could have been modified. Indeed, determined action on the part of the major powers might even have saved the gold standard. What we would stress, therefore, is that some degree of recession was inevitable in 1929–30; that it developed into a global crisis of such magnitude can be attributed not only to the convergence of a combination of unfavourable circumstances but also to the fact that governments, instead of co-operating to rescue the situation, simply resorted to policies which made things worse rather than better.

DEEPENING DEPRESSION AND FINANCIAL CRISIS

By the middle of 1930 most countries were engulfed in depression. Despite the sharpness of the initial downturn the decline in activity through 1929 and 1930 was considered to be little more than an ordinary downward phase in the business cycle. Indeed in the first half of 1930 there were some signs, especially in the United States, that the decline was levelling off and there was also some revival in international lending. But this proved to be nothing more than a temporary respite from depressing forces which soon became overwhelming and which were to be accompanied by financial crisis and monetary disorders on a scale never before experienced in peacetime. The events spelt the end of the gold standard and the liberal economic regimes which had prevailed hitherto.

Throughout the latter half of 1930 and 1931 economic conditions steadily deteriorated everywhere. As incomes fell domestic budgets and external accounts became unbalanced and the first reaction of governments was to introduce deflationary policies which only made things worse. Little assistance was forthcoming from the creditor countries. The main surplus countries, the United States and France, failed to make sufficient funds available to the debtor nations on either a long-term or a short-term basis. This is perhaps not altogether surprising since the creditworthiness of the borrowers was extremely weak and hence the creditors were reluctant to grant further accommodation. France in particular, despite her large reserves, was unwilling to bale out debtor countries and Germany especially, given France's hostility towards that country. In any case the creditor nations themselves were experiencing financial difficulties and monetary disorders during 1930–1.

Thus the European financial crisis which culminated in the summer of 1931 can be seen as a general failure on the part of creditor countries to provide accommodating finance to overcome the effects of depression. The subsequent collapse of confidence was reflected in a virtual cessation of lending and an attempt on the part of creditors to demand repayment of previous loans. Under these pressures debtor countries were forced to pursue deflationary policies and/or repudiate their international obligations, which, being denominated in gold terms, had become vastly more burdensome by 1930–1.

The antecedents of the financial crisis of 1931 can of course be traced back to the late 1920s when overseas lending first contracted and international liquidity became tighter. The financial pressures on debtor countries were increased after the breaking of the American boom which further reduced the flow of dollars to Europe. Despite temporary alleviation in the early months of 1930, by the middle of that year conditions were such that debtor countries could expect little assistance from the creditor nations. During the course of that year the chief creditors began to experience severe monetary problems. The United States suffered a wave of bank failures after the stock market crash; no less than 1,345 banks collapsed in 1930 and another 687 went under in the first half of 1931, the vast majority of them being linked to the fortunes of agriculture. This banking crisis together with a further deterioration in economic conditions forced the United States to reduce its international commitments even further, and by 1931 the former outflow of capital was being transformed into a net inward movement. France also suffered monetary disturbances in the latter half of 1930 which weakened confidence and led to increasing demands for liquidity. This was reflected in a repatriation of commercial bank balances held abroad, especially from Germany and Austria, which put further strain on an already weak financial position in central Europe.

The increasing demand for liquidity in 1930 and 1931 on the part of foreign creditors at a time when European financial institutions were overstretched in their commitments to depressed industries led to a crop of bank failures throughout Europe. In many European countries some one-quarter or more of bank liabilities were foreign owned and this complex interlocking of balances only served to propagate the spread of the crisis. Attempts to meet demands for liquidity led to forced realization of assets and deflationary monetary policies and this weakened the structure of financial institutions and reduced foreign confidence even more. The final phase of the European crisis was played out in the summer of 1931. It began in May with the crash of the Austrian Credit Anstalt which accounted for over two-thirds of the total deposits of the Austrian banking system. The illiquid state of this bank created panic in European banking circles. Within weeks the banking crisis had spread to Germany and eastern Europe and by July the German banking system was on the point of collapse. The crisis enormously increased the demand for liquidity and much of the strain was now transferred to London as one of the few places still prepared to grant accommodation. The outflow of funds from Britain reached panic proportions in July and August when some £200 million left the country. The rapid rate of withdrawal from London was largely occasioned by the European financial crisis; but the situation was undoubtedly aggravated by the loss of confidence in Britain's ability to maintain solvency in the light of her deteriorating balance of payments position and her unfavourable short-term liquidity account. Britain's position was rendered the more difficult by her heavy financial commitments in Europe – the assets being frozen in the crisis – as well as the weak and passive policy of the Bank of England and political instability in 1931. Attempts by New York and Paris to come to the rescue were too little and too late. In the circumstances the authorities could think of little else to do but release the parity of sterling and on 21 September 1931 Britain officially went off gold.

In retrospect the financial panic of 1931 can be seen as a typical crisis of confidence, which had deep-seated causes. The contraction of foreign lending and the impact of depression started the chain of causation in that pressure was put on debtor countries. But it was exacerbated by the widespread foreign ownership of national bank deposits, a large volume of liquid and mobile balances and the misuse of these funds by recipient countries. Once confidence in the monetary institutions of the debtor countries collapsed the demand for liquidity rose sharply and the only prospect of salvation lay in a concerted rescue operation by the creditor countries. When this failed to materialize the disintegration of the international monetary system was a forgone conclusion.

AFTERMATH OF THE CRISIS

The financial panic of 1931 left its mark on the world economy in many ways. Any prospect of an early end to the depression – there had again been some signs of improvement in the first few months of 1931 – was shattered completely since the crisis shook even the strongest countries. As the panic swept from one country to another, hurried measures of national economic defence were taken and these inevitably resulted in further damage to economic activity and international economic relations. Thus output, already at a low level in most countries in the summer of 1931, declined further during the course of the next twelve months. Production in most cases reached its lowest point in the summer and autumn of 1932, at levels ranging between 20 and 55 per cent below previous peaks. Primary producing countries both in eastern Europe and elsewhere did not suffer quite so much from decreased production but were more severely hit by the fall in primary product prices, the effect of which was to reduce incomes by up to 50 per cent or more. Probably the worst-hit sector of the world economy was international trade. Both the volume and value of trade, already seriously diminished before the financial crisis, declined even more as countries resorted to restrictive measures to insulate their domestic economies from the impact of depression. By the third quarter of 1932 the value of world trade was less than 35 per cent of that in the corresponding quarter of 1929; this decline was made up of a fall in average prices of about 50 per cent and a reduction of some 25 per cent in the quantum of goods traded. The decline was not evenly distributed; primary producing countries fared the worst since prices of commodities fell more sharply than those of industrial products which they imported. Thus at the low point in the third quarter of 1932 the trade of European countries fell for the first time below 40 per cent of the 1929 reference level, whereas for the rest of the world it had dropped below 30 per cent.

Perhaps even more serious than the collapse in economic activity was the disorganization and partial destruction of the delicate machinery of international economic and financial co-operation. Indeed, the depression and financial crisis more or less destroyed the former international economic mechanism. Most countries eventually abandoned the gold standard and devalued their currencies. Then in order to shield domestic economies from external influences a battery of protective restrictions was employed including tariffs, import quotas, exchange controls and special devices to iron out fluctuations in the exchanges. This spelt the end of the pre-1914 system of multilateral trade and payments and the free flow of commodities, capital and labour across national borders. Instead nationalistic economic policies and managed currencies became the order of the day. The finishing touch to the previous system came with the breakdown of the World Economic Conference in 1933 which effectively 'signalised the end of any general attempts at international action in the economic field during the inter-war period'.

The most notable manifestation of the decline of the old order was the general abandonment of the gold standard. Several countries had already gone off gold before September 1931 when Britain broke its links with the gold standard. Almost simultaneously with Britain's departure many countries abandoned the standard and devalued their currencies. By the end of 1932 more than one-half the countries of the world had formally abandoned gold and most others maintained it or its semblance only by virtue of rigid exchange controls. When in 1933 the United States gave up the standard only a handful of countries, France, Switzerland, the Netherlands, Belgium, Italy, and Poland, continued to adhere to it and these countries formed a gold bloc for settlement of balances among themselves.

The benefits arising from general abandonment of the gold standard were mixed. It is true that adherence to the system of fixed exchange rates had helped to propagate the spread of the depression, since for countries faced with balance of payments problems it meant a resort to deflationary measures which simply aggravated the depression. Thus for any individual country departure from the gold standard and depreciation of the currency released that country from deflationary constraints and gave a boost to exports. On the other hand, once the same line of action was adopted by many countries then the benefits formerly reaped by the leaders soon disappeared. The gold bloc countries found themselves in an invidious trading position simply because they retained the former fixed exchange values at a time when most other currencies had depreciated. A second possible benefit flowed from the fact that some countries found the burden of external indebtedness reduced in so far as their debt was held in terms of currencies which had depreciated. Conversely, of course, those countries that subsequently went on to depreciate their own currencies below the level of the currencies in which their debts were due found the external burden of their debt was greater than before.

In other words, individual countries, depending on the timing of their departure from the gold standard, the extent of the ensuing currency depreciation and the structure of their debt burden, stood to benefit. Some also gained from a boost given to their exports. Whether the economic situation in 1932 would have been better or worse if the gold standard had not been widely abandoned is more debatable. It is probable that trade would have continued to decline during that year and investment to remain paralysed even had it been possible to retain the standard since the trends were already firmly operational before the breakdown and in fact were among the causes of that breakdown. Moreover, there is little evidence that countries adopted reflationary policies of any moment once they were released from the straitjacket of the gold standard. On the other hand, it is also clear that the widespread exchange instability which arose during 1932 following the general abandonment of gold greatly complicated the economic situation. Fluctuating exchange rates aggravated by speculative and non-economic capital movements, the prospect of competitive depreciation of currencies and restrictive measures of defence thrown up by the threat, together with renewed deflationary pressure, banking crises and rigid exchange controls to protect weaker currencies, created a thoroughly unstable situation. These uncertainties were not only a serious impediment to economic recovery but presented a constant threat of further deterioration. While the countries already off gold experienced temporary relief in their domestic situation, they were confronted by an accelerated fall in gold prices and a further reduction in international trade.

Moreover, efforts to maintain the external values of their currencies were threatened by flights of capital as confidence in the security of various financial centres waxed and waned. Thus, on balance, the relief arising from abandonment of the gold standard both for individual countries and for the world as a whole was fairly small and of limited duration. Prices did not rise and trade continued to dwindle, while exchange instability and various controls imposed fresh obstacles to capital movements and trade recovery.

The circulation of both long-term and short-term capital had been impaired at an early stage in the depression, but by the middle of 1932 the financial panic had led to almost a complete paralysis of capital movements and had done much to restrict the servicing of existing debt. Problems arising from over-borrowing had forced many countries to repudiate debts, to suspend interest payments on them or to impose rigid exchange controls in an effort to achieve currency stability and safeguard the external account. The steady decline in international trade was mainly responsible for this and for the freezing of short-term debts, since amounts of short-term indebtedness adequate to finance trade at its 1929 volume became unnecessary but difficult to repudiate when trade fell to 1932 levels. The stoppage of capital movements, freezing of short-term debts and assets and the use of exchange controls were not confined solely to European countries. By the middle of 1932 there were moratoria on the foreign service of the public debt in seventeen countries and on private debt in seven others. Many other countries, especially among agricultural producers, faced with a crushing burden of external debt payments as export values plunged and their currencies depreciated below those in which the debts were held, were forced to take emergency action to deal with the problem, either by severe domestic deflation or by restrictions on trade and payments or both.

By virtue of increasing restrictions on trade and capital flows there was an obvious danger that the international trading machinery would be smashed as completely as the international monetary system. Increasing resort to restrictive policies had been evident of course before the financial panic but after September 1931 the use made of such measures became far more widespread and severe. It is difficult to summarize briefly the multiplicity and variety of emergency restrictions promulgated to deal with the crisis of 1931. Most countries, as already noted, eventually abandoned gold soon after Britain did and devalued; by the end of 1932, thirty-five countries were already off gold and twenty-seven, including nine still nominally on the gold standard, were officially exercising exchange control, while yet others were exercising unofficial controls or import prohibitions tantamount to exchange control. General tariff increases had been imposed in twenty-three countries, while customs duties had been increased on individual items or groups of commodities by fifty countries. Import quotas, prohibitions, licensing systems and other quantitative restrictions had been applied in thirty-two countries. Import monopolies, mostly for grains, were in existence in twelve countries;

milling or mixing regulations in sixteen others. Export premiums were being paid in nine, while export duties or prohibitions had been imposed in seventeen.

By the summer of 1932 therefore the economic situation in Europe and the wider world appeared very grim. True the immediate panic had subsided but the international economy was badly shattered after three years of depression and crisis. Economic activity almost everywhere was at a very low ebb, capital and labour were seriously underemployed, investment was negligible and international trade had received a very serious battering. The international economic and financial system had been seriously weakened and in some parts destroyed in its original form, and fears were expressed at the time that a general collapse or total breakdown of the economic mechanism would ensue. Yet within a few months, despite continued depression, there were signs that the turning-point was close at hand. Confidence began to revive, albeit slowly, and during the autumn of 1932 the United States economy showed signs of life. Though this proved to be something of a false dawn – a final wave of bank failures in 1932-3 stifled the first signs of revival – the undercurrent of cautious optimism continued and was rewarded early in the New Year when it became apparent that the corner had been turned and most countries had seen the trough in economic activity.

THE EXTENT OF RECOVERY

Though the beginnings of recovery can be detected in some countries late in 1932 it was not until the following year that it took firm hold. Even then the process was by no means rapid and widespread. Some countries, notably France and Czechoslovakia, continued to experience further declines in economic activity, while in the United States the pace of revival was slow and faltering. But during the next two or three years the recovery gathered momentum so that by the middle of the 1930s nearly all countries were registering at least modest gains in activity over the levels reached in the trough of the depression. Recovery was interrupted temporarily in 1937-8 when several countries experienced a mild recession after which it was resumed once more largely under the influence of rearmament for the Second World War.

Despite several years of growth, by the end of the decade recovery from the slump was only partially complete. Most countries still had fairly high unemployment levels, while the agrarian sector acted as a drag on the countries of eastern Europe. Some of the more industrialized countries, France, Austria and Czechoslovakia for example, failed to regain their pre-depression levels of activity, while even the United States barely reached her previous peak of 1929 (see Table 3.1). One of the most successful countries was Germany; she virtually eradicated unemployment and achieved substantial gains in output by dint of policies which were unacceptable to most other countries. Sweden too recorded an impressive performance, largely on the back of strong export growth and continued structural adaptation assisted by sensible government policies, while Finland was another export beneficiary. Britain's achievements were also quite impressive though she still had a large pool of unemployment by the end of the decade. However, the presence of high unemployment does not necessarily denote an abortive recovery since, at least in the case of Britain, much of the unemployment at the end of the 1930s was structural rather than cyclical in character. The most spectacular performance was undoubtedly that of the USSR where industrial output surged ahead under the Five Year Plans. The social costs of this forced industrialization were more dreadful, however, than those experienced in Fascist Germany.

As the scale of recovery varied from one country to another so too did the forces promoting it. Indeed, the diversity of factors involved makes it difficult to generalize about the initiating forces though it is possible to make some broad observations. The first thing that can be said is that recovery owed virtually nothing to international action. International attempts to provide a solution were rare and unsuccessful. Though the League of Nations had played a useful and constructive role in the 1920s its impact in the following decade was negligible. It produced many valuable reports but as far as policy was concerned it had no immediate effect. Attempts at international co-operation to sort out the monetary and trade situation foundered after the failure of the World Economic Conference in London in 1933, and only sporadic and half-hearted efforts were made in the later 1930s, principally by the United States, to ease the restrictions on trade. Indeed, for the most part the restrictions on trade and capital movements tended to increase rather than diminish. Consequently international lending never revived to any extent, trade volumes remained well below their former peak levels and the ratio of trade to national income therefore declined. Not surprisingly exports did not for the most part play a significant part in the recovery process, though there were important exceptions, for example Finland and Sweden. Most countries did of course experience a revival in exports from the low levels reached in the trough, and devaluation frequently gave a temporary boost to exports, but more often than not pre-depression levels of exports proved unobtainable.

One factor common to all countries was the increase in government partici-pation in the economy. Given the severity of the depression it was almost inevitable that this would be the case. Again the methods used varied a great deal as did their impact, which generally was not very significant. As we have seen, the early 1930s were characterized by a wave of currency devaluations followed by the imposition of severe restrictions on trade, payments and capital movements. These were primarily defensive measures designed to insulate domestic economies from unfavourable external influences. In some countries, especially Germany and in eastern Europe, the 'planning' of foreign trade came to be more widely accepted as a normal function of the state, and the weapons originally forged as an emergency defence of prices, production or currency were not discarded but tended to be pressed into service as permanent elements of trade regulation, dovetailed into programmes of national economic development.

Such policies have been regarded as reactionary and restrictive and in many respects they were since they were implemented with little regard as to their effects on other countries. As restrictions increased trade was diverted more and more into bilateral channels, and hence the scope for expansion in foreign intercourse became limited. Ultimately the policies were self-defeating since the gains initially derived from devaluation and restrictive controls or whatever soon disappeared as other countries adopted similar procedures. It is of course easy to be critical of past events; one should bear in mind that, though many policy measures were restrictive and reactionary, at the time in question governments had little choice but to safeguard the external side of the balance sheet as a prelude to the introduction of domestic recovery measures. What can be fairly criticized is the reluctance of governments to relax such restrictions once recovery got under way and the somewhat limited and half-hearted efforts made to stimulate recovery in the first place. More countries it is true adopted cheap money but thereafter constructive policy action was limited and inadequate. Attention was concentrated on bolstering up and protecting established producers and declining staple industries, while expansionary fiscal measures were notable for their absence. Fear of inflation (surprising though it may seem), adherence to the time-honoured principle of balanced budgets, coupled with a general ignorance as to the role of state spending in a depression, inhibited governments from pursuing a policy of deficit financing to stimulate recovery. There were of course some notable exceptions, for example the United States and Sweden, though even in these two cases the policies pursued left something to be desired.

Given the narrow scope of government policies in the 1930s it is not surprising to find that their impact in terms of recovery was often very limited. With the exception of Germany, to a lesser extent Sweden and possibly one or two east European countries which attempted to force industrialization by autarchic planning measures, national economic policies contributed very little to recovery from the depression. Even in Sweden, with its enlightened budgetary policy, the impact was too late to start the initial upturn, while in France and Belgium, both countries clinging to the gold standard until 1936, government policy was positively detrimental. The same applies to the remaining gold bloc countries. One can go further and argue that recovery took place in most countries despite domestic policy measures which, if not actually harmful, were too little and too late to have much bearing on the recovery effort. Again there are exceptions to the rule; one should not totally underestimate the impact that cheap money had on stimulating investment in residential construction in say Britain and Sweden, though generally the favourable influence tends to be exaggerated.

By and large therefore it was real forces rather than policy measures that were instrumental in bringing about recovery. And to a large extent that recovery was based on home rather than export markets. The outstanding case in the latter respect was Britain where the demand for products of the newer industries and the upsurge in building activity provided important stimulants. In part this process reflected a structural transformation which many European countries were experiencing to a greater or lesser degree in the inter-war years and which was by no means complete at the end of the period. Svennilson has stressed the severe structural transformation problem in Europe, which in the industrialized countries was characterized by a shift of resources from old staple industries to newer lines of development, while in the east it was largely a question of effecting the transition from predominately agrarian structures to economies based more solidly on manufacturing activity.

Despite the common features outlined above the diverse nature of the recovery process and the forces responsible therein can only be appreciated properly by looking more closely at the experience of individual countries or regions. In the remainder of this chapter therefore we propose to examine the record of five industrialized countries, Britain, France, Sweden, Germany and Austria, all of which had one-third or more of their active population engaged in industry by the end of the 1930s, and then to turn attention to the problems of eastern Europe where the active labour force was engaged predominantly in agriculture. The final section offers a comparison between the east and the west on the eve of the Second World War.

RECOVERY IN INDUSTRIALIZED COUNTRIES

The five countries selected for treatment in this section all displayed different features: Britain experienced fairly vigorous growth based largely on the domestic market with government policy contributing very little to recovery; France had an abortive recovery largely because of misguided policy measures; Sweden forged ahead under the influence of exports, a housing boom and enlightened government policies; Germany achieved great success but at a price, both politically and socially, while Austria had a very chequered recovery as a result of conflicting forces and policies. The one common feature to all, at least towards the end of the period, was the increasing influence of rearmament in sustaining recovery which showed signs of flagging in 1937–8.

Britain's internal recovery policy was remarkably orthodox. The economic crisis did not give rise to any great programme of public works nor did it produce any marked increase in state interference in, or control of, the economic system. For the most part the government confined itself to providing what it thought were favourable conditions for the recovery of private enterprise. Reliance was therefore placed on indirect measures such as cheap money, protection and other trade controls, and industrial reconstruction schemes aimed at propping up the old staple industries. External policy was perhaps more notable for its departure from traditional liberalism than for its effect on recovery since the initial gains stemming from devaluation, tariffs etc. were soon whittled away as other countries followed suit.

Generally speaking, government policy had only a marginal influence on Britain's economic recovery. The gains from devaluation were weak and short-lived, while the impact of tariff protection and measures of industrial assistance was slight. The stimulus from cheap money was somewhat greater but it was certainly not the chief agent of recovery. Cheap money probably imparted a greater stimulus to the housing market than to industrial investment, yet it cannot be regarded as the major causal factor responsible for the housing boom of the 1930s. There were several important stimulants to housing including falling construction costs, rising real incomes partly as a result of the favourable shift in the terms of trade, and a shift in consumer tastes. Nor did fiscal policy make any notable contribution to recovery. Here government action was extremely orthodox, differing little from practice in the 1920s. Deficit financing was avoided, the size of the budget was not materially increased, and the component most crucial from the stabilization point of view, capital spending, was cut substantially. On balance therefore fiscal policy was at best neutral, though the favourable psychological impact of balanced budgets in an age still conditioned by orthodox finance should not be overlooked. Apart from a small increase in public expenditure between 1929 and 1931, government spending (both at central and local levels) remained remarkably stable until the late 1930s when rearmament began to take effect, and in practically every year the central government's accounts showed a surplus.

Despite the relative ineffectiveness of government policy, recovery in Britain was more pronounced and sustained than in many other countries. Apart from exports most indices of economic activity rose sharply after 1932 and over the decade as a whole Britain's rate of growth compared favourably with that of other industrial countries. Admittedly unemployment still remained a problem in the later 1930s but to a large extent this was a structural matter rather than a cyclical one. The domestic market provided the main basis of recovery; important real forces were at work, namely rising effective demand which led to vigorous growth in housing and consumer durable industries. These sectors were certainly important to the recovery though their role should not be exaggerated. In time it became more broadly based with exports and some of the staple industries staging a revival, especially in the later 1930s when rearmament assumed importance.

If British policy had limited influence on the recovery effort, France's economic policy was little short of disastrous, and it goes far in explaining why the French economy stagnated in this period. Initially France was in a strong position since growth had been vigorous in the 1920s, the downturn in economic activity came late and was less severe than in some countries, and the balance of payments was strong. However, the large gold stocks accumulated in the late 1920s and early 1930s allowed France to pursue an independent policy. Thus even when the defensive policies of other countries began to affect the economy adverseiy France was in a strong enough position to maintain the gold standard, and her fear of the inflationary consequences meant that she was unlikely to abandon it willingly. This line of action had unfortunate implications since in order to get French costs and prices in line with world levels (given the general devaluation of currencies) it was necessary to resort to severe deflation. Between 1931 and 1936 deflationary policies were pursued relentlessly; money wages were reduced by more than 12 per cent, prices fell and government expenditures were cut sharply. At the same time various trade restrictions were imposed to protect the external account. These policies had the opposite effect to what was desired, for until 1936 production and employment continued to decline.

It is not difficult to see why French policy failed to revive the economy. The maintenance of the gold standard at a time of general devaluation inevitably meant that the burden of adjustment was thrown onto the domestic economy. This entailed high interest rates which did little to restore business confidence. Second, economy measures and sharp cuts in government spending only served to aggravate the depression. Third, the efforts made to reduce costs and prices were partly self-defeating since wage cuts reduced effective demand in the short term until prices had adjusted. Moreover, the expectation that costs and prices would fall further coupled with high interest rates induced businessmen to postpone investment.

The adverse consequences of the deflationary package were partly responsible for the sweeping victory of a left-wing coalition in 1936. Between June 1936 and March 1937 the new Blum Government introduced what might be described as a miniature New Deal experiment. It was an expansionist programme which reversed the policies followed in the first half of the 1930s. It entailed the abandonment of the gold standard and devaluation of the franc, a moderate programme of public works, increased money wages and a reduction in hours of work. For a time the French economy experienced a temporary fillip, but growing labour shortages, continued distrust of the franc and the ensuing international recession (1937–8) led to renewed stagnation in the latter half of 1937. Subsequently the Blum policies were modified but a reversal in the trend of economic activity awaited the rapid increase in military expenditures in 1938–9.

French experience demonstrates clearly how disastrous government policy can be. Even by the late 1930s output and production were still below pre-depression levels and unemployment had only been reduced by the artificial manipulation of working hours. In view of the fact that the French economy was in a relatively strong position at the onset of depression one might have expected a reasonably firm recovery in the 1930s. The absence of any marked revival can be attributed chiefly to the severe deflationary policy of the first half of the decade, the effects of which were not easily reversed.

Sweden offers a sharp contrast with the two countries so far considered, not only in respect of the strength of her recovery but also on account of the enlightened policies adopted. Sweden avoided the mistakes of many other countries in that she did not resort to extreme measures of protection nor did she follow the deflationary course of the gold bloc countries. Even better, the government attempted to phase its public expenditure to offset fluctuations in business activity. The country was fortunate too in having experienced strong growth and rapid structural change in the 1920s with plenty of potential still left, and in the fact that the depression was later and weaker than in some countries.

Initially it is true that Sweden, like so many countries, imposed some deflationary measures, for example wage cuts; but public spending continued to rise throughout the depression years, and by 1932-3 nearly one-quarter of the unemployed were being given relief work. Meanwhile the deflationary tendencies were being reversed. During 1931-2 the krona was devalued and cheap money was adopted. In the following year it was announced that budgetary policy was to be made an important instrument of recovery. The Finance Minister's speech of January 1933 is notable not only for its open declaration of an unorthodox budgetary policy but also because it formally acknowledged the state's responsibility for promoting recovery. Accordingly, a large programme of public works was implemented and the resulting budgetary deficit was to be financed by loans amortized over a period of four years. By 1934-5 the proportion of budgetary expenditure, when public works absorbed some 15 to 20 per cent of the total, met by borrowing amounted to one-quarter as against one-twentieth in the four fiscal years between 1928-9 and 1931-2. After 1935, when recovery was well under way, expenditure on public works was sharply reduced and the loans previously incurred were amortized.

By contrast with most other countries Swedish economic policy in the 1930s was impressive and exemplary, but one should be wary about overemphasising its contribution to the recovery. Currency devaluation certainly gave an initial boost to exports which showed vigorous growth from the middle of 1933, though the main stimulus eventually arose from the demand abroad for Sweden's industrial materials as industrial recovery took place elsewhere, and later because of rearmament. Cheap money also gave a boost to the housing market and industrial investment which surged forward after 1933. The public works programme, however, was a carrier of recovery rather than an initial stimulator since it did not really get under way until 1934 by which time economic activity was moving ahead strongly. Moreover, there were strong real or autonomous forces at work as in Britain, notably housing, consumer durables and new industries and exports, the recovery of which owed relatively little to policy action. Thus though policy measures were certainly favourable to Sweden's economy it is probable that the main agents of recovery lay elsewhere. And it should be noted that though Sweden put up an impressive record in this period the recovery was by no means complete, for even by 1937 unemployment still amounted to 11.6 per cent. Nevertheless, such facts should not be allowed to detract from the importance of Swedish policy; Sweden was the first country to acknowledge and use a countercyclical fiscal policy, and in the later 1930s preparations were made to continue the procedure in any future slump.

The German economy had two unique features in the 1930s: the strength of its recovery and the degree of state involvement in economic affairs. Though Germany suffered more than most from the slump she also staged one of the strongest recoveries after 1932. Output rose by more than one-third between 1929 and 1937 while unemployment was abolished, being reduced progressively from a peak of 44 per cent in 1932 to 14.1 per cent in 1934 and to less than 1 per cent in 1938. Few other nations could match such a record and probably few wished to do so given the high political and social price entailed in the process. Following the Nazi seizure of power in 1933 the economy was steadily transformed into a prototype of rigid control and became, in the latter part of the period, dominated by war motives.

Though the degree of state interference in economic affairs was eventually more extensive than in any other country outside Russia, the system of production, distribution and consumption which the Nazis erected defies classification in any of the usual categories of economic systems. It was neither capitalism, socialism nor communism in the traditional sense of these terms; rather the Nazi system was a combination of some of the characteristics of capitalism and a highly planned economy. A comprehensive planning mechanism, which was by no means highly efficient, was imposed on an economy in which private property was not expropriated, in which the distribution of national income remained largely unchanged and in which private entrepreneurs retained some of the prerogatives and responsibilities of traditional capitalism. Moreover, by extensive control over trade and payments the German economy came to exercise considerable influence over the economies of central and southeast Europe.

Initially, however, the economy of the Third Reich was peace-orientated as Nazi economic policy concentrated its attack on the unemployment problem. The deflationary policies of the previous governments (of Brüning and von Papen) had done more to aggravate than alleviate the crisis, though in the middle of 1932 a moderate programme of public works had been instituted. Immediately the Nazis assumed power they extended the relief policy by launching a massive programme of public works involving an outlay of some 6 billion reichsmarks. The employment-creating effects of this expenditure soon set recovery in motion and mopped up a good deal of the unemployment, though before the sum had been fully spent the basis of economic policy shifted dramatically. From November 1934 onwards priority was given to rearmament and preparations for war and as early as 1936 military spending was beginning to dominate certain sectors of the economy, though the really big peacetime build-up in the defence sector did not occur until 1937–8. The shift in policy gave rise to a large increase in government spending, selective economic planning and extensive regulation of many sectors of the economy, including wages and prices, foreign trade and exchange and the money and capital markets. It also entailed higher taxes, selective depreciation of the mark and controls designed to shift resources from consumer to producer goods industries.

A policy geared to rearmament inevitably led to the increased importance of public as opposed to private spending and consumption. Between 1933 and 1939 the Reich government claimed it had spent roughly 90 billion reichsmarks on preparing for war, which was equivalent to one year's income on the standard of 1938. Modern authorities tend to downgrade the sum but it still remains large. Military spending as a proportion of national income rose from 3 per cent in 1933 to 23 per cent in 1939, much of the increase occurring in the last two years when it accounted for over one-third of total government spending (Britain's share, it may be noted, was almost as high in 1939 following a massive armament drive in that year). The state's influence was larger than this of course since these figures refer specifically to military expenditure. By 1938 the public sector accounted for 57 per cent of Germany's gross investment as against 35.2 per cent in 1929, while total state spending as a proportion of national income increased from 11 per cent to over one-half between 1929 and the end of the 1930s. In effect, therefore, the government by the latter date had become the largest investor and consumer in the German economy.

The vast expansion in the size of the military machine and the public sector would not have been possible without extensive controls on private spending designed to shift resources away from this sector. To do this the government maintained tight control over private investment, especially that in consumer goods industries. Effective demand for consumer goods was kept in check by controls over wages and prices, increased taxes and forced savings. Money wages remained more or less stable after 1933 at a level below those of 1929, and given the moderate rise in prices real wages therefore fell slightly. Thus the general consumer failed to benefit from the increase in aggregate national income; per capita income in 1938 was no greater than in 1929, while private consumption as a proportion of national income fell from 72 to 54 per cent between 1929 and 1939. The main beneficiaries were those now in work who had previously been unemployed and the business community who thrived on munitions orders. Much of the increased public spending was financed by higher taxation and borrowing, though the latter rarely accounted for more than one-quarter of total government receipts.

The network of controls was completed by extensive regulations on trade, payments and exchange. The chief aim of these was to restrict inessential imports and where possible boost exports and secure the benefits of favourable trade terms. The results in terms of exports were disappointing despite the fact that eventually some 60 per cent of Germany's exports received a subsidy in one form or another. The import policy was more successful, with essential raw materials comprising an increasing share of the total import bill. At the same time Germany's foreign trade was increasingly directed towards those countries with whom she had concluded bilateral clearing agreements, thereby avoiding the need to release free exchange currency for the payment of imports from such countries. By 1938 some 40 clearing agreements had been negotiated covering about 80 per cent of Germany's imports. This involved a striking shift in the geographical direction of Germany's trade away from western Europe and towards southeastern Europe and countries overseas, notably Latin American, which were favourably disposed to Germany. Eventually, as we shall see, German economic influence over eastern Europe became very strong and it paved the way for subsequent political control. On balance the net cost of German imports (including allowances for quality differences in raw materials) probably rose as a result of her regulated trade policy.

Whatever the social costs of the German system, and they were substantial, there can be little doubt that it was successful in terms of recovery from the depression. Germany was the only country to eliminate unemployment and her record in aggregate output was impressive. It is very probable that some degree of recovery would have taken place without such extensive government intervention but it would not have been anywhere near as strong or as sustained. On the other hand, it should be noted that the state's increasing participation in the economy was motivated, especially after 1934, largely by political considerations rather than by dictates of modern business-cycle theory. Nor should policy action be accorded all the bouquets in the matter of recovery. By the time the first large injection of expenditure in the 1933–4 relief programme had taken place recovery in economic activity had already begun, though the process was markedly speeded up as a result of the new spending. There were too some real forces at work which were largely outside the government's domain. In particular, the 'motorization' of the German economy, namely the widespread use of motor vehicles and the road-building programme, was very important in this period and played a significant part in sustaining if not initiating the upswing in the German economy. However, in so far as Hitler gave it his blessing and active encouragement one might be inclined to argue that it represented yet another arm of the state's influence.

The final case to be considered is rather a sad story. Austria fared badly in the 1920s and little better in the 1930s, so that by 1938 her domestic output was no greater than in 1913. During the 1920s the country had had many problems to contend with including war exhaustion and the task of reconstruction, structural deficiencies in the economy, the loss of industrial areas to Czechoslovakia, the loss of a large customs-free market for her products and a bout of hyperinflation. Before she had time to recover properly Austria was engulfed in depression; this was accompanied by the collapse of the Credit

Anstalt and the financial crisis of the summer of 1931. It left the country almost as prostrate as it had been after the war. The subsequent flight of capital from Austria and the consequent drain on her foreign exchange reserves forced the government to take drastic action in the latter half of 1931. This entailed the adoption of exchange control, import and other trade controls and a deflationary package. Devaluation was ruled out for fear of its inflationary consequences, the memory of the great inflation of the early 1920s being still strong. But such policies were bound to aggravate the depression. By July 1932 industrial production was 43 per cent below the 1929 level and unemployment was in the region of one-quarter. There was also a big trade deficit because of the collapse of exports and a continued high volume of imports due to the overvalued exchange. Foreign capital was not now available to cover the deficits and in the summer of 1932 transfer on foreign debts had to be suspended.

Austria's economic position was therefore extremely serious in 1932. The monetary system had disintegrated as a result of the wave of bank failures, the government had a serious fiscal problem because of the collapse in tax receipts, the foreign exchange position was acute, while entry to traditional markets had been closed by protection. Though signs of an upturn in business activity were apparent in 1933 the recovery was weak and hesitant and the government was precluded from following an expansionary policy, even had it had the inclination to do so, by financial pressures. Fiscal and monetary policy therefore remained deflationary, and the accompanying high interest rates deterred business investment. However, some alleviation was provided by *de facto* devaluation through the use of private 'clearing' whereby certain exporters could sell their foreign exchange directly to importers at a negotiated rate, while in 1933 financial reconstruction measures were taken to prop up the banking system and the public finances with the help of a foreign loan. In addition, the devaluation of the dollar eased the budgetary problem by reducing overseas indebtedness. This enabled a moderate programme of public works to be instituted, but in 1936 public investment had to be cut back sharply because of financial constraints, and it only revived again when rearmament expenditures came into focus.

Austria therefore had little scope for manoeuvre in the 1930s because of her serious financial and monetary problems. It was never possible for the government to carry through a large programme of state spending to boost the economy and real forces were far from strong. Consequently the recovery was weak and erratic, being determined largely by the vagaries of export demand, the impact of the limited public works programme and later by rearmament. Even in 1937–8 the volume of output was barely the same as in 1929 though exports did slightly better. Unemployment remained high at about 17 per cent. Given Austria's weak position it is not surprising that she succumbed to political and economic domination by Germany.

STAGNATION IN EASTERN EUROPE

Apart from Russia which, cut off from the western world, forged ahead economically in the 1930s under the stimulus of the Five Year Plans, the east European countries had a rather chequered performance and achieved little in the way of bridging the gap in income levels compared with the west. Indeed, for the most part per capita income levels stagnated in this period. The severity of the great depression almost wrecked the sickly economies of this area and in the struggle for survival most of the countries were forced to adopt strongly nationalistic policies. Even more pernicious, they were, for want of an alternative escape route, drawn into the German economic sphere.

That the depression should have proved to be a calamity for eastern Europe is not altogether surprising. As noted previously, apart from Czechoslovakia none of the countries had what might be called structurally sound economies. They were heavily dependent on agriculture which in itself was badly organized and inefficient compared with that of the west: too many small farms, limited capital and low productivity. In three countries (Yugoslavia, Bulgaria and Romania) some three-quarters or more of the population was dependent on agriculture, while in Poland and Hungary the proportion was well over one-half; even in Czechoslovakia it accounted for one-third but this country did have a strong industrial base. Agriculture therefore provided the main source of exports, accounting for one-third or more of all exports, while foodstuffs, raw materials and semi-manufactures were responsible for three-quarters or more of all exports. By contrast, finished goods accounted for over 70 per cent of Czechoslovakia's exports.

The vulnerability of eastern Europe to changing fortunes in agriculture can be readily appreciated. During the economic crisis primary product prices collapsed – falling by one-half to two-thirds between 1929 and 1934, the decline being partly accentuated in the early stages by increasing production as farmers sought to maintain their incomes through increased sales. As a result agrarian incomes declined by up to one-half in Romania, Bulgaria, Poland and Yugoslavia and by about one-third in Hungary. This collapse in incomes was little short of disastrous given the already heavy indebtedness of the farming sector; the debt burden increased proportionately to income and the distress was aggravated by the fact that agricultural prices fell faster than those of industrial products purchased by the peasant. Thus by 1932 many peasants were on the verge of bankruptcy. In Yugoslavia, for example, more than one-third of all rural households were seriously in debt – many more being too poor even to obtain credit – and the sum of the indebtedness amounted to 80–90 per cent of their total net incomes. Many farms collapsed altogether and rural communities were put under severe social strain, though the problem was subsequently alleviated to some extent by government relief in the form of credits, debt moratoria and other measures of assistance.

The position was equally serious on the export front. Agricultural exports were hit by falling prices, severe competition and increasing self-sufficiency and protection in former markets. The volume of both cattle and cereal exports fell sharply but the shortfall in incomes was even greater because of the dramatic price decline. For example, in Romania the volume of cereal exports fell by 42 per cent between 1929 and 1934 but export receipts fell by no less than 73 per cent, while for Hungary the percentage changes were 27 and 60. For the area as a whole export incomes fell to about 40 per cent of the pre-crisis level. The collapse in export receipts inevitably affected the ability of these countries to import and resulted in a sharp deterioration in their external accounts. Between 1930 and 1933 Hungary was able to buy on average 15–20 per cent fewer foreign goods for the value of equal quantities of her export articles than in the period 1925–7.

It was little consolation, moreover, that the industrial sector suffered less acutely from the crisis since for most of the countries in this region industry accounted for such a small proportion of total economic activity. Experience here varied more widely than in the case of agriculture depending in part on the structure of each particular economy. In the Balkan countries, for example, industrial overproduction was not particularly pronounced, partly because of the relative insignificance of this sector, and in any case reduced consumption was usually counterbalanced in many fields by import restriction. Thus production declined only moderately in Romania thanks to a large increase in oil output, while Bulgaria experienced a significant advance in manufacturing between 1929 and 1932. The setback was quite severe in Yugoslavia but the most serious industrial consequences occurred in Czechoslovakia, which had the most advanced industrial sector, and to a lesser extent in the mixed agrarian-industrial economies of Hungary and Poland. Even so, for all countries except Czechoslovakia it was the agrarian sector which determined the scale and severity of the crisis.

A further major problem was of course the region's international indebtedness. Most of the countries (again excepting Czechoslovakia) had relied heavily on foreign credit of one sort or another in the 1920s. The drying up of foreign lending between 1928 and 1931 caused acute problems since the servicing of previous debts was dependent on the ability to raise new loans; even by the late 1920s the amount of yearly amortization was usually in excess of new loans. By the time of the European financial crisis in 1931 the situation had become desperate; all external sources of finance had disappeared, incomes and export receipts had plummeted and as gold and foreign exchange reserves drained away the countries faced the threat of complete financial collapse. With the rapid fall in export receipts the interest payments on former debts accounted for one-third or more of these revenues. Only Czechoslovakia, never a large debtor, escaped financial ruin.

The consequences of the crisis in terms of later events and policy may be summarized as follows: (1) emergency measures to deal with the immediate situation; (2) the rise of dictatorships or semi-dictatorial regimes bent on fostering development along autarchic lines; and (3) the increasing stranglehold exercised by Germany over the region's economic and political future.

The problem initially in the early 1930s was not so much one of recovery as of economic salvation. Drastic measures were required to shore up the tottering economies and these were soon forthcoming: they included not only severe deflationary policies but also a battery of restrictions typical of siege economies, which were designed primarily to deal with the external account. Among them were temporary closure of banking institutions, rigorous exchange control, limitation on debt payments and tariffs, quotas and import prohibitions. Thus, for example, by early 1933 the import of almost all finished products into Hungary was prohibited except under special permit. At the same time attempts were made to boost exports by subsidies, special and advantageous exchange facilities in favour of exporters often in place of devaluation, and the widespread use of clearing agreements in foreign trade relations, since the acute shortage of foreign exchange rendered previous methods of foreign trade impossible. Clearing agreements proliferated in the 1930s (by which foreign trade turnover was based on reciprocal exchange of products of approximately equal value wherever possible, with the use of foreign exchange being restricted to the payment of balances where liabilities arose, especially with countries outside such agreements), and by the end of the decade some four-fifths of the trade of most of the eastern countries was settled through bilateral clearing arrangements.

If bilateral trade and barter offered some alleviation to the external problems of these countries, they also presented Germany with an opportunity to increase her economic, and subsequently political, influence in this area. In September 1934 Dr Schacht had launched a plan designed to regulate Germany's trade and payments and to import from countries which did not demand payment in foreign exchange. This was clearly well suited to strengthening economic relations with an area heavily dependent on exporting primary products and importing finished goods, especially producer goods, and which was still facing severe economic difficulties. At first only Hungary was really sympathetic to Germany's new economic foreign policy but in time other countries succumbed to the temptation and signed trade agreements with Germany. By offering a ready market for primary products in exchange for imports of equipment Germany came to exercise increasing dominance over the trade and development of eastern Europe. By 1937 total German trade amounted to only 40 per cent of the 1929 value but that with southeast Europe (Bulgaria, Romania, Yugoslavia and Hungary) had attained the previous peak level; these four countries accounted for about 10 per cent of Germany's trade as against 4 per cent in 1929. Their dependence on Germany as an outlet for their exports rose sharply; exports to Germany as a percentage of the total between 1933 and 1939 increased from 36 to 71 per cent in the case of Bulgaria, 11 to 52 per cent for Hungary, 17 to 43 per cent for Romania and 14 to 46 per cent for Yugoslavia.

Though Germany's economic penetration into the area was not wholly exploitive, in that it provided the eastern countries with a market for their commodities and at the same time allowed them to secure imports of much-needed capital equipment, the balance of advantage lay with Germany. For one thing Germany was able to dictate the prices to be paid for the region's primary products and at the same time she piled up large import surpluses with the countries in question which were not matched by German exports. The accumulating arrears in the German supply of goods meant in effect that Germany was financing part of her rearmament interest-free at the expense of her suppliers in the east. And though the eastern countries did secure some capital equipment from Germany it was too little and too late to do much in the way of transforming the structure of their economies. Finally, economic penetration paved the way for ultimate military and political conquest of Germany's eastern neighbours.

Elsewhere Germany had less success on the economic front in the conquest of territories, though economic factors were not entirely absent in the eventual domination of Poland, Austria and Czechoslovakia. The scope for economic penetration by purchasing agricultural and raw material surpluses was much less in the case of the latter two countries given their more advanced economic structures, while Poland managed to do without German economic assistance. Hitler therefore adopted alternative methods which included overt pressure and military blackmail, economic blockade, prohibition of German tourists from visiting these countries, limitations on foreign trade and conquests of markets supplied by these countries. This policy culminated in the crushing of Austria and Czechoslovakia and their annexation in 1938–9, with Poland following soon after. Thus by the outbreak of war Germany's economic and political domination of central and eastern Europe was almost complete since all the states in the area had succumbed to her offensives, though German ambitions for the area as a whole were only fully realized during the course of the war itself.

Germany's domination of eastern Europe is not particularly surprising given her grandiose military ambitions and the weakness of the states concerned. The fact that the economic crisis subsequently gave rise to dictatorships or quasi-dictatorships in these countries was not necessarily a barrier to these ambitions since the new regimes tended to be more favourably disposed towards German interests and more responsive to pressures than their democratic counterparts of the 1920s. Moreover, despite efforts to foster industrialization their economies remained weak and structurally unsound.

The depression undoubtedly strengthened nationalist sentiments within eastern Europe and gave rise to the increasing involvement of the state in economic affairs. The drift towards *étatism* took different forms but basically the common aim was to improve the economic performance of the countries in question. Accordingly attempts were made to promote exports and industry in an effort to create a shift in the structural format of the economies away from the predominant base of agriculture. Apart from specific measures of protection and subsidy and the like, this policy involved an increase in the state-owned sector of economic activity. The prime example in this respect was Poland. Here the focus of attention was concentrated on the industrialization of the central industrial region within the triangle bounded by Warsaw, Krakow and Lwow. As a result of steady acquisition of undertakings the Polish state owned about 100 industrial enterprises by the end of the 1930s; they included all the armament factories, 80 per cent of the chemical industry, 40 per cent of the iron industry and 50 per cent of other metal industries, and 20 per cent of the oil refineries. The state also held the majority of stock in some fifty companies. The state's direct role was not quite so important in other countries though it certainly increased in this period. In Hungary it accounted for only about 5 per cent of industrial investments in the later 1930s. A notable feature in some eastern countries was the experiments made in medium-term planning of economic development. Hungary, for example, launched a Five Year Plan early in 1938 which included a big programme to develop the armament industries and build up a modern army.

On balance the efforts made to foster industrial development were not an unqualified success. Certainly industry proved to be the most dynamic sector in the 1930s and in most cases the share of this sector increased in importance, albeit rather marginally in most cases. Moreover, industrial expansion was probably faster on average in eastern Europe than in the west, though the most industrialized country, Czechoslovakia, scarcely made up the losses incurred in the depression partly because of the closing of western markets to her industrial products. But the advance on the industrial front was not spectacular when it is recalled how small the industrial sector was in the economies of eastern Europe. More to the point, however, is that certain aspects of the pattern of development give cause for concern. For one thing state policy tended to foster unproductive or non-economic investments. Second, the state's financial resources were limited; it could not replace the role of the foreign capitalist when overseas loans dried up in the early 1930s, and the 'nostrification' policy designed to discourage the influx of foreign funds and ownership did not help matters. Third, efforts to mobilize domestic resources were frequently offset by restrictive monetary and fiscal policies including higher taxation. Fourth, the direction of investment was not especially conducive to promoting rapid development. It was frequently channelled into textiles, food-processing and light industries, where the growth potential was low, to the comparative neglect of modern science-based industries such as chemicals, the electrical trades, telecommunications and the motor industry. One of the most obvious deficiencies in the investment strategy is shown by the failure in eastern Europe to shift from the railway to the motor age. The motor vehicle did not replace the railways as a growth force in the inter-war period. An index of motorization based on the number of cars in use in relation to territory and population gives values of between 0.3 and

0.5 for Poland, Hungary, Yugoslavia and Romania, as against 5.7 for Europe as a whole in 1938. In fact the infrastructure of eastern Europe was probably more backward compared with that of the west than it had been in 1913.

Apart from its rather lop-sided industrial structure, eastern Europe also retained its traditional dual structure, namely many small-scale inefficient firms competing with a few modern large-scale corporations. During the inter-war period small-scale business was as viable as ever partly because of the weakness of large-scale concerns, the abundant labour supply and the predominance of those industrial activities in which small-scale firms tended to thrive. Furthermore, the large-scale corporation failed to make much progress in production and management methods which were a feature of those in the west. Modern mass-production methods made little headway and for the most part the largest companies remained little more than 'general stores' supplying a multiplicity of products in small batches to limited markets within a rigid protectionist framework.

In this period too agriculture acted as a drag on economic progress. Before the war, the agrarian sector, though still far behind western standards, had made significant advances partly as a result of the gradual spread of capitalist farming; hence it provided something of a stimulus to the economy in general. During the inter-war years this sector lost its dynamic role and therefore it could not perform its previous function of capital accumulation. Throughout the 1920s agriculture struggled to recoup its wartime losses only to be dealt another shattering blow in 1929–32. In the 1930s recovery was slow, though output did manage to surpass 1913 levels by the end of the decade. Even so it remained an extremely weak sector: there was no radical transformation in the structure and methods of farming partly because of the shortage of capital and the existence of too many small farming units. Even in countries where large estates still remained important, for example Poland and Hungary, small farms still predominated, while in Yugoslavia over 75 per cent and in Bulgaria over 60 per cent of the farms were under 5 hectares in size. In Poland 47 per cent of the peasant farms consisted of narrow strips. Small-scale peasant holders, often overburdened with debt, were not in a position to farm land profitably and economically, and they lacked the capital and incentive to shift to larger and more efficient units of production. Consequently new techniques, mechanization and the use of fertilizers made relatively little progress, and productivity stagnated. In some cases crop productivity levels were little better than those before 1914 and in most cases they were well below those of western Europe. High rates of population growth in some countries also exerted pressure on the land and helped to press down productivity levels.

Low productivity, capital shortages, low incomes and agrarian overpopulation formed a vicious circle which could only be broken by radical changes in market conditions. But there was little prospect of these occurring since overpopulation, low incomes and a weak industrial sector meant a limited domestic market. Moreover, former export markets for agrarian products disappeared because of protection and reduced cereal consumption in the west – hence the attraction of trade links with Germany. In the 1930s agricultural exports of most eastern countries were still about 20–25 per cent below pre-war levels. Market prospects were somewhat better for certain vegetables, fruits and animal products and some countries adopted intensive market farming to cater for new demands, as for example chickens and fruit in Hungary, tobacco and garden produce in Bulgaria, and oilseeds in Romania, together with a more general shift towards livestock farming. But such changes were insufficient to offset the setback in cereals, nor did they produce a radical transformation in the structure of agriculture. Yet despite its inherent backwardness agriculture remained, except in Czechoslovakia, the most important single factor determining the economic position of eastern countries in every year until the Second World War.

The progress achieved in industry during the 1930s was insufficient to counterbalance the stagnation in agriculture and population growth, with the result that real incomes per head remained unchanged from 1929 to 1938, and in the case of Czechoslovakia they even fell slightly. Over the inter-war period as a whole income growth per head was very modest, less than 1 per cent in many cases, and much less than in the years before 1914. Agriculture stagnated for most of the period while only modest gains were made on the industrial front. The progress in the latter did not produce any significant change in the structural format of the eastern economies. By the end of the 1930s about 75–80 per cent of the active population in the Balkan countries (Romania, Bulgaria and Yugoslavia) was still engaged on the land, a proportion very similar to that in 1910. There was a shift away from agriculture in Hungary and Poland, albeit modest, the proportions engaged in this sector falling from 72 to 65 per cent and from 56 to 51 per cent respectively over the years 1920–40. In terms of the generation of national income the shift from agriculture to industry was a little more pronounced, but in the Balkan countries the proportion of income derived from industry remained less than one-quarter, and only in Czechoslovakia did it surpass one-half.

In short, therefore, up to 1939 eastern Europe remained a backward and predominantly agrarian-based region, and by every conceivable indicator it was less productive, less literate and less healthy than western Europe or even west-central Europe (Austria and Czechoslovakia). It was potentially a rich region stocked with a poor people in which the maldistribution of poverty was the central feature and whose development had been stunted by the vicissitudes of war and the unfavourable economic climate which followed. The depression and its aftermath finally set the seal on any further substantial development. The dynamism apparent at the turn of the century all but petered out in the 1930s and there were no radical changes in the economic structure of the region of a type propitious to rapid economic growth. With the exception of Czechoslovakia, the countries of eastern Europe remained suppliers of food and raw materials and buyers of industrial goods. Politically, economically and socially they were backward and weak, struggling with inner tensions and contradictions, and with little prospect, as war loomed near, of solving their fundamental problems.

EUROPE ON THE EVE OF THE SECOND WORLD WAR

For Europe as a whole the inter-war period was one of chequered growth, crisis, political tension and latterly the threat of war. Some economic advance was made during this period, but at a slower rate than before 1914. Not only was progress severely interrupted by the slump of 1929–32 but most countries faced important structural problems throughout the period as new techniques, changes in tastes and patterns of demand created difficulties for established producers. Recovery from the depression was slow and patchy and even towards the end of the 1930s many economies continued to operate at less than full capacity. Ironically it was the rearmament build-up and war which finally provided a solution to this problem.

From 1914 to 1939 Europe's role in the world economy steadily declined. The war provided opportunities for countries outside Europe, notably the United States and Japan, to strengthen their economic power and subsequent events did little to redress the balance. Western Europe in particular was no longer strong enough to continue to dictate the pattern of world development as she had more or less done in the nineteenth century. America now assumed this role and with fateful consequences in the depression. Politically too Europe had been weakened; it had lost its nineteenth-century cohesiveness; in central and eastern Europe a multiplicity of autonomous but weak and struggling states had arisen from the ruins of the Austro-Hungarian Empire, while bitter political tensions and weak democracies left the west in a disunited state. Ultimately, neither the west nor the east were able to resist alone the designs of Germany, while after 1945 the eastern countries became the prey of a new world power, the USSR.

Within Europe itself the balance of economic power did not change significantly in this period. The richest industrial centre remained firmly in the west, and as one moved south and east the strength of the income and industrial contour lines steadily diminished. On the eve of the Second World War about two-thirds of Europe's industrial output was produced by the UK, Germany and France and the share of the first two countries in industrial production was more than twice their share of Europe's population. There were also several smaller industrially advanced countries, for example the Netherlands, Belgium and Switzerland, with larger proportionate shares in production than population, but their contribution to the European total remained small. Moving into central Europe one finds two relatively advanced countries, Austria and Czechoslovakia, with industry and population shares about equal; then, shifting further east, one reaches Hungary with a 60 per cent gap between industry and population shares and then Poland

and the Balkan countries where the discrepancy was even greater.

Income levels tell a similar story. Per capita national income in constant dollar terms was highest in Britain, Sweden, Germany and Belgium in that order and lowest in the Balkans, with central Europe (Austria and Czechoslovakia) occupying a intermediate position. The average per capita income for the richest four countries in 1937 amounted to $378, whereas in the poorest three (Romania, Yugoslavia and Bulgaria) it was but a mere $79, or just over one-fifth the former. Even the addition of Poland and Hungary to the poorest group only brings the average up to $91. Austrian and Czechoslovak per capita income levels were about double the latter figure but even these only represented one-half the per capita income levels of the west. In fact in every central and eastern European country income per head was lower than the $200 per head average for twenty-four European countries. While such comparisons of constant dollar incomes cannot provide a precise guide to the standard of living within individual countries, they do give a rough idea of the disparity in income levels between the west and the east, a disparity which was probably as great in 1937 as it had been in 1913. Moreover, not only did eastern Europe remain desperately poor compared with the west, but also the fact that incomes were probably more unevenly distributed in the former region must have meant that many people were in very dire straits indeed. It is this contrast between poverty and wealth both between countries and within individual countries in Europe that is the most glaring yet least explored subject.

4

WAR AND RECONSTRUCTION,
1940–1950

THE RISE AND FALL OF HITLER'S EUROPE

The map of Europe underwent a radical transformation in the years immediately following the outbreak of war in September 1939. Hitler's march across the continent, which had already started in a preliminary way before that date, proceeded virtually unchecked and by the latter half of 1942 the new German Empire was practically synonymous with that of continental Europe. It stretched from Brittany in the west to the mountains of the Caucasus in the east, and from the arctic tip of Norway to the shores of the Mediterranean. Independent states and territories disappeared almost overnight under Hitler's onward drive and only a few nations managed to retain their autonomy, and even then it was not always very secure. They comprised the neutral countries of Portugal, Spain, Eire, Switzerland, Sweden and Turkey. In addition, Romania, Bulgaria and Hungary, and possibly Finland which slipped from neutrality to quasi-alliance with Germany, retained a semblance of sovereignty by joining Hitler as military allies, though in practice they became very much satellite dependencies of the German Reich. Italy, ostensibly an equal partner in the exercise of European domination, very soon became more akin to a satellite country since her economic and political structure was no match for that of Germany.

The new Nazi Empire consisted of a rather motley patchwork of territories acquired in a somewhat unsystematic manner and ruled in different ways. As each piece of territory was acquired Hitler assigned to it, in a rather *ad hoc* manner, that type of governance which seemed least likely to pose a threat to the Reich's military plans. There was also probably some attempt, at least initially, to allot a form of administration suitable to its final place in the Nazi conception of the New Order for Europe; this envisaged the formation of a single economic community for the whole of the continent working under German direction and with the Reich as the industrial hub of the system. Thus the central industrial core of Europe was brought under unified control by incorporating into the German Reich such areas as Alsace-Lorraine, Luxembourg and Polish Upper Silesia. Other less highly industrialized areas, including much of the rest of western Europe, were subject to only indirect control. Those regions designated as 'colonial' territories, for example the occupied parts of Russia and the General Government of Poland, though kept apart from the Reich itself, were controlled from Germany and allowed virtually no hand in their own administration. However, apart from this and the centralization of financial dealings in Berlin – the Reichsmark became the main unit of settlement within German-dominated territories – little further progress was made with the New Order despite considerable propaganda on the subject in 1940. Indeed by 1942 the German media had lapsed into silence on it and at this stage the new German Empire was far from being a coherent and efficient economic structure. The reasons for failure on this score are not difficult to discern. For one thing the Nazis never had a very clear idea of what was involved in setting up the New Order. No complete and comprehensive plan for the restructuring of Europe was ever published so that the concept remained vague and confused, being based largely on the somewhat conflicting statements made by Reich ministers from time to time. Second, in the first two years of hostilities the speed of military conquest outran the regime's plan for a new Empire. The success of Hitler's campaigns exceeded even the most optimistic expectations and as a result of the rapid acquisition of new territories the Nazi regime was occupied with the immediate task of administering them. Then, just at the time when the Reich might have been in a position to give more attention to the idea, that is, when it was master of most of Europe, things began to go wrong for the Nazis and the conglomerate Empire began to crumble. In particular, the inability to quell the Russian giant and the coalescence of the Allied powers under US leadership significantly altered the situation; it meant that Hitler was faced with a long campaign requiring the assistance of all European nations. The war now turned into a struggle for survival involving a shift towards immediate objectives and the abandonment of long-term planning for the future of Europe.

The events of the Second World War have been recounted all too frequently and it would be pointless to repeat the exercise in detail here. The following section examines some of the less well-known economic aspects of the war effort, but before turning to these there are one or two general questions that are worth considering: (1) How was it that one country was able to overrun the European continent in so short a time? (2) Why, given the extent of Hitler's power and control by 1942, did his regime eventually collapse? (3) Why, in view of the far greater resources of the Allied powers, was victory for the Allied cause so long delayed?

The first of these questions cannot be answered simply in terms of the greater military and economic potential of Germany prior to the war, though, as we shall see, this was by no means an irrelevant factor. It must be recognized first of all that the peace treaty exercise following the First World War had left a power vacuum in east-central Europe. It had created several independent states all of which were relatively small and weak, both politically and economically, compared with their neighbours to the east and west. They therefore became an obvious target for large predator nations, notably Germany and Russia, once the latter powers had recuperated from the impact of the First World War. By the later 1930s both these countries were conceivably in a position to extend their spheres of influence in Europe and the fact that Germany got there first can be attributed to that country's superior strength and political ambitions under Hitler coupled with the fact that the Soviet Union was still in the throes of sorting out its own development process. But the important point is that the structure of Europe left it vulnerable to attack from any larger power in the 1930s, the two most obvious candidates being Germany and Russia. Moreover, there was no effective bulwark to prevent this taking place. France was weak and herself open to invasion, a point borne out by her precipitous collapse in 1940. Britain, by virtue of her equivocal attitude towards Germany in the 1930s, dithered between appeasement and rearmament and finally ended the decade in no position to prevent the German onslaught. The only power which might conceivably have been able to do justice to the situation, the United States, had retreated into isolation after 1920 and by the time war broke out again her military potential was far from ready to counter the German attack.

Hitler's initial successes derived largely from the strategy employed to conquer Europe. The Blitzkrieg strategy eschewed any commitment to a long-drawn-out war involving armament in depth. Rather it entailed swift attack on specified but limited objectives, a procedure which took his adversaries by surprise and left them debating whether each new conquest would be the last. The key to Germany's sweeping victories lay in her ability to back up threats with force, together with the absence of serious opposition, and this she was able to do because of her greater military build-up before the war. The expenditure of the Axis powers (Germany, Italy and Japan) on armaments in the period 1934–8 increased twice as fast as that of the UK, the Soviet Union and France combined, and it accounted for 52 per cent of all war expenditure of thirty nations in 1938 as against 35 per cent in 1934. The countries which faced Germany in September 1939 – France, Poland, Britain, India and the belligerent Dominions – had budgeted in the previous year for a total armament expenditure little more than a third as great as Germany's. Poland and France of course fell quickly, while Russia, though she had armed rapidly just prior to the war, did not join the Allied cause until two years later. The United States, on the other hand, preserved her neutrality at the onset and in any case her arms expenditure was little greater than that of France. Thus, given the weakness of the Allied position together with the geographical dispersion of the countries which faced the Axis powers it is scarcely surprising that Hitler swept all before him in the first phase of the war.

Though attempts have been made to downgrade the extent of Germany's military preparations prior to the war, there seems little doubt that Germany did hold an initial superiority in terms of military and economic potential. The important point to bear in mind, however, is that her military preparedness was designed primarily for a series of short wars with certainty of victory. One must stress again that Hitler had never any intention of engaging in long drawn-out battles for which the country was definitely not prepared, and this point is borne out by the fact that the onset of war did not produce any significant change in Germany's economic and military priorities. For the most part sufficient preparation had already been made to carry out the type of war contemplated by the Nazi administration. Only when Germany was forced to abandon her 'smash-and-grab' tactics and switch to fighting defensive and rearguard campaigns of indeterminate length did the limitations of her military preparations become apparent. It was unfortunate, at least as far as the Allied cause was concerned, that Britain in particular mistook the nature of the German war plans. Britain had assumed that Germany had been arming heavily for years in order to wage a massive and prolonged attack and it was therefore concluded that little could be done in the short term except defend against invasion until such time as her own military potential had been built up. Priority was therefore given to long-term armament in depth, the consequence of which was to allow Germany a relatively free hand in Europe in the first two years of war.

The elapse of these two years left Germany in what seemed to be an invincible position. Yet during the course of the following year the tide was turning distinctly against the Reich and by the winter of 1942–3 Germany's empire was on the wane. Although it was to be another two years or more before the country was defeated the seeds of decay were sown before the half-way stage.

Several factors can be adduced to explain the demise of the Reich despite its apparently insuperable position at the height of conquest. One of Hitler's early and chief mistakes was to launch an attack on Russia (June 1941). This was at a time when he was still engaged on the western front with Britain, an exercise that was proving costly and not terribly successful. The motive for attacking Russia was Hitler's dissatisfaction with what he regarded as an unco-operative and untrustworthy ally which left him with the conviction that she should be dealt with promptly before she grew any stronger. At the same time Hitler believed that the war in the west was virtually won, and even at this late stage he had not quite abandoned the notion of the possibility of enticing Britain over to the Axis side. Moreover, it never occurred to him that Russia would pose much of a problem. And, indeed, to begin with the Russian campaign went well and once again it appeared that Hitler's strategy was sound. Within five months an area some five times greater than that of Germany proper had been conquered and it seemed only a matter of time before the Russian giant was subdued. Unfortunately Russia simply refused to 'collapse on schedule'; Russian forces put up a stubborn resistance and by the summer of 1942 their continued defence made it clear that the Blitzkrieg phase was over. Meanwhile, the United States had been drawn into the war by the Japanese attack on Pearl Harbour (December 1941). This at the onset proved a useful diversionary move from Hitler's point of view but it was only a matter of time before the United States turned its focus on Europe.

The first half of 1942 therefore marked a crucial turning-point in the Second World War. It spelt the end of the Blitzkrieg strategy on which Germany's whole plan of campaign decisively turned, and it meant in turn that the regime was forced to commit itself to a long drawn-out struggle for which it was neither militarily prepared nor temperamentally suited. In effect the war now turned into a struggle between opposing economic potentials which weighted the odds heavily in the Allies' favour. The United States, UK and USSR alone had accounted for some 60 per cent of world manufacturing production in 1936-8 as against about 17 per cent for the main Axis powers. It is true that the latter could also draw upon the resources of the conquered territories, but so in turn could the major Allies tap the resources of an even wider area beyond Europe.

The commitment to total war on the Allied side prompted a massive build-up of armament strength and extensive mobilization of manpower and economic resources. It also led to a more extensive system of planning and controls than had been the case in the First World War. Thus from early 1942 arms production in Allied countries rose rapidly to reach a peak in 1944. On the Axis side a similar trend was apparent but the commitment to an all-out effort came later and was less energetically pursued. In fact as late as September 1941 Hitler had made the fatal mistake of cutting back war production schedules on the assumption that the war was virtually won, an order that was to prove costly in terms of military supplies for a time in 1942. Even then Hitler remained reluctant to agree to anything like a general mobilization of manpower and resources since he still laboured under the delusion that the war could be won by his previous 'smash-and-grab' policies. Thus although arms production did increase in 1942, thanks largely to Speer's efforts in improving resource ultilization, it remained inadequate, and the failure to mobilize fully meant a continuing shortage of labour for both defence and production purposes. Instead the regime was content to alleviate the labour shortage in some degree by drafting workers from occupied territories.

The Stalingrad disaster at the close of 1942 made it clear, however, that fundamental changes were required in the conduct of the German war economy. Prior to this event, in February 1942, Albert Speer had been appointed Minister of Armaments and Munitions and during the course of that year he had achieved some notable results in boosting production under conditions that were far from propitious. But it was not until September 1943 that a single authority to direct the whole German war economy was realized when Speer was made Minister of Armaments and War Production with powers over both the military and civilian sectors of the economy. Though Speer accomplished spectacular feats against great odds, since Hitler remained unwilling to let the output of civilian goods fall appreciably, the main opportunities for restructuring the economy had been missed. Because of

Germany's initial delay in mobilizing fully the Allies were given a head start in arming in depth, apart from the fact that their combined strength was infinitely greater. Thus by the time it was fully appreciated that a change of direction was required it was too late for Germany to attempt a radical overhaul of her war economy with a view to broadening its industrial base. Germany was now on the defensive and therefore immediate needs were paramount; labour and materials could no longer be spared for projects which did not yield quick returns. In other words, Germany was now forced to concentrate her energy on boosting arms production as best she could, drawing as far as possible on supplies of labour and materials from occupied Europe. In time these supplies began to dry up and by 1944 growing manpower and raw material shortages were seriously hampering the war effort. By the autumn of the same year it was becoming increasingly clear that Germany had insufficient resources to carry on the war much longer. However, even at this late stage Germany had not fully tapped all her own reserves: the mobilization of women, for example, was far less extensive than was the case in Britain. This neglect can again be attributed to Hitler's original conception of war which made him reluctant to sanction an all-out effort as far as mobilization was concerned.

The policy adopted towards the conquered territories was also unsatisfactory in securing the maximum potential for war purposes. The Nazi regime never sought to persuade any one of the nominally allied or conquered countries that their interests were identical to those of the German people. For the most part Hitler treated all non-German countries in Europe alike, that is, as territories to be exploited to serve German needs. This policy had two unfortunate consequences as far as Germany was concerned. It precluded the possibility of securing the voluntary support of non-Germans for Hitler's war effort. How extensive this might have been is a moot point but certainly the inferior treatment of non-Germans did little to encourage such support and it often bred latent hostility. Second, the outright exploitation of occupied territories as opposed to the building up of their productive potential was eventually self-defeating. It is true that Germany acquired considerable resources from the domains she ruled – rough estimates suggest that the foreign contribution to Germany's wartime gross national product was of the order of 14 per cent – but it is more than likely that the contribution would have been even greater had a more humane and constructive attitude been adopted towards these territories. In particular, had they not been seriously weakened by the policy of exploitation their contribution in the later stages of the war could have been crucial to Germany's final effort.

On other grounds too it could be argued that Germany made a serious mistake in not securing the co-operation of the occupied countries, since by the middle stage of the war her main allies, Italy and Japan, were proving something of an incubus. Italy was a weak country, despite Mussolini's valiant attempts to ape the Führer, and the country provided little effective support for the German war effort. Indeed, Mussolini's independent ambitions, especially in Africa, together with the disastrous war record of the Italian economy, meant that Germany was virtually forced to prop up the country until the Fascist experiment collapsed. Japan's record was better, and initially she proved a useful ally in the effort to deflect the United States from Europe. But Japan failed to check the United States and when she subsequently developed wider ambitions within the Pacific area her strategic usefulness to Hitler diminished.

Finally one should note that the German regime itself was far from united. Bitter inter-Nazi feuds and struggles for power went on throughout the war and served to weaken the administrative and organizational effort of the Third Reich. The effects were seen in the relatively inefficient organization of the conquered territories as well as in the disputes about the conduct of the German war economy itself. At one time or another every prominent member of Hitler's entourage indulged in feuding with his immediate adversaries, a practice which Hitler chose largely to ignore for personal reasons. This internecine warfare can have done little to assist the planning and organization of the war effort and it may well have given Germany's opponents an opportunity to break the German hegemony.

Given the weaknesses and mistakes of the Nazi regime and its inferior potential compared with its adversaries it may seem surprising that it took the Allied powers so long to secure victory. The general provision of goods and services for war for Britain and the United States alone probably exceeded those available to Germany in 1944 by some 75 per cent, while in munitions output the ratio was about 5:2. Three years earlier the comparative strength of the two sides had been approximately equal.

There are several reasons to explain the delay. For one thing, after the entry of the United States into the war the Allies were faced for a time with the task of maintaining a holding operation until such time as they were able to build up their military strength to a point at which they could launch a full-scale attack on Germany. This took some time to accomplish, especially the tooling-up operations required for American mass production methods, while heavy shipping losses as a result of German submarine activity played havoc with the movement of supplies. In addition, war on the second front in the east absorbed a large proportion of resources, especially American, thereby reducing the European effort. For a time too the Russian striking force was seriously weakened as a result of Hitler's initial victories. The Soviet Union had also lost a large part of its industrial resources to Germany and it was not until a new industrial base had been created in the Urals and beyond the Volga that Russia was in a position to launch an effective attack from the east. It is also possible that the Allies underestimated the war production potential of Germany after the Blitzkrieg. Despite increasing difficulties German production of munitions did increase rapidly and in the first half of 1944, by which time the Allied superiority was clearly apparent, Germany was able to make one last effort and in the process managed to increase the output of certain vital armaments faster than the Allies. Finally, the rather inefficient Allied bombing strategy contributed to the delay in victory.

After the middle of 1944, however, the defeat of Germany was only a matter of time. Until then Germany's war production had not been too seriously hampered by a shortage of resources. Thereafter the position deteriorated rapidly. The Normandy landings in the summer of 1944 together with excessive bombing put Germany in a state of siege. The supply of raw materials became increasingly tight as the area under German control diminished, while heavy Allied bombing reduced the productive capacity of the Axis powers and their occupied territories. For example, the sustained aerial attacks from May 1944 on German oil resources were extremely successful; they reduced the amount of fuel available by 90 per cent thereby rendering Germany's new tanks and jet planes inoperative. The increasing shortage of resources had a serious impact on production in the latter half of the year. Thus with rapidly dwindling reserves and declining production Germany faced the combined onslaught of the Allied nations on all fronts. Their superior economic and military strength was telling. By the spring of 1945 the position had become desperate and on 7 May Germany surrendered. 'The hard facts of economic power, expressed in the form of military equipment and the men to operate it, in the end overwhelmed both [Hitler] and Germany' (Wright 1968).

ECONOMIC ASPECTS OF THE WAR EFFORT

By the winter of 1943–4 the world economy was far more mobilized for war than at any time in the past, including the period of the First World War. The planning and control of economic resources was far more extensive and detailed than it had been in 1914–18 while the proportion of output devoted to war purposes was also greater. At the peak of activity well over one-third of the world's net output was being devoted to war. Military spending was of course heavily concentrated on a small number of countries. The major belligerents including the British Dominions were spending about £36,000 million to £38,000 million a year on war or defence, while the rest of the world had an annual budget of £1,500 million at the most for such purposes. At the same time the main combat powers were drawing some £3,000 million to £3,500 million from the rest of the world in the form of levies, exactions and loans.

The distribution of war expenditures among the major participants varied considerably. Reckoning on the basis of budgetary responsibility for the war goods and services provided, the United States easily topped the list, her share accounting for 30 per cent of the world total. The next largest spender was Greater Germany with 25 per cent, which includes exactions and levies imposed on occupied territories. The Soviet Union and the UK accounted for one-seventh and one-eighth respectively, while Japan's share was about one-fourteenth. These five countries accounted for some eleven-twelfths of total world expenditure on war though their combined share of world output in 1943–4 was just under 70 per cent. The proportions vary somewhat if based on the countries to whose governments the goods and services were finally made available.

˶ The war effort was sustained by three main factors: increasing output, a fall in consumption and capital depletion. During the course of the war net world output probably rose by between 15 and 25 per cent, though the output record of countries varied enormously, with the biggest gains occurring in North America. The extent of the depletion in capital resources is much more difficult to estimate with any precision but at a rough approximation it may be put at about 2 per cent of total output annually. Global consumption also probably fell but there are no reliable figures on the magnitudes involved. However, the impact of each of these factors varied considerably from one country to another. Most of the main belligerents managed to increase output to some extent, at least for part of the time, though this was often at the expense of consumption. The most impressive performances occurred in the United States and, to a lesser extent, in the Dominion countries. The former was undoubtedly the major beneficiary of war since the American economy was very much stronger in 1945 than it had been at the time of its entry into the war. Industrial production rose at an annual rate of some 15 per cent while new investment increased the capacity of the economy by about 50 per cent. War production, which accounted for a negligible proportion of total output in 1939, rose to 40 per cent in 1943. A rise in real income of more than 50 per cent was sufficient to cover this outlay and leave something over for an improvement in living standards. At the same time the United States became the life-line for the Allied powers, providing some $47 billion of lend-lease goods between 1941 and 1945 (about 5 per cent of US national income in this period), the bulk of which went to Britain and the Soviet Union.

In other words, the war stimulated growth and led to an improvement in living standards in the United States, and the same may be said for some of the Dominions. Elsewhere this was not the case. Though many of the belligerents managed to increase their output it was usually insufficient to meet the demands of war and so something else had to suffer. Net output in the UK, for example, rose by 20 per cent between 1938 and 1944 but this fell far short of the war effort requirements, which absorbed some 50 per cent of total income at the peak. The leeway had therefore to be made up by the disposal of foreign assets, debt accumulation, capital depletion and a fall of 22 per cent in personal consumption. Japan too suffered a cut in consumption despite a considerable rise in net output and an extension of capital equipment.

On the continent of Europe it was Germany, ironically enough, who probably fared the best, at least until the closing stages of the war. In large part this can be explained by the fact that Germany was able to maintain herself by exacting large contributions from occupied territories, and as a consequence the population suffered only moderate inconvenience. The national product of Germany as constituted at the outbreak of war rose quite modestly, 17 per cent between 1938 and 1944, though there had been a sharp increase just prior to the war. However, the total resources available to the Reich were much greater than this figure indicates since foreign contributions and levies accounted for about 14 per cent of Germany's domestic product between 1940 and 1944, while if the contribution of foreign labour is included the total addition to domestic resources was of the order of one-quarter. Speer claimed, in July 1944, that up to that date some 25–30 per cent of Germany's war production had been furnished by the occupied western territories and Italy, though he probably exaggerated the latter's contribution. In fact after 1939 much of the increase in the product available to Germany came from foreign contributions including foreign labour in Germany which accounted for over a fifth of the civilian labour force in the later stages of war. 'Like a gigantic pump, the German Reich sucked in Europe's resources and working population' (Kulischer 1948). Thus despite the fact that the state's share of total output was as high as 63 per cent at the peak, consumption levels were maintained quite well until near the end of the campaign. Drafts on capital equipment were substantial though the extent of the depletion has usually been overstated.

Italy, on the other hand, proved a great disappointment to Hitler, and in more ways than one. From the economic viewpoint the war was a disaster for Italy. Even during the period of victories Italy's output failed to increase while after 1942 it fell sharply, bringing it back by 1945 to a level close to that of the first decade of the century. Consumption was sharply reduced while inflation reached serious dimensions. An interesting contrast is provided by Russia, which for a poor country devoted a high proportion of resources to military activities. The country was badly devastated by the German invasion, losing about half her industrial capacity; as a consequence production slumped to a low point in 1942 and living standards declined seriously from levels already low by western standards. However, the Russians proved incredibly resilient and resourceful; they undertook a massive relocation of industry and workers in the Urals and beyond with the result that by 1945 industrial production had recovered to a level only some 8 per cent below that of 1939.

The impact of the war elsewhere in Europe varied a good deal depending upon the extent of fighting and the degree of exploitation carried out by the Germans. Countries allied with Germany and nominally independent such as Finland, Hungary, Romania and Bulgaria did not do too badly though their living standards fell as they became increasingly dependent on servicing the German war machine. The main brunt fell upon the occupied countries the consequences of which were often little short of disastrous. The main objective of German policy was to extract the maximum benefit from the occupied territories without consideration of the interests of the countries in question. Thus the imposition of heavy levies, looting, the removal of plant and labour, together with general devastation following military operations, led to a fall in output and a general decline in living standards over a large area of Europe. Germany assigned to herself an ever increasing proportion of the total output of the countries concerned, and the financial practices of the Reich vastly increased the means of payment, thereby creating a highly inflationary situation. A large increase in the supply of occupation currency together with a decrease in the supply of goods led to a flight of money and widespread black-market operations, though only in a few countries, notably Greece, did a complete financial breakdown occur. The practices pursued not only increased the resources available to the Reich but also helped to damp down the inflationary potential in Germany.

The worst effects of the occupation were felt in Greece, Poland, France, Belgium, the Netherlands and the occupied parts of the Soviet Union. In all these countries output fell sharply, capital was seriously depleted or damaged, labour resources were exploited and living standards declined, in some cases to subsistence levels. Extensive general damage also occurred in those countries where heavy fighting took place. During the occupation the level of output in France fell to two-thirds of that of 1938; occupation levies absorbed one-third of that total so that consumption declined to less than 50 per cent of pre-war. In Belgium and the Netherlands the experience was similar though not quite so severe. Further east the position was even worse; output declined to very low levels and many consumers struggled along on subsistence rations or less, some dying of starvation and malnutrition. In Poland in the last year of war many urban dwellers were getting only half the quantities of food received by their German counterparts, while in the Athens–Piraeus region the daily food intake of the majority of the population was down to 600–800 calories in 1941 and 1942. By contrast Norway and Denmark did rather better. Denmark suffered little serious privation, while in Norway the fall in output was slight but the cost of troop occupation absorbed a large share of income, thereby reducing the living standards of the indigenous population. Taking continental Europe as a whole it appears that every second consumer obtained only about two-thirds to three-quarters of his pre-war food intake in most years; many received even less and as a consequence substantial numbers died of starvation.

Though German policy in the occupied territories created severe inflationary pressures, price inflation was less severe generally than was the case in the First World War. Despite enormous war expenditures, which involved heavy borrowing and large increases in the money supply, the rate of inflation in most western countries, apart from Belgium, France and Italy, was quite modest in the circumstances. Improvements in monetary and fiscal control, with a larger share of war expenditure being financed by taxation than in 1914–18, were partly responsible for the better out-turn. But the main reason was the extensive use of price controls and rationing which were far more effectively applied than in the previous experience. Only in countries with weak governments or under enemy occupation, for example France, Hungary, Portugal, Greece and China, did it assume alarming proportions. In the Second World War it was left to the Balkan and Middle East countries to suffer inflation comparable with that experienced by some of the major belligerents in 1914–18, and only Greece and China had by the end of the war suffered a fate similar to that which overtook the defeated countries after 1919. On the other hand, the greater success in restraining inflation by controls did create difficulties for peacetime since it meant the build-up of a large suppressed inflationary potential. Fortunately government policies in the early post-war period kept this potential within bounds and only in one or two countries, Hungary and Germany for example, did inflation and currency problems pose a really serious threat.

DEVASTATION OF EUROPE

At the end of the war Europe was in a shambles, and little short of destitute. From Stalingrad to Saint-Nazaire and from Murmansk to Bengazi there was a trail of devastation and destruction, with the worst ravages occurring in central and eastern regions. The extent of the damage and loss of production was more serious than it had been in the First World War. Manufacturing was paralysed, commerce was almost at a standstill, agricultural production was well down and communications were badly disrupted. Shortages of almost everything prevailed over a wide area of the continent. Financially Europe was in an extremely weak state, with huge budgetary deficits, swollen money supplies, a severe shortage of foreign exchange reserves and strong inflationary pressures. Conditions varied of course from country to country but there were few, apart from Sweden and Switzerland, which had not suffered severely from the impact of several years of hostilities. Europe's position stood out in sharp contrast to that of the United States and it soon became apparent that the task of rebuilding Europe would depend very much on the policies adopted by that country, since without external assistance the prospects of an early European revival looked very grim indeed. Fortunately the post-war policies of America were more conducive to recovery than those pursued after the First World War. After some initial hesitation the United States did not, as after 1920, retreat into isolation, but instead became, partly because of political factors, the universal provider of western Europe. As a result the reconstruction and recovery of Europe proved to be more rapid and sustained than anything conceived possible in 1945.

As far as the chief productive assets, labour and capital, are concerned, European losses and damage as a direct result of war were greater than in 1914–18, but the extent of the net depletion of resources is easily exaggerated. The problem in both cases, however, is one of obtaining reliable data. For example, there are several different estimates of population losses. The most acceptable figure for the whole of Europe is one of 40 million which covers military and civilian casualties sustained in the war. Civilian deaths far out-numbered military ones owing to the mass extermination policies of the Nazis. Loss of life through disease, epidemics and civil war was quite modest, while the wartime birth deficit appears to have been quite low. These factors probably account for another 5 million to 7 million persons, excluding the Soviet Union where the birth deficit was fairly high. Thus though direct slaughter was far more severe than in the previous war the toll of life from other factors was very much less. However, apart from actual deaths, some 35 million people were wounded, while millions suffered from malnutrition.

The distribution of the losses varied enormously. On the whole northern and western Europe (excluding Germany) escaped fairly lightly, whereas central and eastern Europe suffered badly. Over half the total, about 25 million persons, was accounted for by Russia, while large absolute losses occurred in Poland, Germany and Yugoslavia. Nearly one-fifth of Poland's population was killed during the war, while Germany's loss may have exceeded 6 million though estimates vary widely. Casualties in some of the smaller eastern countries, though small in absolute numbers, were often quite significant relative to their total populations. Thus on average about 5 per cent of the population of Hungary, Romania, Czechoslovakia, Yugoslavia and Greece perished.

However, few countries, apart from France, Poland and the Soviet Union, emerged from the war with seriously depleted populations. The overall losses were offset by a remarkable excess of births over deaths, the major boost coming from the sharp rise in fertility in northwest Europe (France excepted), so that the total non-Russian European population in 1945–6 was very similar to what it had been just prior to the war. In other words, the war had simply served to wipe out the natural increase in population. Perhaps more important from the economic point of view was the effect on the composition of popula-tions. In countries with large losses such as Germany and Russia there was a serious deficiency of population in the most productive age groups together with a marked sex imbalance. In West Germany, for example, females out-numbered males in the 25–45 age group in the ratio 100:77 in 1950, while over the whole population the excess of females numbered 3 million. Another problem, particularly in some of the badly devastated and poorer countries of the east, was the shortage of skilled workers and people with managerial and professional training. The mass extermination of the Jewish population deprived several countries of valuable financial and business talent.

The war also caused an enormous upheaval in population resulting in the displacement of many nationals from their country of origin. Altogether upwards of 30 million people were transplanted, deported or dispersed. Many of these persons subsequently disappeared from the scene altogether but by the end of the war more than 15 million people were awaiting transfer from one country to another. Thus in the immediate post-war period dispersal and resettlement affected most European countries to some degree, with

Germany, Poland and Czechoslovakia bearing the brunt of the burden. The biggest single transfer consisted of German nationals living outside post-war German territory who were obliged by the Potsdam Agreement of 1945 to return within the new German boundaries. By October 1946 nearly 10 million Germans had been transferred; over two-thirds of the total migrated to the western zones which were later to receive a continuous stream of people from East Germany when the Cold War broke out. Initially this influx posed serious economic and social problems for West Germany, but eventually the expellees provided a valuable addition to the work-force. In relative terms transfers of Polish nationals were even more significant; large numbers of Poles returned from Germany and Russia while the cession of territory to the Soviet Union and territorial gains from Germany led to further movements. The net result was that Poland acquired a more homogeneous population but a much smaller one, 24.8 million in 1950 as against 32.1 million in 1939.

The loss and destruction of capital assets are even more difficult to quantify precisely. Extensive fighting together with heavy bombing and deliberate devastation meant that the damage to land, property and industrial equipment was more severe than it had been in the First World War. A trail of devastation stretched from west to east across the European continent, with some of the worst damage taking place in the occupied countries. In the invaded areas of the Soviet Union, for example, some 17,000 cities and towns and 70,000 villages were devastated, as were 70 per cent of industrial installations and 60 per cent of transportation facilities. Some of the worst damage was to social capital. Cities were particularly vulnerable to aerial bombardment and many large cities, especially in Germany, were virtually obliterated. In most countries including the UK the damage to city structures and property was considerable. The destruction of dwellings as a percentage of pre-war stock was as high as 20 per cent in Germany, Poland and Greece, 6–9 per cent in Austria, Belgium, France, Britain and the Netherlands, 5 per cent in Italy and 3–4 per cent in Czechoslovakia, Norway and Hungary. The range of magnitudes is similar for non-residential properties. The backlog of housing to be made good at the end of the war was enormous since new construction was virtually at a standstill during the war except in neutral countries. To the 10 million houses destroyed or badly damaged in Europe one must add at least 6 million to make up the deficiency from the cessation of building. Buildings generally, both public and private, had suffered badly through neglect of repair and maintenance.

Transportation facilities were also badly damaged and disrupted. In several countries, especially in eastern Europe, over one-half of the railway bridges, junctions, marshalling yards, signalling systems, stations, permanent way and other installations were destroyed or in need of major capital repairs. Rolling stock was also seriously depleted and damaged and much of what was left was scattered throughout Europe. In fact rail transport had almost broken down completely and for some time after the end of the war there was little regular overland traffic in Europe apart from military convoys. The position was little better in other forms of transport. Many ports were blocked or destroyed, waterways were out of action, while the use of road transport was limited. In addition, Europe's merchant fleet was only about 61 per cent of that of pre-war. The west as well as the east was severely affected in transport. In France, the Low Countries and Germany most waterways and harbours were out of action, many bridges were destroyed and a large part of the rail system was temporarily suspended.

The catalogue of disasters was similar in industry and agriculture. Industry's working capital was seriously depleted and almost non-existent in former occupied areas apart from the scattered stocks left by the Germans. Industrial equipment and factory buildings suffered severe damage as well as deterioration through continuous working and neglect of maintenance. But in this sector the impact was much less severe than in the case of transport and housing. The incidence of outright loss was very patchy, being most extensive in major basic sectors such as coal, steel and power. There was moreover an imbalance between consumer and producer goods industries, many of the latter having been expanded at the expense of the former during the war. Against the losses must be set the additions made to capacity during the war which, though not always directly suitable to peacetime needs, were substantial. It is possible therefore that there was little diminution of the capital stock. In fact the United Nations in a report published in 1953 even maintained that Europe's industrial capacity at the end of the war was larger than before and more suited to its new needs. While this report may have sounded a rather optimistic note and almost certainly did not refer to the Russian Empire, nevertheless it does seem that many countries were able to maintain and even increase in some cases their industrial capacity. In Britain, France and the neutral countries manufacturing capacity expanded modestly, while Roskamp (1965) suggests that West Germany actually had a greater industrial capacity in 1946 than a decade earlier, a position that was not fundamentally changed by the dismantling for reparations. Even in eastern countries, where the damage was on balance greater, the aggregate losses often did not exceed the additions to industrial capacity since 1936. Though prolonged fighting and civil war brought great destruction to Yugoslavia and Greece, in Austria, Romania, Bulgaria and Czechoslovakia there were significant additions to capacity which more than offset the losses. And in the case of Czechoslovakia the reduction in population as a result of the expulsion of the Germans led to a large increase in the amount of capital per worker. Even in Poland, where capital losses were heavy, amounting to perhaps a third of the pre-war stock, subsequent additions to capacity plus gains of assets from former German territories together with population losses left Polish industry with a much higher capital–labour ratio than previously. And Russia, with her enormous losses in the invaded areas, was able to make good much of the deficit by the time the war ended.

111

The situation in agriculture is more difficult to assess. Agricultural potential was severely disrupted by the war through damage to the land, the destruction and looting of equipment and the loss of livestock. The extent of the total damage is unknown but it was probably worst in Poland and Russia. Polish estimates suggest that 60 per cent of the livestock was lost, 25 per cent of the forests and 15 per cent of the agricultural buildings. Damage to the land itself entailed a serious loss of fertility often through lack of fertilization. Perhaps most important in the short term was the loss of working capital and livestock. In east and southeast Europe over half the pre-war livestock was lost, while the damage and destruction to farm equipment and buildings was also heavy.

On balance, therefore, the net loss of productive assets during the war was much less serious than often imagined. Certainly the amount of loss and damage was considerable but its incidence was patchy, being more severe in eastern countries than in the west. More often than not the losses were quickly made good so that soon after the end of the war Europe's population and productive capital were back to the pre-war levels even though they were differently distributed between countries and economic activities. There was of course a large amount of restoration and repair work to be undertaken, especially in construction and transport equipment, but the main deficiencies were confined to a few countries.

The setback to current output was very substantial and will require explanation in view of what has already been said about the position with regard to productive resources. Almost everywhere on the continent industrial and agricultural output was well down on pre-war levels by the end of hostilities. Industry was almost at a standstill in several countries. In the summer of 1945 industrial production was less than half that of pre-war in all countries except Britain, Switzerland, Bulgaria and the Scandinavian countries. It was only about one-third in Belgium, the Netherlands, Greece and Yugoslavia, while in Italy, Austria and Germany it was less than one-quarter. Even by the spring of 1946 the general level of production was still only about two-thirds or so that of pre-war, with serious lagging in Greece, Finland, Germany, Italy and Austria, as against an approximation to former levels in the UK and Scandinavia. The shortfall in agriculture was not quite so sharp but it was far from modest. Only one or two countries, notably Denmark and Britain, managed to increase agricultural output during the war. In Europe as a whole the production of bread and coarse grains was running at about 60 per cent of pre-war, with the largest declines in occupied countries; for example Poland had a 60 per cent drop in grain production. Potato output suffered similar declines while the shortage of fats was even more acute. In some countries the domestic production of fats was only a fraction of peacetime levels because of low yields and losses of livestock: 13 per cent of pre-war in Poland, 25 per cent in Yugoslavia, 33 per cent in Belgium and somewhat lower than 50 per cent in France, Austria and Czechoslovakia; only Sweden recorded an increase. Meat and livestock products were also well down. The overall decline in meat production was about one-third but in Poland it was only 14 per cent of pre-war, in the Netherlands one-third and in Belgium, Austria and Yugoslavia two-fifths.

Rough estimates for total national income in real terms suggest a considerable fall in most countries between 1938 and 1946 even though some recovery had taken place in the latter year from the low point reached in 1944–5. The decline was about 50 per cent in Poland and Austria, 40 per cent in Finland, Greece, Hungary, Italy and Yugoslavia, 25 per cent in Czechoslovakia, 10–20 per cent in France, the Netherlands and Belgium, and slight in the UK, with approximately the pre-war level in Switzerland and Sweden.

The general reduction in productive activity was far greater than that which outright physical loss of assets and population would appear to indicate. The discrepancy, however, can be readily explained in terms of the conditions obtaining at the end of the war. Destruction of capital was the least of the worries in 1945. Far more important were the general dislocation and disruption to productive activity as a result of the war: in particular, the winding down of armaments production and the problems involved in converting to peacetime operations; the severe shortage of essential raw materials, components and repair facilities; the scarcity of technical skills and the bottlenecks in communications; and, perhaps most important of all, the sheer exhaustion of a generally undernourished population. The end of the war marked the climax of six years of struggle and privation at the end of which workers were in no fit condition to exert themselves. Serious food shortages meant that per capita food consumption in most countries in 1945–6 was well below peacetime levels, with the shortfall bearing most heavily on urban industrial populations. In Germany and Austria it was less than 60 per cent of normal, in Italy 68 per cent, in Belgium, France, the Netherlands, Finland and Czechoslovakia about three-quarters of the pre-war levels; elsewhere it was somewhat higher but still below normal. Under such conditions it is scarcely surprising that production and productivity levels were low.

The shortage of food, raw materials and consumer goods in general was acute in Europe but it was part of a wider problem. In the immediate post-war period there was a world shortage of materials and foodstuffs. Even by 1947–8 world food production was some 7 per cent below the pre-war level and in the intervening period there had been an addition to global population. In addition, shortages of shipping space and dislocation in inland transport facilities impeded the movement of supplies. But these problems apart, Europe's position was made worse by the fact that she had little means to pay for imports of essential commodities, especially from the dollar area which was the main source of supply. By the end of the war the export trade of many European countries was almost non-existent, and even by the end of 1945 the volume of exports was below 20 per cent of pre-war in all countries except the UK, Switzerland and Scandinavia. In addition, the invisible export earnings of many countries, especially Britain, France and the Netherlands, had been seriously impaired by the decline in trade, the loss of shipping and the liquidation of foreign asssets, while new debt burdens had been incurred. The loss of income on foreign assets alone was serious enough; in 1938 the income earned by western Europe as a whole on foreign holdings was equivalent to 32 per cent of its exports, whereas by 1950–1 it amounted to only 9 per cent of what she sold to the rest of the world. As a result of these factors the volume of imports into Europe in the post-liberation period rarely exceeded 50 per cent of the 1937 level; in many countries it was less than one-quarter and in some eastern countries almost negligible. Thus while physical shortages and transportation bottlenecks presented the immediate problems, it soon became apparent that the overriding difficulty was going to be one of earning sufficient foreign exchange. Europe desperately needed imports but her capacity to export was limited; consequently the ability to carry out reconstruction would depend very much on the amount of assistance derived from the United States, the only country in a position to supply both goods and financial aid on a large scale.

Low production and widespread shortages of goods also exacerbated the inflationary and monetary problems of Europe and these in turn impeded the task of reconstruction. Inflationary pressures rarely reached the serious dimensions of the early 1920s but all European countries suffered from inflation and monetary disorders to a greater or lesser extent in the post-war period. The situation was worst in some of the occupied countries and in the east and several countries were forced to undertake monetary reform. It was less severe in western Europe and Scandinavia where it was suppressed in many cases by physical controls.

Thus in the latter half of 1945 the economic outlook in Europe was far from bright. The immediate problem was not one of a shortage of assets, despite the heavy destruction, but a severe scarcity of essential supplies including food and a weakened and undernourished population. Imports were urgently needed to bring about a recovery in production but because of a low export potential Europe had not the means to pay for them. Europe's position was aggravated by many other factors including large public debts, new waves of inflation, loss of markets and unfavourable terms of trade and by social and political upheavals. It soon became apparent that Europe would not be able to undertake the task of reconstruction unaided. Fortunately the policies of the Allied governments and of the American government in particular proved to be more constructive than was the case after the First World War.

THE POLITICS OF RECONSTRUCTION

Europe's immediate need was aid, which she got on a temporary basis at first and then more permanently under the Marshall Plan. Beyond the short term the strength of European recovery would also depend upon the international economic environment, and in particular upon the institutions devised for improving economic relationships. There were also the questions of boundary changes to be settled and the amount of reparations to be exacted from the vanquished. In all these matters politics determined the final format of the arrangements made. While these were not always ideal some of the most glaring mistakes of the post-1918 period were avoided and as a result a more solid foundation for European recovery was secured.

Though there were some important territorial changes following the Second World War these did not involve the extensive carve-up of Europe that had taken place after 1918. In fact the victors in 1945 did not rush into formal peace treaty negotiations but instead arranged informally among themselves what boundary adjustments should be made. Because of strong political differences between the Allies and the Soviet Union this inevitably resulted in the marking out of spheres of influence in Europe leading to the east–west split.

Nowhere was this more obvious than in the case of Germany. Decisions regarding the future structure of the country were reached piecemeal well before the end of the war. Spheres of influence were worked out by the European Consultative Commission, set up following a conference in Moscow in October 1943 of the Foreign Ministers of the United States, UK and the Soviet Union. This Commission fixed the limits of the zones of occupation in Germany – the three western zones which became the German Federal Republic and the Soviet zone, later to become the German Democratic Republic – and in effect created the east–west split. Russia was placed in a strong position to control the region east of the western line of her occupation zone, and her hand was considerably strengthened after the Yalta and Potsdam conferences of February and July 1945. Russia was allowed to increase her territory considerably, mainly at the expense of Poland, while the western boundary of the Soviet Union was fixed by a line running from the Bay of Danzig north to Braunsberg to a meeting place on the frontiers of Lithuania and Poland. This gave Russia an additional 274,000 square miles and added 25 million to her population.

The rivalry between the west and the Soviet Union was reflected in subsequent peace negotiations with Italy, Romania, Bulgaria, Hungary and Finland. Each side attempted to gain as much as possible, with the Soviet Union further strengthening her position in the east. Romania had to give up Bessarabia and Bukovina to Russia, while Finland ceded one-tenth of her agricultural area and one-eighth of her industrial capacity to that country. Hungary was reduced approximately to its post-First World War size, losing southern Slovakia to Czechoslovakia and northern Transylvania to Romania. Bulgaria surrendered land formerly acquired from Yugoslavia with Nazi support, while the latter gave up Fiume and a large part of the Istrian Peninsula. Italy released its colonies and the Dodecanese islands to Greece. Finally, Trieste was placed under international control but later returned to Italy, while the Saar was incorporated into France until 1957 when it was given back to Germany.

115

While the territorial changes were not enormous they were significant in terms of later political events. They also involved considerable movements in population. The major losers were Germany and Poland, while the Soviet Union was the main beneficiary not only in terms of territory and population, but also by virtue of the fact that she was left in a stronger position to exert control over eastern Europe. However, in some respects this can be seen as a benefit from the point of view of western Europe, since the rivalry between east and west meant a much greater readiness on the part of the United States to assist and strengthen the west European economies.

One big improvement compared with the First World War was that the fiasco over reparations and international war debts was largely avoided. As regards German reparations the major disagreement arose between the Soviet Union and the west over the amount to be levied. The Russians wanted substantial reparations on the grounds that they had suffered badly at the hands of the Germans, whereas the Allies, the United States in particular, were less ambitious in their demands, realizing that to penalize Germany heavily would hinder the latter's recovery and thereby weaken the position of western Europe. Both sides were agreed, however, that Germany should lose her foreign assets and much of her shipping, that she should bear the costs of occupation and the indemnification of injured parties including minority groups, and that her future war potential should be held in check by prohibiting the production of military equipment. Subsequent negotiations established a formula whereby reparations would be paid not from current output but from Germany's existing stock of capital, mainly by dismantling industrial equipment. This procedure had the advantage of avoiding the financial difficulties following the First World War when payments out of current output had involved the transfer of scarce foreign exchange. The original dismantling schedules were fixed at a relatively high level and would probably have crippled German industry for a time. Fortunately they were later reduced substantially and the total value of reparations equipment finally made over was quite modest. On the other hand, the total costs borne by Germany on account of reparations, occupation and indemnification costs and other costs were greater than the Allied aid she received, but they did not cripple the country and for the most part they did not involve a serious loss of foreign exchange. Other enemy countries including East Germany were treated less favourably. The Russians, incensed by the lenient treatment of West Germany, insisted on exacting large payments from the smaller enemy countries including East Germany (see Chapter 6).

War debts proved much less of a problem after the Second World War for most countries with the exception of Britain. America's lend–lease policy meant that no charge would be made for the aid and goods sent to the Allies (principally Britain and the Soviet Union) during the war and for the most part other members of the Allied coalition adopted a similar procedure. When hostilities ceased the lend–lease arrangements were terminated but it soon became clear that the United States would be forced to provide for the relief of poverty-stricken Europe. Thus from July 1945 America began pouring aid into Europe through various organizations, notably the United Nations Relief and Rehabilitation Administration, and by early 1948 some $25 billion had been spread throughout the continent including eastern Europe. The aid was soon depleted, however, and in terms of recovery it appeared to have only a limited effect, at least initially. This was not altogether surprising. For one thing much of the aid was disbursed rather indiscriminately with scant regard, either by lending or borrowing nations, as to the most profitable uses to which it could be put. Second, in the conditions then prevailing a good part of the aid was used simply to keep people alive, especially in eastern Europe. Third, much of the aid was on a loan basis thereby creating debt problems for the borrowing countries; in some cases strings were attached, as with the British loan involving acceptance of currency convertibility and non-discrimination at a specified date (see below). Finally, national policies were not always conducive to immediate recovery; in the early post-war period radical new policies, including extensive nationalization in Britain and France and socialization in eastern Europe, the stultifying effects of the German occupation, as well as financial and monetary disorders generally, meant that many economies were not very receptive initially to foreign aid.

Recognition of the relative ineffectiveness of the relief programme was one factor prompting a change in policy in 1947. But the shift was probably conditioned more by the turn of political events, in particular the expansionist policy of the Soviet Union including its hardening line over Germany which eventually culminated in the blockade of Berlin. Fear of social and political disturbances and the threat of communist regimes in the west played no small part in the formation of the new aid programme. When the new offer was first announced in June 1947, by Secretary of State George Marshall, it became clear, for political reasons, that it would be confined mainly to western Europe. Moreover, it was made conditional on self-help by the recipient nations, that they co-operate for purposes of ensuring that the aid was used in the most effective way possible. The funds were to be administered on the US side through the Economic Co-operation Administration, while on the European side sixteen nations joined together to form the Organization for European Economic Co-operation (OEEC), which had the tasks of estimating national requirements and dividing the aid among members, while acting as a clearing-house for national economic plans so as to avoid countries working at cross-purposes.

The Marshall Plan came into effect in April 1948 and was designed to last for four years, though in actual fact it was merged into the Mutual Defense Assistance programme in 1951 after which the emphasis shifted to military rather than economic aid. The European Recovery Programme (ERP) was based on the principle of helping those who were willing to help themselves. It provided aid to pay dollars for commodities and services required by Europe;

it required recipients to pay for what they received in their own money, with outright grants being confined to emergency cases; while the accumulated funds of local currencies were to be used to promote recovery of national economies. To estimate individual needs the OEEC used deficits in trade and payments, especially dollar deficits, as the main criterion.

On the whole the funds of the programme were well administered; they were not squandered by political mismanagement as much previous aid had been. While in the first year or so a considerable part of the aid was required for food purchases, later on the funds were used for raw materials and rebuilding productive capacity. Altogether the United States paid out $13,365 million for commodities required by the sixteen nations of the ERP of which $5,539 went on food and agricultural products, $6,167 for industrial commodities and the rest for services of one sort or another. To this must be added the total counterpart deposits of $10,509, 95 per cent of which was available to member countries. It is difficult to estimate the impact of the programme with any precision but it is clear that without aid the process of European recovery would have been seriously impeded. The critical problem was Europe's shortage of exchange with which to purchase much-needed imports, and in this respect the aid was crucial in enabling OEEC countries to cover their external deficits. In Germany's case, for example, 57 per cent of that country's imports between 1947 and 1949 were financed by foreign aid. It is true that in the peak year (1948–9) total aid deliveries amounted to less than 5 per cent of Germany's national income, while counterpart investment was equivalent to 9 per cent of gross investment (1950). But as a contribution to total resources over and above minimum requirements the amounts involved are impressive, and at a critical time they provided resources of a kind that Germany would have been hard pressed to obtain. Moreover, the qualitative impact of these additional increments was important, especially in terms of the reconstruction of the basic industries.

However, one can easily overestimate the contribution of the Marshall programme. In many cases recovery was well under way before it was initiated. What it did was to ensure that the recovery would be sustained rather than halted in its tracks through lack of funds. But it did not solve Europe's payments problems overnight. Contrary to original expectations, western Europe continued to remain in deficit on external account, in some cases seriously so, until well into the 1950s. In fact the aid programme may well have retarded progress in this respect since some countries were inclined to view the elimination of external account deficits as less than pressing given that the larger their deficits the greater would be their share of American aid.

Apart from the immediate reconstruction issues, efforts were being made well before the end of the war to secure a greater measure of international economic co-operation among nations on a wider and more permanent scale than anything which had been tried in the past. From the negotiations at Bretton Woods in 1944 two important institutions emerged, the International

Monetary Fund (IMF) and the International Bank for Reconstruction and Development (World Bank), while in 1947, after a meeting of twenty-three nations at Geneva, the General Agreement on Tariffs and Trade (GATT) was signed.

The World Bank may be dealt with briefly since it had little significance in terms of reconstruction. The original intention was that this institution should assist the recovery process by providing loans for productive purposes. In practice its role in this respect was negligible partly because of its limited funds and terms of reference, and because by the time it began operations the task of aiding Europe had already begun under other auspices in a big way. Thus so far as reconstruction and economic co-operation were concerned the World Bank contributed little, though subsequently it did become an important source of long-term loans for projects the world over.

By contrast the IMF and GATT were more concerned with improving international relations within the field of trade and payments. In both cases the general philosophy was one of freedom for trade and payments, the elimination of discrimination between nations and the restoration of currency convertibility. While GATT was primarily concerned with tariff matters, the IMF's main focus of attention was on monetary questions. The Agreement specifically provided for the restoration of exchange stability with exchange rate adjustment taking place only in cases of fundamental disequilibrium in the balance of payments of member countries. Members were to desist from imposing restrictions on current transactions and engaging in discriminatory currency practices without the approval of the Fund. The most important provision was the creation of an international pool of reserves derived from members' quotas which could be drawn upon by individual countries to meet temporary imbalances in their external accounts (see Chapter 5).

Early attempts to restore non-discriminatory multilateral trade proved disappointing. The major initiative in this direction was made by the United States who proposed the creation of an International Trade Organization (ITO) which would embody the objective of moving quickly towards the goal of free trade. This was a premature move simply because most countries were scarcely in a position to abandon controls over trade given their weak external positions. Not surprisingly, therefore, the proposal did not gain a particularly sympathetic hearing outside the United States. In an effort to force the issue the United States laid onerous conditions on the loan agreement concluded with Britain in 1946 which required, among other things, British support for the ITO and the restoration of sterling convertibility. The terms proved disastrous; during the first half of 1947 Britain made a progressive move towards convertibility and by early July full convertibility on all current transactions had been restored. In the process the US loan was quickly dissipated and the reserves fell sharply so that within five weeks the experiment had to be abandoned.

This experience was proof enough that it was too soon to expect much progress in restoring freedom to trade and payments. In the event therefore the ITO was not ratified by a sufficient number of countries but out of subsequent discussions emerged the General Agreement on Tariffs and Trade. This agreement was more limited than the original ITO charter, being confined mainly to tariff policy with emphasis on multilateralism and nondiscrimination. In later years it came to play a key role in negotiating worldwide tariff reductions.

In short, therefore, the reconstruction period following the Second World War was marked by a much more constructive attempt to foster international economic co-operation and establish conditions under which European recovery could thrive and remain sustained than had been the case after 1918. As far as the immediate task was concerned the most important contribution was the stream of American aid which flowed into Europe. It is true that most of the institutions established, apart from the OEEC, did not have a crucial part to play in the reconstruction process since they were not designed specifically to cope with immediate difficulties, or alternatively they had objectives, for example the removal of restrictions on trade and payments, which in the conditions of the early post-war years could never be achieved. Nevertheless, one should not underestimate their importance since they provided a basic framework for post-war international co-operation and in a later period they were to achieve considerable success in promoting the liberalization of trade and payments and also in ensuring a reasonable degree of stability in international monetary relationships. Moreover, they provided the precedent for later co-operative efforts, especially in western Europe in the 1950s with the establishment of the European Payments Union (1950), the European Coal and Steel Community (1952), the European Economic Community (1957) and the European Free Trade Association (1959).

It is important to stress these points since there have been attempts to deride the importance of these experiments in international co-operation and to see the new institutions as being essentially tools of American foreign policy. The facts of the situation cannot be disputed but the realities should be faced squarely. The American approach in Europe was conditioned by the intransigence of the Soviet Union and its satellites which eventually meant a confrontation between two great military and economic powers with designated spheres of influence. Europe needed American aid and assistance and it was natural enough that this should be made contingent upon policies and institutions which would satisfy America's overriding objective of defending the west against the Soviet bloc. The major mistake of American policy was the attempt to force western Europe into adopting policies which were clearly not practical in the difficult years following the war. Nor should the split between the east and the west be regarded as a disaster. Certainly a more harmonious relationship between the two sides would have been preferable, but failing that – a failing that owed as much to American as to Soviet attitudes – it was better to have two equally powerful and self-contained blocs within Europe rather than the power vacuum that existed after the First World War and which paved the way for the holocaust of less than a generation later.

THE ROAD TO RECOVERY

Despite the extensive damage and the substantial check to productive activity the rate of recovery in Europe in the five years or so after the war was impressive. Within two years of the termination of hostilities many countries had already achieved considerable increases in output, albeit from a low base, while by the late 1940s most countries, both in the east and west, had surpassed pre-war levels of activity, in some cases by a substantial margin. However, experience varied considerably both in terms of the progress achieved and in the policies pursued. Until 1948 western Europe did rather better than the east which had suffered more severely in the war and was disrupted in the immediate post-war years by radical changes in political and economic structures. Conversely, between 1948 and the early 1950s it was eastern Europe which set the pace in terms of industrial expansion though agricultural output lagged behind that of the west. Germany, on the other hand, had much the slowest rate of recovery and it was not until 1951 that industrial production surpassed pre-war, while in Berlin the level of activity still remained seriously depressed.

As far as western Europe (including Scandinavia) is concerned the period between the end of the war and 1950-1 was one of fairly continuous expansion, though there were minor interruptions. Positive government policies probably contributed less to this expansion than the successive waves of external stimuli which enabled it to continue each time it was threatened from either the demand or the supply side. Until 1949 there were few signs of serious demand deficiencies because of the large pent-up demand for goods, excess liquidity and inflationary pressures in one form or another in most countries. The main difficulty was that of obtaining adequate supplies of food, raw materials and fuel, because of supply shortages and/or exchange problems. Fortunately the supply difficulties were considerably alleviated by the stream of American aid which provided the most important external stimulus. At the same time inflationary pressures were gradually damped by various means including controls of one sort or another, counterinflationary policies, an improvement in the supply of goods and a reduction in excess liquidity through large import surpluses and improved budgetary positions. During the first half of 1949 inflationary forces were further checked by the backwash of the temporary recession in America, though by the second half of that year a new push to business activity and prices was being felt as a result of the currency devaluations of September 1949. Less than a year later, another external stimulant, the Korean War, produced a violent outburst of speculative demand in the latter half of 1950, to be followed by increasing production and further price increases in 1951 as a result of the demand for military goods.

Western Europe as a whole staged a rapid recovery in the first two years after 1945 so that by 1947 industrial production had surpassed pre-war levels in most countries except Austria, Italy, France and the Netherlands. Agriculture lagged behind, however, being adversely affected by poor crops due to bad weather, especially in 1946–7. The hard winter of 1947 also checked industrial output for a time. Moreover, serious shortages, especially of food and raw materials, continued to prevail throughout 1947 and into 1948. Nevertheless, progress continued and by 1950–1 nearly all countries had increased their industrial output by a third or more above pre-war, with the largest gains taking place in some of the smaller countries, for example Sweden and Denmark (see Table 4.1). One should bear in mind of course that some countries, notably France, Belgium and Austria, had levels of output in 1938 that were the same or slightly lower than in 1929, so that their progress through to 1950 was not as striking when compared with Britain and Sweden for example where pre-war performance had been rather better. Agriculture still continued to lag behind. Indeed, it was not until the turn of the decade that most countries regained or exceeded their pre-war levels and even by 1951–2 the gross agricultural output of western Europe was not much more than 10 per cent above the peacetime level.

Income gains, especially on a per capita basis, were much lower than the

Table 4.1 Western Europe: indices of industrial production (1937–8 = 100) and agricultural production (1934–8 = 100)

	Industrial production 1947	Agricultural production 1946–7	Industrial production 1949	Agricultural production 1948–9	Industrial production 1951	Agricultural production 1950–1
Austria	56	70	123	74	166	98
Belgium	106	84	122	93	143	111
Denmark	123	97	142	97	162	126
Finland	117	75	142	106	177	115
France	92	82	118	95	134	108
Ireland	122	100	151	96	176	106
Italy	86	85	101	97	138	109
Luxembourg	109	–	138	–	175	–
Netherlands	95	87	126	104	145	123
Norway	115	98	140	101	158	118
Portugal	112	99	112	95	125	102
Spain	127	88	130	80	147	86
Sweden	141	104	157	109	171	113
Switzerland	–	107	–	112	–	120
UK	115	117	137	122	155	130

Sources: United Nations, *Economic Survey of Europe in 1950*, p. 43; *Economic Survey of Europe in 1951*, p. 179

Note: The industrial production series exclude building but include electricity, gas and water and mining.

rise in industrial output partly because of the much slower growth in agriculture and the service sectors of the economy. In addition, there was a loss of income on overseas investment equivalent to about 1 per cent of the aggregate product of the main countries; this loss bore most heavily on Britain, France and the Netherlands, though in no country did it exceed 3 per cent of the national product. Furthermore, deterioration in trade terms involved a loss of some 3 per cent of the product of western Europe, the most seriously affected countries being Britain, the Netherlands and Denmark. When these factors are taken into account together with the increase in population the gains in real per capita income up to 1951 turn out to be quite modest in many cases. The rise over the period 1938–51 was less than 10 per cent in the Netherlands, between 10 and 15 per cent in Britain, France and Denmark, 20 per cent in Switzerland and over 30 per cent in Sweden, while for Italy it was about the same as pre-war and in Germany well below the former level.

Owing to the weak external position of western Europe in these years (see below) the recovery effort was very much dependent on the flow of overseas aid. At the same time, however, national policies did have an important contribution to make. The big task of reconstruction together with new government commitments in terms of social welfare, full employment and greater income equality among other things meant that governments generally intervened much more extensively in economic matters than before the war. The need to allocate scarce investment resources also involved close control over economic variables, while problems of inflation and external imbalances required attention.

The range of policies adopted varied considerably and it is only possible to outline some of the most important of these. One of the major tasks was to raise the level of investment, especially in the basic industries, in order to ensure rapid growth in output and exports and improve productivity performance. All countries gave priority to investment at the expense of consumption. Private consumption was restrained by controls while every effort was made to boost investment. Incentives included cheap and easy credit, favourable tax provisions and measures to stimulate savings. The government itself became the largest single investor either directly in its own public enterprises – France and Britain especially where a substantial part of industry was nationalized soon after the war – or through intermediary channels. Thus in France between 1947 and 1951 some 30 per cent of all investments came from government sources and in some countries the proportion was as high as one-half. Overall, investment spending as a proportion of income rose substantially above the pre-war levels, though government policies were not the sole reason for this. A high level of demand, rising prices and an investment backlog were conducive to capital spending and in the event investment demand was so high that it had to be controlled in order to steer resources into priority areas. Some of the policies proved conflicting: for example, incentives to boost savings and investment but heavy taxes on high income earners and corporations. Controls over resource allocation were often piecemeal and too rigid so that the final allocation was not always the most optimal. Generally speaking, however, the investment policies were successful; they encouraged a high level of investment and resources were not seriously misallocated.

The control of inflation was a more difficult task. Given the pressure on scarce resources as a result of heavy reconstruction programmes, the commitment to full employment and social welfare policies, together with excess demand in the economy generally, the authorities could do no more than keep inflation within bounds. Indeed the problem was aggravated by wartime policies of control including subsidization of key commodities which meant the build-up of a latent inflationary potential, while strong pressures came from the import side after the war because of a world shortage of commodities at a time of rising demand. Policy action varied though in no case was it wholly successful. A number of countries, Denmark, the Netherlands, Norway, Sweden and Britain, used a combination of fiscal and physical controls to restrain prices and demand, though in time, as physical controls were gradually dismantled, the emphasis was shifted towards the control of aggregate demand by fiscal measures. Intermittent attempts were also made to control profits and restrain wages. But such controls could only suppress inflation; they could not stop it. Moreover, lax monetary policies worked in the opposite direction. In time, as demand and supply conditions became more normal, inflationary pressures abated, only to be revived by the devaluations of 1949 and the Korean War. Some countries, notably France and Italy, found it more expedient politically to let prices rise and therefore did relatively little to restrain inflation.

Undoubtedly the major priority in the post-war years was the need to improve the external account. In the first three years after the war western Europe's trade deficit exceeded $5 billion as against $2 billion in the years prior to the war. The current account as a whole, which had been roughly in balance in 1938, showed a large though gradually diminishing deficit from $7.4 billion in 1947 to $2.5 billion in 1950. It was principally a dollar imbalance since nearly three-quarters of Europe's cumulative deficit in the period 1946–50 was with the United States. Given the area's inability to earn sufficient dollars it was forced to draw upon reserves and rely on large credits to make up the difference.

Reasons for the large deficits are not difficult to find. The war had shattered Europe's export trade resulting in markets being lost for good, either to local or to North American suppliers. War damage and shortage of resources meant that imports were urgently required in the post-war years when exports were less readily available. The result was that export volumes fell more than imports over the period 1938–47, while unfavourable price trends had the effect of raising the total monetary deficit. In addition, there had been a large drop in invisible earnings through the liquidation of foreign assets, the loss of shipping and tourist trade, and a contraction in financial services, while new debt-servicing burdens had been incurred, notably by the UK. Finally, Europe's external position was affected adversely in the post-war years by a deterioration in the terms of trade and currency overvaluation, at least until 1949.

Adjustments to this new situation could be made in several ways although in practice there were certain difficulties. The opportunities for adjustment in the invisible account were limited given the loss of foreign assets and shipping together with the growth of world fleets. This meant that the burden of adjustment would have to fall on commodity trade and principally exports, since a large part of Europe's imports consisted of food and raw materials and these were bound to rise in the early post-war years given the urgent need for commodities. Thus if the entire adjustment were to take place on the export side, the volume of exports on average would need to be about 80 per cent greater than in 1938 to pay for the same amount of imports, or 60 per cent if there were a 10 per cent saving on 1938 import volumes.

The position was slightly more complicated than this, however, by virtue of the fact that a large part of the deficit was with the dollar area. Unfortunately, it was this area which was the main source of supply for food and raw materials, while Europe's ability to earn dollars to pay for these imports was, for one reason or another, very limited. Apart from domestic supply problems, it was difficult for Europe to earn dollars directly in the North American market largely because of the self-sufficiency of the United States, while indirect dollar earnings from third countries, on which Europe had relied before the war to clear her accounts with the dollar area, were no longer available simply because these countries themselves were now in need of dollars. In other words, the restoration of external equilibrium was not simply a matter of a large increase in exports and a restraint on imports; it required in the main a vast improvement in Europe's dollar trading relationships.

In an effort to deal with the problem most governments took active steps to increase exports and restrain imports. Resources were channelled into export activities, consumption was held down to release as many resources as possible for exports, while vigorous export promotion campaigns were launched. Imports were held in check by tight physical controls, the restraint on consumption and by import substitution wherever possible. The results, while superficially impressive, were not entirely satisfactory. The volume of west European imports remained consistently below the already low level of 1938 – 15 per cent less in 1950 and 10 per cent less in 1951. The shifts in the sources of supply were the exact opposite of what was required, however. The fall in imports reflected the low level of supplies obtained from non-dollar sources (especially eastern Europe), whereas dollar imports were consistently above pre-war, by as much as 31 per cent in 1951. Likewise, export achievements were substantial but inadequate. The total volume of west European exports rose by 40 per cent between 1938 and 1951, but this was insufficient to cover the loss in invisible earnings and the effects of the deterioration in trade terms.

Moreover, performance in the dollar area was not very satisfactory. Though exports to the United States between 1949 and 1951 were well above pre-war they remained below the level of 1925–9, while the share of western Europe's exports going to the dollar area rose only moderately. Thus by the turn of the decade the dollar scarcity still remained an intractable problem. Contemporary estimates suggested that Europe required additional dollar earnings of some $4 billion annually to make a full and effective adjustment in the external accounts. This figure takes into account the removal of restrictions against dollar imports, the elimination of American aid and the need to build up reasonable gold and dollar reserves. At the time this seemed an almost impossible task but during the course of the 1950s Europe's balance of payments position was radically transformed for the better.

On balance, therefore, western Europe staged a remarkable recovery in the period 1945–50, though her external position continued to remain weak. The performance contrasts sharply with the unhappy experience following the First World War. Economic progress rested on the achievement and maintenance of high levels of employment and investment, a large influx of foreign aid and strong demand pressures which were never allowed to get out of hand. However, the high level of demand did give rise to inflationary pressures which aggravated the exchange difficulties – hence the need to retain tight controls on imports and consumption and the resort to devaluation in 1949. In this period the authorities became acutely aware of a problem which incidentally was to remain beyond the reconstruction years; this was their inability to pursue successfully a series of incompatible objectives, namely rapid expansion, full employment, price stability and external equilibrium. At the time many governments were forced to rely on a fairly wide range of direct controls and sharp fiscal measures to suppress inflation, shore up the balance of payments and allocate resources to priority needs. These measures proved unpopular and in time they outlived their usefulness; they produced irrational effects on investment, trade and payments and they could not eliminate inflation when there were strong external forces pushing up prices. Under these conditions it became increasingly difficult to maintain controls and the whole system was seriously weakened by onslaught from the demand side in 1950–1 arising from the 1949 devaluations and the Korean War. Henceforward greater reliance was to be placed on more general methods of controlling inflation and achieving macroeconomic objectives.

Germany deserves separate and more detailed treatment since its recovery experience was quite different from that of any other country in Europe. This in large part stemmed from the Allied and Soviet occupation policies which until 1948 effectively checked any real progress. In 1947 industrial output, in both the eastern and western zones, was not much above what it had been at the end of the war, at 47 per cent and 33 per cent of the 1938 levels respectively.

During 1948 a radical policy change took place which encouraged a rapid recovery so that by 1950-1 pre-war output levels were finally attained. Berlin, for obvious reasons, did not participate in this leap forward.

Initially the occupation forces not only were directed to hold down Germany but also were precluded from undertaking rehabilitation schemes. In practice these directions could not be carried out to the letter, apart from which the orders had an air of unreality at a time when the United States was providing relief aid to prevent starvation. In order to maintain themselves the occupation authorities were obliged to carry out a certain amount of repair and reconstruction work, while they probably felt under some moral obligation to ensure that sufficient supplies of necessities were made available to the indigenous population. Thus a certain amount of restoration work was undertaken in this period, more especially in the US zone. Such relief measures were relatively insignificant, however, against the generally repressive impact of the occupation administrations. The occupation forces ran the zones on military lines, imposing detailed and rigid orders together with stringent controls to suppress inflationary forces. The result was that the economies were almost paralysed.

From the middle of 1947 this hardline attitude was gradually modified. It began to dawn on the Allied powers at last that a prosperous Europe would depend in part on the reconstruction of the German economy. Furthermore, the increasing friction between the east and the west lent greater urgency to the need to strengthen Germany so as to provide a bulwark against the Soviet Union. Accordingly, the policy of repression was steadily abandoned in favour of constructive measures. These comprised the inclusion of Germany in the ERP programme, a sharp reduction in the dismantling schedules, currency reform and the removal of controls, more positive reconstruction measures by the forces of occupation and attempts to fuse the western zones into one. The latter efforts culminated in the formation of the German Federal Republic in September 1949, after which the Allies surrendered a substantial share of their power in Germany.

By far the most urgent task was that of currency reform. The war had left Germany's financial system in chaos, with an enormous oversupply of money in relation to the availability of goods which meant strong inflationary pressures. These were suppressed quite well for a time by the rationing and price control systems of the occupation authorities, but at the expense of strangling economic activity. Moreover, a significant black-market sector developed in which average prices were some fifty times higher than the legal prices. The desirability of reforming the currency was not in dispute but its implementation was delayed by the large number of different plans put forward, and also by political factors. The Potsdam Agreement of 1945 had specified that Germany should be treated as one unit in economic matters, including currency reform. However, disagreement among the Allied powers themselves did little to further this objective in the early years, while the clash between east and west over reparations and the control of German industry held up progress with currency reform. Russian intransigence on this issue ultimately led to separate currency reforms being undertaken in the two sectors, a move which merely served to strengthen the division of the country into two parts. The split involved some short-term losses for West Germany, for example food imports from the east, but it did not have a serious or lasting impact on the economy of West Germany.

When the currency reform was finally enacted in the summer of 1948 it proved extremely rigorous and inequitable. It reduced the money supply from the 122.4 billion Reichsmarks presented for conversion to 10.5 billion new Deutschmarks though this was increased to 13.2 billion Deutschmarks by the end of the year. It heavily penalized people with liquid assets but greatly improved the position of those with non-monetary assets. However, it did markedly increase incentives for business and with the subsequent removal of controls the way was left open for a sharp rise in profits. Thus after two or three years of stagnation industrial output shot forward in the latter half of 1948 and thenceforward Germany's recovery proceeded unchecked. It was assisted by a large influx of foreign aid which provided foreign currency and investment funds, a strong revival in exports and an elastic labour supply, together with policies designed to stimulate investment and profits, hold down wages and ensure monetary stability. However, it was not until 1951 that industrial production exceeded the pre-war level, while agriculture and services lagged behind. Net per capita income still fell short of the pre-war level because of the large influx of population from the east. Nevertheless, the economy was in a much healthier state than it had been a few years earlier.

Eastern Germany fared less well under Soviet domination though even here there was a marked recovery after 1948. Berlin, however, was quite another matter. The city was very badly damaged by the war with the result that its economic and financial activities were seriously impaired. But worse was yet to come. A partial dismantling of industry soon after the war followed by a curtailment of foreign aid and the Russian blockade left Berlin almost prostrate. Industrial production, already at a very low level in 1946 and 1947, declined even further, to just under 20 per cent of pre-war in 1949. Though conditions eased subsequently with the renewal of aid it was not until the middle of the 1950s that the city got within striking distance of former levels of economic activity.

Recovery in eastern Europe was at first slower than in the west, though later the east made up some of the ground lost. The initial lag was not surprising given the fact that eastern Europe had been more severely devastated than the west. When hostilities ceased industrial production in most countries, apart from the Soviet Union, was one-half or less that of pre-war, while agricultural output was extremely depressed. Almost all goods, and especially food, were in short supply and but for relief through UNRRA many people would have starved. Relief supplies were of considerable importance to Poland, Czecho-slovakia, Hungary and Albania in the immediate post-war years; for example, they amounted to about 11 per cent of Polish national income in 1946. How-ever, they declined rapidly after 1946 and eastern Europe, for obvious reasons, was not included in the Marshall Plan. Thus eastern Europe had to struggle along with limited external assistance; the Soviet Union provided little aid and indeed exacted reparations from East Germany and the former allies Hungary and Romania. In 1946 reparations deliveries from East Germany and Hungary amounted to as much as one-fifth and one-tenth respectively of their already low levels of national product. Though the pay-ments were later scaled down they still imposed a serious burden on these impoverished countries.

There were moreover other factors retarding progress. Frontier changes and population movements posed new problems for Czechoslovakia, Poland and East Germany. Inflationary forces were also serious, especially in Hungary and Romania, where the upward price spiral was allowed to assume hyperinflationary proportions before being checked by the introduction of new currencies. Poland also experienced a sharp rise in prices in the first two years after the war, but Czechoslovakia and Bulgaria took early steps to check or suppress inflation. By 1948, when the East German currency was reformed, most countries had regained control of the situation.

Finally, all countries in the eastern sector of Europe underwent a political and social revolution in the post-war period involving a complete change in the system of property relationships and the emergence of the state as the main agent of economic activity. Though these radical changes were ultimately to prove beneficial (at least in terms of economic growth), they did cause a certain amount of dislocation in the short term which probably affected the recovery effort adversely. On the other hand, there were certain advantages in that foreign trade became a state monopoly and dwindled in importance so that external payments problems did not pose the same difficulties as in the west.

In the reconstruction phase between 1946 and 1949 all countries began the expropriation of economic interests, including a start with land reform, and at the same time published reconstruction plans of two to three years' duration. Large-scale industry was appropriated first, followed by banking, insurance, trade and all but the smallest enterprises. By 1949 most major branches of economic activity apart from agriculture were owned and operated by the state. The reconstruction plans focused their attention mainly on large-scale industry, though tentative targets were set for other sectors. In the early stages, however, it was difficult to enforce rigorous planning since the state's power was limited by virtue of the fact that private enterprise still remained extensive. Even so the planned targets for industry as a whole were generally attained, and in Poland and Hungary substantially surpassed. By the end of 1949 the patterns and current rates of production in all eastern countries were broadly in line with the objectives and goals laid down by the authorities. Apart from East Germany, where the repressive policy of the Soviet Union had retarded development and delayed the introduction of the reconstruction plan until 1949, most countries had surpassed their pre-war production levels by 1949, in some cases by a large margin, whereas two years earlier output levels were still well down. On the other hand, agriculture and services lagged far behind; in 1948–9 agricultural production in eastern Europe excluding the Soviet Union was less than 80 per cent of the 1934–8 level. Thus the gains in national income were much more modest, while per capita changes varied considerably from country to country because of differing population movements. Thus in East Germany and Romania per capita income levels were still lower than pre-war because of population increases and relatively slow rates of recovery. Poland benefited from a loss of population but income per head did not improve owing to a serious shortfall in agriculture. On the other hand, Czech income per capita was some way above the pre-war level by 1950 as a result of population losses and a strong industrial base. However, the tentative nature of the income estimates for this period do not permit very precise comparisons to be made. On balance, it seems unlikely that eastern Europe as a whole had regained pre-war per capita income levels by the end of the 1940s.

At the end of that decade, when the reconstruction phase was drawing to a close, the governments of eastern Europe turned their attention to more comprehensive long-term planning of their economies along the lines of the Soviet system. The main objective was to build up powerful economies by means of central planning and direction of economic activity. This involved a final offensive against private enterprise together with the extension of socialization to agriculture. By 1952 only traces of private enterprise remained outside agriculture, though in the latter case socialized operations still remained quite limited except in Bulgaria, Czechoslovakia and Hungary. A second feature was the shift in the tax structure towards the Soviet model, that is, the adoption of the turnover tax which became the main source of revenue. The most important aspect of the policy change was the implementation of centrally drawn-up plans which set out in detail the targets to be met in different sectors of the economy. Thus in the Czech Five Year Plan issued in 1949 output targets were set for each branch of activity, while 'norms' for labour productivity and conversion ratios between resource inputs and final output were specified in detail. Wage rates and material allocations were to be related to these norms. The plans laid heavy emphasis on the need to boost investment with priority being given to producer durable goods industries. In terms of the objectives set these early planning exercises proved highly successful and were to be followed by a succession of plans throughout the 1950s and 1960s (see Chapter 6).

The Soviet Union's recovery was even more impressive given the fact that the country had suffered enormous damage during the war. Apart from large industrial losses in the occupied areas, there had been serious damage in the agrarian sector including substantial livestock losses. Industry, however, proved more resilient and, as already noted, Soviet industrial production staged a marked recovery after the low point in 1942 largely as a result of the creation of a new industrial base in the east. Thus by the end of the war industrial output in Russia was much closer to the pre-war level than in any of the eastern countries. The Fourth Five Year Plan (the third had been started in the late 1930s but was interrupted by the war) was to cover the period 1946–50 and gave priority to the reconstruction of devastated areas and the continued build-up of heavy industry especially in the newer regions not damaged by war. The results were impressive in the industrial sector though agriculture failed to meet its targets. By 1950 industrial production was very much higher than before the war with the main expansion taking place in producer goods. Agriculture, however, barely managed to attain its former peacetime level of production. There was also a large rise in national income, but the bulk of this increase was devoted to investment and defence and very little went to raising the levels of consumption which remained close to or slightly below those of pre-war.

5

WESTERN EUROPE'S SUSTAINED EXPANSION, 1950–1970

POST-WAR GROWTH AND INTER-WAR COMPARISONS

Probably the most outstanding economic feature of the European continent as a whole in the two decades to 1970 has been the sustained and high level of economic growth. After the initial post-war recovery, which by 1949–50 had brought most countries back to, or beyond, their pre-war output levels, a sustained rise in output and industrial production occurred in all regions – industrial western Europe, southern Europe (Greece, Portugal, Spain and Turkey), and the eastern sector. There were in fact few significant interruptions to progress and Europe's advance was more rapid than that of the rest of the world. Between 1950 and 1970 European gross domestic product grew on average at about 5.5 per cent per annum and 4.4. per cent on a per capita basis, as against world average rates of 5.0 per cent and 3.0 per cent respectively. Industrial production rose even faster, at 7.1 per cent a year compared with a world rate of 5.9 per cent. Thus by the later date output per head in Europe was almost two and one half times greater than in 1950. The pace of advance contrasts sharply with the long-term rate of growth prior to 1950. According to Bairoch's recent calculations, European income per capita growth barely reached 1 per cent per annum from 1800 through to 1950 as against 4.5 per cent since. In other words, in the generation from the late 1940s, per capita income has made greater progress than in the 150 years or so before 1950. It also compares very favourably with the post-war record of the United States, a country which emerged much stronger from the two world wars; after 1950 per capita output growth was only one half that of Europe at 2.2 per cent per annum. Only Japan of the major countries outperformed Europe in the 1950s and 1960s.

The net result of this striking performance has been a considerable strengthening of Europe's economic position in the world economy. Whereas during the inter-war years and through to 1950 Europe's economic influence was declining as a result of the effects of two world wars and a great depression, since 1950 or thereabouts her share of global economic activity has increased quite noticeably. During the period 1950–70 her share of world output of goods and services (gross domestic product (GDP)) rose from 37 to 41 per cent, while in the case of industrial production the increase was even greater, from 39 to 48 per cent. By contrast Europe's population grew at only about one-half the world rate (1.1 as against 2 per cent per annum) so that by 1970 she accounted for some 26 per cent of the world's population compared with 31 per cent in 1950.

An important feature of the post-war period has been the widespread diffusion of growth throughout Europe generally. Virtually all countries experienced continuous growth and at a much higher level than anything achieved in the previous half century. Though differences in national income accounting practices and data discrepancies make precise comparisons hazardous, it would seem that on balance eastern and southern Europe did slightly better than the industrial west. The growth of output in the eastern communist countries (including the USSR) averaged 7.0 per cent per annum in the 1950s and 1960s, that in southern Europe was between 5 and 6 per cent while in the industrial west it was of the order of 4.6 per cent. In per capita terms, however, the differences are rather less on account of the somewhat faster rate of population increase in southern and eastern Europe. Nevertheless, differences in output growth of the order of magnitude shown here have not been sufficient to close the gap in income levels between the rich industrial west and the rest of Europe. This chapter is concerned primarily with the dozen or so countries in the former area while the one following examines the experience of the east European countries which operated within a rather different political and economic institutional framework.

Table 5.1 provides some key data on the countries of the industrial west. It can be readily seen that the growth in output was fairly uniform between the 1950s and 1960s though a slight acceleration is apparent from the late 1950s. The fastest-growing countries were Austria, West Germany, France, Italy and the Netherlands though there were some contrasts between the two decades. France, for example, stepped up her growth rate quite appreciably in the 1960s, whereas Austria and Germany both recorded a deceleration in output expansion. At the other extreme Britain and Ireland, though improving on past performance, did badly in comparison with all other countries in western Europe, with growth rates less than half those of the most successful nations. The remaining countries expanded at close to the average for the region as a whole or slightly below. On balance there was some tendency over time for output growth rates to converge towards the average of around 4.5 per cent.

The growth of output per capita was also fairly rapid partly as a result of the very modest increases in population. Apart from Switzerland, most countries had population growth rates of less than 1 per cent per annum. The overall average for the region was just under 0.8 per cent per annum giving a per capita output growth of nearly 4 per cent. Though slightly less than the average for all Europe this was still very high by historical standards and it

Table 5.1 Industrial western Europe: total output, employment, labour productivity and population, 1950–69 (annual percentage compound rates of growth)

	Output (GDP at 1963 f.c.)			Employment			Output per person employed			Population, 1950–70
	1950/2–1967/9	1950/2–1958/60	1958/60–1967/9	1950/2–1967/9	1950/2–1958/60	1958/60–1967/9	1950/2–1967/9	1950/2–1958/60	1958/60–1967/9	
Austria	5.0	5.7	4.5	0.1	0.4	−0.2	5.0	5.3	4.7	0.3
Belgium	3.5	2.5	4.5	0.4	0.2	0.6	3.1	2.4	3.8	0.6
Denmark	4.0	3.2	4.7	1.1	1.0	1.2	2.8	2.2	3.4	0.7
West Germany	6.2	7.5	5.1	1.2	2.2	0.3	5.0	5.2	4.8	0.9
Finland	4.4	4.3	4.6	0.9	1.0	0.9	3.5	3.3	3.7	0.7
France	5.0	4.3	5.5	0.4	0.0	0.7	4.6	4.4	4.8	0.9
Ireland	2.5	0.8	4.0	−0.7	−1.6	0.1	3.2	2.5	3.9	0.0
Italy	5.4	5.3	5.5	0.4	0.7	0.2	5.0	4.6	5.3	0.7
Netherlands	5.0	4.5	5.5	1.1	1.1	1.2	3.9	3.4	4.3	1.3
Norway	4.1	3.0	4.9	0.3	0.0	0.6	3.7	3.1	4.3	0.9
Sweden	4.1	3.6	4.5	0.3	0.2	0.4	3.8	3.4	4.1	0.7
Switzerland	4.2	4.0	4.4	1.6	1.4	1.8	2.5	2.6	2.5	1.5
UK	2.7	2.4	2.9	0.5	0.5	0.4	2.2	1.8	2.5	0.5
Average	4.6	4.5	4.7	0.6	0.8	0.5	3.9	3.6	4.2	0.8

Source: United Nations (Economic Commission for Europe), *Economic Survey of Europe in 1971*, Part 1, *The European Economy from the 1950s to the 1970s*, New York, 1972, p. 6, Table 1.2

implied a considerable advance in real living standards for the majority of the population. Low population growth also meant that the annual additions to the labour force were modest, about 0.6 per cent per annum, though a few countries, Germany, Switzerland and the Netherlands, had labour inputs above 1 per cent per annum. From this it follows that the main output gains were derived from increased labour productivity (see Table 5.1 and below).

As one might expect with such rapid growth there were significant broad structural changes within the economies in question. Agriculture almost everywhere declined in importance in terms of both output and employment shares. The increase in agricultural output has only been about one-third to one-half of the rate recorded for domestic output as a whole, at approximately 2 per cent per annum for industrial western Europe (though somewhat faster in the east), ranging from a fall in Norway to 2.5 per cent in the UK and Sweden. Employment in agriculture fell rapidly in most countries, averaging about 3.5 per cent a year, with the result that agriculture's share of employment declined faster than its output share. For some countries, notably Britain and Belgium, the change was not very significant since agriculture only accounted for a very small proportion of both output and employment at the beginning of the period. But in the case of Finland, Ireland, Italy and to a lesser extent France the shift from agriculture was of some significance because of the greater weight of this sector initially. By 1980 few industrial countries in western Europe had an agrarian sector which accounted for a large share of income and employment.

The most rapidly growing sector of the economy has been industry though mainly in terms of output rather than employment. This sector gained most of the loss of output share by agriculture but its share of employment remained fairly constant except in Italy and Ireland where it rose rapidly. In few countries, apart from Britain and Germany, did it account for more than 40 per cent of total employment by the end of the 1960s. By contrast, the service trades (construction, transport and communications and other services) absorbed an increasing share of employment while maintaining a fairly stable output share, a reflection in part of the low rate of productivity growth in this sector. Thus its overall share of employment in the industrial west rose from 45 to 54 per cent and in most cases big declines in agriculture's share of employment were accompanied by a corresponding rise in the service sector's share of this factor. Investment patterns have also been characterized by a shift towards services at the expense of industry.

Apart from high growth and structural change there are several features of Europe's development since 1950 which contrast sharply with experience in the inter-war period. As already noted, there were few interruptions to the growth process. Rarely have countries in the post-war period experienced absolute contractions in output in any one year, and the old trade cycle of the past, which involved severe declines in economic activity in the recessionary phases of 1921, 1929–32 and 1937–8, have disappeared. This does not mean of course that economies were perfectly stable throughout the period; fluctuations in activity have occurred frequently but these have always been against the backdrop of continually rising output. Thus recessions have been characterized by decelerations in output growth rather than by absolute contractions, while boom periods were those when output was advancing more rapidly than the secular trend. This has prompted some commentators to suggest that the former trade cycle has been replaced by a growth cycle for which the peaks and troughs can be determined by the rates of acceleration or deceleration in aggregate growth. The concept of the growth cycle has also been linked with the policy reactions to changes in growth rates, giving rise to a political growth cycle or policy-induced instability. While many would not be happy with the latter interpretation there are also some writers who have challenged the very concept of the growth cycle itself. Recent tests of the growth cycle hypothesis for the period 1950–69 for sixteen OECD countries proved to be statistically insignificant (Licari and Gilbert 1974). In other words, the fluctuations observed in practice were found to be not statistically distinguishable from those generated by a random process. There was no systematic regularity akin to the pre-war cycle and exogenous influences, particularly policy-dominated ones, may have been responsible for producing these random fluctuations. In which case the growth cycle may be, as the authors note, more of an interpretative myth than an empirical reality.

Even if this interpretation is correct it does not alter the fact that there have been fluctuations in economic activity in all countries in the post-war period which are fairly readily distinguishable. On average they have occurred every four to five years, and while there has been a certain degree of divergence in timing between countries it is also possible to discern a fairly close pattern of synchronization in the movements of various countries. The first major boom following the immediate post-war recovery phase culminated in 1950–1 with the Korean War. It was dominated, as might be expected, by reconstruction and final recovery from the war, assisted by American aid and later by rearmament. Reaction after the Korean War brought a recession in 1952 when rates of growth fell sharply. In the following year expansionary forces set in again and these reached a peak in the middle of the 1950s after which the rate of expansion tailed off through to 1958. The recession of that year was severe by post-war standards; gross domestic product grew by less than 2 per cent in western Europe and in one or two countries – Belgium, Norway and Ireland – it actually fell. During 1959 a strong recovery set in and this ushered in a fairly longish period of steady expansion though with minor peaks in 1960 and 1964 and troughs in 1963 and 1967. The expansion was fed by a massive movement of workers from Mediterranean regions to the industrial areas of Europe involving the migration of about 5 million workers between 1959 and 1965. Late in 1967 a new cycle of expansion began, culminating in a peak two years later and then followed by two years of slow growth. An important feature of these years was the almost universal pressure of inflationary forces;

inflation followed output expansion more rapidly than in earlier cycles, it was much stronger, and it persisted and even accelerated when rates of growth declined and unemployment increased in the early 1970s. It not only delayed re-expansionary policies to deal with the recession but it marked a new and alarming pattern of relationships between output, employment and prices for the future.

Inflationary pressures provide another marked contrast with the pre-war period. Whereas for much of the inter-war period prices (apart from during the European inflations of the early 1920s) were trending downward on balance, during the 1950s and 1960s there was a persistent tendency for prices to increase, with some acceleration in the rate of increase towards the end of the 1960s. On average prices in western Europe rose by 3–4 per cent per annum through to the end of the period, with low rates of increase being recorded in Germany and Belgium and high rates in France, Denmark and the Netherlands. However, variations about the average were nowhere near as large as they were to become in the first half of the 1970s. At the same time there was a continuous upward drift in wages and inflexibility in a downward direction which helped to set a floor to consumption levels in recessionary periods.

The level of unemployment was also much lower than in the inter-war years. It is true that in the first half of the 1950s some countries, notably Austria, Denmark, Belgium, Germany and Italy, were still experiencing quite high rates of unemployment, but in most other countries unemployment was less than 2 per cent of the labour force during the 1950s, and throughout the decade unemployment was declining everywhere. The average unemployment rate in western Europe during the 1950s was 2.9 per cent and this dropped to 1.5 per cent in the following decade, with only Italy and Belgium recording rates above 2 per cent. Precise comparisons with the earlier period are difficult to make because of changes in the basis of compiling unemployment data in the post-war period. But there is no doubt of the marked improvement compared with the inter-war years when unemployment rates on average were double or treble those of the post-1950 period. Concomitant with the shift to full employment there has been a much greater utilization of capacity and far less drag exerted by declining basic sector industries than was the case before 1939.

The volume of commodity trade has grown very rapidly in the post-war years in contrast with the near stagnation in the period 1913–50. Since 1948 the volume of imports and exports of western Europe has risen about twice as fast as gross domestic product, with exports rising by between 8 and 9 per cent per annum during the 1950s and 1960s. This expansion has been facilitated by a much more favourable international environment, in particular the greater degree of international economic co-operation on trade and payments matters which, among other things, has ensured the requisite amount of international liquidity to finance the growing trade volumes. This is not to say that the international financial machinery has always worked smoothly, for some countries have experienced periodic payments problems, but until the early 1970s there was nothing akin to the severe monetary and financial disorders of the inter-war period. For example, there was an absence of severe deflationary shocks to the international system, either government induced or otherwise, of the type imparted say by the collapse of American lending in the late 1920s.

Finally, and perhaps most important of all, the government's role in the economy has changed dramatically in the post-war period. Not only has the state absorbed a much greater, and increasing, share of national resources which in some cases has involved an extension of public ownership of economic activities, but it has also accepted responsibility for maintaining full employment and achieving faster growth and greater stability, among other things. Such policy objectives were not regarded as falling within the province of governments during the inter-war years. Then the basic aims of policy were of a kind which would now be regarded as of a second order of magnitude, namely the restoration of currency stability, maintenance of the gold standard and balancing budgets. The tools of economic policy were also more limited in the earlier period; the main weapon of economic management, at least until it became discredited in the early 1930s, was monetary policy, whereas an important new dimension in the form of fiscal policy was added in the post-war period, as well as a number of smaller, more specific measures which previously would have been considered inappropriate. In effect, therefore, governments in the post-war period have accepted a wider range of responsibilities including overall management of economic activity and they have used a greater variety of policy measures to achieve their objectives than their counterparts before 1939. The extent to which the greater degree of state involvement has been responsible for the more satisfactory economic out-turn in the 1950s and 1960s remains to be seen.

Some of the above points will be taken up later in this chapter when the forces affecting the process of development are examined. First, however, we propose to pursue a more formal analysis of the role of factor inputs in the growth process to see what contribution labour, capital and technical progress made to the growth of output.

SOURCES OF GROWTH: FACTOR INPUTS AND TECHNOLOGY

In recent years the debate about the sources of growth has reached gigantic proportions. Various writers have stressed the importance of different factors in trying to explain Europe's post-war growth; for example, Kindleberger has espoused the role of abundant labour supplies, Maddison emphasizes the importance of investment, while Denison allocates a large part to technical progress. While from a theoretical point of view it may seem relatively easy to state the determinants of growth, in practice it is a somewhat complex task to allocate to particular factors their specific contribution to total output growth.

Basically the direct sources of growth may be divided into two broad categories. First, there are changes in the volume of resources used to produce the national product; these include inputs of labour, capital and land, the last of which is normally excluded on the grounds that its contribution to growth is very small. Second, growth may occur as a result of increases in output per unit of input. This is commonly described as the residual element being that part of the growth of output which cannot be attributed directly to changes in factor inputs. This category covers a wide range of variables which influence productivity, the most important of which are advances in knowledge and new techniques, improved allocation of resources and economies of scale. Growth may therefore be achieved either by raising the inputs of capital and labour or by changes in the residual items which improve the productivity performance of the factor inputs. In practice growth occurs as a result of simultaneous movements in all the variables.

Any attempt to explain differences in rates of economic growth must in part be based on an examination of the interrelation between increases in output and additional inputs of capital and labour. As a preliminary to such an exercise some key data on output, employment and investment have been assembled in Table 5.2.

As far as employment is concerned this input over the longer term will be largely determined by the natural increase in population. Over shorter periods of time, however, a number of factors serve to cause a divergence in the rates of change between the two: these include migration, the age distribution of the population, the rate of participation in the labour force of those of working age and the level of unemployment. The impact of these factors varied from country to country. In some countries, Austria, France, Ireland, Italy, Norway, Portugal and Spain, employment grew at a rate at least 50 per cent less than the native population, whereas in Denmark, West Germany and Switzerland the reverse was the case. However, since for most of the period agriculture was losing labour as manpower shifted into other activities, a more useful series is that for non-agricultural employment. This shows a much more rapid growth than that for total employment, and on average it was more than twice the latter for western Europe as a whole. Only in Britain, where there was a little surplus labour in agriculture, were the rates of growth the same. The labour flowing from agriculture went into both the industrial and service sectors, principally the latter. The shift into services was especially marked in France, Belgium and Denmark.

One explanation of the better growth performance post-war compared with the period 1913–50 can be found in the employment data. Because of the better utilization of labour through reduced unemployment, the drift out of agriculture and the shift of surplus labour from southern Europe (Italy, Spain, Greece and Turkey) to northern Europe (especially Germany), non-agricultural employment between 1950 and 1970 grew very much faster than hitherto; the average for western Europe was 1.6 per cent per annum as

Table 5.2 Industrial western Europe: output, employment and investment, 1950–70

	Output growth		Employment growth			Investment ratios		
	GDP	Manufacturing	Total	Manufacturing	Non-agricultural employment	Total economy	Excluding dwellings	Manufacturing
Austria	5.0	5.6	0.1	0.6	0.5	26.2	21.1	15.9a
Belgium	3.5	5.3	0.4	0.2	1.0	22.4	16.2	18.1
Denmark	4.0	4.6	1.1	1.2	2.0	21.0	17.1	8.5
Finland	4.4	5.7	0.9	1.5	3.2	27.3	21.2	19.6
France	5.0	5.8	0.4	0.5	1.6	23.7	17.8	21.1b
Germany	6.2	8.0	1.2	2.1	2.4	27.0	20.2	18.3b
Greece	6.0	8.1	0.9	1.5	2.3	23.1	19.4	20.3
Ireland	2.5	4.7	-0.7	1.0	0.4	21.9c	18.2c	19.8c
Italy	5.4	7.9	0.4	1.7	2.3	22.1	15.6	19.6
Netherlands	5.0	6.3	1.1	1.0	1.4	26.0	20.8	20.3
Norway	4.1	4.7	0.3	0.7	1.4	32.0	26.7	18.5
Portugal	5.1	8.6	0.2	1.9	1.1	18.8	14.8	15.1
Spain	6.1	8.4	0.8	2.9	2.5	22.6	16.7	n.a.
Sweden	4.1	5.1	0.3	0.3	1.2	24.4	18.4	16.4
Switzerland	4.2	4.6	1.6	1.8	1.8	23.9	18.3	n.a.
UK	2.7	3.3	0.5	0.4	0.5	17.5	14.0	12.6

Sources: United Nations, *Economic Survey of Europe in 1971*, Part 1, *The European Economy from the 1950s to the 1970s*, New York, 1972, pp. 12–14; A. Maddison, *Economic Policy and Performance in Europe 1913–1970*, London: Collins/Fontana, 1973, p. 51

Notes: a 1960–9; includes mining and construction.
b Includes construction.
c 1960–9; investment ratio for manufacturing includes construction.

against only 1 per cent in the years 1913–50. Only Austria, the Netherlands, Sweden and the UK went against the trend. Several countries were major beneficiaries: France, West Germany, Italy and Switzerland in particular, where non-agricultural employment grew very much faster than in the earlier period.

When we turn to an examination of the relationship between output and employment growth the position is less clear-cut. There is a positive association between the two, that is, high rates of output growth tend to be accompanied by high rates of employment growth and vice versa, but it is by no means perfect. The association was stronger in the 1950s than the 1960s which may partly reflect the reduction in unemployment in the earlier period. Moreover, relatively high rates of growth in the labour force tended to be associated with fairly high labour productivity growth rates as well as with gross domestic product, which suggest the importance of demand forces – that is, rapid expansion of demand encourages the fuller use of resources than would obtain in conditions of slow expansion.

Closer inspection reveals several discrepancies which make it impossible to state categorically that labour inputs were always of crucial significance in explaining growth performance. Thus while Germany at one end of the spectrum obviously secured substantial gains through rapid employment growth, and the UK at the other end experienced slow growth in both output and employment, several countries ran counter to the trend. Thus Austria's employment record was no better than that of Britain yet her output performance was considerably superior. Both France and Belgium experienced higher growth rates of output and non-agricultural employment than before 1950, though most of the increase in the latter went into the service sector so that manufacturing employment grew very slowly indeed, at about the British rate. Sweden, with growth rates comparable with those of Switzerland for total output and manufacturing activity, had a much lower rate of employment growth especially in manufacturing. Clearly therefore employment growth, while not unassociated with output performance, cannot fully explain inter-country differences in output growth.

To what extent therefore can these differences be explained by varying rates of capital accumulation? Investment may contribute to growth in various ways: it provides increasing employment opportunities; by providing more equipment per worker it raises the productivity of labour; and it is an important vehicle by which new techniques and processes become embodied in the production process. While the general character of the relationships are well established there are serious problems regarding the measurement of their relative importance. Furthermore, there are practical difficulties relating to the definition and measurement of the capital stock. Capital stock accounting procedures are still in their infancy and consequently a sufficiently reliable series of data for all countries for the period 1950–70 which would allow a meaningful cross-country comparison to be made is not readily available. For want of a better indicator the shares of gross investment in gross domestic output and in manufacturing were used as proxies in order to determine the relationship between capital accumulation and the growth of output. The method is not ideal since investment ratios among nations may vary for reasons other than the requirements of growth but it should allow a first approximation of the importance of the variable.

One thing is certain: investment ratios in all countries were much higher than in the inter-war period. They rose between the 1950s and 1960s almost everywhere and averaged 15–20 per cent (excluding dwellings) as against about 10 per cent between 1920 and 1938. As with employment growth, therefore, the higher rates of investment compared with the inter-war years helped to improve the growth performance in recent decades. The net effect of generally higher investment ratios and fairly stable rates of output growth between the 1950s and 1960s was that in most countries the marginal capital–output ratios rose, suggesting lower returns to investment, although productivity growth rates improved because of greater capital intensity per worker.

What is noticeable from the data in Table 5.2 is the wide spread of investment ratios among western nations, ranging from a high of 32 per cent in Norway to 17.5 per cent in the case of the UK. The range is almost as great if investment in dwellings is excluded or if manufacturing investment ratios alone are considered. The main conclusion to be drawn from the data is that there is a positive association between investment and growth but that it is not as strong or as uniform as one might expect. Countries with high investment ratios tended to grow rapidly (Germany and the Netherlands) whereas those with low ratios grew slowly (the UK). But that is about all one can say since there are so many cases which do not conform closely to the pattern. Thus Norway had the highest overall investment ratio but was in the bottom half of the growth league table, while Portugal was first in terms of manufacturing growth but twelfth in terms of the respective investment ratio. Italy's total investment ratio was very low in comparison with her high ranking in output growth, though the correspondence was closer in the case of manufacturing, while France's excellent investment record in manufacturing was not matched by her placing in the growth stakes. Of course there is no special reason why investment ratios and growth rates should correspond exactly since so much depends on the composition of investment, the way in which it is utilized and the structure and pattern of development of the countries in question. Thus, for example, Norway's very high investment ratio is explained by the large proportion of capital formation in shipping, while Portugal's good growth record with a relatively low investment ratio may partly reflect the early stage of development of that country where large output gains were derived from the more efficient utilization of existing resources.

So far therefore we may conclude that in general high rates of employment and investment were conducive to rapid growth while low rates tended to produce the reverse, but that the relationship between growth and factor inputs is not consistently and uniformly strong over a broad cross-section of countries. Such an analysis does not tell us anything about the respective contributions of capital and labour imputs to the growth of output, however, nor does it provide any indication of the relative importance of technical progress in the growth process.

A number of attempts have been made to estimate more precisely the contributions of capital and labour to economic growth in western countries by testing the data for consistency with a production function incorporating pre-determined estimates of the 'true' marginal productivities of labour and capital. The residual increments of output in individual countries not explained by the production function can then be regarded as indicative of the contribution to output growth of all influences other than those two inputs, though at the same time also reflecting any failure to estimate correctly the true contribution to growth of increases in labour and capital. The analyses made to date have been confined to a select number of western countries for the 1950s and early 1960s. The most elaborate study is that by Denison for northwestern Europe for the period 1950–62. Table 5.3 presents a summary of the key figures for eight countries, which show the estimated contributions to growth of capital and labour inputs together with the contribution arising from changes in output per unit of input.

The main conclusion to emerge from these figures is that factor productivity improvements were the most important source of growth in all countries, accounting in some cases for two-thirds to three-quarters of the rise in national income. The UK is the major exception with only around one-half coming from this source. The productivity improvements were derived mainly from advances in knowledge, reallocation of labour resources and economies of scale. What should be stressed is that while fast-growing countries such as Germany, Italy, France and the Netherlands had high contributions from these factors and from productivity improvements in general it was also true that the contribution from the increase in factor inputs was a good deal larger in absolute percentage point terms than was the case in slow-growing countries, for example the UK and Belgium. This would seem to imply that countries with high rates of labour and capital input were in a better position to exploit productivity gains than were countries with low factor input growth.

Several points of reservation may be made with respect to this type of analysis. First, Denison assumes that advances in knowledge and techniques made a uniform contribution to growth in all countries. While one would not disagree with the relatively high value accorded to this factor since rapid technical progress has been a marked feature of the period, it is somewhat doubtful whether all countries benefited to the same extent. True the diffusion of new technologies and ideas has been far more rapid than before 1939 but the advances among the countries are unlikely to have been as uniform as Denison suggests.

Table 5.3 Sources of growth of total national income, 1950–62 (contributions to growth in percentage points)

	Belgium	Denmark	France	Germany	Italy	Netherlands	Norway	UK	NW Europe
National income	3.20	3.51	4.92	7.26	5.96	4.73	3.45	2.29	4.78
Total factor input	1.17	1.55	1.24	2.78	1.66	1.91	1.04	1.11	1.69
Labour	0.76	0.59	0.45	1.37	0.96	0.87	0.15	0.60	0.83
Capital	0.41	0.96	0.79	1.41	0.70	1.04	0.89	0.51	0.86
Output per unit of input	2.03	1.96	3.68	4.48	4.30	2.82	2.41	1.18	3.07
Advances in knowledge	0.76	0.76	0.76	0.76	0.76	0.76	0.76	0.76	0.76
Reallocation of labour	0.35	0.59	0.88	0.91	1.26	0.47	0.77	0.10	0.60
Gains from trade	0.16	0.09	0.07	0.10	0.16	0.16	0.15	0.02	0.08
Scale economies and income elasticities	0.51	0.65	1.00	1.61	1.22	0.78	0.57	0.36	0.93
Residual items	0.25	−0.13	0.97	1.10	0.90	0.65	0.16	−0.06	0.70

Source: E. F. Denison, *Why Growth Rates Differ*, Washington, DC: Brookings Institution, 1967, pp. 300–18.

A more substantial point concerns the validity of the mode of analysis itself. The results suggest a downgrading of the role of factor inputs in the growth process but the question remains whether the findings are particularly meaningful. Measurement of the contribution of factor inputs requires calculation of the quality of inputs which may involve a degree of circularity. Furthermore, attempts to measure the contribution of separate factor inputs have usually rested on the assumption that factor income shares reflect the marginal productivity of those factors. The validity of this procedure, given the extent of non-competitive and institutional factors in the process of income determination, has frequently been questioned and is still the subject of serious controversy. But the main area of debate and uncertainty, both in theory and measurement, really centres on the question whether it is possible to allocate growth precisely to particular factors given the degree of overlap and interrelationship among the factors concerned. What this amounts to is that the technique of apportioning growth to factor inputs and productivity improvements may well understate the role of capital in particular if, as is often the case, technical advances are embodied in investment, part of which comprises the replacement of assets. This would imply therefore that gross investment, rather than simply net additions to the capital stock, is of greater significance. It is very probable that improvements in many of the residual items are dependent on capital accumulation to some degree. For example, the enhancement of the quality of the labour force, by such means as better education, vocational training, and improved health services and housing standards, is likely to be dependent on a certain minimum rate of capital formation. In so far as this is the case there is an inherent danger of underestimating the role of capital in any attempts at measuring the sources of growth using the production function method. In reality, therefore, the residual item, or that part of growth not attributable to factor inputs, must be interpreted, as noted earlier, not only as an indication of the influence of 'technical and organizational progress' but also as an indication of the errors embodied in the allocation process itself.

The possibilities of reinterpretation are illustrated by Maddison's (1972) reworking of Denison's basic data for the same countries. The main difference is the larger weight assigned to capital by making allowances for the input of government capital and the effects of education and by assuming that technical progress (advances in knowledge in Denison's case) is all embodied in either capital or labour, in which case it disappears as a separate item. On this basis Maddison concludes that factor inputs played a much larger role, explaining on average about three-quarters of the growth in west European countries as against less than half in Denison's calculations.

Clearly therefore the dispute over the weights to be attached to particular factors leaves the growth problem very much unresolved. That factor contributions to growth differed considerably among the several countries is stating the obvious, but at least there is one point of significance, namely that high

145

income growth countries such as Germany, Italy and the Netherlands tended to secure larger absolute contributions from all factors than slow-growing countries such as Britain. Perhaps of greater relevance at this stage then than the proximate causes of growth is to determine what forces influenced changes in the growth factors: that is, what determined the rate of technical progress and organizational change, the high levels of investment and variations in the labour supply.

There were several favourable influences bearing on supply factors in the post-war period. These were both general and specific in nature and the strength of their impact varied from one country to another. In the first half of the 1950s for example some countries, notably Germany and Italy, were still under the influence of reconstruction from the war. These countries had only just surpassed their pre-war levels of output by 1950 and there was still consider-able slack to be taken up. Unemployment was still very high in both Germany and Italy but it was declining steadily with the result that employment growth was fairly rapid. Moreover, extensive reconstruction of productive facilities, especially in Germany, had to be carried out, which meant rapid capital accumulation and a more efficient and up-to-date capital stock than in countries less seriously damaged by the war. By the mid-1950s the special circumstances associated with the aftermath of war ceased to be very important and therefore they cannot be used as an explanatory factor for high growth countries in the later 1950s and 1960s.

Several countries experienced high rates of employment growth in both the 1950s and 1960s. These included advanced industrial countries such as Germany, the Netherlands and Switzerland as well as some of the smaller and poorer countries – Portugal, Greece, Spain. In part this can be accounted for by the reduction in unemployment especially in the 1950s, and the removal of disguised unemployment, in particular in agriculture, which in turn was associated with a reallocation of labour resources. Some countries also benefited considerably from increased immigration in both the 1950s and 1960s, together with an improvement in the quality of the labour force. In France, Germany and Switzerland total population grew at a rate at least 50 per cent higher than the native population as a consequence of a continual stream of immigrants into these countries. They were the chief host nations to migrating workers from the European south and by the end of the 1960s foreign workers constituted between 5 and 7 per cent of their respective work-forces. Sweden too absorbed foreign workers on a considerable scale. Germany was probably the major beneficiary with a large influx of refugees and expellees from eastern Europe in the 1950s followed by the migration of workers from southern Europe in the 1960s. By 1961 West Germany had absorbed some 12 million refugees and expellees, 7 million of whom had become active participants in the labour force. By contrast employment growth in the Netherlands was boosted by the natural increase in population which was one of the highest in Europe. In all these countries the demand for labour remained fairly high but the supply was reasonably elastic so that pressure on the labour market never acted as a serious brake upon the economy. This in turn kept demand buoyant and increased the need for new investment in both productive facilities and social overhead capital.

Several European countries, Italy and to a lesser extent France and of course the southern European countries, were less highly developed than Britain and Sweden at the beginning of the period. Their levels of income per head were lower and structurally they still had a relatively large proportion of resources tied up in low productivity sectors such as agriculture. In the process of catching up they were bound to reap substantial gains from the reallocation of resources and economies of scale associated with large-scale industrial development. There was also greater scope for the adoption of best practice techniques and general improvements in efficiency. Both France and Italy gained substantially from these influences. According to Denison's calculations, 2.48 percentage points (42 per cent of the total) of Italy's income growth between 1950 and 1962 came from resource reallocation, while a further 0.9 was derived from changes in the lag in the application of knowledge and general efficiency. During the 1950s the industrial sector in Italy absorbed some 2 million additional workers most of them coming from agriculture. In the same way France gained about 1.90 percentage points (39 per cent of the total income growth) from the first two factors, 0.65 of which came from the reduction in agricultural inputs. In fact most European countries stood to gain more from resource reallocation than a country such as Britain where the opportunities for shifting labour out of agriculture were virtually exhausted. Even in the 1960s the reallocation of labour from the primary sector to industry and the service trades continued strongly in some of the major countries. In Germany farm employment dropped by more than 1.2 million between 1960 and 1970, while non-agricultural employment rose by 2 million; in France the figures were 1.3 and 3.0 million and in Italy 2.9 and 1.7 million respectively. The importance of this movement can be expected to diminish in the future, however.

The post-war period has been characterized by a high level of technological innovation, especially in science-based industries such as chemicals and electronics, and rapid diffusion of technical developments among the major industrial countries. There have been several strong forces at work to explain the accelerated rate in the application of new inventions and the diffusion of techniques. These include the high rate of capital formation, the larger proportion of resources devoted to research and development and the continuing growth of education at all levels, to all of which governments have contributed considerably. Furthermore, the transmission of ideas and techniques and their rapid spread and diffusion throughout western countries have been facilitated by the removal of trade barriers and the growth of trade, especially that in manufactured products, the general improvement in communications, the expansion of international investment and the exploitation of new products by multinational companies. The high level of demand has also helped to encourage the adoption of new products especially in the consumer durable goods field.

More generally it can be argued that the greater internal stability within Europe compared with the pre-war period has been favourable to growth. This is a difficult factor to measure but both in a political and economic sense the climate has been more favourable to international economic progress. The political situation, despite the east–west split, has been more stable than in the inter-war years and this in turn has encouraged a greater degree of international economic co-operation among western nations. This has assisted the removal of many restrictions on trade and payments (see below). The east–west split itself probably encouraged a greater degree of co-operation and at the same time prompted America to give as much assistance to western Europe as possible. Perhaps even more important has been the fact that economic fluctuations and crises have been much milder than previously, possibly because of the more active participation of government in economic affairs (see below). These more stable conditions provided a climate conducive to high investment and sustained growth.

However, possibly the major reason for western Europe's good showing in the 1950s and 1960s has been the high and sustained level of demand. Nearly all countries experienced both a rapid increase in exports and an increasing volume of domestic consumption. The importance of demand, and especially export demand, has been stressed frequently by economists and it would be difficult to deny that a high level of demand is a necessary condition of growth. Buoyant markets raise businessmen's expectations about future profits and this in turn encourages investment. Whether demand is the autonomous element which induces changes in supply or whether it is autonomous changes in the latter that govern the rate at which demand increases is still a matter for debate. Nevertheless, the fact remains that demand has been sustained throughout the period. It is therefore important to analyse the determinants of export demand and its impact on growth and also to examine the influence of government operations on the level and pattern of domestic consumption.

THE ROLE OF EXPORTS

The unprecedented growth in western Europe in the 1950s and 1960s was accompanied by an even better performance in the trading sphere. This was also true of the world in general. The volume of west European exports rose by between 8 and 9 per cent in the two decades with a slight acceleration in the 1960s. All countries except the UK achieved rates of export growth in excess of 5 per cent per annum and in the case of Germany and Italy the rates ran into double figures. In fact western Europe's trade performance was better than that of the world as a whole and very much better than the near stagnation in trade in the period 1913–50. Trade grew considerably faster than output and it was most buoyant in manufactured goods. The effect of this was to raise the trade-output ratio above unity whereas in the past it had been close to unity except in the 1930s. Europe's trade with outside regions grew only slightly more than output in Europe. The main part of the expansion was concentrated on intra-European exchange and was dominated by the exchange of manufactured products among countries having not very dissimilar levels of income per head. The growth of trade volumes was also accompanied by an increasing flow of international capital, both short term and long term. This was dominated in the first decade by American lending and investment in Europe but in the 1960s the flow of portfolio investment from Europe to the United States assumed increasing importance, as did short-term capital movements once freed from administrative regulations. Direct investment by international corporations also increased in importance which was advantageous from the point of view of trade growth and for the diffusion of technical advances.

There are several reasons why trade expanded rapidly in the post-war period. As noted in the previous chapter, western Europe's trade was sharply reduced during the war and even in the immediate post-war years it remained well below the pre-war level, largely because of supply difficulties. Intra-European trade in fact only regained the 1913 level in 1950. Yet because of severe payments imbalances, especially with the dollar area, it was vitally important that Europe should increase her exports substantially. Hence it is not surprising that first priority was given to exporting since, given Europe's dependence on dollar supplies in particular, this was the only way of clearing the accounts once American aid ceased to flow. In fact by 1950, as a result of increased production, the control of inflation and the correction of currency overvaluation in 1949, the European current account deficit had been cut by two-thirds to $2.5 billion. The balance of payments problem still remained acute, however, and it worsened during 1951 on account of the Korean War which caused a sharp rise in the price of commodities. If Europe was to dispense with external aid and liberalize her trade, as well as compensate for a deterioration in terms of trade and loss of invisible earnings, the requirement in terms of increased exports remained very large. Fortunately continued US aid and rising American military expenditure in Europe contributed to Europe's dollar receipts, and these together with rapidly rising exports meant that some countries achieved a surplus on their current accounts by the middle of the 1950s. At the end of 1955, eleven OEEC countries felt strong enough to restore currency convertibility for non-residents and in 1958 a general move to full currency convertibility was made by most countries. By that time, though certain payments problems remained, the dollar scarcity was all but over, and rather sooner than most people would have believed possible at the beginning of the decade. During the 1960s the position was reversed; America incurred large deficits on current account and western European countries recorded an aggregate surplus on current account of about $2.5 billion dollars.

Meanwhile other influences were beginning to have a favourable impact on trade, especially within Europe, where the prospects for the exchange of manufactures became increasingly apparent. These prospects were enhanced by the improving payments position, the liberalization of trade and payments and the creation of new trading blocs. Among the more important developments affecting international trading relations in the period were the removal of trade restrictions by the OEEC liberalization programme of the 1950s, the general reduction in tariffs through GATT, and the formation of new trading communities (EEC and EFTA) in the later 1950s.

In the early post-war years not only was the volume of intra-European trade at a low level but the trade and payments between western European countries tended to be along bilateral channels and backed up by rigorous quantitative restrictions. In an attempt to break down these obstacles to trade the United States made its aid conditional upon the removal of trade and payments restrictions by fostering economic co-operation among western nations. Thus in July 1950 the European Payments Union (EPU) was established which, by providing effective means for clearing intra-European payments, paved the way for the termination of bilateral trade agreements and trade restrictions. The latter became the province of the OEEC and its Code of Liberalization set out a programme for the progressive removal of trade restrictions. Progress was fairly rapid and, by 1955, 84 per cent of the quantitative restrictions had been removed. Subsequently the easing of tariff policies was taken in hand by GATT and in the later 1950s and 1960s several rounds of general tariff reductions were made.

The late 1950s saw the development of closer and more intricate co-operation among the western nations. In 1958, following the signing of the Rome Treaty in the previous year, the European Economic Community (EEC) was established. Its founder members consisted of France, West Germany, Italy, the Netherlands, Belgium and Luxembourg. The Community's long-term objectives are ambitious and wide-ranging but it is as a customs unit that the most significant advances have been made to date. By 1968 intra-community trade in non-agricultural products had been freed of duties and a common external tariff had been established. Agricultural products, on the other hand, enjoy considerable protection especially from outside competition. The following year also saw the creation of the European Free Trade Area (EFTA); its members included Austria, Denmark, Norway, Portugal, Sweden, Switzerland and the UK, with Finland becoming an associate member in 1961 (in the early 1970s the UK and Denmark withdrew on joining the EEC). The aims of the Association were more limited than those of the EEC, being largely confined to trade matters. The abolition of restrictions on trade between member countries proceeded rapidly and by the mid-1960s quantitative restrictions and customs duties had all but disappeared.

Thus substantial and rapid progress was made in the 1950s and 1960s in abolishing barriers to foreign trade. The impact of the liberalization policy is difficult to estimate precisely but there seems little doubt that it has created greater trade opportunities. The progressive relaxation of quantitative restrictions in the 1950s and early 1960s was an important factor encouraging the growth of exports, while the establishment of the two trading communities in the late 1950s produced both trade creation and trade diversion effects. Trade of the member countries grew more rapidly than the world average until the early 1970s. Among the countries of the EEC it rose by nearly 13 per cent per annum between 1955 and 1969, with manufactures recording a higher rate and agricultural products about 10 per cent a year. The most dynamic sector was intra-EEC trade which by 1969 accounted for one-third of the total intra-European trade compared with one-quarter in 1955. The performance of the EFTA countries was not so strong but this was principally because of the sluggish growth of UK exports. If the latter are excluded, intra-EFTA trade rose by 11.5 per cent per annum over the same period, with the Nordic countries showing the most spectacular gains.

The trade diversion effects are much less easy to demonstrate but the general consensus seems to be that the diversion of trade in manufactures from third countries as a result of enhanced intra-European trade was roughly balanced by the creation of new trade with non-members. But in the case of agrarian products the agricultural policy of the EEC has probably entailed a net loss in trade for outside members. Apart from the specific trade effects an important by-product of the Community was its negotiating strength *vis-à-vis* non-members. The importance of the Community as a trading partner, for example, was recognized by the United States in the 1960s when unilateral tariff cuts of about one-third were agreed in the Kennedy Round of GATT negotiations.

It is important to recognize that the international economic environment as a whole has been distinctly more favourable to the growth of trade than it was in the inter-war years. In this respect the strong and sustained economic co-operation between nations since the end of the war, which contrasts sharply with the breakdown in international economic relations in the 1930s, must be accorded an important role. It has been manifested in several ways. Initially the United States was instrumental in fostering European reconstruction and recovery with its enormous aid programmes, amounting to some $43 billion net. Subsequently there were big payments both on military and private accounts to Europe including the large US payments deficit in the 1960s which facilitated European expansion. Second, western European co-operation has been fostered by several organizations including the EPU, GATT, OEEC and later the EEC and EFTA, the main impact of which, as already noted, has been the progressive elimination of trade barriers. Finally, international monetary co-operation has been more in evidence and more effective than before the war. Even before the war had ended an international governmental conference at Bretton Woods had drafted the Articles of Agreement of the International Monetary Fund (IMF) which was to become the main institution responsible for international financial and monetary matters. Three main provisions emerged from the complex negotiations at Bretton Woods. Fixed exchange rates were to be introduced and currency parities altered only to correct fundamental disequilibrium; a pool of international credit derived from members' quotas to the Fund was available to finance temporary balance of payments difficulties, including those caused by speculative raids; and, third, there was provision for currency convertibility on current transactions and prohibition of discriminatory currency practices, the payments equivalent to non-discrimination in trade.

It would be wrong of course to assume that the existence of the IMF provided a solution to all international monetary problems. Indeed, in the early years and through the 1950s the IMF pursued a somewhat passive policy, partly because its reserves were never large enough to offer more than token support to countries in difficulties. During the following decade its lending activities became more pronounced, partly as a consequence of the increase in members' quotas in 1958 and 1962 and the institution of Special Drawing Rights (SDRs) in 1969. Moreover, the work of the IMF was greatly assisted in this decade by arrangements for short-term support and swap facilities among the central bankers of the major countries, while the international liquidity position was boosted by the recycling of dollars arising from the large US payments deficit in what became known as the Eurodollar market.

Even with these arrangements periodic strains in the international financial mechanism did occur. The most important sources of disequilibrium were the ever-increasing surplus of continental Europe, Germany in particular, and the intractable deficit of the UK, and later the United States. Eventually such disequilibria reached the scale where no amount of liquidity would obviate the need for adjusting exchange rates. But even before the upheavals of the early 1970s, when rate adjustments and floating rates became commonplace, there had been several disturbances caused by payments imbalances which involved major realignments of exchange rates in several cases, including the French devaluations of 1957–8 and 1969, the British devaluation of 1967 and the German and Dutch revaluations in the early 1960s.

Despite these upsets it would be fair to say that in the post-war period through to the end of the 1960s the international financial machinery conferred net benefits on the economic system. Certainly it was a vast improvement on anything that had gone before. Its inherent weaknesses were masked by a regime of relatively stable exchange rates, moderate inflation and a reasonable supply of international liquidity. The international monetary climate has been generally favourable to growth and the expansion of trade and with notable exceptions, the UK in particular, governments have not felt the need to check output severely because of a lack of liquidity. International financial co-operation between the major powers has meant a continuous expansion in the supply of liquidity which in turn has bolstered confidence among businessmen and traders. The strains in the international mechanism which did occur from time to time were not severe enough to cause permanent damage or were repaired before they could do so. It was not until the early 1970s that the foundations of successful post-war monetary co-operation were undermined, but that is part of another story.

If international co-operation in its many forms has been conducive to trade expansion, so too has the growth process itself within the major economies. Rapid growth brought scale economies and considerable output diversification. This in turn encouraged the increasing exchange of industrial products among the wealthier nations, a process no doubt facilitated in some fields, for example consumer durables, by demonstration effects. Rapidly expanding domestic markets, especially in Germany and Italy, enabled these countries to benefit considerably from scale economies in the production of consumer durables, thereby reducing units costs and providing a strong launching-pad for export penetration into overseas markets. In addition, high technology investment, notably in Germany, provided a medium for expanding the exports of producer goods to other advanced nations.

This of course more or less brings us back to the original point of departure in this section, namely, are exports good for growth or does the causal link flow in the reverse direction? It has been very fashionable in recent years to talk about export-led growth and some economists have assigned an independent role to the export component in the growth process. The main crux of the argument rests on the following premises: that export growth stimulates industries with significant scale economies and, second, that by inducing strong external accounts it encourages investment. The evidence is somewhat conflicting, however; although most analyses confirm a general positive association between exports and growth the direction of the causal mechanism is frequently disputed. Recent statistical tests on data for eleven leading manufacturing exporters for the period 1950-69 (Lubitz 1973) does cast doubt on the alleged export-led mechanisms. Rates of economic growth were found to be correlated more strongly with total export growth than with manufacturing export growth, thereby raising doubt as to the strength of the scale economies effect in manufacturing. Moreover, when the investment ratio was used alongside export growth as a second independent variable in the regression equations it turned out to be statistically significant, implying that exports did not stimulate growth through their effects on investment. In other words, the results are more consistent with a theory of growth-induced exports rather than with one that ascribes an independent and dynamic role to the export component. This would be quite a plausible interpretation; high growth countries gained competitive strength through rapid domestic investment, while slow growth countries, Britain in particular, ran up against supply constraints because of low investment which in turn reduced their competitive edge.

POLICY VARIABLES

Any survey of economic development in modern industrial economies cannot be complete without a discussion of the role of government in economic affairs. This is not simply because the goals and instruments of economic policy are now much greater than before 1939 but also on account of the sheer scale of government economic operations in the post-war period. The war of 1939–45 even more so than that of 1914–18 led to a vast increase in the size of public sector activities. Only part of this increase was reversed afterwards since the shift upwards during the war in what were regarded as tolerable levels of taxation allowed governments to retain part of the increase in peacetime, while in more recent years the public sector's share of resources has been increasing again by a stealthy incremental approach. Thus since 1945 the government sector has been a major component in every western economy. The ratio of public sector outlays (including transfer payments) to gross national income ranged between 30 and 40 per cent in the 1950s rising steadily to exceed 50 per cent by the early 1970s in Scandinavia, the Netherlands and Britain, most of the later increase being accounted for by transfer payments. These high rates, which on average are more than twice those attained pre-war, have given governments enormous leverage over their economies.

Not only has the increase in government operations itself inevitably resulted in the state's greater involvement in economic affairs, but changes in attitudes as to the state's responsibilities with regard to economic matters have also played an important part. In some cases, for instance, ideological commitments led to a significant increase in the public ownership of economic enterprise, notably in France and Britain where several important sectors of the economy were nationalized shortly after the war. Perhaps of more general importance was the natural unwillingness of societies to contemplate a return to pre-war conditions as they had been disposed to do after the First World War. This is not very surprising given the high unemployment and poor performance of most economies during the 1930s. Thus instead of opting for a return to 'normalcy' as after the first war, governments in the mid-1940s were inclined towards planning for the future, a shift of opinion well illustrated by the British Labour Party's 1945 election manifesto entitled 'Let us face the future'. In effect, therefore, what this implied was that governments would have to accept greater responsibility for achieving full employment and faster growth among other things than had been the case before the war. Not that policy aims had been entirely absent prior to 1939 but for the most part they were of a kind which came to be regarded as secondary, if not irrelevant, in the different climate of the post-1945 period.

Changes in economic thinking and statistical reporting also gave governments greater scope for manoeuvre. Whereas inter-war governments, at least until the 1930s, had relied primarily on monetary policy as a policy weapon, post-war governments, partly as a result of the revolution in economic thinking wrought by Keynes, have been able to add fiscal policy to their armoury of weapons. Not that fiscal action was absent in the pre-war period but for the most part it involved passive and often perverse adjustments of expenditures and taxes for purposes of balancing budgets, with little contemplation of using the fiscal device as a means to influence changes in broad economic aggregates – in fact at the time there were very few references to aggregate demand as a factor determining employment etc. Thus although the inter-war years saw substantial stabilization action on the part of governments it was generally of a restrictive type which had an adverse influence on the economy. As Lundberg rightly observes: 'The measures taken were more inappropriate, more badly timed, or more obviously wrong than most measures of similar importance adopted in the post-war period' (Lundberg 1968).

Apart from improvements in theoretical analysis and practical policy application there was also a concomitant improvement in the gathering and processing of economic data and its evaluation. The policy debate prior to 1939 had to make do with a limited range of imperfect statistics and for this reason the debate was limited in scope since the data available did not allow a proper evaluation of aggregate magnitudes. During and after the Second World War the quality and range of statistical reporting, both official and otherwise, improved enormously, most notably in the field of national income accounting. In addition, technical expertise in the assessment of the material became very much better, allowing the construction and testing of increasingly complex models of the economy. Whether this has always been as beneficial in terms of policy performance as we should like to think is another matter, but at least it provided a basis for a more positive and realistic assessment of how economies worked in practice.

These then are some of the main reasons why governments since the war have become such active agents in the economic sphere, and indeed increasingly so until nowadays their electoral prestige depends very much on how well they can manage the economy. In the main they have been concerned with two basic issues: the growth and the stability of economic systems, the ideal aimed for being fast growth with relative stability. These two broad dimensions may be expanded into four main responsibilities or objectives: fast growth, full employment, price stability and external equilibrium. To these may be added others such as the more equitable distribution of income, the modification of structural or regional imbalances and the development of specific sectors, for example social security systems, as well as a host of smaller issues, for example environmental betterment. But, generally speaking, the latter have tended to be regarded as matters of secondary importance given the commitment to the first four objectives, though experience in this matter varies from one country to another. In any case, fulfilment of the basic aims may well assist in realizing the second-order priorities; for example, rapid economic growth will make it easier to improve social security services and reduce income inequalities – a fact which the zero growth enthusiasts would do well to bear in mind. In practice, however, things have not always worked out quite so favourably since for all but a few countries the range of objectives has proved incompatible. Few countries have been able to achieve fast growth combined with price stability, while others have found that growth and balance of payments equilibrium do not make happy marriage partners. One possible problem apart from inherent structural weaknesses in particular economies such as Britain's is that the number of objectives has generally been larger than the number of major policy weapons, the assumption being that there must be a one-for-one relationship between aims and policies, or as many control measures as there are objectives. This is probably true up to a point, but more so for basically unsound economies as in the British case than for strong and vigorous economies such as the German. The one-for-one relationship also poses something of a prescription problem because of the difficulty in defining what constitutes a major policy control weapon. Is fiscal policy to be counted merely as one lever or does it consist of a series of instruments, for example tax changes, investment incentives, aggregate spending volumes etc., which in total form an omnibus holding labelled fiscal policy?

In fact in a sense some countries have neatly sidestepped some of the above difficulties by ordering their priorities in terms of both objectives and instruments of control. Not all countries for instance have given first priority to full employment and growth. The German neo-liberals argue, and for the most part the authorities have accepted their basic premise, that these two goals would be achieved by ensuring internal and external stability, or price stability and balance of payments equilibrium, which in the German case has usually been interpreted to mean a surplus. Accordingly, economic management has been geared primarily to achieving the latter objectives even if at times it might run counter to full employment and growth. In the event this type of policy direction has proved to be correct since Germany was blessed with success on all fronts. Possibly the one area where there has been some lagging has been in social matters and particularly the achievement of a more equitable distribution of income, but then Germany has never regarded these as being high on its list of priorities, and given the rapid overall growth it could afford such a deferment. France, on the other hand, encouraged by faith in her planning ventures, hedged her bets on growth for most of the period but at the expense of monetary stability. The final out-turn has been good but not as favourable as the German since France's rapid growth led to more severe inflationary pressures and at times a precarious balance of payments situation.

Now contrast the position and practice of the above two countries with that of Britain. In this case the authorities never seem to have been able to decide upon any scale of priorities among the main objectives listed, in addition to which they flirted, and very seriously at times, with a fifth – social progress and equality. This proved a dangerous exercise for a country whose economy was basically weaker than those of most other west European countries. They tried something which few other countries dared to contemplate, namely to march along on four or five fronts simultaneously with an inadequate armoury of weapons, primarily fiscal policy, a somewhat weak and negative monetary policy and a dead-set against using external regulators (though eventually they were forced to devalue in 1967), together with an almost deliberate refusal to recognize that under such conditions the objectives were bound to be incompatible. Not surprisingly the results have been poor: slow growth, inflationary pressures, a precarious balance of payments and, one bright spot, fairly full employment. But the last of these was achieved more by accident than design as a result of a very slow growth in the labour force and a bad track record in productivity. It is true that policy mistakes cannot be held solely responsible for the sad failings of the British economy, but it is difficult to resist the conclusion that the out-turn might have been very much better had the authorities launched a frontal attack on one or two objectives rather than spreading their efforts so widely. Perhaps the British authorities have heeded too closely the warning about placing 'all one's eggs in one basket'.

As hinted above, the methods used to manage economic systems have varied from one country to another. Though most countries at one time or another have tended to use a variety of policy measures, in practice there has been a specific predilection for one particular set of policy instruments. Thus, for example, Germany, Belgium and Italy have generally placed their faith in monetary controls of one sort or another, whereas the UK has given first preference to fiscal regulators though backed up by credit and discount controls from time to time. Indeed, contrary to general impressions, Britain has been somewhat exceptional in her emphasis on fiscal policy since most continental countries, until recently, have been less ready to use fiscal weapons specifically for purposes of counter-cyclical manipulation. As might be expected Sweden, as a pioneer in this field of policy, continued to be in the forefront in the development of Keynesian methods of economic management, though perhaps her most distinctive and well-known contribution has been her labour market policy. Norway's policies have been rather similar. Some countries have been strong on planning in one form or another. The best known is France with her heavy emphasis on government investment planning and active sponsorship of investment projects by subsidies and licensing systems, together with the periodic use of import controls and devaluations. The Dutch followed a similar path, but they use a much more sophisticated econometric model for forecasting and planning purposes, and until the mid-1960s they also had the bonus of a remarkable wages policy. However, planning as such cannot act as a substitute for policy control; it only provides the basis on which action may be taken so that ultimately the French and Dutch have had to utilize the main weapons of control to achieve the aims or targets outlined in their plans.

Other policy instruments have been used much less frequently. Direct physical controls were employed extensively during the war and the immediate post-war years but most of the detailed system of controls of these years had been abandoned by the early 1950s. Price and income controls of one sort or another have been used from time to time but apart from the Dutch case they have rarely formed part of the permanent policy package of governments. The major policy gap has probably been on the external side, that is, the absence of a specific policy weapon for dealing with balance of payments disequilibrium. Exchange rate adjustments have of course been made on occasions and the French have probably made more use of external regulators than most other countries; but by and large, until the early 1970s, currency realignment was regarded as a policy of last resort. For much of the period exchange rate adjustment was out of favour as a policy instrument – and indeed it did not accord with the IMF rules – so that it was only employed in cases of fundamental disequilibrium. The same goes for trade controls of one sort or another since these conflicted with the general movement towards trade liberalization. One should add, however, that until general currency convertibility in 1958 many countries employed protective devices to safeguard their external accounts, while in the 1960s special measures to control the movement of short-term capital were widespread.

While individual countries tended to pursue one type of policy in preference to others this was not to the complete exclusion of the other alternatives. Indeed, in the 1960s there was some tendency towards policy convergence among the European countries. One reason why some continental countries have preferred to give priority to monetary weapons is because their budgetary systems are less centralized and therefore less efficient for purposes of fiscal regulation than is the case in Britain or France. The complex political and administrative procedures involved often hampered the speedy introduction of tax and spending changes. For example, the German public financial system is highly decentralized; in 1959 the central government accounted for only 20 per cent of total public expenditure (current and capital) as against 59 per cent in France and Britain, while local authorities and social security agencies controlled 41 per cent and 39 per cent respectively. Clearly this gave the central government far less scope for pursuing an active fiscal policy, and even if it did so there was always the danger that, as in America in the 1930s, its actions would be offset by reverse spending patterns of the financially autonomous Länder governments. In the case of Italy the reluctance to resort to fiscal policy arose from the inherent weakness of the whole budgetary system, including the structure of the tax system and its general inefficiency, the defective procedural, institutional and administrative framework within which budgetary policy was formulated and implemented, and the antiquated and overcautious attitudes towards deliberately using budgetary deficits as a policy measure to induce expansion. Yet in both countries there was a move away from too heavy reliance on monetary policy in the later 1960s. After 1965 Italy used budgetary policy more strenuously than hitherto though not always to very good effect, while in 1967 Germany deliberately adopted an expansionary fiscal policy to prevent the then current recession, severe by post-war standards, from developing into a full recession. Up to that time Germany had never taken major fiscal policy measures to stimulate the economy, since the post-war slowdowns were regarded as useful cooling-off periods and they had normally been reversed by an upswing in exports before becoming really serious.

Similar shifts in policy direction were evident in other countries. Britain in the later 1960s began to pay more attention to monetary policy than had previously been the case. Not that reliance on fiscal policy had ever meant the complete exclusion of monetary controls, but in this case the authorities had had some difficulty in sorting out their attitudes towards monetary policy, partly because of influences stemming from historical experience with monetary policy (for example in the 1920s) and partly because of the uncertainty as to the role and impact of monetary controls, not helped on this score by the rather ambivalent attitude of the Radcliffe Committee of 1959, which by emphasizing the 'general liquidity position' above all else tended to send the authorities along interest rate and credit control channels at the expense of monetary aggregates. Thus the change when it came was not simply a shift from fiscal to monetary controls. It also involved a shift of emphasis within the monetary spectrum, that is, away from credit and interest rate weapons *per se* towards broad monetary aggregates – first domestic credit expansion and later the growth of the money stock, equivalent to domestic credit expansion but inclusive of the monetary counterpart of any overall surplus or deficit on the balance of payments. This redirection of emphasis, which was partly conditioned by academic arguments and analyses of various monetary authorities, most notably the IMF, was consummated in the credit reforms of 1971.

The process of policy convergence was apparent in other respects in the 1960s. While the French began from the mid-1960s to place decreasing emphasis on the detailed design of their investment plans and at the same time gave greater weight to monetary and fiscal controls, Britain became somewhat more planning conscious, as did Germany and Italy in the later 1960s, though few concrete results emerged from these forays into uncharted waters. Similarly the Dutch attachment to complex and sophisticated model-building for purposes of prediction, which had yielded rather mixed results, softened somewhat and they began to pay more attention to surveys of business expectations of the type used in Sweden. Ironically at the very same time the Swedes were beginning to make increasing use of the techniques of econometric analysis. The Dutch centralized wage-bargaining system also broke down in the middle of the 1960s when other countries were starting to think seriously about the expediency of wages and incomes policies. The process of policy convergence became even stronger in the early 1970s when the system of fixed exchange rates partly disintegrated and the upheavals of these years prompted the adoption of rather similar emergency measures in many countries.

Shifts in policy emphasis in part reflected the dissatisfaction of individual countries with prevailing policies; in part they were determined by changes in the order of priorities and by the changing fortunes of economic events. Few countries were able to retain throughout the period unrelenting reliance on one particular set of policies since there was a continuing need to adapt them to changing circumstances. The next step is to determine how effective these policies were in achieving the main macroeconomic aims and here we shall pay particular attention to the questions of growth and stability. It should be borne in mind of course that the two are closely interrelated: measures to achieve greater stability say in investment or consumer spending or the balance of payments may also contribute to the long-term growth of the economy. Conversely, a too rapid promotion of investment for growth purposes may create greater instability. A distinction should also be made between longer-term policies designed to promote growth, especially those relating to the supply side, and the essentially short-term policies of demand management for purposes of achieving a greater measure of stability. In practice of course the distinction is sometimes difficult to make, though it would be true to say that successful long-term growth depends very much on effective demand management policies.

The high and sustained level of demand in the post-war period is generally regarded as an important factor in the rapid growth of most European countries. There were strong autonomous forces at work which promoted consumption, for example the widespread desire to accumulate consumer durables; but at the same time government budgetary operations have contributed to the continued high level of demand. Not only has government spending itself on goods and services been much higher than before the war but the level and pattern of private consumption has been partly determined by the fiscal process. In particular, the enlarged importance of taxes and transfer payments has created a built-in stabilizing mechanism or compensatory device which has led to greater stability in consumption and set a floor to consumption in times of recession. Thus disposable incomes and hence consumption have fallen less than national income in recessionary periods compared with the inter-war period because of higher marginal tax rates and compensatory welfare payments, while conversely they rise less than total income during boom periods because of rising tax rates and reduced transfer payments. At the same time the long-run tendency towards greater income equality through taxation has meant a shift in the distribution of income towards those people with a high marginal propensity to consume, which in turn has helped to maintain consumption levels. Also the greater security involved under the post-war welfare society has probably meant a stronger inclination to maintain consumer spending in difficult times.

The impact of compensatory budgetary forces has varied between nations. It has been strongest in those countries with rigorous fiscal policies and in which direct taxes and social security systems are well developed. In this category would be included Sweden, Norway and the UK at least. It has been estimated that in Sweden over 50 per cent of the 'primary' gross national product (GNP) recession impulse may be neutralized by built-in budgetary responses, though this is taking a fairly broad definition of the stabilizing properties including the starting of relief works. However, a strong compensatory fiscal mechanism does not automatically lead to a high rate of growth in consumption in the long run as the British case shows. Here the problem has been that, despite the high floor to consumption in recessions through the working of the fiscal adjustment mechanism, the expansion of consumption in the upswing phases of the cycle has had to be squeezed prematurely by restrictive action in order to deal with balance of payments problems.

In many continental countries the compensatory mechanism has not been as strong. This is because of the greater reliance on indirect taxes and also on account of the structure of social security payments. Though welfare schemes are well developed they are generally less compensatory than those of the UK or Sweden. Many of the social transfer payments are fixed and they are financed by fixed charges which are insensitive to income fluctuations. Similarly, a large proportion of European tax receipts are insensitive to cyclical changes and many taxes are collected in arrears.

It seems probable therefore that consumption as a whole has been maintained at a higher and more stable level by compensatory adjustment and the higher level of government spending on goods and services. In turn this has helped to make conditions more favourable for investment. But governments have also been active in this regard. After 1945 most European governments took steps to encourage productive investment for purposes of reconstruction and such policies were continued during the 1950s. In the 1960s, however, less importance was attached to increasing aggregate investment ratios which were already high, and so few new measures were taken to that effect, though attempts were made to influence investment for countercyclical purposes.

The methods used to influence the course of investment have varied a great deal and quite often they have been designed to achieve greater stability rather than expressly for the purpose of raising the long-term rate of investment. Moreover, the state's own capital outlays have been large especially in those countries in which public ownership is significant, while the housing sector has been influenced strongly by government policy. There has been a wide range of measures to encourage investment by private enterprise including loans and grants, subsidies and various types of tax incentives. In addition, most countries have created schemes for mobilizing savings, especially those of the lower-income groups.

The most readily identifiable attempt to influence seriously the course of investment over the long term has been made by France. Perhaps more than any other country France has been concerned with the question of long-term growth and investment to the neglect at times of short-term disturbances in the economic system. Since 1946 the authorities have regularly instituted a series of major investment plans which, among other things, defined targets for private and public investment and for housing. The state has not only been an important investor in its own right but it has also done much to foster private investment by way of loans, subsidies and guarantees. The investment programme needs to be seen within the wider context of the planning mechanism which has cemented relationships within the mixed economy by involving the active participation of the main corporate interests in the economy – business, trade unions and government departments. Planning in fact has become a way of life in France and it has given valuable guidance and direction to an economy that had previously suffered from years of stagnation. The active investment strategy has provided business with the much-needed assurance of the long-term future. Judged by the record the experiment paid off; France has enjoyed rapid growth and a fairly high investment ratio (especially in manufacturing) even if these were achieved at the expense of price and monetary stability.

While most other countries have provided various incentives for investment few have had the same overriding long-term aims in view as the French. Indeed, many of the measures, though ostensibly designed to stimulate private investment, tended to fall foul of short-term stabilization policies. Thus Britain in the 1950s and early 1960s provided several investment incentives, including investment allowances, investment grants and changes in tax rates, but their impact was mixed and often slow to materialize, partly no doubt because there were frequent switches in policy which often counteracted their beneficial effect. Monetary policy was also used for the same purpose from time to time though its influence on investment tended to be weak and indirect and certainly less than in some continental countries, for instance Germany, where institutional (bank and government) financing was more important. Moreover, until 1958 Britain still operated a negative control over investment through the Capital Issues Committee. In Germany direct state investment has been relatively less important than in Britain but the government has made loans to private industries operating in key areas and fiscal policy has been used for purposes of encouraging a high level of investment. Monetary policy, on the other hand, has been employed mainly for countercyclical purposes but it has sometimes had a considerable impact on investment because of the wide range of monetary weapons used, the illiquidity of German business after the currency reform of 1948 and the important part played by the banks in the supply of long-term capital.

Both Sweden and the Netherlands have employed a variety of fiscal devices to encourage investment and budgetary policies have been formulated with a view to satisfying savings needs, especially of the public sector which is quite large. Here again, however, the devices seem to have been used more for short-term stabilization purposes than as a long-term stimulus to investment. The Swedes, for example, employed an investment reserves fund scheme by which taxes levied on investment in boom periods were released when the economy was moving into recession.

The measures used to stimulate investment in west European countries have been very different and it is difficult to assess their impact precisely. One of the main problems is the difficulty of distinguishing between long-term incentives and short-term stabilization measures, though it seems that much of the policy action was designed to achieve the latter rather than the former. Certainly public investment was at a much higher level than pre-war and in some cases loans and tax incentives played an important part in boosting investment in certain sectors, and probably the general level of investment as well. In the Netherlands, for example, investment was increased by tax rules favouring the use of retained business earnings for reinvestment and allowing unrestricted compensation for initial losses. But it is difficult to believe that policy measures were instrumental in securing the high investment ratios recorded in the post-war period, except possibly in the case of France. Throughout the period these ratios have remained fairly stable, and if anything they increased slightly in the 1960s when deliberate investment stimulation became less pronounced. One might also at this point take the contrast between Italy and the UK as a reflection of the weakness of the impact of policies on investment. Italy achieved a high rate of growth and a relatively high investment ratio despite a fiscal policy which was basically unfriendly towards growth and investment. In the case of the UK, however, investment incentives, especially in the 1950s, were high by international standards, yet her investment ratio and rate of growth were very low in comparison with those of other major countries. That investment ratios were high generally during this period can be attributed to the basically favourable economic climate rather than to active stimulation on the part of governments.

Finally we turn to the general question of economic stability; it is in this area that governments have been most active, that is, in short-term demand management rather than in the longer-term field of raising supply potential. One of the central issues in economic policy since the war has been that of demand management, the aim being to secure a reasonable degree of economic stability within the context of the desired objectives. The dilemma facing governments was that they were committed, in a greater or lesser degree, to achieving a series of basically incompatible objectives, namely growth, full employment, price stability and external equilibrium, and possibly greater social equality. Thus it was found in practice that full employment could only be achieved at the cost of creeping inflation, or conversely price stability was only possible with a degree of unemployment that was politically unacceptable. Alternatively, in some cases rapid growth proved incompatible with balance of payments equilibrium. Some countries of course opted for one or two objectives, notably Germany with her concentration on monetary stability and external equilibrium, and in so doing managed to achieve a fair degree of success on all fronts. Nevertheless, even these countries had from time to time to face an alternate tightening and slackening of pressure on resources and as a consequence were forced to take action to stabilize the level of activity. In practice, therefore, it became a question of trading one objective off against another – price stability versus employment, growth versus the balance of payments – in order to maintain a reasonable degree of overall stability in the level of economic activity.

The task of economic stabilization has involved the use of a wide range of fiscal and monetary instruments, and sometimes more direct controls, in order to influence both consumption and investment. As far as fiscal policy is concerned the general practice, especially in continental Europe, has been to use budgetary policy selectively to effect particular types of demand rather than to rely on budgetary surpluses or deficits as a macro regulator. Selective measures have therefore been used to influence the level of activity in the private sector though at times governments have also varied their own spending programmes. The fiscal instruments used have been varied and include investment allowances, subsidies, variations in tax rates on distributed and undistributed profits, changes in consumer taxes, tax rebates for exports etc. As already noted, some countries placed greater emphasis on monetary policy. This has proved to be an easier and more flexible instrument especially in those countries where the fiscal process does not make it easy to achieve rapid changes in the policy mix. The range of monetary instruments has been wide including variations in discount rates, open market operations, selective credit controls, reserve ratios, the imposition of ceilings on advances and rediscounts of commercial banks and moral suasion. The first two have been the most popular though not in every country. Sweden had little faith in the efficacy of discount rates, while the absence of an adequate and efficient bond market in Italy meant that that country made relatively little use of open market operations. A few countries have also at times limited the borrowing of local authorities and restricted the flow of capital issues. Special measures to control the movement of short-term capital have been fairly widespread. From the middle of the 1960s onwards nearly all countries began to pay greater attention to the question of the aggregate money supply as opposed to the question of liquidity and credit facilities where the task of control became increasingly complex as a result of the growth of non-bank financial institutions.

Given the fact that fluctuations in economic activity have been very much less pronounced in the post-war years compared with previous experience one might argue that government policies have had a beneficial impact. The much larger share of government purchases of goods and services and public investment could have led to greater stability of incomes and resistance of GNP to fluctuations in private investment, while the enlarged importance of taxes and transfer payments promoted greater income stability via the stabilization of consumer incomes. This is in accordance with the hypothesis of policy-induced stability expounded by Lundberg. On the other hand, Maddison has suggested an alternative interpretation: that economic systems have become basically more stable than previously as a result of endogenous influences but that policy factors have caused the minor oscillations around the trend. These two views are not necessarily incompatible, however. It could be that the post-war cycle has been modified by the greater impact of government operations within the economy which have ensured that fluctuations occurred at a higher level of output and employment than was previously the case, but that at the same time policy factors were the cause of fluctuations within a limited range of deviations.

Evidence suggests that on balance governments have not been very adept at what has been termed 'fine-tuning' their economies. Quite frequently policy action has been both badly timed and of the wrong order of magnitude so that it turned out to be destabilizing. The classic example is that of Britain where periodic balance of payments crises in 1947, 1949, 1951, 1955, 1957, 1960–1, 1964–5 and 1967–8, which were partly caused by allowing the economy to overheat in the first place, forced the authorities to adopt restrictive policies. But the timing of the policy action was usually mismanaged and quite often the authorities exerted too much pressure in both the upswing and the recessionary phases of the cycle. For the most part therefore policies tended to have a destabilizing effect in both the 1950s and the 1960s. The situation was not helped by the fact that the authorities lacked effective instruments with which to act directly on the balance of payments and hence they were forced to aim at a level of economic activity compatible with balance of payments equilibrium. Denmark faced a rather similar situation until the late 1950s with frequent exchange difficulties giving rise to restrictive policies which in turn damped down the growth of the economy. On the other hand, France, who suffered from similar problems in the 1950s, did not resort to the restriction of internal demand in the way Britain and Denmark did but used import controls and devaluation to deal with the external problem. Between 1949 and 1958 France devalued her currency no less than seven times. Consequently French economic policy did not act as a serious brake on the domestic economy.

Countries without serious balance of payments problems have not necessarily had a better record with their stabilization policies. In Sweden the main concern has been with demand pressures and inflationary developments. Generally speaking the government has had greater difficulty in preventing expansions from developing into inflationary boom conditions than in counteracting recessionary tendencies. Thus the strong expansions that got under way in 1954, 1959 and 1963 were badly controlled with the result that rather drastic action had to be taken which caused disruption and jerkiness in the process of expansion. Despite some degree of success with the more even phasing of investment through the investment reserves fund scheme, budget-ary policy was badly co-ordinated with the cycle. In years of rapid expansion there was no significant tendency for rising surpluses or reduced deficits in the total budget, and in some cases, for example the mid-1950s, large budgetary deficits created surplus liquidity that had to be mopped up by credit restric-tions. Countercyclical measures to deal with recessionary phases were rather more successful though in part these may have been favoured by the inherent strength of the Swedish economy and the lack of a serious balance of payments constraint. Not that the Dutch, with the aid of their sophisticated econometric forecasting model, have been any more successful in stabilization policy. The model is used partly for the purpose of inferring short-term disturbances in the economy but unfortunately it has not provided a very reliable guide for policy decisions. Tensions within the Dutch economy were revealed by the model only when there were already clear indications of disequilibrium by which time it was too late for the authorities to take the appropriate policy action.

The German record has also been somewhat mixed. The authorities relied heavily on monetary policy to curb expansionary and inflationary tendencies in the later stages of the upswing, as for example in 1956 and 1965-6, since budgetary policy was not actively used for countercyclical purposes. On the whole monetary restriction was fairly effective in damping boom conditions though usually it went too far, thereby aggravating the recessionary down-turn. But the subsequent revivals owed little to policy stimulus; they were initiated primarily by an upsurge in the demand for exports. In the more severe recession of 1967 the government for the first time adopted an expansionary fiscal policy to back up its monetary measures. The slowness of the economy to respond to the measures prompted the authorities to contemplate an incursion into medium-term growth planning.

Italy's experience in demand management in the 1950s and 1960s was not dissimilar to that of other countries. Action was usually hesitant and belated with the measures being taken in an *ad hoc* manner in response to predictions of economic events which often reflected past rather than current trends. As with other countries relying primarily on monetary weapons, these tended to invoke a strong response in periods of restraint but a weak and slow response in times of recessions. The increasing inadequacy of monetary control, in the 1963-4 recession in particular, forced the authorities to turn increasingly to fiscal policy, though the record of achievement on this score in the later 1960s was not very promising. The timing of reversals in policy was such that their impact came when the opposite influence would have been more appropriate.

The mixed success of governments in dealing with short-term fluctuations in economic activity is not altogether surprising. Though state control over national resources is large and the automatic stabilizing element within the fiscal process may be quite significant, nevertheless the budgetary operations of governments have often been destabilizing. Even though not all countries have used fiscal spending deliberately as a countercyclical device, many items of budgetary expenditure have been quite volatile and they have frequently moved in a destabilizing manner. This is particularly true of defence expenditure and investment which have fluctuated sharply and often in the wrong direction, most notably in 1950-1. Up to a point the same is also true of public spending on goods and services. It should of course be recognized that government spending, and especially investment expenditure on public utilities, is very difficult to regulate sharply in response to sudden changes in activity, and for this reason governments have often thrust the burden of adjustment onto the private sector under the curious assumption that it is easier for this sector to respond in the way required. The task of regulating state spending is greater of course in countries where financial control is fragmented, for example in Germany where local authorities and social security agencies account for a large part of public spending, and in countries such as Italy where administrative and constitutional difficulties pose a restraint, one reason no doubt why these countries have preferred monetary controls.

A further difficulty may have been that some governments had too few control levers for the tasks in hand. This is particularly relevant to countries with serious balance of payments problems such as Britain since it involved juggling with a series of objectives and trying to maintain a semblance of stability with an inadequate armoury of weapons. The main problem has been the want of an effective external regulator, and it is interesting to contrast this with France's readiness in the 1950s to use external controls to deal with the balance of payments. It is also important to note that in the 1960s both Italy and Germany became aware of the need to broaden the range of their policy weapons.

Perhaps the major problem, however, is the inherent time-lags involved in the process of formulating and applying stabilization policies. The initial perception of the need for policy action may be delayed because of the difficulty of obtaining the requisite statistics promptly. Another delay is incurred in the time taken to interpret the data once obtained since it is often difficult to distinguish, on the basis of weekly or monthly data, whether, for example, there is a basic underlying change in the trend of economic activity. Then when a policy change is eventually decided upon there can be a severe time-lag before it begins to take effect. All these lags can involve a considerable period of time which may result in policies which are the reverse of what are required because of an intervening change in circumstances, or alternatively it may lead to policy action which is either too severe or too moderate. It is difficult to know how this problem can be readily overcome although a solution is essential if short-term stabilization management is to be successful. Unfortunately the task has not been made any the easier in recent years by the welter of contradictory forecasts of short-term trends in economic activity.

CONCLUSION

Western Europe's successful economic performance in the post-war period contrasts sharply with that of the inter-war period. The marked acceleration in growth in the 1950s and 1960s can be attributed to a number of factors, including higher rates of input of capital and labour, rapid technical progress and a high level of demand. The greater degree of international economic co-operation and better macroeconomic policies have had a favourable impact on growth generally, and especially on demand though there were also strong autonomous forces stimulating the latter. Differences in growth rates among nations can only be partly explained by differing rates in the growth of factor inputs since much depended upon the way in which resources were utilized. It is important to note, however, that countries with high rates of factor input also tended to reap large productivity gains and they also did well in exports. It is unlikely that variations in growth rates can be attributed in any significant degree to differences in government policies, though again it should be stressed that countries which concentrated on one or two objectives were more successful than those that attempted to do too much. The record of governments with regard to stabilization has been rather mixed but the much greater stability of the post-war decades compared with pre-war can be set on the credit side.

6

THE SOCIALIST ECONOMIES OF EASTERN EUROPE, 1950–1970

Eastern Europe – comprising the eight socialist countries of Bulgaria, Czechoslovakia, East Germany (German Democratic Republic), Hungary, Poland, Romania, the Soviet Union and Yugoslavia – achieved an even better economic performance than the west in the 1950s and 1960s. But this was accomplished under a quite different political and economic institutional framework. Whereas in the west the mixed social market economy prevailed, in the eastern bloc the means of production were owned and operated by the state. After the war the eastern countries followed the Soviet model, though with some variations, of economic and political control, and by the early 1950s they had emerged as fully fledged socialist states, firmly embraced within the Soviet sphere of influence.

SOCIALISM IN MORE THAN ONE COUNTRY

For a second time war shattered the economic and social life of central and eastern Europe including the Soviet Union (see Chapter 4). The unification of a considerable part of central-east Europe within the Third Reich collapsed on the expiry of Hitler's regime and the result was another redefining of national frontiers together with the migration of millions of people. But the geographical carve-up of territory was less extensive and less damaging than that after the First World War, and the area did not return to the fragmented state which prevailed after 1918. Instead the countries drew inspiration from their larger eastern neighbour (the USSR) and very quickly established themselves as socialist states using the Soviet model as a benchmark. The main objectives were seen to be industrialization and the transformation of the social structure, tasks which could best be carried out by the abolition of private ownership of the means of production and the creation of a centrally administered and planned economic system.

Consequently, during the immediate post-war years when these countries were engaged in fostering economic recovery the state was steadily acquiring ownership of the means of production. The focus of attention initially was on the nationalization of industry. This proceeded more slowly than had been the case in the Soviet Union after the 1917 Revolution, partly because it took time to eliminate non-communist interests from power, but at least there was no policy reversal as in the USSR in the early 1920s. Nationalization occurred more rapidly in the former allied countries (Czechoslovakia, Poland and Yugoslavia) than in the ex-enemy territories (Bulgaria, Hungary and Romania). The former, having suffered German occupation, emerged from the war in a devastated condition and this left the way open for the state to extend its influence through the appropriation of ex-enemy property. By 1948, however, the socialization of the industrial sector was almost complete in all countries except East Germany (the Soviet zone of occupation). Here the transition was efffected rapidly when the German Democratic Republic was formally established in 1949. By this time considerable progress had been made in the takeover of other sectors of the economy, including banking and finance, the distributive trades and other services. Thus by the early 1950s nationalization had been extended to most of the main branches of economic activity apart from agriculture.

The agrarian sector posed a more difficult problem. Though early attempts were made to nationalize the land, especially in Bulgaria, for the most part this had not got very far by the end of the 1940s. In fact it was soon recognized that outright state ownership was impractical on account of the peasants' strong attachment to the soil. They regarded the land as rightfully theirs and expected one thing only: expropriation of the land and its redistribution among themselves. The obvious solution was therefore to allow the peasants to retain ownership but to organize their activities into collective enterprises, which in some ways would be a logical follow-up to the partial reforms of the inter-war years. Thus land, in varying amounts, was confiscated from the former owners without compensation and redistributed free among the peasantry, with the state retaining a part for its own purposes. This inevitably led to an extreme fragmentation of holdings and hence the next step was to group holdings into larger units. Accordingly the co-operative pooling of farm units became the dominant form, though the process of reorganization was slower and less brutally administered than had been the case in the Soviet Union before the war. It was accomplished steadily during the course of the 1950s and by the beginning of the following decade the bulk of agricultural production was under collectivized methods. State farms, on the other hand, accounted for only between 5 and 10 per cent of the land. In two countries, however, Poland and Yugoslavia, where opposition to agricultural socialism was very strong, very little progress was achieved. By the end of the 1960s only about 15 per cent of the land in these two countries was run by collectives or state farms. Yugoslavia, it should be noted, had since 1948 deviated from the Soviet camp and followed a nonconformist brand of socialism.

Taking the countries as a whole, therefore, little was left of private enterprise by the early 1960s except in some small-scale minor activities such as handicrafts and catering. Virtually all mining, agriculture, industry, transport, trading and financial activities were socially owned and operated. Some 95 per cent of the total national income of the eastern countries was derived from the socialized sector and an even higher proportion of industrial output and retail turnover. Only in agriculture was the socialized component less, though even here it accounted for 92 per cent of the land. The deviations from the average were quite small except in Poland and Yugoslavia where the income derived from the state sector was about 75 per cent, and this was largely on account of the fact that in these two countries agriculture was largely outwith the socialized sector of control.

Apart from state ownership and control the second major feature of the socialist countries was the emphasis on central planning. In contrast to the situation in most west European countries all decisions affecting the economic process were planned and determined centrally, the functions being carried out in each case by the State Planning Commission or Office. The methods of planning did vary of course from country to country and, as noted above, Yugoslavia deviated from the other socialist countries in her mode of operation at a very early stage. Moreover, significant changes in the planning mechanism, especially the radical economic reforms enacted in the 1960s, were introduced from time to time. Nevertheless, throughout the period to 1970 the major economic variables strategic to the process of economic development continued to be determined by the central planning authorities. These included the determination of the proportions between consumption and saving and between productive and non-productive investment and the allocation of investment among the major sectors and branches of the economy. In practice the planning process went much deeper than this since detailed targets were set for each sector and branch of activity in the central plans which were drawn up periodically, on the basis of which allocations of factor inputs were made. While this type of planning may not always have been efficient, it was possible to implement it in practice simply because of the absence of a significant private sector within the economy.

By virtue of their ideological commitments as well as recognition of their relative backwardness compared with the west, the socialist countries were conscious of the need to achieve a fast rate of development. To further this aim priorities were accorded to capital formation and industrialization and in the case of the latter emphasis was placed on the heavy producer goods industries, especially iron and steel, machinery, chemicals and electronics. Inevitably this meant some neglect of other sectors, notably agriculture, consumer goods industries and certain services, while it also entailed a slower rate of improvement in personal consumption and general welfare than in western countries. In addition, the strong emphasis placed on boosting growth by raising factor inputs, capital especially, particularly in the 1950s and early 1960s, probably led to a wasteful and inefficient use of resources. Later, however, greater attention was given to improving both the quality and productivity of factor inputs.

The planning process and the reforms of the 1960s will be discussed at greater length later in this chapter. First we must take a look at the socialist record in terms of growth and structural change.

GROWTH AND STRUCTURAL CHANGE

Although the growth of output was rapid in eastern Europe in the post-war period – and on balance somewhat better than in the west – it does not appear at first glance that centralized planning made that much difference to the performance of the socialist countries in comparison with their free market counterparts in the west. This could in part be explained by the fact that, though growth was a central objective, it entailed too great a priority being accorded to some sectors of the economy, for example heavy industry, while too little attention was paid to improving the efficiency with which resources were used. Furthermore, given the backward state of these countries and the slower recovery from the war compared with western Europe, one might have expected a fairly strong performance in subsequent years. In 1950 most western economies had well exceeded their pre-war output levels, whereas eastern Europe as a whole had only just about managed to regain the pre-war position. Apart from the Soviet Union only Czechoslovakia and Bulgaria had surpassed the pre-war benchmark in 1950, though Poland also showed significant advance as a result of boundary changes. But in East Germany, Hungary and Romania output fell short of the former level by amounts varying between 2 and 15 per cent. In other words, the differences in income levels between east and west in 1950 were even greater than they had been in 1938 so that socialist countries had a big task in hand if they were to approach the living standards of their capitalist neighbours.

Any discussion of growth performance is a somewhat hazardous exercise given the reliance one is forced to place on aggregate statistics which may contain substantial errors. Even in the west the methods of calculating income generated by the service sectors are far from perfect. In the case of the socialist countries the difficulties encountered are greater since national income accounting procedures differed substantially from those used in western countries. One of the main differences is that socialist countries only recorded material production in their national income accounts, thereby excluding most of the income generated by the service sectors, while they valued the product at realized sale prices (that is, inclusive of turnover taxes) as against the western practice of valuation 'at factor cost'. This means that official socialist income data are not directly comparable with those of western countries unless adjustments are made. Unfortunately scholars themselves disagree as to the adjustments required, though most would take the view that the official figures on material production tend to overstate the growth performance of the communist countries.

For our purposes we shall use the estimates of GDP compiled by the

United Nations which as far as possible conform to a standardized system of national accounting. Because of the obvious difficulties involved in adjusting the accounts the data are subject to margins of error so that too much reliance should not be placed on the precise accuracy of individual figures. Nevertheless, the magnitudes involved are broadly comparable with other estimates of income and output for these countries, and they do correspond to the data on western Europe used in the previous chapter.

Data on output, employment, productivity and population growth are given in Table 6.1 for the eight countries. In eastern Europe as a whole domestic output grew at 7 per cent per annum through the 1950s and 1960s, a rate considerably in excess of that in the west (4.6 per cent). However, population rose more rapidly in the east, especially in the Soviet Union and Poland, so that the differential in per capita output growth rates was narrower, 5.7 per cent per annum as against nearly 4 per cent in the west. The higher rates of population growth (the main exception being the German Democratic Republic) also led to a rather more rapid growth in the labour force, while the productivity record was also superior to that of the west.

In general there was not a very wide spread between countries in growth performance. It was fastest in the Soviet Union and in the least developed countries, Romania and Bulgaria, while Hungary's performance was relatively poor by the standards of the east. Between the two decades there was a tendency for rates of expansion to decline, especially in the more advanced economies of the USSR, Czechoslovakia and East Germany, whereas Hungary and the two least developed countries, Romania and Bulgaria, achieved some acceleration. In fact during the early 1960s there were signs of a slowing down in growth in most of the socialist countries except Romania, a feature which prompted the introduction of economic reforms in the planning and management of these economies (see below).

As one might expect given the ideological commitment of these countries, there was a substantial sectoral imbalance in rates of expansion. Priority was given to industry and especially the heavy sector including producer durables with the result that there was a more marked disparity than in the west between the rates of growth of different sectors of the economy. Thus in eastern Europe as a whole industrial output over the period 1950–70 rose by just under 10 per cent per annum with Bulgaria, Romania and the Soviet Union recording double figure increases. By contrast agriculture, with a low priority, expanded by only 3 per cent a year, with Czechoslovakia actually recording a slight fall in the output of this sector. Indeed, the agrarian sector generally proved to be a persistent weak spot in what otherwise was a splendid record of achievement, though in part the authorities had only themselves to blame through their neglect of this branch of activity. It was a decade or more before agricultural production in the east surpassed the pre-war levels, as against a 50 per cent rise in the west, while even by the early 1960s the more developed countries of East Germany and Czechoslovakia still fell short of the

173

Table 6.1 Eastern Europe: output, employment and labour productivity growth, 1950–69 (annual percentage compound rates of growth)

	Output (GDP at 1963 f.c.)			Employment			Output per person employed			Population, 1950–70
	1950/2–1967/9	1950/2–1958/60	1958/60–1967/9	1950/2–1967/9	1950/2–1958/60	1958/60–1967/9	1950/2–1967/9	1950/2–1958/60	1958/60–1967/9	
Bulgaria	6.9	6.4	7.4	0.5	0.7	0.4	6.4	5.7	7.0	0.8
Czechoslovakia	5.2	5.7	4.8	1.2	1.0	1.3	4.0	4.7	3.5	0.8
German Democratic Republic	5.7	7.1	4.5	0.4	0.7	0.1	5.3	6.4	4.4	-0.2
Hungary	4.8	4.1	5.5	1.0	1.2	0.7	3.8	2.9	4.8	0.8
Poland	6.1	6.2	6.0	1.8	1.7	1.9	4.2	4.4	4.0	1.4
Romania	7.2	6.3	8.0	0.9	1.4	0.4	6.2	4.8	7.6	1.1
Soviet Union	7.6	8.3	6.9	2.0	1.9	2.1	5.5	6.3	4.7	1.5
Yugoslavia	6.2	6.4	6.1	0.8	0.5	1.1	5.4	5.9	5.0	1.1
Eastern Europe	7.0	7.6	6.5	1.7	1.7	1.7	5.2	5.8	4.7	1.3

Source: United Nations (Economic Commission for Europe), *Economic Survey of Europe in 1971*, Part 1, *The European Economy from the 1950s to the 1970s*, New York, 1972, p. 6, Table 1.2

pre-war targets. The remaining sectors of the economy – transport, trade, construction and personal and government services – grew in aggregate slightly less rapidly than the economy as a whole, though there were considerable variations between different branches. Government services, for example, expanded faster than direct personal services and housing, and in some cases the output of personal services actually declined. Transport also expanded more rapidly than most of the other activities in this group.

These differences in performance reflected the order of priorities accorded to particular sectors. Industry, for example, received a large part – sometimes one-half or more – of the available investment resources, whereas agriculture was somewhat starved of capital. Moreover, within the broad sectors certain branches were singled out for top priority treatment. This was particularly the case with the industrial sector where the emphasis was placed on producer durables to the neglect of consumer goods. Consequently, industries such as chemicals, metals and machine-building grew twice as rapidly as food-processing and considerably faster than industry as a whole, while three branches, electric power, mechanical engineering and chemicals, accounted on average for about one-third of industrial production in the mid-1960s. The share of capital goods as a whole in gross industrial production had risen to over 60 per cent in most countries by the 1960s compared with 40 per cent or less in the immediate pre-war years (1938–9). The increasing orientation towards the heavy industrial sector is reflected in the capital formation figures. From a relatively low level at the beginning of the period investment ratios rose steadily to reach around 30 per cent by 1970 in most cases. It has also been noted that if socialist income figures were put on a comparable western basis the proportion of saving in national income would range between 20 and 40 per cent as against 10–25 per cent in capitalist economies at a similar stage of development (Wilczynski 1972).

Not surprisingly rapid growth brought about significant structural changes in the socialist economies, which were more pronounced and diverse than those in western Europe during the same period. The data in Table 6.2, showing the composition of national income and employment by main sectors of the economy, provide a broad idea of the main trends. The figures purport to be no more than approximate measures, but those for the composition of the national product have been adjusted to correspond more closely than the official estimates with those used in western countries. They are based on independent estimates of GNP at factor cost, and unlike the official figures they include the service sectors. Unfortunately comparable estimates for the Soviet Union are not available.

The most significant change was in the shares of industry and agriculture in income and employment. All countries experienced a shift from agriculture to industry and in some cases this was substantial, more particularly in the Balkan countries (Yugoslavia, Romania and Bulgaria) where industry eventually accounted for one-third or more of total income, while agriculture's share

Table 6.2 Composition of gross national product and structure of employment (in percentages of total)

		Industry and handicraft		Agriculture and forestry		Construction		Transport and communication		Trade		Other services	
		GNP	Employment	GNP	Employment	GNP	Employment	GNP	Employment	GNP	Employment	GNP	Employment
Bulgaria	1939	9.5		55.1		3.0		2.5		6.9		23.0	
	1950	18.1	7.9a	39.4	82.1	5.6	2.0	5.9	1.5	4.8	2.2	26.2	4.3
	1967	42.7	28.2	15.6	41.8	9.3	7.5	10.4	5.3	7.2	5.4	14.8	11.8
Czechoslovakia	1937	30.6		28.9		7.5		4.4		7.4		21.2	
	1950	34.8	27.9	23.9	36.9	6.7	6.0	7.3	4.9	7.1	8.0	20.2	16.3
	1967	45.0	38.0	12.4	19.1	7.7	8.0	12.8	6.2	7.7	8.0	14.5	20.7
East Germany	1950	36.8	39.7b	11.3	22.9	4.7	5.8	10.4	7.0	7.3	10.7	29.5	13.8
	1967	50.8	41.1	8.7	15.6	7.8	5.8	9.2	7.1	8.5	11.5	14.8	18.9
Hungary	1938	20.7		37.3		4.3		5.0		6.7		26.0	
	1950	25.3	19.7	29.7	49.8	6.2	5.3	9.5	4.2	6.2	4.8	23.1	16.2
	1967	36.0	33.5	20.6	30.0	7.1	6.3	13.2	6.3	8.1	7.2	15.0	16.6
Poland	1937	18.9		36.6		4.0		3.4		12.3		24.8	
	1950	22.0	20.7	36.9	53.5	4.5	5.1	5.7	4.7	6.2	6.0	24.7	10.0
	1967	36.0	27.3	24.2	39.9	6.2	6.9	8.7	6.1	7.1	5.9	17.8	14.0
Romania	1939		9.1		80.0						2.9		8.0c
	1950	19.2	12.0	31.3	74.3	4.1	2.2	6.5	2.2	7.4	2.5	31.5	6.8
	1967	32.9	20.0	22.0	53.8	11.1	7.1	8.8	4.0	5.4	4.2	19.8	10.9
Yugoslavia	1939	10.0		76.3							4.2		9.5c
	1950	22.7	9.3b	27.6	78.3	5.9	3.2	8.6	2.0	5.2	2.3	30.0	4.9
	1967	37.2	19.6	22.6	56.7	3.4	5.4	10.2	3.3	7.9	4.9	18.7	10.0
USSR	1950	22.0		46.0		4.0		7.0		5.2		21.0d	
	1967	29.0		30.0		7.0		8.0		7.9		26.0d	

Sources: T. P. Alton, 'Economic structure and growth in eastern Europe', in Joint Economic Committee, US Congress, Economic Developments in Countries of Eastern Europe, Washington, DC: US Government Printing Office, 1970, pp. 54, 58; J. C. Wilczynski, Socialist Economic Development and Reforms, London: Macmillan, 1972, p. 190

Notes: a1948.   b1952.   cIncludes construction and transport and communications.   dIncludes trade.

declined to one-quarter or less. The same trends are illustrated by the employment data though in the less developed countries some 40 per cent or more of total employment was still located in the agrarian sector. However, this was a substantial improvement on the pre-war period when between 75 and 80 per cent of all employment in Yugoslavia, Bulgaria and Romania was to be found in the primary sector. These countries were in fact fast losing their predominantly agrarian base against which they had struggled for so long. The trend away from agriculture was also significant in the more advanced economies of East Germany, Czechoslovakia and the Soviet Union, and in the case of the first two countries their economic structures were then very similar to the west European pattern. One should also note the marked difference between the income and employment shares in agriculture. The much higher share of the latter reflects the substantial difference in productivity levels between industry and agriculture. As for construction and trade there were no marked trends in these two sectors but transport and communications tended to increase in importance in terms of both income and employment except in the German Democratic Republic. The last category in the table, which includes government and personal and miscellaneous services, displayed contrary tendencies. The income share of this sector declined in all countries, reflecting no doubt the low priority accorded to the provision of personal and private services, but in most cases the employment share rose, suggesting a rather poor productivity performance in these activities.

In sum, therefore, though most of the socialist countries still had some way to go before the structural format of their economies resembled closely that of the advanced capitalist economies, it is quite clear that the rapid development of the post-war period had already brought about a considerable transformation of economies which not many years previously had been basically agrarian.

CONSUMPTION AND INCOME LEVELS

Despite rapid growth and structural change the consumer in eastern Europe did not benefit commensurately. Income levels moreover still remained far below those of the western world. It is true that the standard of living of most people in the socialist countries improved substantially between 1950 and 1970 and in some cases by appreciable amounts. In the German Democratic Republic, for example, real wages more than tripled in this period, while in Bulgaria, Yugoslavia and Romania they rose by over 150 per cent. By contrast the real income gains of the workers in Poland, Hungary and Czechoslovakia were considerably less. However, real wages did not keep pace with the growth in national income, while personal consumption was held back to an even greater extent through the emphasis on savings and investment and the limited range of choice as regards consumer products. Whereas in the west personal consumption advanced almost in step with national income, in the

the east this was far from being the case. On average the increase in per capita consumption in eastern countries was probably only about one-half that of the west, though there were considerable variations between countries. Czechoslovakia recorded one of the lowest increases, whereas in Bulgaria and Romania consumption advanced quite rapidly. Political factors in part determined the speed with which consumer welfare was satisfied. For example, the Hungarian revolt of 1956 led to a sharp increase in living standards which had been held back severely prior to that event. Conversely, the closing of the German border between east and west led to a restriction on the growth of consumption in East Germany since there was no longer any pressure to try and maintain the standards of the west. Similarly, fluctuations in Polish living standards were partly dependent on political circumstances.

The compression of personal consumption levels reflects of course the socialist order of priorities, particularly the emphasis on building up investment at the expense of consumption. In effect therefore it meant that the socialist consumer benefited far less than his western counterpart from rapid growth in economic activity. Moreover, for some countries it meant a widening gap in consumption levels compared with western countries where formerly there had been fairly close parity. For instance, before the war East German consumption levels were not far removed from those of the western half of the country, with Czechoslovakia not too far behind. By the middle of the 1960s per capita consumption in East Germany and Czechoslovakia was only about 60 per cent of the West German level, and they also trailed Austria by a large margin whereas there had been a clear lead before the war. Or again, whereas Hungary and Austria had similar levels of consumption before the war, in the mid-1960s there was a 40 per cent gap between the two, with Hungary's consumption not much above the Polish.

The bare statistics of consumption do not of course fully reflect consumer welfare in the socialist countries since there are a number of other relevant factors that need to be taken into account. These affect both sides of the balance sheet. Adverse features include the limited range of product choice especially in consumer durables, the frequent shortages of goods and in some cases the need for rationing or queuing. On the other hand, the population did benefit from a big increase in the supply of free or nearly free social services, probably at least equal to those in the west. Lower paid and less skilled workers gained through a narrowing of pay differentials, while the peasants, despite an initial squeeze on their incomes, were major beneficiaries as a result of the shortage of agricultural products. Agricultural wages generally were brought more closely in line with industrial earnings during the period. Furthermore, lower paid workers in general benefited substantially from the low prices of necessities, the letting of housing at nominal rents and the greater security of employment compared with before the war. By contrast, skilled and white-collar workers suffered a relative decline in their living standards, while middle-class professional and managerial groups fared worst of all.

If the consumer did not benefit fully from the impressive growth record of the socialist countries, at least some consolation may be derived from the fact that in this period the income gap between the eastern countries and the advanced countries of the west began to narrow noticeably for the first time. This of course was only to be expected given the higher rate of income growth in eastern Europe compared with most other countries except Japan. Even so the leeway to be made up still remained large by the end of the 1960s. While levels of national income per capita in the eastern countries taken together were nearly double those of all capitalist countries and the world in general, they fell far short of American and western European income levels. They ranged from about one-quarter to less than one-half those in the United States with the highest being recorded in Czechoslovakia, East Germany and the USSR and the lowest in Bulgaria, Romania and Yugoslavia.

GROWTH FACTORS

For much of the period, at least until the economic reforms of the 1960s, the countries of eastern Europe concentrated their attention on what has been termed *extensive growth*, that is, boosting output by raising the inputs of labour and capital. This probably involved some loss of efficiency and was one of the reasons for the move for economic reform in management, but it did mean that these countries achieved faster rates of input growth than was the case in western Europe. Employment, for example, grew at an annual rate of 1.7 per cent in the area as a whole compared with 0.6 per cent in the west (1950–70), and apart from East Germany all the socialist countries experienced fairly high rates of labour input. This can partly be explained by the more rapid rate of increase in population in the east (the major exception being the German Democratic Republic), but policy factors were also instrumental in securing the maximum use of the available labour reserves. Thus there was a determined effort to eliminate unemployment and increase the participation rates, especially among women who now provided a larger proportion of the labour force than in western Europe. At the same time the effective labour force was augmented by long hours of work, the shift of labour out of agriculture and the squeeze on the growth of the service sectors which are labour-intensive activities. Despite these measures labour shortages did occur from time to time owing to the high growth targets set, capital shortages or bottlenecks and the emphasis on output rather than efficiency.

Capital inputs also rose sharply in the post-war period. Though Marxist theory may hold that the only source of growth is labour the socialist authorities were never under any delusion as to the indirect contribution of capital growth in terms of raising labour productivity. Consequently a determined effort was made to raise investment ratios at the expense of consumption, and investment resources were directed to what the socialists regarded as the productive sector, namely industry and especially producer durables, to

Table 6.3 Eastern Europe: contribution of factor inputs and factor productivity to growth in output of major sectors

| | Output growth (annual rate) | | | Percentage contribution to output growth of | | | | | | | | | Output per unit of input | | |
| | | | | Employment | | | Capital | | | Total factor input | | | | | |
	A	B	C	A	B	C	A	B	C	A	B	C	A	B	C
Industry															
Bulgaria	13.3	15.5	11.5	31.6	33.4	29.2	30.9	25.9	36.5	62.5	59.3	65.7	37.5	40.7	34.3
Czechoslovakia	6.7	8.0	5.5	24.0	23.6	25.5	21.5	17.3	27.8	45.5	40.9	53.3	54.5	59.1	46.7
German Democratic Republic	7.5	10.1	5.2	5.6	9.0	-1.4	18.8	10.7	32.9	24.4	19.7	31.5	75.6	80.3	68.5
Hungary	7.9	7.1	8.7	33.7	47.3	24.1	30.7	35.9	26.9	64.4	83.2	51.0	35.6	16.8	49.0
Poland	8.9	9.4	8.3	29.1	29.8	29.5	17.2	9.9	25.3	46.3	39.7	54.8	53.7	60.3	45.2
Romania	12.6	11.9	13.2	23.9	22.3	25.5	22.9	21.2	24.3	46.8	43.5	49.8	53.2	56.5	50.2
Soviet Union	10.3	11.2	9.4	21.7	17.5	26.1	31.5	31.6	31.9	53.2	49.1	58.0	46.8	50.9	42.0
Eastern Europe	9.6	10.6	8.8	22.6	19.2	25.5	25.9	22.4	29.3	48.5	41.5	54.8	51.5	58.5	45.2
Agriculture															
Bulgaria	1.6	1.3	1.8	-131.3	-102.3	-151.7	129.4	117.7	143.3	-1.9	15.4	-8.4	101.9	84.6	108.4
Czechoslovakia	-0.4	-0.5	-0.3	-455.0	-294.0	-700.0	375.0	258.0	560.0	-80.0	-36.0	-140.0	-20.0	-64.0	40.0
German Democratic Republic	2.0	2.3	1.7	-84.0	-79.1	-94.7	73.5	41.7	112.9	-10.5	-37.4	18.2	110.5	137.4	81.8
Hungary	1.1	2.0	0.5	-120.9	-28.0	-392.0	120.0	66.0	270.0	-0.9	38.0	-122.0	100.9	62.0	222.0
Poland	1.9	2.2	1.6	0.0	-3.2	0.0	37.9	24.5	56.3	37.9	21.4	56.3	62.1	78.6	43.7
Romania	2.8	3.3	2.2	-27.5	8.5	-73.2	39.6	21.8	65.5	12.1	30.0	-7.7	87.9	69.7	107.7
Soviet Union	3.8	5.7	2.1	-16.6	-2.5	-53.3	58.4	42.1	98.5	41.8	39.6	45.2	58.1	60.4	54.8
Eastern Europe	3.1	4.4	1.9	-22.6	-4.8	-62.6	54.2	36.1	93.2	31.6	31.3	30.6	68.4	68.7	69.4

Construction and services

Bulgaria	6.8	6.4	7.2	45.3	48.1	42.8	20.3	17.8	22.1	65.6	65.9	64.9	34.4	34.1	35.1
	5.7	6.1	5.4	34.4	28.7	41.5	14.7	12.8	17.2	49.1	41.5	58.7	50.9	58.5	41.3
Czechoslovakia															
German Democratic Republic	4.5	5.1	4.0	24.9	26.1	22.8	11.3	6.5	16.5	36.2	32.5	39.3	63.8	67.5	60.7
Hungary	3.3	2.6	3.9	42.4	40.4	43.1	26.4	26.5	26.9	68.8	66.9	70.0	31.2	33.1	30.0
Poland	6.1	6.4	5.8	36.7	33.9	39.8	14.8	13.1	16.6	51.5	47.0	56.4	48.5	53.0	43.6
Romania	6.2	5.5	6.8	49.7	49.6	50.4	24.2	23.5	24.7	73.9	73.1	75.1	26.1	26.9	24.9
Soviet Union	6.9	7.5	6.3	43.6	39.2	50.0	36.1	34.4	38.1	79.7	73.6	88.1	20.3	26.4	11.9
Eastern Europe	6.4	6.8	6.0	42.7	38.1	47.8	25.3	22.1	29.0	68.0	60.2	76.8	32.0	39.8	23.2

Source: Calculations based on data in United Nations (*Economic Commission for Europe*) *Economic Survey of Europe in 1971*, Part 1, *The European Economy From the 1950s to the 1970s*, New York, 1972, p. 6, Table 1.2

Notes: A, 1950/2–1967/9; B, 1950/2–1958/60; C, 1958/60–1967/9.

the neglect of services and agriculture. Thus the fixed capital stock in industry in the eight socialist countries rose on average by 8.3 per cent per annum over the years 1950–70, with the Soviet Union and Bulgaria recording double-figure increases. In the service sector and agriculture on the other hand fixed capital stock rose by only just over 5 per cent a year. Yet despite the strong emphasis given to capital accumulation the stock of fixed assets in the economy as a whole rose at a slightly slower rate than national output, at 6.1 per cent per annum, though there were times, especially in the 1950s, when it expanded more rapidly than output. Taken in conjunction with employment growth of 1.7 per cent a year this suggests that of the combined growth rate in output of 7 per cent for the east, some 3 percentage points can be accounted for by the increase in factor inputs, while the remainder was a result of increases in output per unit of input. In other words, factor productivity accounted for some 57 per cent of the growth achieved, a share not very much less than that for west European countries.

However, in terms of major sectors and countries there were some marked differences in the relative contribution to growth of the various factors. Table 6.3 gives details of the growth attributable to employment, capital and productivity in percentage terms in the three main sectors of the economy for the several countries in question. The first thing to notice is the sharp contrast between the different sectors in terms of the sources of growth. In the case of industry total factor inputs and factor productivity were roughly equally responsible for the overall growth in output during the 1950s and 1960s. But in agriculture less than one-third of the growth in output was derived from increases in inputs, and in some cases, notably Czechoslovakia, Hungary and the German Democratic Republic this source produced a negative contribution. The reason in this case of course is the large negative contribution from employment as a result of the substantial shift of labour out of the sector. Though agricultural expansion was relatively modest in most countries, the loss of labour resources was often beneficial to productivity since it relieved the land of low or zero marginal productivity workers. The third sector – construction and services – also shows some interesting features. Here factor inputs were far more important than productivity as a growth source. This is perhaps not altogether surprising given the traditionally low productivity growth in many of the branches of this sector. What is noteworthy, however, is the high rates of employment and capital growth in the sector as a whole. In fact employment expanded more rapidly in services than in industry, which implies that the socialist authorities were not as successful as often imagined in containing the movement of resources into what they regarded as the non-productive areas of the economy.

Country differences within the major sectors were also significant. Bulgaria and Hungary, for example, derived about two-thirds of their industrial growth from factor increases, with labour and capital contributing roughly equal proportions, whereas in East Germany it was productivity change which accounted for most of the growth recorded. East Germany also had a similar experience in construction and services. For most other countries, however, the major contribution to growth in the latter sector was employment with productivity accounting for one-third or less in Bulgaria, Romania and the Soviet Union. The biggest inter-country variations occurred in agriculture and these were partly occasioned by the sharp and general contraction in labour inputs. As a result the contribution of total factor inputs to growth was negative in several cases and only Poland and the USSR secured a substantial positive contribution from resource expansion. Inevitably, therefore, productivity accounted for most of the output growth in agriculture, ranging from over 100 per cent in the case of Bulgaria, Hungary and East Germany to about one-half or more in the USSR, while in the case of Czechoslovakia it was a negative quantity, a reflection of the disastrous record of Czech agriculture.

Though for the economy at large the relative contributions to growth of factor inputs and productivity were not all that different from those of western industrial countries, it should be stressed that eastern countries did experience faster rates of expansion in the inputs of capital and labour. Moreover, if anything the input intensity of total output tended to increase between the 1950s and 1960s as a result of an acceleration in capital growth. In fact in all countries apart from the Soviet Union fixed capital per person employed increased in all three sectors during the period. This led to declining efficiency; with the major exception of Hungary, most countries experienced a deceleration in the growth of labour productivity and output per unit of input, a trend which is reflected in the declining contribution of factor productivity to overall growth (see Table 6.3). This adverse movement in productivity was mainly responsible for the fairly general decline in rates of output growth in several countries during the 1960s, a matter of some concern to the authorities and one which prompted an overhaul of the basis of economic management.

THE COSTS OF ECONOMIC GROWTH

In view of the extremely backward state of eastern Europe generally, both before the war under capitalist regimes and in the immediate transitional post-war years, the socialist countries of this area achieved little short of a miracle in the generation or so after 1945. Their record of achievement was certainly more impressive than anything in the west given the initial starting disparities. Formerly low-income, agrarian-based economies with limited growth potential had been transformed into relatively modern and dynamic structures with a solid industrial foundation. Rapid economic growth, high by virtually any standard, led to a more than fourfold increase in national income and a sevenfold increase in industrial output within the space of two decades. By 1970 the eight socialist countries accounted for some 30 per cent of world industrial output as against 18 per cent in the early 1950s.

The development strategy adopted to achieve this result inevitably entailed considerable costs. Whether such results could have been achieved without them or whether the benefits outweighed the costs are matters which have given rise to endless debate. It is important to recognize, however, that the growth strategy imposed several costs on the community.

In the first place, as noted earlier, the consumer did not reap the full benefits of the economic advance. The investment and growth strategy of the authorities dictated a restriction on the expansion of consumer spending and a low priority for consumer goods and service industries. This meant that not only did consumption rise by considerably less than national income but that the range and quality of goods and services available were much inferior to those in western countries. Shortages of goods were also common and this led to queuing, rationing and black-market activities. The market situation for many consumer products resembled that in western democracies in the immediate post-war years when rationing, shortages and low quality products were common features. On the other hand, one must bear in mind that under socialism the economic position of the masses has improved substantially, and that an alternative growth strategy, with a lower growth profile, might not have brought any greater benefits to the individual consumer.

Perhaps more serious is the way in which the socialist development strategy led to an extravagant use of resources. Labour, capital and natural resources were used in a profligate manner. In part this was the inevitable result of the original socialist conception that quantity not quality provided the key to faster growth. Thus under the extensive growth phase the emphasis was directed towards increasing the inputs of labour and capital, especially the latter, at the expense of productivity or the efficiency of input use. This may have led in some cases to the injection of labour inputs to the point of zero marginal productivity, while with increasing capital intensity per worker and rising capital–output ratios the marginal productivity of capital declined. These trends are reflected in the deceleration of factor productivity growth in the 1960s. Moreover, by western standards resources were inefficiently utilized in the socialist economies. Ernst (1966) reckoned that investment costs (that is, the ratio of gross fixed investment to increments in output) were higher than in western Europe by an average of 25 per cent for the total economy, and up to 40 per cent in industry. Productivity levels were also much lower than in the advanced capitalist economies. Wilczynski (1972) maintains that productivity in the USSR in the early 1960s was only 40 per cent of the American level despite the fact that the rate of capital accumulation was three times the US rate.

Apart from the overriding belief of the socialist authorities in the importance of the quantity of resources, the planning mechanism itself, at least until the reforms of the 1960s, tended to encourage the wasteful use of resources. The high and often increasing targets set by the plans provided an incentive for managers of plants and factories to secure as large an allocation of resource inputs as possible even though they sometimes remained under-utilized. The hoarding of labour by enterprises was a common occurrence, a result partly of the general excess demand for labour. Moreover, slack labour discipline, increasing absenteeism and high labour turnover led to poor utilization of the available manpower resources. Capital resources were also hoarded and used inefficiently. This partly stemmed from the fact that, until the mid-1960s, capital was allocated to enterprises without charge except for depreciation rates which were kept low. But it was also a product of the planning and management process. Investment planning was highly centralized and largely divorced from current production activities. The absence of a market mechanism and the inherent socialist antipathy to the concept of cost and scarcity as criteria for allocation purposes meant that investment resources were allocated in a somewhat arbitrary and bureaucratic manner, often without reference to real needs. Inevitably therefore this led to a misallocation of investment and often, as a consequence, the under-utilization of capital. For example, on grounds of prestige and propaganda the planners often made extravagant provisions for space per worker. The insistence on high rates of investment sometimes strained the capacity of the construction and machinery industries which in turn entailed long gestation periods and the accumulation of half-finished projects. New plant facilities often ran well below capacity because of poor planning of locations and the lack of complementary and back-up supplies and facilities. In the industrial sector, for example, a substantial part of the investment was earmarked for new plants in previously undeveloped sites. This involved an excessive amount of capital for infrastructure and complementary facilities which sometimes meant that there were insufficient resources for modernizing or maintaining plants in already established industrial areas. Finally, there is the possibility that the investment requirements of the least developed heavy sectors, chemicals, metallurgy and fuels, were accorded too great a priority to the neglect of light industry and industries producing materials, which often provided supplies of intermediate products for the heavy sector.

It is possibly inevitable that a centralized planning system divorced from the market will give rise to discontinuities and a sub-optimal allocation of resources. Furthermore, the socialist emphasis, at least in the earlier part of the period, on growth at any cost also had adverse implications for technological progress. Generally speaking, a growth policy based on raising the quantity of inputs was not conducive to rapid technical progress. In theory the relative backwardness of eastern Europe should have provided opportunities for more rapid technical transformation than in the west. And the possibilities for taking advantage of such opportunities were good given the high levels of investment and the scope this provided for technical change and scale economies. Yet eastern Europe remained far behind the west in the application of new technology and there is some evidence that the gap was increasing up to the 1960s. Wilczynski (1972) suggests that the Soviet lag in civilian technology behind the United States was greater in 1962 than in 1940, while Poland was some forty years or more behind Britain and nine behind France. The proportions of national income spent on science and technology were generally lower than in the west, while the growth derived from technological improvement was also lower.

In the lesser developed economies of eastern Europe one would expect of course that the level of technological development would be less strong than in the more mature countries. One should also bear in mind too that the socialist countries had limited access to the best western technology simply by virtue of their restricted trade and cultural contacts with the west. Yet the lag was also serious in the most industrialized of the eastern countries, namely Czechoslovakia and East Germany, which suggests that there may have been other factors at work. Certainly under the extensive phase of socialist growth technology was not accorded a very high priority, while poor planning and management of investment resources did little to offset the emphasis on quantity rather than quality. The high proportion of investment resources earmarked for buildings and construction – up to one-half of productive investment in the period before the reforms – as opposed to investment in plant and machinery which provide the source of new technology did not help matters either. It is true that the large share of investment devoted to construction can be partly explained by climatic conditions and the need for extensive infrastructure facilities in economies at an early stage of development. But there is evidence to suggest that a rather excessive amount of investment was devoted to buildings and other construction works to the detriment of alternative types of investment.

Finally, and on a rather different matter, one might expect that in centrally planned economies fluctuations in economic activity would be less evident than in the market-oriented economies of the west. It is true that employment remained at a continuously high level and that unemployment was rarely a serious problem except in one or two cases such as Yugoslavia. On the other hand, there were some large variations in rates of growth from year to year (as in the west absolute contractions in output were rare), though there were no clearly defined cycles akin to the policy-influenced ones in western Europe. But on balance the socialist economies appear to have been no more stable than those of the west. In a study of eight planned economies and eighteen free market ones for the period 1950–60, Staller (1964) found that the planned economies of the eastern communist bloc were subject to fluctuations in economic activity equal to or greater than those experienced by the market economies of the OECD. No consistent pattern was apparent between fluctuations and rates of growth though the lesser developed countries of Bulgaria, Yugoslavia and Romania did tend to be subject to greater instability. Thus central planning and control were not able to eliminate fluctuations in economic activity though, as with management policies in western countries, it has done something to modify their severity.

ECONOMIC REFORM

During the 1950s several attempts, notably in Yugoslavia, Hungary, Czechoslovakia and the German Democratic Republic, were made to reform the economic planning mechanism. However, many of the more ambitious reforms were blocked by the opposition from Stalinist hardliners. Except in Yugoslavia, where considerable progress was made in decentralizing the planning mechanism, the reforms only made fairly minor modifications to the economic systems of socialist countries. For the most part they remained, as in the original conception on the Soviet model, command economies with highly centralized planning and management. But during the 1960s a new wave of reforms achieved much greater success and led to a radical overhaul of the planning mechanism.

One of the main forces behind these reforms was the realization that fast rates of growth could not be obtained indefinitely under the original policy of extensive growth with its emphasis on boosting factor inputs. Indeed, by the early 1960s there were already signs, especially in the more advanced countries of East Germany and Czechoslovakia, that resources, particularly labour, were becoming scarce and that efforts would have to be made to tap *intensive* sources of growth (productivity) if high rates of growth were to be maintained. The gradual decline in rates of growth in the late 1950s and early 1960s (except in Romania) together with a deceleration in productivity performance gave additional weight to pressures for reform. In addition, the desultory performance of agriculture, the crises in which never ceased to surprise the socialist authorities despite the fact that the problems of this sector stemmed largely from resource neglect and the inhibiting effects of socialization, gave further impetus to the reform movement. At the same time several enlightened economists in the socialist countries pressed the need for reform on the grounds that the rigid and centralized planning system led to waste, inefficiency and the misallocation of resources. Czech economists in particular argued that the policy of extensive growth tended to retard technical progress and created disequilibrium between different sectors of the economy. Finally, it may be noted that political disturbances, for example in Hungary and Poland in the 1950s, and increasing consumer dissatisfaction also played a part in the growing pressure for reform.

Such factors eventually convinced the authorities of the basic deficiencies of the Soviet-type economic management which, with minor modifications, had been followed by the satellite countries of eastern Europe with the main exception of Yugoslavia. Basically there was a twofold problem: (1) the planning mechanism was not based sufficiently on rational economic considerations; and (2) management was not flexible enough to adapt to changing needs and circumstances. In short, the system lacked flexibility. If therefore these countries were to move to a more intensive phase of growth and thereby secure the gains of more efficient production, it was essential to decentralize the planning mechanism to make it more flexible, and at the same time adapt the structure of production to demand conditions by strengthening incentives through competitive forces and the market mechanism.

Thus the economic reforms, which began in the early 1960s and continued for much of the decade, were designed to loosen up the system and make it more flexible in the manner indicated above. The changes were first applied to industrial enterprise and then gradually extended to trade, transport and agriculture. The pace and timing of the reforms varied from country to country and there were considerable differences in detail. Nevertheless, it is possible to summarize some of the chief features of the reforms which were common to most of the eastern countries.

The first major change occurred in the planning and management of economic activity. Detailed planning directives were replaced by broad indicative plans with the number of compulsory targets being considerably reduced. The planned targets were now expressed partly in value terms rather than solely in physical ones as previously and a greater role was accorded to branch associations and enterprises in the planning progress. The plan was no longer simply a blueprint formulated and handed down by the central authorities without participation of the executive agents. At the same time individual enterprises, branch associations etc. were given a much greater degree of independence in the management process. Instead of the detailed system of commands and directives handed down by the central planners to the local units of industry, the central authorities concentrated their attention on overall co-ordination of economic resources, leaving the individual enterprise much greater latitude and initiative in managing its activities.

Former detailed directives, which were often unrelated to economic considerations, were replaced by a series of incentives of the market variety. Profits became the criterion of success and flexible price systems allowed prices to be determined to a much greater degree than hitherto by market conditions. It was now in the interests of enterprises to minimize costs of operation and maximize output for which there was a demand since profits were calculated on output sold, not that produced. Similar incentives were introduced for workers. Differentials in pay were increased to reflect variations in levels of skill and responsibility, while in some cases profit bonuses were paid.

The third main revision related to investment and financial facilities. The former practice of allocating capital to enterprises free of charge was drastically reduced and even abolished in some cases. Enterprises were encouraged to finance a larger share of investment out of their cash flows, while capital charges were introduced to secure an optimal allocation of investment resources. Depreciation charges were raised from their previously low levels, and the cost of credit facilities was varied according to the credit rating of the borrower.

The reforms were also accompanied by some relaxation on the activities of private enterprise. Greater freedom was allowed to private initiative in some areas including certain branches of retailing, catering, laundering, house construction and transport. The private sector of the economy still remained very small of course though its contribution to national income is somewhat greater than the official figures suggest simply because most of the private enterprise activity took place in services which are not included in the national income accounts of socialist countries. Private enterprise was also given a new lease of life in agriculture. As noted earlier, in some countries, Poland and Yugoslavia particularly, socialized agriculture had never been very strong and during the 1950s a process of decollectivization occurred. Elsewhere socialized agriculture (state farms and collectives) remained predominant but more scope was allowed to private initiative. In all countries the restriction on private plots was lifted and compulsory state deliveries were reduced or even abolished. Agriculture generally participated in the reforms. Agricultural prices, which for many years had been artificially depressed, were adjusted to reflect market conditions more closely, and even in some cases in line with world prices. As with industrial enterprises, detailed central control of agrarian activities was reduced and was replaced by market incentives and new accounting procedures.

Finally, control over foreign trade was eased. The state monopoly on trading activities was relaxed and greater freedom was allowed to individual trading enterprises to negotiate directly in foreign markets. These changes were accompanied by an attempt to improve trading connections, not only with the western world but also through greater economic co-operation within the eastern bloc as a whole. These aspects are dealt with more fully in the next section of this chapter.

These reforms represented a radical departure from the centralized and bureaucratic planning and management methods which prevailed throughout the 1950s and which were very similar in each country with the exception of Yugoslavia where the strict orthodox line had been abandoned at an early stage. The extent of reform varied from country to country; it was most radical in Hungary and Czechoslovakia but less extensive in the USSR, East Germany and Romania, though in some cases it was still not complete by the end of the decade. In place of the former rather identical versions of economic planning and control in each country there emerged almost as many variants as countries in the socialist bloc. However, while there were now no longer any examples of extreme centralized command economies neither were there any market economies of the western type. The changes wrought by the reforms might be seen to represent a synthesis of what is regarded as the best of socialism and capitalism. In effect an attempt was made to use the market mechanism to varying degrees in order to enhance the efficiency of economic operations, while leaving the long-term planning of the main macro goals and targets to the central authorities. In the process planning lost much of its rigidity and inflexibility, and the combination of broad central planning of the main aggregates combined with decentralized operations geared to the market

189

may have provided a better reflection of consumer needs, while at the same time ensuring a more efficient allocation of resources and improved efficiency.

At first sight the post-reform economies of eastern Europe may appear to have moved to a position similar to those of western Europe. In fact, however, though there had been a considerable convergence between the two there was no evidence that any of the socialist countries, even Yugoslavia, the most liberalized and westernized of them all, was approaching a capitalist state. Indeed, though the reforms brought into being many facets of the capitalist market system it should not be forgotten that the bulk of productive activity was still owned and operated by the state, while the central planning authorities retained a firm control over the broad objectives of policy and over the main aggregate variables in the economic system. The ultimate aim of these countries was still that of moving towards pure communism and the liberal phase was seen as a transitional interlude in some ways similar to that of the New Economic Policy in the USSR in the 1920s.

In fact debate on further reform continued, since ironically the reforms of the 1960s did not have the favourable impact anticipated by the authorities, at least not initially. Indeed, at first they often had a depressing effect on growth performance, though this could no doubt be partly explained by the rather lengthy process involved in completing the reforms and the attendant disruption which they caused, and partly it was a reflection of the degree of opposition to the new policies. The growth record generally improved in the later 1960s, though it was not as strong as in the 1950s, and possibly this could be attributed partly to the revisions in economic management. There is also some evidence to suggest that a slightly larger share of that growth was a result of improvements in factor productivity, a trend in keeping with the new intensive growth policy. The changes in planning and management procedure and the new financial incentives also appear to have provided greater stimulus to technological improvement. It is noticeable for example that the central plans of the early 1970s laid greater stress on the scientific and technical aspects of development. During the 1960s as a whole the indications point to a greater interest generally, both at central and local level, in technological and scientific progress and in most countries the number of expert personnel and amounts spent on science and technological research increased considerably. Thus the USSR could boast as many research workers as the United States by the end of the decade, while some countries, notably Czechoslovakia, East Germany and also the Soviet Union, were spending as much on scientific and technological research as a proportion of national income as some western countries. But again, in their effort to match the west there was an overriding obsession with quantity which tended to be at the expense of quality.

FOREIGN TRADE AND INTERNATIONAL CO-OPERATION

So far little has been said about the external aspects of socialist development. It is true that foreign trade and intercourse with other nations in a wider sense featured much less prominently than was the case with western Europe. Nevertheless, the external activities of the eastern countries increased considerably in the post-war period, especially after the middle of the 1950s, while there were some important developments in international co-operation among the socialist countries themselves.

In the immediate post-war years and in fact well into the 1950s conditions were not particularly favourable for the development of international relations, at least as far as the eastern countries were concerned. Political differences tended to isolate the eastern bloc from the western capitalist nations and thereby effectively limited access to foreign goods and western technology. What trade there was between east and west was conducted on a bilateral basis and even this was subject to the dictates of the political climate. Relations among the socialist countries were also far from cordial. The main problem here was the Soviet Union's exaction of payments from her satellites. Unlike western countries, which received substantial aid from the United States, the eastern bloc countries were forced to make large net payments to the USSR to cover reparations, dismantlings and occupation costs. Altogether the Soviet takings on these counts amounted to between $15 and $20 billion at post-war prices, some two-thirds of which were derived from East Germany. Hungary and Romania also suffered considerably from the appropriation of fixed assets and current production by the Soviet Union, while Poland delivered large quantities of coal to her neighbour at nominal prices. Most of the reparation payments were made in the period between the end of the war and the early 1950s and the burden declined over time. During the same period Soviet aid to eastern Europe (mainly in the form of credits) was fairly small – probably just over $1 billion.

The absence of close trading relationships also reflected the prevailing ideology regarding development. Foreign trade did not have a significant part to play in the extensive growth phase of socialist development. It was regarded at best as a necessary evil to be dispensed with as much as possible since each country was bent on achieving self-sufficiency. Hence imports were rigidly controlled while exports were looked upon as a sacrifice to pay for those imports, especially producer goods, which could not be supplied indigenously.

Thus for a decade or more after the war external forces were scarcely conducive to socialist growth. Indeed, for some countries they were positively harmful. Soviet exactions certainly retarded recovery in Hungary, Romania and East Germany, especially the latter. That the German Democratic Republic lagged seriously behind West Germany can be attributed, among other things, to the heavy payments she was forced to make to the USSR which amounted to some 10–15 per cent of her GNP. Investment was stifled and it was not until the later 1950s, when reparations ceased, that East Germany was able to undertake a substantial investment programme. The burden on Hungary and Romania was rather less but it still impeded their development in the early years.

More generally, the drive towards self-sufficiency meant that socialist countries could not readily draw upon the expertise and technology of the west. This was particularly unfortunate at the time since these developing countries were urgently in need of supplies of advanced machinery and technical expertise. It meant in effect that there were continued shortages of certain types of advanced equipment and as a result attempts were made to develop high-cost substitutes. Moreover, the rigidity of foreign trade management, under the state trading monopolies, did little to ease matters. Imports of key products rarely occurred in the quantity and quality desired, while slack delivery dates led to bottlenecks. The Soviet Union, the one country in a position to assist its lesser developed neighbours, was more interested at this stage in exploiting them for her own benefit. In addition, the virtual absence of any co-ordination among member countries in their planning severely limited the prospects of gain from inter-country specialization and inevitably led to the duplication of high-cost production facilities especially in the heavy industries. Spulber (1966) goes as far as to suggest that the duplication of similar facilities in each country was greater than under pre-war protectionist policies.

The apparent lack of co-operation among the socialist countries in this period is perhaps somewhat surprising given the fact that soon after the war a move was made in this direction. In 1949 the Council for Mutual Economic Assistance (CMEA or Comecon) was established for the purpose of achieving closer relations and more integrated development among the countries of the socialist camp. It seems to have achieved very little of substance in its early years, possibly because each country was trying, in slavish imitation of the earlier Soviet model, to become as self-sufficient as possible. But of greater importance at this particular time was the fact that relations were soured somewhat by the uncompromising Soviet policy on reparations and its hard-line attitude towards deviationists and political disturbances within the socialist bloc, for example Poland and Hungary.

During the latter half of the 1950s external relations generally, both within the eastern bloc and with the west, took a turn for the better. The first step was made towards obtaining greater unity within the socialist camp by the co-ordination of national plans through the CMEA, leading to the 1962 agreement on basic principles for the international socialist division of labour. It was recognized that future growth would depend increasingly on greater mutual co-operation and specialization in industry and technology in place of the autarchic policies hitherto pursued. Thus instead of launching their plans separately and independently of each other most countries began to initiate their plans simultaneously and for the first time attempted to co-ordinate them to some degree on the basis of international specialization. While the degree of co-ordination attained should not be exaggerated, the new policy did presuppose that foreign trade and exchange would come to play a greater role in subsequent development. The reforms in management and pricing systems in the 1960s, which strengthened the incentives for the efficient allocation of resources, also opened up greater opportunities for international trade. At the same time, the rigid control over trading activities was relaxed and bilateral trade agreements were operated in a more flexible manner. Furthermore, instead of subordinating foreign trade to the plan as was formerly the case, the plans were drawn up to take account of the requirements of foreign trade. Bilateral trade balancing among member countries was not abandoned completely but there was a noticeable increase in multilateralism, through credit and clearing arrangements, a process encouraged by the establishment of the Bank for International Economic Co-operation in 1964. The policy of closer integration within the eastern bloc continued under the aegis of the CMEA during the latter half of the 1960s and early 1970s.

Relations with the west also improved from the later 1950s onwards as the political climate became more favourable. At this stage most of the dealings remained on a bilateral basis but during the 1960s trade between east and west was increasingly liberalized and several long-term contracts were concluded. The process of relaxation was facilitated by the work of various international associations or organizations including the EEC and GATT, several of the eastern countries being members of the latter by the early 1970s. Even so, the socialist countries still retained restrictions on trade with western countries, especially on goods which eastern Europe could readily provide. Conversely, western countries have been forced from time to time to raise barriers against 'dumped goods' from eastern Europe.

Despite the impediments to intercourse in the early years the trade of the eastern bloc grew rapidly through the period up to 1970, though it began from a very low base. On average it increased by about 10 per cent per annum, a rate somewhat faster than the growth of national income, and slightly in excess of world trade. The share of world trade of the eight socialist countries increased steadily from 5 per cent in 1948 to about 10–11 per cent by the later 1960s, compared with around 6.5 per cent in 1938. Moreover, if anything the trade of these countries with non-socialist countries increased more rapidly than intra-eastern trade. The most active sector was trade in manufactured products, reflecting the increasing industrialization of these countries.

The rate of trade expansion was rapid both in per capita terms and in relation to national income. The share of trade in national income in some countries doubled between the early 1950s and the late 1960s. Moreover, imports more than kept pace with national income growth, which suggests that economic development was not seriously impeded by a restriction on imports though initially import ratios were well below the pre-war level. However, trade levels, in per capita or national income terms, were still low by western standards. Surprisingly, perhaps, the economic reforms and

193

liberalization of trade in the 1960s do not appear to have led to any marked acceleration in foreign trade growth. This in part may be explained by the fact that very high rates of expansion were recorded in the later 1950s following the low levels at the peak of the Cold War earlier in the decade.

7

WESTERN CAPITALISM IN THE 1970s

INTRODUCTION

The first half of the 1970s will probably come to be regarded as a watershed in the development of western capitalist economies. Effectively the period marked the end of the 'super-growth' phase of the post-war period which culminated in the somewhat feverish and speculative boom of the early 1970s. From which time, according to Samuel Brittan (*Financial Times*, 14 February 1980), 'everything seems to have gone sour and we have had slower growth, rising unemployment, faster inflation, creeping trade restrictions and all the symptoms of stagflation'. Indeed, compared with the relatively placid and successful decades of the 1950s and 1960s, that of the 1970s was an extremely turbulent period, reminiscent in some respects of the inter-war years, though parallels between the two periods can easily be pushed too far.

Europeans might be forgiven if they felt in the later 1960s or even in the early 1970s, as their American counterparts undoubtedly did in the later 1920s, that they had entered an era of perpetual prosperity. Certainly at that time there were signs, for example on the price front, that difficulties were accumulating, but few people probably suspected that such problems were more than temporary in nature, and few would have envisaged that the leading economies would soon be faced with a severe recession together with a host of other problems, many of which were quite unfamiliar to a post-war generation of young people who had experienced sustained and fairly stable real income growth, low unemployment and gently rising prices throughout their lifetime.

The recession following the boom of 1972–3 was in itself a shock, since for the first time in the post-war period output actually contracted quite sharply in most countries, though certainly not to the same extent as in the slump of 1929–32. The recessionary phases prior to this time had been both shorter and milder, involving for the most part a deceleration in the rate of growth rather than an absolute decline in economic activity. Moreover, the recession of 1974–5 was accompanied not only by rising unemployment on a scale not previously experienced since the inter-war years, but also by very strong inflationary pressures. The latter were exacerbated by resource problems, particularly in the energy sector, which became more or less a permanent feature of the whole decade, and these in turn led to severe balance of payments difficulties and exchange crises in a number of countries. Given the convergence of so many unfavourable factors it is perhaps not surprising that the strength of the subsequent recovery was somewhat less pronounced than that from other recessions of the post-war period, nor that policy-makers began to question the practicality of using traditional demand-management tools to stimulate economic activity. After a brief spurt in 1976, the growth in output remained weak and hesitant in the later 1970s, being constrained at times by inflation, resource bottlenecks, particularly in energy, and policy factors. The direction of government policy shifted away from the traditional priorities of full employment and growth towards the more urgent ones of controlling inflation, maintaining balance of payments stability and securing an adequate supply of resources. At the same time there was perhaps an ever increasing awareness that some of the problems of the 1970s, notably the continued pressure on energy resources, were of a more long-term nature, and that the real forces of growth were entering a phase of weakness as the technological opportunities of the post-war period became partly exhausted.

One of the main questions to be considered therefore is why things went so wrong for the market economies of the western world in the 1970s, and also why governments were able to do so little to restore the *status quo*. In turn this will entail a recapitulation of some of the factors which were responsible for the high and sustained growth experience of the period prior to the early 1970s. First, however, it is useful to gain some perspective from a brief review of the performance of the western economies during the decade in question.

GROWTH AND INSTABILITY IN THE 1970s

Although the major events of the 1970s are no doubt familiar, the main economic trends of the period are less well known. The data given in Tables 7.1 and 7.2 illustrate clearly that growth was far less vigorous in the 1970s than it was in the previous decade or for that matter in the 1950s. For all OECD countries the rate of growth of real gross domestic product fell from 5.0 per cent per annum in the 1960s to 3.5 per cent during the years 1970–8, while the corresponding figures for industrial production were 5.9 and 3.5 per cent respectively. All countries without exception experienced a marked deceleration in growth performance; in some cases the rates were one-half or less of those recorded in the 1960s, while at the lower extreme Switzerland barely managed to attain one-tenth of its earlier performance in industrial production. Another notable feature was the wider dispersion of growth rates among countries compared with previously; during the 1960s most countries, with the exception of the UK and Japan, had clustered around the 4–5 per cent range for GDP growth, whereas in the 1970s values varied from a low of 1.3 per cent

Table 7.1 Growth of real gross domestic product at market prices (annual percentage changes)

| | Average | | 1970 | 1971 | 1972 | 1973 | 1974 | 1975 | 1976 | 1977 | 1978 | 1979a |
	1960–9	1970–8										
Austria	4.8	4.2	7.8	5.3	6.4	5.8	4.1	-2.0	5.2	3.7	1.5	5.2
Belgium	4.9	3.9	6.3	4.1	5.8	6.5	4.7	-2.1	5.7	1.3	2.5	3.0
Denmark	5.1	2.7	2.6	2.4	5.4	5.2	-0.9	-0.4	7.0	1.9	1.0	2.5
West Germany	5.1	3.2	6.0	3.2	3.7	4.9	0.5	-2.1	5.6	2.8	3.5	4.2
Finland	5.4	3.5	8.3	2.4	7.0	6.5	4.3	0.9	0.3	0.4	1.4	7.2
France	5.8	4.1	5.7	5.4	5.9	5.4	3.2	0.2	4.9	2.8	3.3	3.0
Ireland	4.6	3.9	3.2	4.1	5.7	4.6	2.1	1.2	2.9	5.5	6.1	3.2
Italy	5.7	3.0	5.0	1.6	3.1	6.9	4.2	-3.5	5.7	1.7	2.6	4.0
Netherlands	5.4	3.7	6.7	4.3	3.4	5.7	3.5	-1.0	5.3	2.8	2.4	3.2
Norway	5.2	4.3	2.0	4.6	5.2	4.1	5.2	4.2	5.8	4.1	3.5	2.7
Sweden	4.4	1.8	5.3	-0.2	1.6	3.4	4.2	0.8	1.3	-2.7	2.8	4.0
Switzerland	4.6	1.3	6.4	4.1	3.2	3.0	1.5	-7.3	-1.4	2.4	0.2	0.2
UK	3.1	2.4	2.3	2.8	2.4	8.0	-1.5	-1.0	3.7	1.3	3.3	0.5
United States	4.1	2.9	-0.1	2.9	5.8	5.4	-1.3	-1.0	5.5	4.8	4.4	2.0
Japan	11.1	6.1	10.9	7.3	8.9	9.8	-1.0	2.4	6.0	5.4	5.6	6.0
Total OECDb	5.0	3.5	3.1	3.8	5.5	6.3	0.5	-0.4	5.2	3.7	3.9	3.2
OECD Europe	5.1	3.4	5.2	3.6	4.4	5.9	2.2	-1.0	4.6	2.3	3.0	3.0
EC	4.9	3.2	5.0	3.5	4.0	5.9	1.7	-1.4	5.1	2.3	3.1	3.0

Source: OECD, *Economic Outlook*, no. 26, December 1979

Notes: a Estimates.
b Total OECD includes above countries plus Canada, Greece, Iceland, Luxembourg, Portugal, Spain, Australia and New Zealand.

Table 7.2 Growth of industrial production (annual percentage changes)

	Average		1971	1972	1973	1974	1975	1976	1977	1978	1979a
	1960–70	1971–8									
Austria	5.7	3.6	6.0	7.5	5.3	5.0	−6.3	6.0	3.7	1.8	8.9
Belgium	5.1	2.5	3.0	5.8	6.4	3.4	−9.2	9.0	0.0	1.8	4.5
West Germany	5.8	2.2	2.0	3.9	6.6	−1.8	−5.4	7.0	2.8	2.7	4.4
Finland	7.4	3.3	2.0	11.8	7.0	4.9	−3.9	2.0	0.0	2.9	6.6
France	5.9	3.2	4.0	7.7	7.1	2.5	−8.1	9.0	0.9	2.7	1.3
Ireland	6.8	5.0	4.0	4.8	9.2	2.5	−6.6	9.0	8.2	9.3	n.a.
Italy	7.2	2.8	0.0	4.0	9.6	4.4	−9.2	12.0	0.0	1.8	6.1
Netherlands	7.2	3.2	6.0	4.7	6.3	5.9	−4.8	6.0	0.9	0.9	1.9
Norway	5.2	5.1	4.0	4.8	5.5	4.3	6.7	6.0	−0.9	10.5	n.a.
Sweden	6.2	2.0	1.0	3.0	6.7	5.4	−1.7	−2.0	−6.1	0.0	6.5
Switzerland	5.2	0.5	2.0	2.0	5.8	0.9	−12.6	1.0	5.0	0.0	0.5
UK	2.8	1.7	0.0	2.0	8.8	−1.8	−6.4	3.0	4.9	2.8	2.7
United States	4.9	3.6	0.0	8.0	9.3	1.7	−9.2	11.0	2.8	5.5	4.0
Japan	13.1	4.1	3.0	6.8	15.5	−3.9	−9.8	11.0	4.5	6.0	6.5
Total OECDb	5.9	3.5	1.1	6.9	9.3	1.7	−8.3	9.0	3.7	4.4	4.2
OECD Europe	5.6	2.7	2.0	4.9	8.4	1.7	−6.8	7.0	2.8	1.8	3.6
EEC	5.2	2.5	2.0	3.9	8.5	0.0	−6.1	8.0	1.9	1.8	3.6

Sources: OECD, Industrial Production: Historical Statistics 1960–75 and Main Economic Indicators

Notes: a Estimates based on nine months only.
b Total OECD includes above countries plus Canada, Denmark, Greece, Iceland, Luxembourg, Portugal, Spain, Australia and New Zealand.

per annum in the case of Switzerland to 4.3 per cent for Norway and 6.1 per cent in Japan.

Not only was economic growth slower generally than in the two decades prior to the 1970s – though, it should be added, still very respectable compared with the longer term – but it was also far less stable than previously. Rates of activity varied quite significantly from year to year and in 1975 there was a sharp absolute contraction in most countries, an unusual feature by post-war standards since recessionary phases had normally been characterized by decelerations in growth rates rather than by absolute contractions.

The recession of 1974–5 can be regarded in part as an automatic reaction to the vigorous boom of 1972–3 when activity in the major industrial countries synchronized rather more closely than in previous post-war upswings. Rates of expansion were also running well above trend, especially in 1973; in that year OECD industrial production expanded at a rate which was over 50 per cent higher than the average for the 1960s. Such a high rate of growth was clearly not sustainable for long since capacity constraints soon began to bite, in some cases in the form of balance of payments disequilibrium. But at the same time several unfavourable factors, notably accelerating inflation and the dramatic oil price rise late on in 1973, did much to erode business confidence. By 1974 expansion had almost ground to a halt in OECD countries taken as a whole, though performance varied a great deal from country to country; the largest economies, namely Japan, the United States, Britain and Germany, fared the worst, whereas some of the smaller countries, Austria, Belgium, Finland, Italy, Norway and Sweden, maintained a very creditable performance. The following year was very much worse. Many countries experienced an absolute decline in GDP while all countries apart from Norway recorded sharp falls in industrial production. In Europe as a whole the fall in industrial production averaged nearly 7 per cent, while outside Europe (Japan and the United States), it was over 9 per cent. Such steep declines in production had never before been experienced in the post-war period and they were more reminiscent, though by no means as severe, of those recorded in the early 1930s (Capie and Collins 1977). The first year of recovery, 1976, witnessed equally steep rises in activity, with industrial production in particular growing well above trend at a rate very similar to that of the boom year of 1973. Thereafter growth wilted again below the long-term trend and by the end of the decade the rate of expansion of total output was only marginally higher than in the slack years of the early 1970s, and trending downwards.

Thus throughout most of the 1970s, but more especially in the latter half of the decade, the growth in output of most European countries, as well as countries outside Europe, fell well below full capacity potential. Not surprisingly this shortfall was reflected in rising unemployment levels and under-utilized capacity. In the later 1970s the average unemployment rate for the OECD area was roughly twice the level of the period 1962–73 (over 5 per cent compared with 2.8 per cent), while current output was running at between

5 and 15 per cent below full capacity. At the same time export and pro-ductivity growth slackened noticeably, though the downward shift was by no means as marked as in the case of output. According to data assembled by Maddison, GDP per man-hour grew at the rate of 3.8 per cent a year between 1970 and 1977, compared with 4.4 per cent over the period 1950–70, while the respective figures for export volume were 6 per cent and 8.6 per cent, being the average for sixteen countries (Maddison 1979).

Probably the most notable feature of the 1970s, and one which was largely responsible for policy constraints, was the pervasive nature of inflation. Though experience varied a great deal between countries, it can be readily seen from Table 7.3 that the rate of increase in consumer prices during the decade was well over twice that of the 1960s. Inflationary pressures had been building up in the later 1960s and early 1970s but the big upsurge came in the middle of the 1970s when most countries, apart from Germany and Switzer-land, recorded double-digit inflation. After 1975 there was a noticeable moderation in inflationary pressures in most countries, though by the end of the decade the rate of inflation was again creeping upwards and was averaging some three times that of the previous decade.

In fact it is the high and sustained level of inflation of this period which really makes the 1970s unique, the nearest parallel being the European experi-ence of the early 1920s. In longer-term perspective the growth of western economies during the 1970s was quite respectable and it is only against the background of the sustained boom of the 1950s and 1960s that it appears mediocre. By comparison, moreover, with the desultory performance of the inter-war years the record of the 1970s, in terms of both output growth and employment, is infinitely better. One might therefore hypothesize that the growth rates of the 1950s and 1960s were highly abnormal by long-term historical standards, and that the downward shift in the 1970s represents a move back towards the more sustainable long-term rates. This assumption raises important implications not only about the determinants of growth in the 1970s and beyond, but also from the point of view of policy, since any attempt to stimulate activity in an effort to restore the high growth levels of earlier decades would merely increase inflationary pressures.

However, before dealing with the policy dilemmas facing governments, we need to look more closely at the factors responsible for the weaker economic performance of the 1970s. It would be all too easy to see the difficulties of the period as a response to cyclical disturbances and/or specific shocks, for example the energy crunch and inflation, and the dampening effects these had on growth and policy formation. On the other hand, it may well be argued that the shift to lower rates of growth in the 1970s was partly an inevitable consequence of long-term forces involving some reversal of the growth-promoting factors of previous decades. In effect this would imply some weakening of the real forces of growth in the 1970s which in turn were aggravated by specific problems and policy factors.

Table 7.3 Consumer prices (annual percentage changes, not seasonally adjusted)

	Average											
	1961–70	1970–8	1970	1971	1972	1973	1974	1975	1976	1977	1978	1979[a]
Austria	3.6	6.4	4.4	4.7	6.3	7.6	9.5	8.4	7.3	5.5	3.6	3.7
Belgium	3.0	7.4	3.9	4.3	5.5	7.0	12.7	12.8	9.2	7.1	4.5	4.6
Denmark	5.9	9.2	5.8	5.8	6.6	9.3	15.3	9.6	9.0	11.1	10.0	12.8
West Germany	2.7	5.0	3.4	5.3	5.5	6.9	7.0	6.0	4.5	3.9	2.6	5.3
Finland	5.0	10.7	2.8	6.5	7.1	10.7	16.9	17.9	14.4	12.2	7.8	7.7
France	4.0	8.6	4.8	5.5	6.2	7.3	13.7	11.8	9.6	9.4	9.1	11.0
Ireland	4.8	12.7	8.2	8.9	8.7	11.4	17.0	20.9	18.0	13.6	7.6	13.6
Italy	3.9	12.0	5.0	4.8	5.7	10.8	19.1	17.0	16.8	17.0	12.1	15.8
Netherlands	4.1	7.3	3.6	7.5	7.8	8.0	9.6	10.2	8.8	6.4	4.1	3.9
Norway	4.5	8.8	10.6	6.2	7.2	7.5	9.4	11.7	9.1	9.1	8.1	3.5
Sweden	4.0	8.7	7.0	7.4	6.0	6.7	9.9	9.8	10.3	11.4	10.0	7.9
Switzerland	3.3	5.7	3.6	6.6	6.7	8.7	9.8	6.7	1.7	1.3	1.1	4.9
UK	4.1	12.6	6.4	9.4	7.1	9.2	16.0	24.2	16.5	15.9	8.3	16.5
United States	2.8	6.6	5.9	4.3	3.3	6.2	11.0	9.1	5.8	6.5	7.7	12.1
Japan	5.8	9.7	7.7	6.1	4.5	11.7	24.5	11.8	9.3	8.1	3.8	3.1
Total OECD[b]	3.4	8.2	5.6	5.3	4.8	7.9	13.4	11.4	8.6	8.7	7.9	10.6
OECD Europe	3.8	9.8[c]										
EEC	3.7	9.3[c]										

Source: OECD, Economic Outlook, no. 26, December 1979

Notes: [a] Twelve months to September 1979.
[b] Total OECD includes above countries plus Canada, Greece, Iceland, Luxembourg, Portugal, Spain, Turkey, Australia and New Zealand.
[c] 1971–6.

It is obvious of course that the several factors mentioned above are not mutually exclusive. However, since the problems of the 1970s have been readily identified in terms of the specific shocks imparted by energy and inflation, it is essential to begin by examining the implications of these two factors before analysing the extent to which the secular growth forces of the post-war boom years have waned in strength over the course of time.

ENERGY AND COMMODITY PROBLEMS

Energy, and oil in particular, is the key element in this sector, and the reader should need no reminding of why this is so. Raw materials and food also posed intermittent problems during the 1970s but on a far lesser scale than energy.

An important factor in the remarkable rise in output and real incomes during the 1950s and 1960s must undoubtedly be the favourable terms of trade experienced by industrial countries. After the sharp rise in commodity prices during the Korean War boom (1950–1) the costs of energy, food and raw materials declined and remained low relative to those of industrial products until the early 1970s. Even by the later 1960s, when upward pressure on commodity prices was becoming apparent, the price of food, raw materials and energy was on average lower than in the early 1950s, whereas manufactured prices had risen slightly during this period. This resulted in a significant gain in the terms of trade for industrial Europe to the consequent benefit of real incomes and growth.

An important aspect of the favourable position with regard to the supply and price of energy and raw materials was that it led to the rapid development of energy-intensive sectors, not only in terms of the most obvious mass penetration of cars, consumer durables and chemical products throughout the income ranges, but also in terms of the intensive use of petroleum as a fuel and source of heat in industry and for domestic purposes. This response was scarcely surprising given the relative cheapness and abundance of energy supplies but it did render the industrial world extremely vulnerable to any sudden distortion in supplies and prices such as that which occurred in 1972–4. Primary product prices rose on average by 160 per cent during this period and then oscillated at the enhanced level over the next few years. Fuel prices, on the other hand, under the impact of the new OPEC crude prices announced late in 1973, rose by 300 per cent or more. Subsequently the pressure on oil prices abated somewhat until the later 1970s when there was a renewed upward thrust, though less severe than that of the earlier period.

A sudden uplift in commodity prices of this order of magnitude could scarcely fail to have an adverse impact on the major industrial countries, more especially since they had been accustomed for some time to gently falling or fairly stable commodity prices. Manufactured goods prices reacted much more slowly to the price upsurge and hence the terms of trade of the advanced industrial countries deteriorated sharply. Britain, for example, suffered a

27 per cent deterioration in her terms of trade within a period of two years, and even by 1978 a unit of imports still absorbed 17 per cent more exports than in 1972 (Rostow 1979).

The global price explosion of the early 1970s was partly engendered by the strong and heavily synchronized boom in industrial countries at this time and by supply deficiencies in some commodities, and it must be remembered that it took place against the background of accumulating inflationary pressures extending back to the later 1960s (see below). But it was the oil price shock of 1973 and the continuing tenuous nature of the sources of supply which were to wreak the most havoc on the industrial west. While the oil price increase was not the proximate cause of the initial price upsurge nor the only factor contributing to the subsequent recession in economic activity, it certainly aggravated both tendencies and had both inflationary and deflationary implications for the main industrial countries. While, on the one hand, the oil price rise put direct pressure on costs and thereby intensified the inflationary process and squeezed industrial profit margins, it had, on the other hand, at least two important deflationary implications. First, it checked the growth of energy-intensive sectors which had underpinned the post-war boom, and second, it transferred a large block of purchasing power to OPEC countries which took time to recycle given their fairly low capacity to absorb industrial imports. The real income effects were partly reflected in large balance of payments deficits in some of the major oil-importing countries as the oil producers amassed substantial current account surpluses. These peaked at about $60 billion in 1974 and thereafter fell to about one-half that level during 1975–7. By the latter half of 1978, when the accumulations had dwindled to small proportions and had ceased to have significant effects on the trade and activity of industrial countries, a new wave of oil price increases and supply difficulties threatened to start the process off once again. However, at least to the turn of the decade, the pressures were less severe than those experienced in the first round of price changes.

Largely as a result of the oil price increases, OECD countries taken as a whole swung from surplus into deficit on external account between 1973–4 and continued to remain in overall deficit for the next three years. However, the impact varied a great deal from country to country. Britain, Italy and France together with some of the smaller, less industrialized European countries were very badly hit and they were forced to take severe deflationary action in order to try and reduce their large external deficits and at the same time stabilize their weak exchange rates. By contrast, Germany, the United States and Japan were able to absorb the oil deficits without too much difficulty thanks to a strong upsurge in exports, particularly to OPEC countries. For a time these three countries were able to accumulate surpluses on their current accounts, though these began to disappear towards the end of the decade under the impact of further oil price rises and a weakening dollar.

It is difficult to estimate with any great precision the full economic impact of the oil pressures of the 1970s since there are so many indirect repercussions which cannot be quantified very accurately, apart from the fact that the energy problem was only one of several which adversely affected economic activity in this period. Estimates by OECD suggest that the real income loss stemming from the oil price shock of the early 1970s may have been of the order of 2 per cent of OECD area GNP, with a similar magnitude for the second oil shock (see Chapter 8). Rostow (1979) maintains that the OECD area suffered declines in total output in 1974–5 of about twice the level that could be directly attributed to the rise in oil prices. The size of the price effects was probably of a similar order of magnitude. However, while the overall impact on the industrial west should not be overdramatized, it should be noted that such estimates do not allow for the many indirect effects, for example the deterioration in business confidence and domestic investment as a result of continued cost pressures, nor do they take account of the adverse impact on economic activity of restrictive government policy to deal with external deficits and inflation. Moreover, a large part of the OPEC oil balances were initially placed on deposit in the leading banks of the western nations which helped to augment liquidity and gave a further boost to the inflationary spiral.

INFLATIONARY PRESSURES

Though the leap in oil prices in the first half of the 1970s added a further twist to the inflationary spiral, it cannot be regarded as the initial cause of the acceleration of inflation nor even the main contributor to the continued high level of inflation throughout the 1970s. For one thing inflation has been a persistent feature of the whole post-war period, though the relatively moderate and creeping inflation following the Korean War has generally been regarded as beneficial on balance, even if at times it caused some degree of concern. Second, inflation began to accelerate noticeably in the later 1960s and was already approaching double figures in a number of countries before the oil price explosion of late 1973. Moreover, in the later 1970s, when the pressure on oil prices eased, the rate of inflation, though much reduced from the peak level of 1974, remained very much higher than in the 1950s and first half of the 1960s.

Since inflation was one of the overriding issues of the decade its causes and implications require close inspection. It is not an easy task to unravel precisely the proximate causes of the price inflation of the 1970s since several inter-related factors were at work. For example, while it is clear enough that there were special forces at work in the very sharp price upsurge in the early 1970s, it is also evident that longer-term forces were operating to push up the underlying rate of inflation. Thus a secular upward trend in inflation from the mid-1960s had superimposed on it a cyclically or partly cyclically generated price boom in the early 1970s – hence the very high rates of inflation in these years. The subsequent fallback from those very high rates may be regarded as a reaction to the cyclical downturn and also to policy effects, but the inflation rate remained obstinately high throughout the rest of the decade partly because the underlying long-term pressures had not been removed and partly because of certain ratchet effects which prevented a rapid reversal to previous inflation levels.

An important element in the price explosion in the early part of the decade was of course the strong and synchronized upswing in economic activity among the major industrial countries in 1972–3. In these years output was growing well above trend which put pressure on commodity prices and led to shortages and speculation. Two other factors compounded the situation: first, since the middle of the 1960s there had been growing tension in some commodity markets, notably grain, as a result of declining reserve stocks in America and poor harvests in Asia and Russia; by 1974 US grain reserves had been reduced to about one-third the level of the early 1960s. Second, at the end of 1973 came the dramatic hike in oil prices.

However, it must be noted that the strong industrial boom of 1972–3 was in part engendered by policy action and that it took place against a background of substantial growth in international liquidity. As a result of slack conditions and stubbornly high unemployment at the beginning of the 1970s, attempts were made in several countries to stimulate economic activity. These erred on the side of generosity partly because an abundance of international monetary reserves made it possible for governments to pursue highly expansionary policies. World exchange reserves, which had grown only slowly in the previous two decades at between 2 and 3 per cent per annum, shot up into double figures in 1970 and between 1969 and 1973 total international reserves rose by some 136 per cent. This explosion was occasioned primarily by the enormous outpouring of American dollars as a result of the policy of benign neglect on the part of the US authorities with regard to the country's heavy external deficits. In turn, these dollars were absorbed into the European banking system – in 1971 alone foreign monetary authorities added more dollars to their official reserves than in all of human history up to that date – and were used as a basis for domestic monetary expansion. It is a somewhat ironic fact that the Bretton Woods fixed exchange rate system, which formerly had been a source of maintaining international monetary stability, became, in its final years, a destabilizing element and a source of inflation as central banks outside the United States sought to prevent the collapse of the system and the depreciation of the dollar, and resisted the appreciation of their own currencies. Eventually of course the strains imposed upon the system proved to be too large to be absorbed. The dollar was devalued and Britain, partly for domestic and political reasons, adopted a floating rate in 1972. This ushered in a period of floating exchange rates tempered periodically by attempts among several European countries to circumscribe the range of the floating.

In most countries therefore the price explosion was preceded or accompanied by reflationary measures and monetary expansion. The combined growth of the nominal money supply (M1) in eleven major industrial countries almost doubled between 1970 and 1972, from 7.5 to 14.0 per cent a year, while in the case of the EEC countries it rose from 9.9 to 18.3 per cent per annum. The highest rates were recorded in Italy, averaging 23 per cent a year between 1970 and 1973, and Japan where it peaked at 30 per cent in 1971. Even in Germany, the high architect of monetary probity, the rate of expansion doubled between 1970 and 1972 (7.1–14.5 per cent) though it fell back sharply thereafter. After 1972 rates of monetary expansion tended to slacken off in most countries though they still remained substantially above those of the 1960s. It should be noted, however, that monetary expansion was tending to rise on balance during the course of the 1960s.

If the immediate causes of the price upsurge of the early 1970s are apparent, the continued high level of inflation throughout the remainder of the decade is less readily so. It is true that inflation rates eased off quite markedly after 1975 under the influence of tighter monetary control, including a shift to monetary targeting, fiscal restraint and various forms of prices and incomes policies. Nevertheless, it was not possible to revert to the modest levels of inflation of the 1950s and early 1960s, and this presented governments with an important policy dilemma with respect to growth versus inflation (see below).

Several possible reasons can be adduced to explain the continuing unfavourable situation on the price front. For one thing monetary growth still remained excessive in comparison with past standards. In fact throughout most of the decade the rate of monetary growth in many countries was inconsistent with exchange stability and price inflation of the German order of magnitude of around 5 per cent. This situation partly reflected the large public sector deficits and borrowing requirements of governments as they attempted to fulfil commitments in terms of collective goods and welfare payments at a time when the budgetary revenue base was weakening. The share of government spending has of course been rising steadily since the war, putting increasing strain on available resources and at the same time possibly influencing the nature of wage claims and the allocation of resources.

During the course of the 1970s wage claims were increasingly based upon past price changes and expected inflation rates which created a built-in rigidity in the cost system. Moreover, with increasing union power and the disappearance of the traditional trade-off between unemployment and wage demands, high claims were more readily conceded and validated in monetary terms than was the case in the past. This tendency was most apparent in Britain, despite periodic declarations of intent about monetary control, and wage pressures became the main stumbling block to regaining price stability. At the same time the wage problem may be seen as part of an accumulating long-term pressure arising from the government's increasing demands on incomes during the post-war period. A study by Thornton (1979) showed that over the period 1952–75 the income retention ratio of the average manufacturing worker in Britain (that is, after deductions of income tax, national insurance contributions etc.) declined from 96.8 to 77 per cent, with the major part of the fall occurring in the 1960s and the first half of the 1970s. What is particularly important is that the increasing deductions encouraged unions to bargain on the basis of the growth of net real earnings, thus necessitating higher demands in terms of gross earnings, while price variables had an increasingly stronger influence on these demands over time.

Intermittent pressure on resources, mainly raw materials and oil again later in the 1970s, coupled with doubts about supply prospects, did little to ease the situation. At the same time slower economic growth and lower productivity meant a reduced rate of offset to cost pressures. Some countries were affected particularly severely by specific problems. For instance between 1973 and 1976 both Britain and Italy experienced a sharp wage-price exchange rate spiral arising largely from excessive monetary creation, while in the later 1970s the dollar was subject to excessive weakness. In some countries very large government deficits posed a problem. This was especially true of Britain where, in the later 1970s, these were being funded at high nominal interest rates into the twenty-first century. This made it difficult to reduce inflation rapidly, since it would erode the tax revenue base for servicing the high-cost debt.

It is difficult of course to eradicate inflation quickly, even though technically not impossible. It would require a very sharp tightening of monetary and fiscal policy which would have serious implications for the real economy and unemployment. It is doubtful whether in most countries there was sufficient political consensus as to the priority for such action. This may stem from the fact that the reduced inflation rates of the later 1970s were more acceptable to the majority of people than further increases in unemployment, at least until the money illusion effects finally wore off.

Nevertheless, governments for most of the 1970s regarded inflation control as the number one priority and to all intents and purposes policy shifted in the direction of dealing with this problem. This of course raised a serious policy dilemma, in that emphasis given to checking inflation made governments reluctant to stimulate activity even at a time of under-used resources and high unemployment. Thus in a sense the loss of output growth in the 1970s may be regarded as a result of inflation in so far as policy measures were directed towards restraint, apart from the fact that business confidence was eroded by the difficulties of coping with cost pressures and weakened markets. On the other hand, it may well be the case that the underlying growth potential was less strong than in the 1950s and 1960s and that the real forces of growth were insufficient to regain the growth momentum of the super-boom years. If this assumption is correct, it would follow that any attempt to regain former output levels by stimulatory measures would simply produce more inflation. For the long term, therefore, the main problem would be how to absorb additional resources, particularly labour, without running up against the constraint of inflation. These policy implications will be explored more fully in the last section.

HOW STRONG WERE REAL GROWTH FORCES?

Energy problems and inflation may be regarded as two important constraints on growth pertaining specifically to the 1970s. In effect, they lowered the equilibrium growth rate of the major industrial nations, an equilibrium growth rate being defined as a sustainable rate of growth consistent with balance of payments equilibrium and price stability.[1] These constraints were likely to remain operative for some time. However, whether the sluggish growth performance of the major economies after 1973 can be wholly attributed to such special factors is more debatable. Certainly they had important depressive effects on activity but at the same time there is reason to believe that this period also experienced a secular decline in the growth generators of the post-war boom. If these forces provided a once-and-for-all thrust to growth in the 1950s and 1960s, then the shift to a lower growth profile would not be unexpected and would largely represent a return to the sustainable historical growth trend.

In some respects this hypothesis has affinity with views expressed by several writers as to the role of real forces in growth, for example, Rostow's leading sectors, Schumpeter's clustering of innovational activity and Hansen's dearth of investment opportunities. Basically such theses tend to stress the apparent lumpiness of investment as a derivative of the strength of innovational opportunities. In turn they can be linked to the structural transformation theses of the type postulated by Svennilson for the inter-war years and by Cornwall for the post-war period, the latter arguing the case for manufacturing as the engine of growth. More recently, the concept of 'deindustrialization' and the size of the public sector would be of relevance to the events of the 1970s.

As a starting point to the discussion, it may be convenient to identify again the main forces of growth relevant to the boom years of the 1950s and 1960s. Apart from relatively cheap and plentiful supplies of raw materials and energy, low rates of inflation and monetary stability which we have already dealt with, the following factors may be enumerated: (1) rapid diffusion of technical backlogs in Europe associated in particular with leading manufacturing sectors; (2) elastic supplies of labour, resource reallocation and the favourable effects on productivity growth; (3) high rates of investment; and (4) high levels of demand bolstered by demand-management policies. It is important of course to recognize that these factors are closely interrelated. While their strength may have diminished in more recent years, they were also adversely affected by the specific difficulties of the 1970s. Moreover, the growth of the public sector and signs of deindustrialization may in part be regarded as a reflection of the weakening of the above forces of growth, and at the same time have an adverse effect on growth potential.

At the end of the war, or perhaps more appropriately in 1950 when the main reconstruction phase was complete, it is clear that European countries had a unique opportunity to grow rapidly given favourable international conditions, since at that time European income and productivity levels were well below those of America. Such conditions were largely met in the period through to the early 1970s in that there was no serious pressure on the supply and price of commodities, inflation rates were modest, monetary disturbances were few and mild in nature, and the progressive dismantling of trade barriers gave ample opportunities to exploit the gains from international trade. Thus by the middle of the 1970s average productivity levels in many European countries were 80 per cent or more of those of America as against an average of 50 per cent in 1950 (Maddison 1979). In other words, during this period European countries were able to close the gap significantly and by the later date the scope for substantial gains from moving towards best practice techniques was diminishing.

The process of catching up involved a significant structural transformation based on key sectors of activity. Manufacturing was the really dynamic sector and within this branch of activity there was a rapid diffusion of techniques in energy-intensive industries including automobiles, consumer durable goods, electronics and chemicals. This stimulated high levels of investment in these sectors and at the same time it led to a substantial shift of resources, especially labour, from low productivity agriculture to the high growth, high productivity areas in manufacturing. The high and sustained level of demand, maintained in part by post-war demand-management policies, provided a favourable climate for investment which, in turn, enabled the backlog of opportunities to be exploited.

Now it is true that the basis of the post-war super-growth was severely undermined in the 1970s. Energy-intensive sectors were badly hit by the pressure on oil supplies, while the income transfer effects reduced demand in the oil-importing countries. This, coupled with severe inflation, obviously created an uncertain and less attractive climate for investment. Not surprisingly, therefore, the revival of investment from the recession of 1974–5 was noticeably weaker than during similar phases of previous post-war cycles. However, although the adverse cyclical influences on investment were undoubtedly important, there are grounds for arguing that the underlying growth forces were weakening at this time.

This argument is based upon several premises. First, as already noted, the scope for further large gains from the catching up process was limited by the 1970s, and the opportunities for further rapid expansion in the high-growth, energy-intensive sectors were less apparent as markets became saturated. Second, by the early 1970s the scope for large productivity gains from shifting labour from agriculture to industry was much diminished. As a result of two decades or so of structural transformation, agricultural employment was less than 10 per cent of the labour force in six of the twelve countries analysed by Cornwall, compared with two at the beginning of the 1950s, and only three countries, Austria, Italy and Japan, still had fairly large labour reserves in this sector. Indeed, in several countries the rate of growth of the industrial labour force tended to decline or stagnate from the later 1960s, with adverse effects on productivity growth. For a time the reduced supply of labour to this sector may have acted as a supply constraint though it is difficult to invoke this argument for the later 1970s given the high level of unemployment generally (cf. Knox 1979). But perhaps more important, though the scope for resource reallocation was dwindling, as time went on the shift of labour took on a more complex pattern involving a proportionate increase in the share of service trades and the public sector at the expense of both agriculture and industry. If, as is frequently argued, productivity levels and growth rates are low in these sectors this would tend further to depress growth potential.

The change in the pattern of labour deployment is important since it involved the stagnation or even decline of manufacturing employment in some countries – hence the term 'deindustrialization'. The trend was most apparent in Britain, though there is evidence that other major industrial countries were beginning to experience similar tendencies by the early 1970s (Cornwall 1977). In the British case, a forceful argument was put forward to the effect that manufacturing had been subject to a 'crowding out' effect as a result of the growth of non-marketable services, primarily public sector services (Bacon and Eltis 1976). The growth of the latter, of course, reflects shifts in tastes and patterns of demand which have required a greater provision of public services in terms of education, medical and welfare care and housing, as well as private services such as tourism and leisure pursuits.

Most countries in the west experienced a rapid expansion of these sectors from the middle of the 1960s, and an OECD report (1978) on *Public Expenditure Trends* argued that 'beyond a certain point too rapid an increase in public expenditure can reduce productive potential by increasing the likelihood of inefficient allocation of resources and by lowering incentives to work and invest'. An increasing public sector share could also have important financial, balance of payments and productivity implications. On the other hand, while such repercussions may be very important, it is not altogether convincing to argue that the erosion of the manufacturing base can be attributed to supply constraints (capital and labour) as a result of diversion to the expanding service and public sectors.

It is clear of course that the public sector may very well entice resources away from manufacturing because its market signals for labour and capital are more attractive. For example, in the case of labour, the public sector may offer higher rates of pay and cleaner and more secure jobs than in manufacturing, while one must not forget the status attraction of white-collar employment. Similarly, high interest rates offered on government stock at a time of reduced margins in manufacturing may have lured capital away from the latter sector. Furthermore, the indirect implications of higher government spending in terms of deficit financing, money supply and inflation may also be important for determining the climate of expectations for private enterprise.

However, there is no firm evidence to suggest that manufacturing has been starved of resources and in terms of labour recruitment, at least, the stagnation in manufacturing employment may reflect a combination of greater productivity gains and/or diminished opportunities for expansion.

This last point seems a more plausible proposition given the massive application of new and known technologies in the post-war years and the rate at which the technology and productivity gap between Europe and America was being closed during this period. The dynamics of the post-war boom in manufacturing began to diminish as markets in the leading sectors became increasingly saturated and diminishing returns to existing technologies set in (Rostow 1979; Giarini and Loubergé 1978). Whether innovational opportunities are subject to some long-wave movement as several writers suggest is still a matter for debate, but it does seem possible that the weakening of manufacturing performance during the 1970s may in part reflect the relative lack of large new fields of endeavour.

The sluggishness of manufacturing investment in the later 1970s may also be attributed to the cumulative effects of the long-term deterioration in profit shares and rates of return, and the concomitant rise in the wage–income share which has been going on since the war. Cross-country comparisons of rates of return are fraught with difficulty because of definitional problems and differences in accounting practices between countries. Even studies within individual countries can often throw up conflicting results. By and large, however, most analyses appear to indicate that economic enterprise has experienced a secular downward shift in rates of return in the post-war period, though the magnitude of the decline varies somewhat from country to country. One of the comparative studies sponsored by OECD (Hill 1979) concluded that the trend towards declining profit shares and rates of return in the major European countries had been unmistakable though, apart from Canada, the same could not be said of the non-European countries analysed, that is, Japan, Australia and the United States. The decline was most noticeable in Germany and the UK where the share of net profits in net value added fell from 37 to 16 per cent and 30 to 7 per cent respectively over the period 1955–76. During the same time net rates of return in manufacturing declined from 31 to 11 per cent in Germany and from 20 to 3 per cent in the UK. These are indeed quite remarkable falls and, as Hill points out, the extent of the deterioration was not fully appreciated by many observers largely because it was obscured by the continuing practice of calculating profits and rates of return on the basis of historic costs. The distortion created by using historic cost accounting principles is particularly serious in times of strong inflation of the type experienced in the 1970s.

Variations in trend rates of return between countries have little significance, in the short term at least, in terms of explaining inter-country differences in economic performance. This point is readily demonstrated from the obvious lack of correlation between the two variables in three major countries, namely the United States, the UK and Germany. But from the point of view of the long-term growth potential of the major economies, the trends in these variables are disturbing as are those for wage–income shares which, by virtue of their essentially reciprocal quality, tend to substantiate the above data. In contrast to the stability of the wage share in total income prior to 1939, the post-war period has seen a dramatic rise in wage shares in all countries, amounting on average to some 20 percentage points for OECD countries as a whole during the period 1948–75 (Paldam 1979). Almost one-third of this change represents a genuine fall in the share of capital, about one-half of which took place in the years 1970–5, more especially in the last two. It is interesting to note the contrasting reactions of the shares during the two price shocks of 1950–1 (Korean War) and 1974–5. In the former case, wage earners bore the brunt of the loss with a consequent rise in the share going to capital, whereas in the more recent price upsurge it was capital that suffered the loss as wage earners sought successfully to insulate themselves, thereby pushing up the wage–income ratio. At the same time, the steady advance in the wage–income share may have been aggravated by the declining proportion of gross earnings retained by the average worker after state deductions.

The implications of these trends are disquieting to say the least. The genesis of the growth crisis of the 1970s can be seen partly in terms of a long-run deterioration in the income share of capital which markedly accelerated in the 1970s as the strengthening bargaining power of labour operated to push up the wage–income share. During this later period the critical point may well have been reached in several countries in which the capital share declined to around 15 per cent or less, that is, to a level insufficient to sustain long-run full employment growth rates, which Paldam puts at between 3–4 per cent per annum, but which may have even be higher in some cases. In other words, if the critical level of distributional shares between labour and capital had been reached or was fast approaching, the main problem would be to restrain any further rise in the wage–income ratio before it suffocated the share of capital. Again this posed an awkward policy issue, since any attempt to stimulate economic activity may push up the wage–income share which, after two decades or more of Keynesian demand-management policies, had shown a consistent tendency to move in an upward direction. To the policy problems of the 1970s we now turn.

MACROECONOMIC MANAGEMENT UNDER STAGFLATION

The events of the 1970s presented governments with a far more difficult task, in terms of economic management, by comparison with the 1950s and 1960s. They were faced with a whole host of problems, many of them occurring simultaneously, namely inflation, rising unemployment, stagnating output, balance of payments difficulties, rising public sector deficits, currency disorders, not to mention specific supply problems. Although their severity and incidence varied from country to country, most countries experienced several, if not all, these unfavourable forces during the course of the decade. Not since the inter-war period, and even then prices and unemployment had not risen together, had there been a period in peacetime when so many adverse influences converged at one and the same time.

Inevitably the extent and magnitude of the problems led to a significant shift in the balance of policy objectives and instruments of control from those which had been in use hitherto. During the 1950s and 1960s the art of economic management had been primarily concerned with trying to achieve a stable economic framework and this entailed governments juggling with a series of basically incompatible objectives, that is, growth, full employment, external equilibrium and price stability. Few countries, apart from perhaps Germany, were able to achieve all four goals simultaneously. Thus, though in practice priority was generally given to maintaining growth and full employment, it was frequently necessary to temper these ideals when considerations with regard to price stability and balance of payments equilibrium became pressing. Fortunately, pressures with regard to the latter rarely became acute enough, the UK excepted, to jeopardize the advancement of growth and full employ-ment for any length of time. Hence reliance on demand-management policies, involving a combination of fiscal and monetary policies with varying degrees of emphasis, while never regarded as ideal, was not seriously brought into question. Occasionally resort was made to other policies – changes in exchange rates, incomes policies etc. – but these never became permanent policy weapons, while very little serious attention was given to supply con-siderations.

Though critics have sometimes argued that such policies were as much a cause of instability as a cure for it, on the surface at least demand-management policies seemed to work fairly well in so far as it would be diffi-cult to deny that the first two post-war decades were the most successful in terms of economic growth and stability in all human history. Not that one can credit governments with much of the honour for the economic growth success of this period, since, as Knox has pointed out: 'Apart from national and inter-national measures to maintain the level of total demand, the influence of government policy in the acceleration of overall economic growth in the non-Communist countries has been negligible' (Knox 1976). Indeed, it may in fact be argued that it was the underlying strength of the major economies and the relative absence of fundamental disequilibrium which made for successful management, rather than the other way round. Given strong real growth forces and consequently a shift of the supply schedule to the right, it was perfectly possible to sustain high equilibrium growth rates without, in most cases, running into serious balance of payments or price problems, a situation helped in part by some trade-off between wages and unemployment.

Once these good conditions evaporated, as they did progressively during the

1970s, the practicality of using traditional demand-management tools to achieve former objectives became less meaningful. During this period, priority had to be increasingly given to controlling inflation and dealing with external imbalances in preference to encouraging growth and maintaining full employment. These now became residual objectives, if that, since under conditions of high inflation and diminished growth potential, it was felt that any attempt to stimulate activity and employment, by fiscal or other means, would simply set off the inflationary spiral again. In line with this reasoning, the tools of economic management underwent a re-evaluation. The delicate combination of fiscal and monetary 'fine-tuning' gave way initially to direct policies in the form of income and price controls, but subsequently attention was shifted towards a more vigorous control of monetary aggregates, including monetary targeting. The new approach to management, though very much conditioned by immediate events, had, like its Keynesian counterpart, a respectable intellectual lineage stemming back to the 1950s under the pervasive influence of Milton Friedman.

Though the explosive inflation of the first half of the 1970s caused many countries to turn at first to direct price and income controls, it soon became clear that these not only caused distortions to market economies but also were regarded, for the most part, as temporary expedients which merely held back movements in wages and prices until the time when they were lifted or relaxed. Given their anticipated temporary nature they could do little to provide a long-term solution to the underlying causes of inflation, though in some cases they formed an important adjunct to the introduction of monetary targeting. In the UK, for example, the government did not begin to use monetary targets until it had managed, against a background of incomes policy, to stabilize the growth of the money supply at around 10 per cent.

In many respects it was logical that governments should turn attention to more rigorous control of monetary aggregates as an intermediary policy objective. It was not simply that the conditions of the time demanded a new initiative or that monetarism had suddenly become more respectable, though both factors played a part. It was rather the more pragmatic response to earlier events that exerted the crucial influence. The shift to monetary weapons focused attention on areas which had been allowed to run out of control in the early 1970s, namely excessive monetary growth associated in part with the willingness of governments to run exceptionally large deficits and resort to financing these through the banking system. Thus the increasing respectability of monetary policies reflected the lessons of past mistakes. The timing and nature of the move to more rigorous monetary control, involving basically the setting of targets or projections for the growth in the money supply or domestic credit aggregates, varied substantially from country to country, as did the instruments of control to achieve these targets (see McClam 1978). But most major countries in the later 1970s adopted some form of control of monetary aggregates, together with fiscal policies designed to stabilize or lower public sector deficits.

The more rigorous approach to monetary policy coupled with fiscal restraint was not overwhelmingly successful in terms of inflation control and there were of course important side effects for the real economy. Most countries did achieve some success in reducing the rate of monetary growth from the high levels experienced earlier in the decade, while the pace of inflation was moderated considerably through to 1978. But the process was a slow and uneven one; inflation remained at a very high level compared with post-war standards prior to the 1970s, and it began to accelerate again in 1979. There are several reasons why the policies only achieved partial success. To have secured a quick and complete check to inflation would have required much more drastic monetary and fiscal action which, given the implications in terms of the real economy, would not have been politically feasible. The second best option of moderate restraint was bound to take time given the lags inherent in policy action and the residual cost pressures still in the system. Second, the monetary targets were by no means firmly adhered to, with the result that monetary growth was allowed to deviate from the target path, often in a procyclical manner. This laxity in control derived in part from the accommodation of cost pressures, as for example in Italy between 1975 and 1976 when substantial overshooting of the total credit target occurred as a result of the wages explosion of 1975 being validated in monetary terms. The British authorities were confronted with similar pressures in 1979–80 which led to the spectacle of high public sector wage claims being validated in monetary terms despite the new Conservative Government's determination to bring monetary expansion under control. Corresponding awards in the private sector were made possible by the high volume of bank lending to the corporate sector, but with serious implications for company liquidity. A further difficulty arose from the technical problems associated with monetary control. Generally speaking, the authorities found it very difficult to get a firm grip on the monetary base because of the development of intermediary finance and the effects of international capital flows, while the problems associated with the financing of large public sector deficits caused short-term fluctuations in the money supply. The latter problem became almost a permanent feature in the UK from 1975, reflecting the fact that 'official sales of gilt-edged tend to be rather tidal, periods of very large sales alternating with periods of very small sales. The institutional structure of the UK is such that when sales are deficient, the government's residual financing tends to be supplied by the banking system, usually in the form of Treasury bills, increasing both the money stock and the banks' reserve assets' (McClam 1978).

In the last resort of course the degree of monetary restraint can only go as far as the political consensus allows. Rostow (1979) has neatly summarized the political and social constraints involved in this context: 'Taxes, public expenditure, interest rates, and the supply of money are not determined antiseptically by men free to move economies along a Phillips curve to an optimum trade-off between the rate of unemployment and the rate of inflation. Fiscal and monetary policy are, inevitably, living parts of the democratic political process.' This clearly tempered the rigour with which the authorities pushed the new policies given the cost implications which they entailed in terms of output and employment, even though policies erred on the side of restraint. What this meant in practice is that the authorities for the most part supplied the amount of inflation demanded by the public and it appears that over time the upper bound to what were regarded as tolerable levels of inflation rose, making it that much more difficult to bring it fully under control.

In purely technical terms it would be fairly easy to prescribe the right policies to eradicate inflation, but since the economic and social implications of these would, in the short term at least, be so horrendous it is not surprising that governments were reluctant to contemplate them. Consequently, while the control of inflation was generally regarded as the number one priority, there was also some attempt to 'minimise macroeconomic misery' in conditions of stagflation (see Perkins 1980). Inevitably this meant an awkward policy compromise in an effort to resolve the dilemma of high unemployment and rapid inflation. Some would argue, however, that the policies of restraint designed to reduce inflation were pushed too far to the consequent detriment of the real economy. It is certainly true that output growth in most countries was well below capacity potential for some time and since this resulted in higher unit costs and lower productivity growth it exacerbated the inflationary problem. Moreover, in so far as policy restraint leads to income destruction it diminishes the tax revenue base of governments and thereby makes it more difficult for the authorities to reduce budgetary deficits which are regarded as a source of inflation. If a solution to the budgetary problem is sought through higher taxes this adds a further cost-push element to inflation.

As far as policy is concerned the authorities faced something of a dilemma in the 1970s and in trying to solve it they became 'boxed in' by their own exertions. In an ideal world a short sharp shock treatment was the obvious way out of the inflationary spiral, but politically this was not a viable solution at the time. Hence governments were forced to adopt an uneasy compromise mix of policies in an attempt to gain some trade-off between inflation, employment and growth. The problem with this approach was that it failed to eradicate inflation and left a residue of unemployment and slow growth. In the process the authorities became confused as to the objectives and specification of different policy weapons.

In an inflationary climate there is clearly a need for a consistent monetary policy, that is, one where monetary expansion is compatible with the underlying growth potential of the economy and an acceptable rate of inflation. Indeed, any worthwhile attempt to deal with the price problem must involve the use of monetary weapons and the control of monetary aggregates. While it may not be essential to adhere to a very rigid target for monetary expansion, it is important that the authorities adopt a figure which is consistent with the growth potential of the economy and the target for inflation. The specification of a monetary target is important for several reasons: it provides the monetary authorities with a firm yardstick with which to operate and should thereby prevent undue laxity in monetary control; at the same time it can act as a useful public information signal, provided the authorities advertise the fact sufficiently, which in time will serve to impress upon the nation the need for restraint; and, finally, it should ensure that nominal interest rates move closer to their natural level. The latter aspect, as Perkins has recognized, is very important, since in the past the refusal to allow nominal interest rates to rise sufficiently has had adverse effects on both inflation and output. When in times of high inflation interest rates are artificially depressed, the returns on financial assets become unattractive and this leads to a process of portfolio readjustment from financial to real assets, including goods and commodities, which raises the price of the latter. Moreover, in their efforts to hold down nominal interest rates below the natural level the authorities may be forced to allow a faster growth of the money supply than would otherwise be the case. Then if any attempt is made to restrain demand and prices by resort to higher taxes, as some governments did between 1974 and 1976, this would add a further cost-push element to the system. These influences will of course serve to dampen real activity but low real interest rates in themselves may have a similar effect through consumption. If returns on financial assets become negative in real terms the propensity to save may rise, as was the case in the mid-1970s despite rapid inflation, as people attempted to restore their stock of savings in real terms. This in turn tended to depress consumption and out-weighed any advantage in terms of investment derived from artificially low interest rates.

If monetary policy had been directed consistently towards achieving price stability, it would have been possible to follow a more constructive fiscal policy. For the reasons stated earlier it may have been too much to expect a return to the high growth rates of earlier years, but given the degree of under-utilized capacity some moderate fiscal stimulus would not have been out of place, provided that it was financed in a non-inflationary manner. Unfortunately the authorities became constrained in their actions by an obsessive fear of the inflationary implications of any fiscal relaxation. This was primarily a result of their failure to adhere to a firm monetary policy, a misconception about the role of fiscal policy, and a neglect of supply variables. What was required was not the traditional consumption-based tax remissions, but fiscal incentives which boosted investment and encouraged structural transformation, especially since the energy shocks had rendered obsolete part of the former capital stock. Yet this was the very time when public investment, especially in infrastructure, was being pruned. Second, in conjunction with a constructive fiscal policy more attention needed to be devoted to the supply

217

side, or the microeconomic foundations of growth, including improved resource allocation, the sponsoring of new technologies, the retraining and redeployment of labour, and the removal of restraints on trade and economic activity to improve the competitive environment, rather than the defensive strategies of the later 1970s which had as their main objective the propping up of declining sectors of activity and the preservation of jobs. As the OECD warned in 1979 (*The Case for Positive Adjustment Policies*), without such new initiatives there was a danger of western capitalism becoming locked into 'a vicious circle whereby slow growth generates behaviour and policies which impair productivity and accentuate inflation; this prompts governments to adopt more cautious demand management policies and hence leads, directly or indirectly, to even slower growth'.

In other words, while priority should have been given to combating inflation by tight monetary control, it was also crucial that an effort be made to break out of the vicious circle of stagflation by shifting progressively away from the defensive policies adopted following the recession of 1974–5. The implications of the failure to solve the policy dilemma are explored further in the following chapter.

NOTE

1 For this purpose price stability is defined as a non-accelerating or gently decelerating rate of inflation. In the short term, the equilibrium growth rate with policies to effect a sharp reduction in inflation may be negative. Under these conditions employment is a residual.

8

WESTERN EUROPE IN THE 1980s

The search for stability

Since the Second World War European nations have experienced two fairly distinct periods of economic change. First there was the long period of very high and sustained growth from the late 1940s through to the early 1970s, which narrowed significantly the gap between American and west European levels of output that had existed at the start of the period. By the late 1960s rapid growth and structural change seemed to be the natural order of things and the old trade cycle depressions a thing of the past.

Yet within a few years this golden age scenario was all but at an end. Rising inflation, wage explosions, student unrest and political disturbances at the turn of the decade were the initial manifestations of a long period of chequered growth and economic gloom. Problems and shocks appeared with almost regular monotony. Commodity shortages, exchange disturbances following the break-up of the Bretton Woods system, oil shocks as a result of the machinations of the OPEC oil cartel, and strong labour resistance to economic adversity combined to produce recession or sluggish growth, high inflation, rising unemployment, and balance of payments and budgetary difficulties. The convergence of favourable factors which had characterized the post-war boom had been transformed into an equally strong convergence of disincentives to sustained growth.

As we saw in Chapter 7, western Europe was slowly struggling to extricate itself from these problems when the second oil shock undermined her fragile recuperation. This time there was little cause for optimism that the disturbance could be accommodated without serious consequences. Because of a host of unresolved problems stemming from earlier shocks – for example inflation, budgetary deficits and wage pressures – governments could no longer afford to contemplate accommodating the external shock as they had done previously. Thus macroeconomic policy almost everywhere turned restrictive and hence recessionary forces were thereby compounded.

The 1980s therefore opened on a very inauspicious note. Governments no longer dreamed of trying to restore the golden age and even their citizens were slowly acclimatizing themselves to a less favourable economic outlook. The main task now became one of searching for a new equilibrium, if need be at a lower level of activity and employment, that was consistent with low inflation, reduced budgetary deficits and external equilibrium. The rise in unemployment which this inevitably entailed was the price to be paid for failure to adjust fully to the disturbances of the previous decade. Unfortunately, the higher levels of unemployment proved to be far from transitory. In the process of tackling the other issues high unemployment became a permanent feature of most western nations. Even by the end of the decade, after several years of quite strong growth, unemployment remained as intractable as ever, so much so that it began to be questioned whether it was more of a structural or micro problem than a consequence of macroeconomic forces. By this time, however, the cycle of events was again moving adversely, prompting governments once more to revert to a cautionary policy stance. So by the turn of the decade, western nations were again teetering on the brink of recession, the duration and severity of which seemed likely to match that of the previous cyclical downturn.

GENERAL TRENDS

A glance at Table 8.1 reveals that after 1973 growth in Europe was less than half that in the super-boom years, while employment virtually stagnated. The 1980s proved to be even weaker than the turbulent 1970s. Apart from southeast Asia and China, growth was in fact slower everywhere than in the previous decade, and much slower of course than in the post-war golden age. World output (GDP) grew by just over 30 per cent in the 1980s compared with over 45 per cent in the 1970s: in per capita terms this represented a mere 1 per cent per annum (2 per cent in the 1970s) as a consequence of a 20 per cent rise in world population. The developed market economies did somewhat better since their population growth was very modest. Though the growth of GDP slowed down to 2.6 per annum compared with 3.1 per cent in the 1970s, real per capita incomes still rose by around 2 per cent a year.

Slower growth was accompanied by a greater degree of convergence in rates

Table 8.1 Growth rates of gross domestic product and employment, 1950-87

	1950–73			1973–87		
	GDP	Employment	Output/ employment	GDP	Employment	Output/ employment
Europe 12	4.7	0.6	4.1	1.9	0.1	1.8
United States	3.7	1.5	2.2	2.5	1.9	0.6
Japan	9.6	1.7	4.1	3.8	0.8	3.0

Source: D. Henderson, 'Comparative economic performance of the OECD countries, 1950–87: a summary of evidence', in A. Graham and A. Seldon (eds) *Government and Economies in the Postwar World: Economic Policies and Comparative Performance 1945–85*, London: Routledge, 1990, p. 207

of performance among the major nations compared with the previous decade. This partly reflects the closer integration of western European nations during the course of the 1980s (see Table 8.2). In addition, there is a noticeable trend improvement in most economic indicators during the latter half of the decade. At the start of the period most economic variables were highly unfavourable, with stagnant or falling output, rising inflation, negative investment, large government deficits and current account imbalances, and high unemployment. By the end of the decade the picture had much improved. On average price inflation had been halved, the growth of GDP was running at around 3 per cent a year, investment was strongly positive and in most cases external deficits had been eliminated and budgetary positions had been consolidated. Only the unemployment scene remained as black as it had been ten years earlier (Table 8.3, Table 8.5 and the Appendix Tables).

Table 8.2 Growth rates of gross domestic product and industrial production (per cent per annum)

	1961–70		1971–80		1981–90	
	GDP	Industrial production	GDP	Industrial production	GDP	Industrial production
Belgium	4.9	5.0	3.2	2.2	1.9	2.1
Denmark	4.5	6.2	2.2	1.9	1.7	2.6
Germany	4.5	5.7	2.7	2.3	2.1	2.0
Greece	7.6	–	4.7	6.9	1.5	1.3
Spain	7.3	–	3.5	5.0	2.9	1.7
France	5.5	5.3	3.2	3.0	2.1	1.2
Ireland	4.2	6.6	4.7	4.5	3.1	7.1
Italy	5.7	7.1	3.8	3.3	2.3	1.6
Luxembourg	3.6	2.4	2.6	0.0	3.3	3.9
Netherlands	5.1	6.2	2.9	2.8	1.8	1.7
Portugal	6.4	–	4.7	6.5	2.7	4.2
UK	2.9	2.9	1.9	1.0	2.6	1.7
Europe 12	4.8	4.9	3.0	2.7	2.3	1.8
United States	3.8	4.9	2.7	3.2	2.9	2.6
Japan	10.5	13.6	4.6	4.1	4.3	3.9

Source: Commission of the European Communities, *European Economy* 46, December 1990

The data in Table 8.3 illustrate clearly the marked difference between the first and second halves of the decade. Performance everywhere was much stronger in the later 1980s than in the first half of the period. In fact in some areas, notably inflation, investment and current account balances, many European countries by the later 1980s had regained the levels achieved before the onset of the first oil crisis. Whether this marked the start of a new equilibrium

Table 8.3 Key indicators of economic performance: Europe 12 (percentage change)

	1973/1960	*1980/1973*	*1985/1980*	*1990/1985*
Real GDP	4.8	2.2	1.5	3.1
Employment	0.3	0.1	– 0.4	1.2
Investment	5.6	0.3	– 0.6	5.7
Prices	4.6	12.4	8.8	4.1
Annual average (% of GDP)				
Current account balance	0.5	– 0.5	– 0.2	0.6
General government net borrowing/lending	– 0.6	– 3.5	– 5.3	– 3.7

Source: Commission of the European Communities, *European Economy* 42, 1989, p. 111

as some observers have suggested is open to doubt. Commenting on the long recovery from 1982, the United Nations in their *World Economic Survey for 1990* were encouraged to believe that western nations 'are now on a track where, barring domestic or external shocks, they can look forward to continuing moderate expansion interrupted by no more than, at worst, moderate cyclical downturns. If so, the world economy could be more stable and dynamic in the 1990s than it was in the 1980s.' Yet as these words were being written recession was about to strike again and it was soon apparent that some of the old problems had not been finally laid to rest.

IMPACT OF THE SECOND OIL SHOCK

The second oil crisis at the end of the 1970s had a broadly similar impact to that of the first, accounting for some 2 per cent of OECD's GDP and with similar price and recessionary effects. But the cyclical experience following the two shocks was not identical by any means. The cyclical swings during OPEC 1 were rather sharper than those accompanying the second crisis. In 1973, prior to the first shock, there had been a strong boom in activity with pronounced synchronization among the major industrial countries, whereas in the later 1970s the upswing was weaker and less heavily synchronized, with the United States lagging western Europe. Moreover, whereas in 1975 there was a sharp drop in activity in most countries followed by an equally sharp rebound the following year, the later cyclical experience was somewhat more attenuated. Many countries experienced falls in output but these were spread over three years while on average growth was maintained, albeit at very low rates. Nor was there any sharp rebound similar to that of 1976. This may be explained partly by the fact that following the erratic recovery after 1975 the underlying economic position was much weaker by the early 1980s, while the contrasting policy stance of the major countries compared with earlier also has relevance in this context (see below).

Price changes were broadly similar at the consumer level despite the fact that non-oil commodity prices were much less buoyant than in the earlier period. On the other hand, several indicators, notably budgetary deficits, unemployment and external accounts, visibly deteriorated. By contrast, the volume of international trade held up rather better than previously.

The policy reaction of governments to the second oil crisis differed somewhat from that following the first. There was both a greater degree of policy convergence and more continuity in policy-making among the western nations. There was no repetition of the accommodating policies to offset real income losses of the oil price hike as happened in the 1970s. This time both fiscal and monetary policies were tightened progressively in most countries, the main exception being France between 1981 and 1982 which undertook a short-lived expansion programme. Thus on balance macroeconomic policy reinforced the recessionary effects of the oil shock. The impact was reflected in the sharp rise in real interest rates, negative in the later 1970s but turning strongly positive with real rates averaging around 5 per cent by 1982 and 1983. Estimates in Table 8.4 suggest that by 1981 the negative impact of policy was substantially greater than that of oil, and in the following year it was probably even stronger.

Table 8.4 Estimates of main forces on OECD output, 1978–81 (percentage contribution to change in real GDP)

	1978	1979	1980	1981
Oil	0.0	− 0.5	− 2.25	− 0.5
Fiscal policy	0.5	− 0.5	− 0.5	− 1.5
Monetary policy	0.0	0.0	0.0	− 0.75
Change in GNP	4.0	3.0	1.25	1.5

Source: J. Llewellyn, 'Resource prices and macroeconomic policies: lessons from two oil price shocks', *OECD Economic Studies* 1, 1983, p. 207

This period marks the final break with conventional post-war policy thinking. Recessionary impulses would normally have signalled a move towards expansionary policies as in the past, and as occurred initially after the first oil shock. Arguably, however, there were strong pragmatic reasons why this was no longer appropriate in the conditions of the early 1980s despite the perception that a change in policy stance would aggravate recessionary forces and raise unemployment. First, the rise in oil prices was equivalent to an external tax for the oil-importing nations and it could only be offset at the expense of adverse repercussions elsewhere in the economies which bore the brunt of it. By the second oil crisis it was realized that real income losses had to be borne by the oil importers in one form or another since they represented a process of income redistribution among nations. Far better, it was felt, that these losses should be incurred directly and without the inflationary consequences that accompanied the first oil shock. Governments were clearly anxious this time to avoid a repetition of the previous wage–price spiral and the ensuing currency depreciation. Moreover, there was also the possibility that the oil market might remain difficult for some time to come in which case slower growth would help to conserve energy use.

Most governments were also very concerned about their budgetary positions at this time. Large deficits had accumulated during the 1970s, and for several years efforts had been made, albeit with not a great deal of success, to reduce or stabilize them. Renewed recession weakened these efforts for a time since automatic stabilizers put renewed upward pressure on public spending at a time when the revenue base was shrinking. Thus there was obviously no ardent desire to add to the problems by expansionary fiscal policies. In any case, fiscal laxness was regarded as a sign of financial weakness which would have repercussions on exchange rates and inflation and help to undermine general confidence. In this regard, lessons were drawn from the German and Japanese experience following the first oil crisis. These two countries adopted the most stringent policy stance which appeared to have met with considerable success in the later 1970s in terms of growth, inflation, exchange rates and current account balances. Italy, France and Britain, on the other hand, had rather the reverse experience.

Two other factors constrained expansionary policy initiatives. First, there was the increasingly popular belief that strong real wage resistance and the re-emergence of the real wage gap (see below), together with structural rigidities in labour markets and elsewhere, would tend to nullify the effects of any demand stimuli, which would therefore show up principally in higher inflation rather than increased output and employment. Second, there was the conviction that countries could not unilaterally stimulate their economies because of the adverse effects this would have on their exchange rates and balance of payments. This was vividly demonstrated in 1981–2 when France attempted a unilateral policy of expansion which soon had to be reversed for these very reasons. In some countries, Germany in particular, policy-makers also believed that renewed expansion would only occur through export-led growth as a result of rising world demand. Since Germany was the key economy in Europe with a strong currency this clearly made it difficult for other nations to act independently.

Given the greater stringency of policy in the early 1980s and the unfavourable trends in several key indicators, it is perhaps surprising that economic activity remained as resilient as it did, and somewhat more robust than in 1974–5. A combination of high real interest rates, adverse terms of trade, high unit labour costs, a significant decline in factor productivity and weak final demand drove down rates of return on capital to their lowest levels of the post-war period. The profitability of business by the early 1980s averaged only two-thirds that of the 1960s and early 1970s. In some countries, notably Italy and the UK, rates of return on industrial capital dropped below

Figure 8.1 EEC: net rate of return on capital invested and real long-term interest rate (per cent)
Source: OECD 1987

the real interest rate for the first time in history (Figure 8.1).

In addition, there was growing competition from Asian countries, deepening debt crises in the developing nations, and creeping trade restrictions, mainly of the non-tariff variety. Furthermore, there were thought to be worrying problems on the supply side relating not only to the flexibility of factor markets and structural impediments to growth, but also regarding the rate at which western nations were taking up modern technology. The climate was therefore not conducive to business investment and this is reflected in the marked slowdown in the growth of the capital stock and the decline in investment ratios.

Yet apart from one or two countries, notably the UK where a combination of policy factors and an oil-induced rise in the exchange rate resulted in a sharp contraction in economic activity, few countries suffered significant falls in GDP, though industrial production setbacks were common in 1981. On balance there was somewhat greater resilience than in the previous crisis even though recovery took longer to materialize. Boltho (1984: 17) suggests that the resilience in consumer spending, partly through a decline in the propensity to save, was an important factor in explaining the avoidance of a major recession.

225

In fact, however, real consumer spending was weaker than in 1974–5, as was public consumption. He also points to the better performance in investment but again the figures for western Europe through to 1983 do not appear to bear out this assertion either (see the Appendix Tables). Rather, the main factor seems to have been the relative buoyancy of exports which continued to expand, albeit at a reduced rate, throughout the recession, whereas there was a fall in volume of some 4 per cent in 1975.

THE LONG RECOVERY

Despite the poor outlook for economic growth in the recessionary conditions of the early 1980s, nevertheless western Europe subsequently experienced nearly a decade of unbroken growth, weak at first in 1982–3, but averaging around 2.5 per cent (of GDP) a year over 1984–7 and then rising to 3 per cent or more in the latter years of the 1980s. Inflation dropped sharply to levels comparable with those of the later 1960s, while wage pressures moderated and there was some advance in productivity. These improvements helped to restore profitability and so investment rose strongly in the latter half of the decade. At the same time the European Community's external position returned to equilibrium following the large deficits occasioned by the second oil price hike, while there was a measure of consolidation in public finances. From the middle of the decade there was even some net employment creation, unemployment levels generally peaking in 1984.

Yet whether the basis had been laid for sound and lasting growth is another matter. There were still several worrying problems which refused to go away, or which remained temporarily hidden just below the surface. Unemployment was one of these. Inflation was another; despite the substantial progress achieved in reducing it there were signs towards the end of the period that it was about to rear its ugly head once again. Nor had the problem of public sector finances been laid to rest; many countries were still in deficit, and longer term there was cause for concern regarding the funding of public commitments. Furthermore, there were frequent suggestions, not least by the OECD (1987), that Europe was suffering from structural rigidities and inflexible markets and that until these were eliminated there could be no real basis for sound growth and full employment. There was even a hint that some European countries were not keeping abreast of modern technology. Finally, at the turn of the decade, external disturbances, for example the collapse of eastern Europe and the Gulf War, once again looked set to impart another setback to western progress. And so an all too familiar pattern appeared to be repeating itself, as the beginning of the new decade opened on a recessionary note.

Some of these problems will be taken up later in the chapter, after a more detailed discussion of the achievements of the decade and the forces making for recovery.

DISINFLATION

One of the most notable achievements of the 1980s was the abatement of inflation. For much of the 1970s and early 1980s inflation in western Europe had been both high and volatile, often running into double figures. For the years 1979–82 it averaged well over 10 per cent a year, though with marked variations between countries. Italy and the UK had the highest rates, around 20 per cent at the peak, whereas at the other extreme Germany and Switzerland experienced quite modest inflation. A conscious decision was taken early on by the authorities in most countries not to tolerate the persistence of the high inflation rates of the past which, by distorting the price mechanism, shortening time horizons and generally undermining confidence, were thought to have been responsible for the sluggish economic performance. Accordingly, monetary policy became increasingly restrictive and it was backed up by fiscal restraint, with the result that the recessionary impulses were intensified or prolonged. Two other factors also weighed heavily in the balance. First, the concern over the state of public finances and the growing burden of interest payments prompted governments to take action to consolidate their finances. Second, macroeconomic policy was strongly influenced by the course of events in the United States. Monetary restraint and growing fiscal deficits in the latter case led to high real interest rates and a strong appreciation of the dollar, so that European countries were forced to maintain a restrictive monetary stance and high real interest rates in order to defend their currencies against the dollar. Yet while American policy certainly put pressure on Europe in this respect, the Federal deficit probably helped to sustain growth elsewhere through rising American imports, even though in time the fiscal problem of the United States became a matter of increasing concern both at home and abroad (Schafer 1988).

The tight policy stance coupled with the declared intention not to repeat the experience of the 1970s certainly helped to reduce inflationary expectations. Non-accommodating monetary policy, rather than fiscal restraint, probably made the major contribution to disinflation. In general fiscal restraint tended to be rather less widespread, important in Germany, the UK and Japan, expansionary for a time in France and Italy, and broadly stable in the smaller European countries. Taking the OECD as a whole, there was little significant change in structural budget balances between 1980 and 1983 because increases in debt service payments and transfers tended to offset action to reduce budget deficits in many cases.

The disinflationary process was greatly assisted by the more favourable trend in commodity prices. Oil prices collapsed dramatically once the OPEC pricing cartel ceased to be effective; from a peak of $36 a barrel early in 1981 they fell to $26 in late 1985 and to a low of $11 early in 1986, before rising gently to around $16 a barrel. Raw material prices also fell back sharply until 1987 as a result of substantial additions to capacity, the slow recovery in world industrial activity and the development of substitutes. Thus between 1980 and 1988 the real price of non-fuel commodity exports from developing countries declined by some 40 per cent. Fluctuations in exchange rates, especially the sharp appreciation of the dollar in the first half of the 1980s, complicated the position somewhat, since it tended to offset part of the gain from falling commodity prices in so far as European imports were denominated in dollar terms. This position was reversed in the second half of the decade, however, when the dollar depreciated.

The third main factor bearing favourably on inflation was the shift in wage-setting behaviour, though in turn it should be stressed that the latter was considerably influenced by the first two factors. During the 1970s a significant influence sustaining the inflationary momentum had been the tendency for wages to rise not only in response to price changes but also in anticipation of future changes. Wage earners, long accustomed to steady annual increases in real incomes, were not prepared to forgo these when the economy could no longer deliver them because of external shocks and declining productivity. Hence they bargained for high nominal wage awards which for the most part were accommodated by monetary expansion, and so wage gains outstripped those warranted by changes in productivity and the terms of trade, leading to the emergence of a real wage gap. Wage-setting behaviour in this period was also adversely affected by the increasing inflexibility of labour markets through protective labour legislation and structural problems.

From 1982 there was a distinct improvement in the functioning of labour markets. Real wage resistance declined under the influence of recession and policy factors, helped also by the downward trend in commodity prices. Weak markets made it difficult for manufacturers to pass on cost increases and therefore stiffened their resistance to unjustified wage demands. Hence real earnings growth abated and the real wage gap became favourable to an improvement in profitability. Moderation may also have been assisted by a greater degree of flexibility in labour markets through more part-time work, the reduction in union participation and a shift away from highly organized staple industries, and also in some cases, the UK in particular, by legislation affecting industrial relations and wage bargaining.

By the middle of the 1980s the disinflationary process had more or less run its course. Consumer price inflation in western Europe averaged 2.5 per cent or less in 1986–7, very similar to that of the 1960s. Whether the problem had really been exorcized is another matter, however. It is noticeable that inflation began to creep up again in the later 1980s as the easing of the policy regime made way for an expansion in activity. The danger of expansionary policies being dispersed mainly in higher wages and prices rather than in real output may have lessened, but it had by no means been extinguished, a fact amply demonstrated by the sharp rise in UK inflation in 1989–90, largely as a consequence of over-exuberant policy relaxation. Few other countries were prepared to jeopardize the gains already made by injudicious action since the costs of disinflation had been heavy. What the experience of the past two decades had brought home, above all, was that 'it is less costly to maintain low inflation through non-accommodation of shocks as they occur, rather than to allow what might appear *ex ante* to be discrete, perhaps innocuous, increases in inflation to cumulate to levels that become economically and politically intolerable. This is the most important lesson from the disinflation of the 1980s' (Coe *et al.* 1988: 114).

CONSUMER SPENDING AND SAVING

The improvement in the inflationary situation encouraged a more confident stance on the part of consumers. Consumer spending was very flat in the recession of the early 1980s, while savings were at record levels as households attempted to restore their real savings balances during a period of high inflation. But consumption began to pick up slowly after 1982 and from 1985 onwards it was averaging more than 3 per cent per annum, being especially buoyant between 1986 and 1988. The rise in consumption was more stable and better sustained than in the previous cyclical recovery for several reasons. First, there was a general decline in household savings from the peak levels reached at the beginning of the decade. The decline in savings was especially marked in France, Britain and Italy. This can be attributed to the gradual erosion of the real balance effect on savings because of the fall in inflation, a high rate of family formation which gave rise to a strong demand for housing and consumer durables, and a wealth effect as house prices and stock market values rose faster than incomes, thereby encouraging households to increase borrowing and spending and reduce savings. The strong rise in residential property values encouraged borrowing on the basis of enhanced asset values, as did the liberalization and innovations in financial markets. In fact much of the fall in the savings ratio in the latter half of the decade, in the UK at least, was due to a surge in borrowing induced by a lax monetary policy and the ease with which new credit could be secured under a more liberal financial regime. Two other factors further strengthened the forces of spending: the continued weakness in commodity prices and a widespread shift in fiscal policy towards lower taxation in the latter part of the decade, both of which helped to sustain real income growth.

The effect of these combined forces was to make households feel considerably better off than before. Falling inflation and rapidly rising asset prices resulted in an improved wealth position, while rising real incomes through the improvement in economic activity, declining taxes and a favourable trend in the terms of trade improved the current income stream. This proved a potent and dangerous concoction which sparked off a spending and borrowing spree, rising real debt levels and the erosion of savings.

FIXED INVESTMENT

The rate of gross domestic capital formation also began to pick up significantly in most countries from 1984 onwards, after falls in 1981 and 1982 and a very modest increase in 1983. By the latter half of the decade investment was rising very strongly indeed and at a rate not seen since the early 1970s. The rate of growth of the capital stock began to increase once again, as did investment ratios, though the latter still remained a few percentage points below the levels reached in the early 1970s: 22 as against 26 per cent for the twelve Community countries.

One of the major factors in the revival of investment was of course the recovery in profitability. By the early 1980s rates of return in some countries had sunk to very low levels indeed, and on average the profitability of business was down on the 1960s by over 30 per cent. The main influence behind the decline, apart from the sluggish rate of activity, was the trend deterioration in the relationship between wages and productivity growth, so that real unit labour costs rose at a time of weak final output prices. Additionally, the unit costs of raw materials also rose sharply following the second oil crisis. At the same time capital productivity had deteriorated quite sharply through the 1970s and early 1980s, owing to lower rates of capital formation, lower capacity utilization, possibly some slowing down of technical advance and impediments to efficient capital use due to structural factors and increasing government regulations. The result was that total factor productivity declined markedly, to only about one-quarter that of the 1960s.

The steady unwinding of these adverse trends during the 1980s led to a general improvement in profitability. Wage moderation was undoubtedly a major factor in the process. Real labour costs, which had previously been rising faster than productivity, were reversed after the early 1980s so that between 1981 and 1990 real unit labour costs fell on average by about 8 per cent. The growth in the productivity of labour remained well below the level of the 1960s, but at least the adverse gap between wages and productivity had been closed. Capital productivity also improved in the later 1980s, partly as a result of better capacity utilization and an increase in capital formation, as did total factor productivity, though still at rates one-half those of the 1960s. Profits were also boosted by more favourable terms of trade, leading to lower input costs, and by a strengthening of final output prices.

Though profitability levels undoubtedly improved they still remained below those of the 1960s. Nevertheless the recovery was sufficient to encourage a revival of investment. The latter was also stimulated by considerable rationalization and modernization of capacity and investment in new technology following a long period of sluggish investment. What is even more significant is that in the latter half of the decade investment was becoming more employment creating, whereas previously, owing to the configuration of relative factor prices, it had been primarily labour saving. Thus in the years 1984–90 net employment creation in the European Community was of the order of 8 million persons. This of course only had a very modest impact on the level of unemployment since other adverse influences were at work (see below).

INTERNATIONAL TRADE

One area that remained relatively buoyant in the recession of the early 1980s was international trade. The volume of exports of goods and services from western Europe, though well down on the level of the later 1970s, continued to expand on average at around 2 per cent per annum, which was a far better performance than in the case of most other key economic indicators – and this despite serious balance of payments difficulties in many countries due to the oil shock (the major exception being the UK because of North Sea oil coming on stream), serious debt crises in the Third World, and a growing protectionist sentiment, reflected mainly in the proliferation of non-tariff barriers. Fortunately, however, unlike the 1930s, the major trading nations avoided a lurch into stringent policy protection which did so much damage to trade and activity in the earlier period.

From 1983 trade once again became something of an engine of growth though less strongly than in the boom years after the war. Total exports grew more rapidly than output, at around 5 per cent or more in western Europe through to 1990, with manufactured exports rising even faster. Closer integration among western nations, the liberalization of international capital movements, the stabilization of exchange rates, and the maintenance of a fairly liberal trading environment, all helped to promote the recovery in trade. But perhaps of more significance as far as the initial upsurge was concerned was the strong demand generated for imports from the United States as a result of that country's domestic boom and the appreciation of the dollar. Thus between 1983 and 1985 total US demand outpaced the growth of domestic output, whereas in most other countries except the UK and Italy the reverse occurred. This led to a sharp rise in American imports and an increasing trade deficit, the counterpart of which was equally large trade surpluses in Germany and Japan. By contrast, later in the decade the position was partly reversed. Though the United States still recorded large external deficits, total domestic demand grew more slowly than output and the dollar depreciated so that increased exports helped to take up the slack. Japanese exports, on the other hand, slowed down as a result of the appreciation of the yen while those of the European Community remained fairly buoyant.

BUDGET DEFICITS AND POLICY FORMATION

Given the overriding problems of inflation and budgetary deficits it was scarcely to be expected that government policy would play a crucial role in recovery from the recession. Indeed, as already noted, macroeconomic policy for a good part of the time concentrated on squeezing inflation out of the system and it was only later in the decade that some modest relaxation was allowed.

An equally, if not more important, factor influencing the conduct of policy was the need to consolidate public finances. During the 1970s and early 1980s most countries saw the emergence of large and growing budgetary deficits (5–10 per cent of GDP) and rapidly rising public debt to GDP ratios. The marked deterioration in budgetary positions was due to an explosion of public expenditure unmatched by revenue, largely resulting from the reallocation of resources arising from the two oil shocks, the slowing down of growth and the rise in unemployment, together with the inflexibility of expenditure commitments incurred in the good years of the 1960s. By the early 1980s the problem had become sufficiently serious to prompt a fundamental reassessment of budgetary practices. Several considerations influenced the shift towards corrective action. First, large public sector deficits were thought to undermine confidence, especially in financial markets, since they were often associated with inflation. Second, there was serious concern about the future sustainability of such deficits and their financing given the increasing inflexibility in expenditures and the rising burden of interest payments and transfer benefits. A third factor was the conviction that large public sectors per se had adverse effects on growth and employment, principally through the crowding out of private sector activity and the alleged adverse effects of transfer payments and high taxation on savings and investment. The evidence on this matter is very mixed and conflicting (Katz et al. 1983; Friedlander and Sanders 1985), and policy response was dictated more by ideological and political conviction than by sound economic reasoning, though concern about the size of budget deficits was genuine enough. Additionally, there was a growing belief that even a balanced expansion of revenue and expenditure might be bad for growth since the rising tax burden could put pressure on wage costs which would adversely affect profitability.

Despite firm resolve to deal with the problem, achieving fiscal correction was quite another matter. Because of the effects of the recession the early years of the decade saw upward pressure on public spending at a time when revenues were far from buoyant. It was not until near the middle of the decade therefore that government attempts to rein back spending began to have some impact on the share of public spending in GDP, so that initially tax revenues bore the brunt of the adjustment process. Even in the latter part of the decade, when firmer control over spending was attained, increased tax revenues, as a result of the upswing in economic activity, were more important than the containment of spending in restoring public finances. Even so, fiscal consolidation was far from complete by the end of the period. No less than thirteen OECD countries were still in deficit, four of which recorded deficits of more than 5 per cent of GDP, while the size of the public sector was on average still greater than at the previous cyclical peak. In 1990 government spending as a share of GDP in the OECD area averaged more than 3 percentage points above that of 1979 (Oxley and Martin 1991: 175).

The experience of the 1980s demonstrates the difficulty of correcting public finances. There is an upward limit to taxation levels beyond which they have an adverse impact on activity, while spending, once committed, is very difficult to reverse. Many of the spending cuts were either cosmetic or marginal, being concentrated on public investment (the most detrimental as far as future growth is concerned), subsidies and wage bills, the latter partly as a result of wage moderation and the containment of public sector employment growth. Moreover, the longer term outlook is not encouraging since spending pressures are likely to increase in the future because of increasing dependence ratios, the restoration of public investment especially on infrastructure facilities, the demand for more resources for health, education and pensions, and the relaxation of wage restraint in the public sector. In time, as the OECD recognized in one of its recent reports (1987), this may force governments to consider making fundamental changes in the way in which collective goods and services are financed. Alternatively, improvements in revenue collection and tax enforcement may be another possibility. Tax evasion is a growing problem everywhere, no more so than in Italy where it has long been a problem of serious magnitude. It has been estimated that tax revenue lost through evasion would have been sufficient to eliminate the whole of the Italian budgetary deficit in 1984 (Sassoon 1990: 119).

On balance, therefore, there was little scope for significant leverage to economic activity coming from macroeconomic policy. Both fiscal and monetary policy remained tight throughout the first half of the 1980s. In the later 1980s there was some relaxation in monetary policy through a fall in interest rates and an expansion of the money supply, while in some countries tax reductions were implemented. The stock market collapse of October 1987 prompted some easing of monetary policy, but the timing may have been inappropriate from the point of view of the real economy given the strength of the recovery and the speculative asset situation. In the UK, for example, an over-expansionary monetary policy helped to fuel a housing boom and consumer spending spree which had to be capped late in 1988. Thus relaxation tended to be short-lived and the turn of the decade saw a shift towards policy tightening as the fear of old problems resurfaced.

THE UNEMPLOYMENT PROBLEM

One problem that refused to go away in the 1980s was unemployment. In fact until the middle of the decade unemployment was on an upward trend, rising into double figures in several countries. Even the sustained growth of the later 1980s failed to make much impact on the levels despite some net employment creation. Unemployment percentages remained close to double figures in some of the larger countries. However, there was considerable divergence in rates of unemployment among countries, in contrast to the situation with respect to inflation and output growth. Germany's unemployment remained consistently below that of many of her Community partners, while several of the smaller countries, notably Austria, Norway, Sweden and Switzerland, had an even better record, with rates not too far removed from those of the 1960s. The relative position of the United States also improved in the latter half of the decade, while Japan's record was quite exceptional throughout the period. The differences and the contrast with earlier periods are shown in Table 8.5.

Table 8.5 Unemployment in Europe, 1960–90 (per cent)

	1960–8	1969–73	1974–9	1980–5	1986–90
Belgium	2.3	2.4	6.3	11.3	9.5
Denmark	2.0	1.4	5.5	9.3	8.6
France	1.7	2.6	4.5	8.3	9.8
West Germany	0.7	0.8	3.2	6.0	5.9
Ireland	5.0	5.6	7.6	12.6	16.2
Italy	3.8	4.2	4.6	6.4	7.7
Netherlands	1.2	2.0	5.1	10.1	8.8
Spain	2.4	2.7	5.3	16.6	18.7
UK	2.6	3.4	5.1	10.5	8.8
Austria	1.6	1.1	1.5	3.0	3.4
Finland	1.8	2.3	4.4	5.1	4.3
Norway	2.0	1.7	1.8	2.6	3.5
Sweden	1.3	1.8	1.5	2.4	1.7
Switzerland	0.1	0.0	1.0	1.7	1.9
United States	4.7	4.9	6.7	8.0	5.8
Japan	1.4	1.2	1.9	2.4	2.5

Source: R. Layard, S. Nickell and R. Jackman, *Unemployment: Macroeconomic Performance and the Labour Market*, Oxford: Oxford University Press, 1991, p. 398

Not since the 1930s had such high levels of unemployment been seen. As then, some of the characteristics of the unemployment problem were familiar: the large regional differences, the sustained rise in the number of long-term unemployed, and the disproportionate incidence of unemployment among certain groups: the young and older workers, unskilled and the handicapped. One major difference with the earlier period, however, was that changes in the level of economic activity seemed to have less impact on reducing the numbers of unemployed.

In fact what is most noticeable is how limited the employment impact of growth has been over the longer term, even back to the 1960s. Between 1960 and 1973 GDP growth in the European Community averaged 4.8 per cent a year, whereas employment expanded by only 0.2–0.3 per cent per annum. A growth rate of 2.4 per cent in the years 1973–9 had virtually no effect on employment, while in subsequent years through to 1986 employment growth was either negative or flat. Thus for the whole of the period 1973–87 some three-quarters of the rise in the labour force was reflected in higher unemployment since the net growth in numbers employed was negligible. By contrast the United States and Japan, and some of the smaller European countries, managed to generate substantial new employment with the result that their unemployment rates were not much higher than in the early 1970s.

Jobless growth therefore seems to have been a peculiar feature of the major western European nations. Estimates suggest that a rate of growth of around 2–2.5 per cent a year is required before employment responds positively (Commission of the European Communities 1989: 119). Thus on the basis of a continuation of growth rates of around 3 per cent a year, as experienced in the later 1980s, and a labour force growth of 0.4 per cent a year, unemployment levels would continue to remain high, around 6 per cent, through to the mid-1990s, unless the employment-to-growth ratio changed for the better. In other words, a return to the former low levels of unemployment of the postwar years would require very much higher rates of economic growth than have been seen over the last few years.

Attempts to explain the unemployment conundrum have taken several forms. They include the Keynesian aggregate demand version, the neoclassical real wage effect, the influence of structural rigidities in labour markets, and the impact of hysteresis. There are also the long-term changes in the growth of the labour supply to take into account. No one factor can explain the persistence of unemployment or differences between countries.

A higher level of aggregate demand and output would no doubt have eased the unemployment situation through greater employment creation had the authorities been disposed to impart a significant fiscal boost to their economies. Given the concern over inflation and budgetary deficits this line of action was never seriously contemplated. Moreover, if, as was suspected, demand stimuli were more likely to feed through to prices than to output and employment, then there would be little point in taking such action. Indeed, if the relationship between output and employment growth of the 1960s and early 1970s had continued to prevail, then raising the rate of growth would not have had a marked impact on unemployment. However, one should also bear in mind that at a time when economic growth was fairly sluggish labour force growth was actually accelerating. Because of demographic factors that led to an increase in the proportion of the population of working age, together with an increase in female participation, the active labour force was growing more rapidly in the 1970s and 1980s than it had done previously. As the data in Table 8.6 show, it was growing at a rate of between 0.6 and 0.8 per cent per annum in these years compared with only 0.2 per cent in the 1960s. Since employment growth, apart from the later 1980s, remained fairly constant at very low levels (0.2 per cent) it was inevitable that most of the increase in the labour force would be translated into unemployment. And had the relationships between employment and output growth of the 1960s continued to hold in the later 1980s the unemployment situation would have been very much worse than it actually was.

Table 8.6 Population, active population and employment in the Europe 12, 1970–90

	Percentage change per annum					
	1970/ 1960	1980/ 1970	1990/ 1980	1984/ 1980	1988/ 1984	1990/ 1988
Population	0.8	0.5	0.3	0.3	0.3	0.3
Active population	0.2	0.6	0.8	0.8	0.8	0.6
Employment	0.2	0.2	0.3	– 0.6	0.9	1.2
	1960	*1970*	*1980*	*1984*	*1988*	*1990*
Unemployment rate	2.0	2.5	6.4	10.8	10.0	8.7

Source: Commission of the European Communities, *European Economy* 42, 1989, p. 120

Clearly then, forces on the labour supply side largely unconnected with the state of economic activity would have put considerable pressure on the labour market whatever the rate of growth. However, this does not mean that we have fully solved the paradox of high unemployment in the major European Community countries. The fact is that unemployment was a good deal higher than in many of the smaller countries and than in Japan and the United States. Moreover, labour force growth was even more rapid in the latter countries, though only in the case of the smaller countries did it accelerate compared with the 1960s (OECD 1991).

Essentially, then, what we have to explain is why the larger European countries had an inferior employment record than the other countries. In seeking clarification of the differences frequent recourse has been made to supply-side considerations. In very broad terms the main contention here is that European labour markets, for one reason or another, work less efficiently than those elsewhere. This could be because of stronger real wage resistance, structural rigidities in labour markets, and the effect of hysteresis (lagged response to a past event). The consequence would be to raise the non-accelerating inflation rate of unemployment (NAIRU), which would make it difficult to reduce unemployment without aggravating inflation.

There is some substance in all these points. Wages have been less responsive to changes in unemployment, productivity and to a lesser extent prices in several of the major European countries than they have been in the United States and Japan. Within Europe Germany, Austria and Switzerland have had a more flexible wage pattern than most other countries (Coe 1985: 117–19; OECD 1987: 132–4). This would be consistent with their better unemployment record. The corollary would be that in other countries labour was too expensive, with wages rising faster than productivity and leading to a real wage gap which dampened labour recruitment. This gap certainly appeared in the major countries during the 1970s and early 1980s, but thereafter it was eliminated as real wages moderated and profits were allowed to recover. This seems to imply that excessive real wages were not a potent force in constraining employment growth after the early 1980s. However, NAIRU estimates remained high for much of the decade which seems to indicate that factors other than real wage rigidity may have been a hindrance to employment creation. Incidentally, the fact that the NAIRU rates tended to be lower than actual rates of unemployment by the mid-1980s suggests that there may have been some leeway for modest fiscal expansion.

Structural factors can partly explain the increasing rigidities of European labour markets which reduce their flexibility and efficiency in allocating labour among competing uses. These would include impediments which reduce labour mobility among firms, industries, regions and occupations and into and out of unemployment, thereby resulting in a rise of the unemployment-to-vacancies ratio (Beveridge curve). This in turn would account for regional differences in unemployment and the disproportionate incidence of unemployment among different groups of workers.

The increasing rigidity of European labour markets was a consequence of two main factors: administrative regulations and the pattern of collective bargaining and wage determination. During the later 1960s and 1970s various legislative enactments served to impede the microeconomic functioning of labour markets. These included minimum wage legislation, employment protection laws and generous benefit systems, some of which were only partly liberalized in the following decade. Second, restrictive work practices and inefficient methods of labour utilization have been perpetuated by unsatisfactory bargaining systems which have hindered both the internal and the external mobility of labour and reinforced the protective employment regulations.

It is significant that labour market outcomes have been consistently poorer in countries such as the UK, France, Belgium and Italy, where collective bargaining systems have neither been subject to the direct constraints of decentralized bargaining at the enterprise level and competitive labour markets as in the United States and Japan, nor been influenced by a recognition of national responsibility as occurs under the more co-ordinated and centralized negotiating procedures in the Nordic countries, Austria and Germany. Instead, 'the setting of wages and of the conditions of employment have typically functioned through a multiplicity of overlapping and competing levels, fragmenting employer solidarity and encouraging inflationary spirals of bargaining around long established pay relativities; and where the legal framework for bargaining has been poorly spelt out in terms of the rights and duties of the parties to collective agreements' (OECD 1987: 41).

Such fragmented systems of bargaining reduce the flexibility of labour markets both in terms of the allocative force of the price mechanism, for example through a narrowing of pay differentials between regions, occupations, skilled and unskilled workers, and through restrictive covenants which limit choice and protect 'insiders' (those in employment). They may also affect the level of skill formation in so far as pay relativities favour the unskilled and untrained, notably in Britain. Effectively what happens is that labour markets become segmented principally between the 'insiders', that is, those with jobs who benefit through higher wages and greater job security by virtue of restrictions on competition in the labour market, and the 'outsiders', or those unemployed who are excluded from effective participation in the labour market and who ultimately bear the cost of the system.

This combination of forces sets the pattern whereby unemployment can feed upon itself through a process known as hysteresis. What might start out as a short-term demand problem transforms itself into a long-term supply phenomenon as the unemployed increasingly become a ghetto group marginalized out of the labour market through demoralization, loss of skill, age disability and lack of training. They therefore cease to be an effective competitive force in the labour market and hence their influence on wage determination is reduced. This in turn reinforces rigidities and restrictive practices by 'insiders', who seek to safeguard the position of the majority even at the expense of more unemployment through early retirement, part-time working, reduced recruitment of young workers and the like. In this way high unemployment can create the conditions for its own perpetuation (Lawrence and Schultz 1987: 45).

In their detailed cross-section study of unemployment patterns in nineteen OECD countries over the last three decades, Layard et al. (1991) argue that, while in the short term demand is a powerful determinant of unemployment, in the long run it is the supply side which dominates. Their supply-oriented model takes as a starting point the recent supply-side shocks to the system and then traces the relationships between prices, wages and unemployment within the framework of different institutional settings. Once equilibrium is disturbed and unemployment rises, it is difficult to return to the *status quo* because of inflexible labour markets and institutional constraints. These imperfections distort the efficient working of the labour market and thereby prevent unemployment, or the level of employment, being determined by optimal allocation processes. The most important impediments to efficient labour markets were found to be the system of wage determination and unemployment benefit provisions, both of which serve to stiffen real wage resistance and restrictive practices in times of difficulty, with adverse effects on employment.

Variations in levels of unemployment among countries can therefore be attributed, in part at least, to differences in bargaining structures and institutional settings. Economies adapt better to external shocks where benefit systems discourage long-term unemployment (short-duration benefits) and where union densities are low, labour markets are competitive and there is a high degree of enterprise bargaining, as in the United States, Canada, Switzerland and Japan. Conversely, highly unionized labour markets may also perform satisfactorily provided that bargaining is co-ordinated and centralized (a relatively small number of agreements with broad coverage) and unemployment compensation schemes are restricted, and preferably where there are active labour market policies. The Scandinavian countries, Germany and Austria would fall into this category. The worst scenario is one in which bargaining procedures are loosely co-ordinated, fragmented and decentralized, and benefit systems are generous. This generates conditions which encourage involuntary unemployment, structural rigidities in labour markets and mismatch unemployment. Several European countries fall into this category including Britain, France, Italy, Spain and to a lesser extent the Netherlands.

There would therefore appear to be a sufficiently strong association between labour market characteristics and levels of unemployment (see Table 8.5) to suggest that supply-side factors were important in determining variations in unemployment across countries. In the major European countries labour markets tended to function less efficiently than elsewhere. Haberler, quoting Marris (Haberler 1986: 67–8), stresses the basic structural impediments in European labour markets which rendered them less flexible than the American labour market and hence weaker employment generators. Europe therefore experienced higher unemployment, while at the same time the scope for effective macroeconomic policy action to deal with the problem was more limited.

STRUCTURAL RIGIDITIES, INNOVATION AND COMPETITIVENESS

It may be, as some writers have suggested, that the slowdown in Europe's growth since the mid-1970s was not a sign of deep-rooted economic problems but simply an inevitable return to more sustainable rates of growth following the exhaustion or partial exhaustion of many of the favourable factors which had powered the post-war boom. Some of these had clearly passed their peak, for example the effects of catch-up, the gains from trade liberalization and labour force reallocation, the diffusion of new technologies and favourable terms of trade. In this case, therefore, one would have expected some slowing down of growth at some stage irrespective of the influence of random shocks and government policies. Nevertheless, one should also bear in mind that the supply shocks severely undermined the energy-intensive basis of post-war growth, while the slowness and ineptitude with which governments adjusted to the supply shocks served to aggravate the deceleration in economic activity.

Notwithstanding these events, however, there were also some worrying signs that European countries were losing their former dynamism and experiencing perhaps a touch of sclerosis which comes with old age. The signs may be seen in increasing structural rigidities and the response to new technology.

The structural issue has been well aired in recent years. The OECD published a weighty tome on this very subject in 1987, *Structural Adjustment and Economic Performance*, arguing that a return to sustainable growth in the longer term was dependent on a broad range of reforms of its microeconomic foundations in order to rejuvenate the efficiency with which economic systems worked. They claimed that 'experience has shown time and again that expansions cannot be maintained, and the cost of ensuing recessions is greatest, when the structural components of economies are functioning poorly' (1987: 49). The report dwelt upon virtually every conceivable supply-side aspect of economies including education and skill formation, research, labour markets and industrial relations, financial markets, agriculture, industrial adjustment, trade, social policies and the public sector.

What was perhaps most remarkable was the extent of the problem: 'the range of areas in which policy reform is needed is so great' (OECD 1987: 49). Some obvious candidates of course were agriculture, labour markets, social policies and industrial adjustment policies, where structural reform or the removal of inefficient subsidies and disincentives was urgently required. In other cases, for example education and training, the need was more for a reform of the structure and pattern of skill formation to cater for the requirements of new transferable skill technologies. Increasing the forces of competition both in trade and production were also deemed to be important, and here it should be noted that the European Community does not always live up to its declared intentions. If anything it may be a source of structural rigidities and regulatory impediments in its own right.

Throughout the 1980s governments tended to favour greater liberalization in markets and a certain degree of structural reform. This was reflected in measures taken to liberalize financial and transport markets, labour market reforms, modifications to minimum wage legislation, the tightening up of transfer payments and the privatization of state enterprises. The extent of the reforms varied from country to country but in few cases did they make a significant contribution to the more efficient working of markets. Governments also attempted to stabilize their budgetary finances and reduce the size of the public sector component, though with somewhat limited and mixed results (see above). This was in accord with the growing conviction, quite widespread among economists and policy-makers, that government spending, taxes, deficits and debt might be harmful to economic growth. Unfortunately there was little agreement as to the nature, size and scope of the relationships.

Nevertheless, there was probably some justification for the growing concern about the size of the public sector. It has grown inexorably over the past three decades, so that by the mid-1980s government outlays averaged over 50 per cent of GDP as against 32 per cent in 1960, creating problems of financing, eroding incentives, distorting choice and reducing resource efficiency. Moreover, since a large part of budgetary revenue – up to 40 per cent or more – consisted of revenue 'churning', that is, revenue returned to the original taxpayers mainly through transfers and subsidies, the cynically minded could well feel that its main function was to keep an army of bureaucrats in jobs! That apart, there was reason to believe that the costs of financing programmes at the margin could be quite steep at high levels of expenditure and taxation, 'so that the costs of increasing the size of the public sector, as well as the gains from reducing it, are significantly larger than the average economic cost of public sector spending' (OECD 1987: 47).

Unfortunately, with public sector spending, as with structural issues, it is very easy to point to anomalies, distortions, disincentives and impediments, but very difficult to quantify their significance. Moreover, many of the relevant matters give rise to strong emotional, ideological or sectional feelings which make analytical logic difficult to swallow. But sooner or later most countries will have to face up to some difficult decisions on these issues, especially with respect to the size, structure and financing of the public sector (see above).

The other area that could be the cause for some concern is Europe's competitive position within the high technology field. There is some evidence, admittedly scrappy, that in the 1970s and 1980s technical progress and innovation slowed down somewhat, more especially in the older energy-intensive sectors affected adversely by the oil shocks. This would be consistent with the decline in effectiveness of research and development spending in such sectors, especially in terms of productivity growth, although aggregate research and development expenditure as a share of output held up quite well. This may therefore simply represent a hiatus as economies transform from one technological scenario to another, for example from energy-intensive sectors to information technology and electronic systems. However, rather more disturbing is the possibility that some of the major European countries may have been losing ground in the high technology race. Data in Table 8.7 on comparative export shares in technology-intensive products does suggest that Europe may have been losing out to more dynamic Far Eastern competitors. This point can be amplified by reference to world trade in electronic products where Japan and the four 'little tigers' (Hong Kong, Taiwan, Singapore and South Korea) are coming to dominate the scene, with large positive trade balances as against growing deficits in European Community countries. This is a worrying trend since high technology skill-intensive fields of endeavour are one of the few comparative advantages left to high income countries in world markets.

According to the OECD (1987: 214) European countries have tended to lose out in international specialization since they have increased their competitive advantage in sectors of activity with low intensity of research and development, while losing ground in medium and high research and development sectors, especially the latter where their position worsened rapidly after the 1970s. This could be attributed mainly to 'slower and less judicious technological adjustment' than in other competitor countries with the result that

Table 8.7 Comparative changes in world export shares of technology-intensive products[a]

	1965	1975	1984
United States	27.5	24.5	25.2
Japan	7.3	11.6	20.2
France	7.3	8.4	7.7
Germany	16.9	16.8	14.5
UK	12.0	9.6	8.5
Italy			3.6

Source: F. Duchene and G. Shepherd (eds), *Managing Industrial Change in Western Europe*, London: Pinter, 1987, p. 36

Note: [a]Technology-intensive products are defined as those for which research and development expenditures exceed 2.36 per cent of value added.

Europe's share of world trade in manufactures has declined since the mid-1970s, while the shares of the United States and Japan have remained fairly constant and non-OECD members increased their shares. Technological progress in Europe has been impeded by structural rigidities and impediments in product and factor markets. These cover a wide area including fragmentation of markets, insufficient competition especially in sectors regulated by governments, slow adaptation of the industrial fabric and its related infrastructure, bottlenecks in skill formation, imperfections in capital markets, price and tax distortions inhibiting efficient resource allocation and technological diffusion, and severe labour market rigidities. The last of these is seen as one of the major impediments to progress on which the OECD (1987: 258) dilated at some length in forceful terms:

> By reducing job mobility, labour market rigidities inhibit technological development and dissemination. By retarding organisational innovation, they slow down the process of application of new technologies, and by distorting relative factor price movements, they set the process in the wrong direction by placing excessive emphasis on the defensive strategies for controlling costs through capital/labour substitution. In doing so, they are likely to prevent a virtuous circle of technical progress, qualitatively balanced growth of investment, enhancing of the stock of human capital and net creation of jobs, from forming or operating fully. They may even help to create a vicious circle in which technological backwardness, investment centred on rationalisation, depreciation of the stock of human capital, and a net decrease in job opportunities, reinforce one another.

LASTING STABILITY?

By the end of the decade official organizations were expressing guarded optimism about the future of the western economic system, the implication being that it had achieved a measure of stability whence sound growth could proceed. The equilibrium may have been more apparent than real, however, possibly no more robust than that perceived to obtain in the late 1920s. It is true that steady progress had been made during the 1980s in controlling inflation, stabilizing exchange rates and, to a lesser extent, consolidating budgetary accounts. There was also a greater degree of convergence in economic matters among European economies. However, it is far from clear that all the problems had been solved, and economies were by no means immune to the impact of disturbances. In other words, there was little ground for supposing that European nations were in a strong enough position to return to the high growth and full employment of the post-war years.

It may be unrealistic anyway to anticipate a resumption of a past performance since the long boom of 1948–73 can be regarded as something of an aberration. The high growth rates of that period were far out of line with long-term trend values and it is difficult to conceive of a repetition of so many favourable factors converging in time and space in the near future. Again, low unemployment is not a pervasive phenomenon through time, nor is the absence of depressions. Historical record suggests that neither are the natural order of things.

An alternative hypothesis might suggest that sustained high growth and low unemployment cannot be recaptured until full adjustment has been made to the supply shocks of the past. This is true in so far as the problems arising from these shocks, such as inflation, wage determination, structural rigidities and budgetary problems, have not been completely solved. On the surface the progress of the period looks solid enough, yet there are grounds for suspecting that not all is well underneath. It is significant, for example, that inflationary pressures soon began to re-assert themselves once activity picked up, while labour market rigidities and other structural problems continued to prevail. Budgetary problems, too, were far from over. Consolidation was at best partial, and given the inflexibility of expenditures and the longer-term commitments envisaged, it is clear that they could become very much more serious in the future. This fact alone would act as a serious constraint on the use of the fiscal weapon as a means of raising growth and employment. In any case there are serious doubts as to how far expansionary fiscal policies of the type traditionally contemplated by governments can secure a permanent and viable increase in employment given the structural rigidities and weak real growth forces that now seem to be prevalent in western economies. Indeed, such policies may even exacerbate the existing problems while doing little to restore the competitive strength of the countries in question. Managing modern economies in the future is clearly going to tax the ingenuity of policy-makers to the limits for there will be no easy and readily acceptable solutions.

A third possibility is that Europe is becoming more sclerotic and therefore is less adaptable to changing circumstances. There is certainly some evidence of increasing structural rigidity and loss of technological dynamism, although it is too early to say whether these constitute major constraints on progress. The European Community itself may also constitute a barrier to flexibility and adaptation to change in the future as it enlarges and becomes increasingly bogged down with regulatory provisions.

Finally, there is no doubt that western Europe is becoming increasingly dependent on and constrained by what happens in a small number of key economies, namely those of the United States, Japan and Germany. The 'follow my leader' principle has been all too apparent in recent years, especially with respect to the movements in key exchange rates and the reaction to US deficits. These countries will continue to set the standards for exchange rates and inflation.

Be that as it may for the longer term, the early 1990s opened on almost as inauspicious a note as the beginning of the previous decade. The elements were similar, though perhaps not quite so strong: one or two disturbances, for example the collapse of Eastern Europe, German reunification and the Iraq–Kuwait conflict, increasing inflation and a drift into recession, plus a cautionary policy stance for good measure. One can be forgiven a feeling of déjà vu.

Appendix Table 8A.1 Gross domestic product (annual percentage change)

	1970	1971	1972	1973	1974	1975	1976	1977	1978	1979	1980	1981	1982	1983	1984	1985	1986	1987	1988	1989	1990
France	5.7	4.8	4.4	5.4	3.1	-0.3	4.2	3.2	3.4	3.2	1.6	1.2	2.5	0.7	1.3	1.9	2.5	2.2	3.9	3.7	2.6
Germany, Federal Republic of	5.1	2.9	4.2	4.7	0.3	-1.6	5.4	3.0	2.9	4.2	1.4	0.2	-0.6	1.5	2.8	2.0	2.3	1.7	3.7	3.3	4.7
Italy	5.3	1.6	2.7	7.1	5.4	-2.7	6.6	3.4	3.7	6.0	4.2	1.0	0.3	1.1	3.0	2.6	2.5	3.0	4.2	3.2	2.5
UK	1.8	1.4	3.0	5.9	-1.5	-1.9	2.0	2.8	3.4	3.0	-2.9	-1.0	2.0	3.3	2.8	3.4	3.2	4.3	4.3	2.2	0.9
Total of four countries	4.6	2.8	3.7	5.7	1.7	-1.5	4.6	3.1	3.3	4.0	1.1	0.3	1.0	1.6	2.5	2.4	2.6	2.7	4.0	3.1	2.8
Austria	7.1	5.1	6.2	4.9	3.9	-0.4	4.6	4.5	0.1	4.7	2.9	-0.3	1.1	2.0	1.4	2.5	1.2	2.0	3.9	4.0	4.5
Belgium	6.4	3.7	5.4	6.0	4.2	-1.4	5.7	0.6	2.9	2.2	4.2	-0.9	1.5	0.4	2.0	0.8	1.6	2.3	4.6	4.0	3.9
Denmark	2.0	2.7	5.3	3.6	-0.9	-0.7	6.5	1.6	1.5	3.5	-0.4	-0.9	3.0	2.5	4.4	4.3	3.6	0.3	0.5	1.2	1.0
Finland	7.5	2.1	7.6	6.7	3.0	1.2	0.3	0.1	2.2	7.3	5.3	1.6	3.6	3.0	3.1	3.3	2.1	4.0	5.4	5.2	0.3
Ireland	3.5	3.4	6.4	4.7	4.3	3.7	1.4	8.2	7.2	3.1	3.1	3.3	2.3	-0.2	4.4	2.5	-0.4	4.4	3.9	5.9	4.7
Netherlands	5.7	4.2	3.3	4.7	4.0	-0.1	5.1	2.3	2.5	2.4	0.9	-0.7	-1.4	1.4	3.1	2.7	2.0	0.8	2.7	4.0	3.2
Norway	2.0	4.6	5.2	4.1	5.2	4.2	6.8	3.6	4.5	5.1	4.2	0.9	0.3	4.6	5.7	5.4	4.2	2.0	0.1	1.2	1.8
Sweden	6.5	0.9	2.3	4.0	3.2	2.6	1.1	-1.6	1.8	3.8	1.7	-	1.1	1.8	4.0	2.2	2.2	2.8	2.3	2.1	1.1
Switzerland	6.4	4.1	3.2	3.0	1.5	-7.3	-1.4	2.4	0.4	2.5	4.6	1.5	-0.9	1.0	1.8	3.7	2.9	2.0	2.9	3.5	2.7
Total of nine countries	5.6	3.4	4.3	4.5	3.0	-0.6	3.3	1.7	2.0	3.5	2.7	0.1	0.7	1.8	3.1	2.9	2.3	2.0	2.9	3.3	2.5
Total western Europe	4.8	2.9	3.8	5.4	2.0	-1.3	4.3	2.7	3.0	3.9	1.5	0.3	0.9	1.7	2.6	2.5	2.5	2.5	3.7	3.2	2.8
Greece	8.0	7.1	8.9	7.3	-3.6	6.1	6.4	3.4	6.7	3.7	1.8	0.1	0.4	0.4	2.8	3.1	0.8	-0.1	4.1	2.8	1.2
Portugal	9.1	6.6	8.0	11.2	1.1	-4.3	6.9	5.6	2.8	5.6	4.6	1.6	2.1	-0.2	-1.9	2.8	4.1	5.3	3.9	5.4	3.9
Spain	4.1	5.0	8.1	7.9	5.7	1.1	3.0	3.3	1.8	0.2	1.5	-0.2	1.2	1.8	1.8	2.3	3.3	5.5	5.2	5.0	3.5
Turkey	4.9	9.1	6.4	4.4	8.5	7.5	8.7	4.3	2.8	-0.9	-0.7	4.4	5.0	3.7	5.7	5.1	8.3	7.4	3.6	1.6	9.0
Yugoslavia	5.6	8.1	4.2	5.0	8.5	3.6	3.9	8.0	6.9	7.0	2.2	1.5	0.7	-1.2	2.0	0.5	3.6	-1.1	-1.7	0.6	-7.6
Total southern Europe	5.1	6.2	7.5	7.2	5.1	2.4	4.5	4.2	3.2	1.7	1.5	0.8	1.7	1.4	2.3	2.6	4.0	4.4	3.8	3.6	3.0
Total Europe	4.9	3.3	4.2	5.6	2.3	-0.9	4.3	2.9	3.0	3.7	1.5	0.3	1.0	1.6	2.6	2.6	2.7	2.7	3.7	3.2	2.8
United States	-0.3	2.7	4.9	4.9	-0.7	-1.0	4.8	4.6	5.2	2.1	-0.2	2.0	-2.5	3.7	7.0	3.6	2.9	3.6	4.4	2.5	0.9
Canada	2.6	5.8	5.7	7.7	4.4	2.6	6.2	3.6	4.6	3.9	1.5	3.7	-3.2	3.2	6.3	4.8	3.3	4.0	4.4	3.0	1.1
North America	-0.1	2.9	5.0	5.1	-0.3	-0.8	4.9	4.5	5.1	2.2	-	2.1	-2.5	3.7	6.9	3.7	3.0	3.6	4.4	2.5	1.0
Total	1.9	3.1	4.7	5.3	0.8	-0.8	4.7	3.8	4.3	2.8	0.6	1.4	-1.1	2.8	5.2	3.2	2.9	3.3	4.1	2.8	1.7

Source: Economic Commission for Europe, *Economic Survey of Europe in 1990–1991*, New York, 1991

Appendix Table 8A.2 Industrial production (annual percentage change)

	1970	1971	1972	1973	1974	1975	1976	1977	1978	1979	1980	1981	1982	1983	1984	1985	1986	1987	1988	1989	1990
France	5.6	6.5	5.5	6.8	2.4	-7.3	8.9	1.4	2.4	4.4	-0.1	-1.5	-0.2	-0.1	0.4	0.5	0.9	1.9	4.7	4.2	1.5
Germany, Federal Republic of	5.9	0.9	3.7	6.3	-1.7	-6.2	6.9	2.6	1.9	5.1	–	-1.9	-3.2	0.7	3.0	4.5	2.0	0.4	3.6	4.9	5.5
Italy	6.6	-0.5	4.9	9.8	3.9	-8.8	11.6	–	2.0	6.6	5.2	-2.2	-3.1	-2.4	3.4	1.3	4.1	2.6	6.9	3.9	-1.0
UK	0.4	-0.5	1.8	9.0	-2.0	-5.4	3.4	5.1	2.9	3.9	-6.7	-3.2	1.7	4.1	0.1	5.5	2.4	3.3	3.6	0.4	-0.5
Total of four countries	4.6	1.5	3.9	7.6	0.2	-6.8	7.4	2.4	2.3	5.0	-0.5	-2.1	-1.5	0.6	1.8	3.2	2.3	1.8	4.5	3.5	2.0
Austria	8.6	5.9	8.1	3.7	5.5	-6.3	6.6	3.8	2.1	7.7	2.7	-1.6	-0.8	1.0	5.3	4.5	1.1	1.0	4.4	5.9	8.5
Belgium	2.9	1.7	7.7	6.0	4.0	-9.8	7.7	0.4	2.4	4.5	-1.2	-2.7	–	1.9	2.4	2.6	0.8	2.2	5.7	3.5	4.5
Denmark	–	–	–	–	–	–	–	–	–	–	–	–	–	–	–	–	–	–	–	–	–
Finland	10.2	5.6	8.8	6.5	4.5	-1.4	–	1.5	4.3	11.1	7.5	2.3	1.1	3.4	4.3	4.2	1.7	5.1	3.7	2.6	-1.5
Ireland	3.4	3.9	4.5	10.6	1.6	-4.0	8.8	8.0	7.8	7.8	-4.8	5.4	-0.7	7.9	9.9	3.5	3.2	9.8	10.9	12.4	4.5
Netherlands	9.2	5.6	5.3	6.3	6.0	-5.6	8.3	–	1.1	3.3	–	-2.1	-4.3	2.2	4.4	5.3	–	1.2	0.1	5.1	2.5
Norway	4.3	4.2	8.0	5.6	3.5	5.1	6.5	–	10.6	6.8	5.1	–	–	8.5	6.7	5.3	3.5	7.5	5.1	16.3	3.5
Sweden	5.1	1.2	2.4	7.1	4.4	-2.1	-2.2	-5.5	-1.2	7.1	-1.1	-1.1	-2.2	4.6	6.6	3.1	–	2.2	1.1	2.8	-3.0
Switzerland	8.7	2.3	2.2	5.5	1.0	-12.4	–	5.9	–	2.2	5.4	-1.0	-3.1	-1.1	3.3	5.3	4.0	1.0	6.7	1.8	3.5
Total of nine countries	6.9	3.5	5.3	6.0	4.0	-5.8	4.0	0.9	2.2	5.4	1.9	-1.0	-1.8	2.8	4.8	4.3	1.5	2.8	3.8	5.6	2.7
Total western Europe	5.1	1.9	4.1	7.3	1.0	-6.6	6.7	2.1	2.2	5.1	–	-1.9	-1.6	1.0	2.5	3.4	2.1	2.0	4.4	4.0	2.1
Greece	10.3	11.2	14.3	15.3	-1.6	4.4	10.5	2.0	7.6	6.0	1.0	0.9	0.9	-0.3	2.3	4.2	-1.0	-1.5	5.1	1.9	-2.0
Portugal	6.4	7.7	12.9	11.8	2.8	-4.9	3.3	13.2	6.8	7.2	5.5	2.4	7.7	3.5	2.5	0.7	6.1	2.4	6.2	5.0	7.5
Spain	10.5	2.9	16.1	15.1	9.3	-8.8	5.1	5.3	2.3	0.7	1.3	-1.0	-1.1	2.7	0.9	1.9	3.1	4.6	3.1	4.5	–
Turkey	–	–	–	–	–	–	–	–	–	–	–	–	–	–	–	–	–	–	–	–	–
Yugoslavia	7.5	9.3	8.5	5.9	11.1	5.0	3.2	10.8	8.3	9.0	3.5	3.4	–	1.1	5.4	3.1	4.0	1.0	-1.0	1.0	-10.5
Total southern Europe	9.5	5.3	13.9	12.8	8.3	-4.7	5.0	6.8	4.5	3.7	2.1	0.5	–	2.1	2.4	2.3	3.3	2.9	2.4	3.4	-2.2
Total Europe	5.4	2.1	4.9	7.8	1.6	-6.4	6.6	2.5	2.4	4.9	0.2	-1.7	-1.4	1.1	2.5	3.3	2.2	2.1	4.2	3.9	1.7
United States	-3.4	1.4	9.8	8.1	-1.4	-8.8	9.2	7.9	6.6	3.9	-1.9	2.2	-7.1	6.0	11.1	1.9	0.9	5.0	5.5	2.5	1.0
Canada	-1.6	5.7	8.8	11.9	1.9	-7.3	6.7	3.4	3.4	4.8	-3.4	2.1	-9.9	6.5	12.2	5.4	-0.8	4.5	4.9	0.1	-3.0
North America	-3.2	1.7	9.7	8.3	-1.2	-8.7	9.0	7.5	6.3	4.0	-2.0	2.2	-7.3	6.0	11.2	2.2	0.8	4.9	5.4	2.3	0.7
Total	0.7	1.9	7.4	8.1	0.1	-7.6	7.8	5.2	4.6	4.4	-1.0	0.4	-4.7	3.8	7.2	2.7	1.4	3.7	4.9	3.0	1.1

Source: Economic Commission for Europe, Economic Survey of Europe in 1990–1991, New York, 1991

Appendix Table 8A.3 Gross domestic fixed capital formation (annual percentage change)

	1970	1971	1972	1973	1974	1975	1976	1977	1978	1979	1980	1981	1982	1983	1984	1985	1986	1987	1988	1989	1990
France	4.6	7.3	6.0	8.5	1.3	-6.4	3.3	-1.8	2.1	3.1	2.6	-1.9	-1.4	-3.6	-2.6	3.2	4.5	4.1	8.6	5.9	4.7
Germany, Federal Republic of	9.4	6.1	2.7	-0.3	-9.6	-5.3	3.6	3.6	4.7	7.2	2.8	-4.8	-5.3	3.2	0.8	0.1	3.3	2.2	5.1	7.1	8.2
Italy	3.0	0.2	1.3	8.8	2.0	-7.3	-	1.8	0.6	5.7	8.7	-3.2	-5.2	-0.9	4.5	1.4	1.6	5.8	6.7	5.1	3.8
UK	2.5	1.8	-0.2	6.5	-2.4	-2.0	1.7	-1.8	3.0	2.8	-5.4	-9.6	5.4	5.0	8.5	4.0	1.9	9.5	14.8	4.2	-1.5
Total of four countries	5.4	4.2	2.7	5.2	-2.8	-5.5	2.3	0.6	2.8	4.9	2.5	-4.5	-2.4	0.7	2.1	2.0	2.9	4.9	8.4	5.7	4.2
Austria	9.8	13.8	12.1	0.3	4.0	-5.0	3.8	5.1	-4.1	3.5	3.0	-1.4	-8.2	-0.6	2.1	5.0	3.7	2.8	6.0	5.5	7.0
Belgium	8.8	-2.0	2.9	7.0	7.4	-1.8	3.8	0.1	2.6	-2.6	4.6	-15.9	-2.0	-4.5	1.8	0.7	4.5	5.8	13.4	13.6	11.0
Denmark	2.2	1.9	9.3	3.5	-8.9	-12.4	17.1	-2.4	1.1	-0.4	-12.6	-19.2	7.1	1.9	12.9	12.6	17.1	-3.8	-6.6	0.2	-0.8
Finland	12.5	3.8	6.5	8.5	3.5	5.9	-8.8	-3.5	-6.9	3.0	10.4	2.2	4.4	4.1	-2.1	2.9	-	5.4	10.5	13.1	-1.9
Ireland	0.3	8.8	7.4	16.2	-11.6	-2.6	13.6	4.1	18.9	13.6	-3.2	7.3	-3.3	-9.0	-2.7	-7.4	-1.3	-3.7	2.6	12.0	9.0
Netherlands	7.5	1.5	-2.3	4.2	-4.0	-4.4	-2.2	9.7	2.5	-1.7	-0.9	-10.4	-4.1	2.1	5.2	7.0	7.4	1.1	9.2	3.9	3.2
Norway	14.9	18.8	-4.1	13.6	5.1	11.9	10.1	3.6	-11.2	-5.0	-1.5	17.9	-11.0	5.8	10.9	-21.0	23.9	-2.1	0.7	-4.8	-26.5
Sweden	3.3	-0.6	4.2	2.7	-3.0	3.1	1.9	-2.9	-6.8	4.5	3.5	-5.8	-0.3	1.9	6.0	7.3	0.7	7.6	6.0	10.9	1.8
Switzerland	8.9	9.9	5.0	2.9	-4.3	-13.6	-10.5	1.6	6.1	5.1	9.9	2.4	-2.5	4.1	4.1	5.3	7.9	7.4	6.9	6.0	3.3
Total of nine countries	7.7	5.1	3.6	5.0	-1.0	-2.7	1.1	2.1	-1.2	1.1	2.0	-3.6	-2.9	1.6	4.7	2.1	7.2	3.1	6.2	6.3	0.9
Total western Europe	6.0	4.4	2.9	5.1	-2.3	-4.8	2.0	1.0	1.7	3.9	2.4	-4.3	-2.5	0.9	2.8	2.0	4.0	4.5	7.8	5.9	3.4
Greece	-1.4	14.0	15.4	7.7	-25.6	0.2	6.8	7.8	6.0	8.8	-6.5	-7.5	-1.9	-1.3	-5.7	5.2	-6.2	-7.8	8.8	8.6	4.3
Portugal	11.5	9.8	13.5	9.5	-7.0	-11.3	0.8	12.0	6.2	-1.3	8.5	5.5	2.3	-7.1	-17.4	-3.5	10.9	15.1	15.0	7.5	9.0
Spain	3.0	-2.9	15.8	14.3	6.6	-3.9	-2.0	-0.2	-2.3	-4.5	1.3	-3.3	0.5	-2.5	-5.8	4.1	10.0	14.6	14.2	13.2	8.6
Turkey	13.5	-4.9	14.8	13.2	10.7	24.7	17.7	3.9	-10.0	-3.6	-10.0	1.7	3.5	3.0	0.5	16.7	11.0	5.6	-1.2	-0.8	8.6
Yugoslavia	12.8	4.6	1.8	4.2	9.1	9.7	8.1	9.5	10.5	6.4	-5.9	-9.8	-5.5	-9.7	-9.6	-3.7	3.5	-5.1	-5.8	0.5	-7.0
Total southern Europe	5.6	1.0	13.1	11.4	2.4	1.1	3.3	3.6	0.3	-0.6	-2.1	-3.7	-0.4	-3.4	-6.6	4.3	7.6	8.1	8.6	8.7	6.7
Total Europe	5.9	4.1	3.9	5.8	-1.8	-4.1	2.2	1.3	1.5	3.4	1.8	-4.2	-2.3	0.4	1.7	2.2	4.4	4.9	7.9	6.2	3.8
United States	-3.1	7.1	11.0	8.4	-6.8	-11.6	8.9	14.1	9.8	3.7	-7.9	1.1	-9.6	8.2	16.8	5.3	1.0	1.9	5.6	1.6	-0.2
Canada	0.3	7.9	4.3	9.9	6.6	5.8	4.6	2.1	3.1	8.5	10.1	11.8	-11.0	-0.7	2.1	9.5	6.2	10.3	10.2	4.5	-0.6
North America	-2.8	7.1	10.4	8.5	-5.7	-10.0	8.5	12.9	9.1	4.1	-6.2	2.2	-9.7	7.2	15.2	5.7	1.5	2.8	6.1	1.9	-0.3
Total	1.8	5.5	6.9	7.1	-3.7	-6.9	5.0	6.7	5.3	3.8	-2.3	-1.0	-6.1	3.7	8.5	4.1	2.8	3.7	6.9	4.0	1.7

Source: Economic Commission for Europe, *Economic Survey of Europe in 1990–1991*, New York, 1991

Appendix Table 8A.4 Private consumption (annual percentage change)

	1970	1971	1972	1973	1974	1975	1976	1977	1978	1979	1980	1981	1982	1983	1984	1985	1986	1987	1988	1989	1990
France	4.3	4.9	4.9	5.3	1.2	2.8	4.9	2.7	3.7	3.0	1.2	2.1	3.5	0.9	1.1	2.4	3.9	2.7	3.2	3.1	2.9
Germany, Federal Republic of	7.6	5.2	4.5	3.1	0.7	3.2	3.7	4.3	3.8	3.6	1.2	-0.5	-1.3	1.7	1.5	1.4	3.4	3.3	2.7	1.7	4.4
Italy	8.4	3.5	3.7	6.9	3.7	0.3	5.2	4.1	3.4	7.3	5.6	1.4	1.3	0.6	2.1	3.1	3.8	4.2	4.1	3.8	2.7
UK	2.8	3.1	6.1	5.1	-1.5	-0.5	0.3	-0.5	5.6	4.2	–	1.1	1.0	4.6	1.6	3.5	6.3	5.2	6.9	3.9	2.5
Total of four countries	5.6	4.3	4.8	4.9	0.9	1.6	3.5	2.7	4.1	4.3	1.9	0.9	1.0	1.9	1.6	2.5	4.3	3.8	4.1	3.0	3.2
Austria	4.2	6.7	6.1	5.4	3.0	3.2	4.5	5.4	-1.5	4.4	1.5	0.3	1.2	5.0	-0.1	2.4	1.8	2.9	3.1	3.2	4.3
Belgium	4.4	4.7	6.2	7.8	2.7	0.6	4.9	2.4	2.5	4.8	1.9	-0.9	1.4	-1.6	1.1	2.0	2.6	3.1	2.8	3.8	4.0
Denmark	3.5	-0.8	1.7	4.8	-2.9	3.7	7.9	1.1	0.7	1.4	-3.7	-2.3	1.4	2.6	3.4	5.0	5.7	-1.5	-0.8	-0.8	0.7
Finland	7.6	1.7	8.4	5.9	1.8	3.1	0.9	-1.2	2.5	5.5	2.0	1.2	4.7	2.6	2.7	3.2	4.1	5.7	5.0	3.9	0.4
Ireland	2.9	3.2	5.1	7.2	1.6	-2.7	2.8	6.8	9.1	4.4	0.4	1.7	-7.1	0.9	2.0	3.5	2.0	2.2	2.4	5.2	3.2
Netherlands	7.4	3.3	3.5	4.0	3.7	3.3	5.3	4.6	4.3	3.0	–	-2.5	-1.2	0.9	0.9	2.5	2.7	3.5	1.3	2.5	4.0
Norway	–	4.6	2.9	2.9	3.9	5.1	6.1	6.9	-1.6	3.2	2.3	1.1	1.8	1.5	2.7	10.4	5.6	-1.0	-2.5	-1.9	3.1
Sweden	3.5	0.1	3.4	2.6	3.4	2.8	4.2	-1.0	-0.7	2.4	-0.8	-0.5	0.7	-2.2	1.7	2.8	5.2	4.6	2.5	1.1	0.6
Switzerland	5.4	4.8	5.4	2.8	-0.5	-2.9	1.1	3.0	2.2	1.3	2.6	0.4	–	1.7	1.6	1.4	2.8	2.1	2.1	2.1	2.0
Total of nine countries	4.8	3.1	4.6	4.5	2.0	1.8	4.2	2.7	1.7	3.1	0.7	-0.6	0.5	0.9	1.5	3.2	3.5	2.7	1.9	2.1	2.6
Total western Europe	5.4	4.0	4.8	4.8	1.1	1.7	3.7	2.7	3.5	4.0	1.6	0.6	0.9	1.7	1.6	2.7	4.1	3.5	3.6	2.8	3.0
Greece	8.8	5.6	7.0	7.6	0.7	5.5	5.3	4.6	5.7	2.6	0.2	2.0	3.9	0.3	1.7	3.9	0.3	0.9	3.4	3.9	2.1
Portugal	2.6	12.7	4.0	12.0	9.7	-0.9	3.5	0.6	-2.0	–	3.7	2.9	2.4	-1.4	-2.9	0.7	5.6	5.4	6.6	3.1	4.5
Spain	4.2	4.9	8.3	8.0	5.2	2.4	4.7	2.5	1.3	1.2	1.3	-0.6	0.2	0.3	-0.4	2.4	3.6	5.4	5.5	5.9	3.7
Turkey	2.2	13.5	6.4	0.2	9.0	7.7	10.1	6.7	-3.9	-3.1	-5.2	0.6	4.2	5.0	6.8	1.3	11.5	6.5	2.6	3.7	11.0
Yugoslavia	14.6	8.3	4.6	2.7	7.3	3.4	4.4	7.0	7.0	5.6	0.7	-1.0	-0.1	-1.7	-1.0	–	4.5	0.3	-1.3	1.0	2.5
Total southern Europe	5.2	7.4	7.1	6.3	5.9	3.5	5.6	3.8	1.1	0.9	0.1	0.1	1.4	0.8	0.9	2.0	5.0	4.6	4.1	4.6	5.0
Total Europe	5.4	4.3	5.0	5.0	1.7	1.9	3.9	2.9	3.2	3.7	1.4	0.5	1.0	1.6	1.5	2.6	4.2	3.7	3.7	3.0	3.3
United States	2.4	3.1	5.4	4.2	-0.9	2.3	5.4	4.4	4.1	2.2	-0.2	1.2	1.3	4.6	4.8	4.7	3.9	2.8	3.6	1.9	1.0
Canada	2.0	5.9	7.5	7.5	5.8	4.7	6.5	3.2	3.4	2.9	2.2	2.3	-2.6	3.4	4.6	5.2	4.4	4.5	4.3	3.8	1.4
North America	2.4	3.3	5.5	4.4	-0.5	2.4	5.5	4.3	4.0	2.3	–	1.3	1.0	4.6	4.8	4.7	3.9	3.0	3.7	2.1	1.0
Total	3.6	3.7	5.3	4.6	0.4	2.2	4.8	3.7	3.7	2.8	0.6	1.0	1.0	3.3	3.5	3.9	4.0	3.2	3.7	2.4	1.9

Source: Economic Commission for Europe, *Economic Survey of Europe in 1990–1991*, New York, 1991

Appendix Table 8A.5 Consumer prices (annual percentage change)

	1970	1971	1972	1973	1974	1975	1976	1977	1978	1979	1980	1981	1982	1983	1984	1985	1986	1987	1988	1989	1990
France	5.2	5.5	6.2	7.3	13.7	11.8	9.6	9.4	9.1	10.8	13.6	13.4	11.8	9.6	7.4	5.8	2.5	3.3	2.8	3.6	3.3
Germany, Federal Republic of	3.3	5.4	5.5	7.0	7.0	5.9	4.3	3.7	2.7	4.1	5.5	6.3	5.2	3.3	2.4	2.0	-0.1	0.2	1.3	2.8	2.7
Italy	4.9	4.8	5.8	10.8	19.1	17.0	16.8	17.0	12.1	14.8	21.2	17.8	16.5	14.6	10.8	9.2	5.9	4.7	5.0	6.3	6.3
UK	6.4	9.4	7.1	9.1	16.0	24.2	16.5	15.8	8.3	13.4	18.0	11.9	8.6	4.6	5.0	6.1	3.4	4.1	4.9	7.8	9.5
Total of four countries	4.8	6.2	6.1	8.4	13.5	14.0	11.2	10.8	7.7	10.3	13.9	11.9	10.2	7.7	6.1	5.5	2.7	2.9	3.3	4.9	5.2
Austria	4.4	4.7	6.3	7.6	9.5	8.4	7.3	5.5	3.6	3.7	6.3	6.8	5.4	3.3	5.7	3.2	1.7	1.4	2.0	2.5	3.2
Belgium	3.9	4.3	5.4	6.9	12.7	12.8	9.2	7.1	4.5	4.5	6.6	8.2	8.2	7.7	6.3	4.9	1.3	1.6	1.1	3.2	3.4
Denmark	6.5	5.8	6.6	9.3	15.2	9.6	9.0	11.1	10.1	9.6	12.3	6.8	5.4	3.3	5.6	3.2	1.7	4.0	4.6	4.8	2.7
Finland	2.7	6.1	7.4	11.4	17.8	17.4	14.4	12.5	7.7	7.1	11.7	12.2	9.6	8.3	7.1	5.9	2.9	4.1	5.1	6.6	6.2
Ireland	8.2	9.0	8.6	11.4	17.0	20.9	18.0	13.6	7.6	13.2	18.2	20.4	17.1	10.5	8.6	5.4	3.8	3.2	2.1	4.0	3.4
Netherlands	3.6	7.5	7.8	8.0	9.6	10.2	8.8	6.7	4.1	4.2	6.5	6.7	5.7	2.8	3.2	2.3	0.3	-0.2	0.7	1.1	2.4
Norway	10.7	6.0	7.2	7.6	9.4	11.6	9.2	9.0	8.2	4.8	10.9	13.6	11.3	8.4	6.3	5.7	7.2	8.7	6.7	4.6	4.1
Sweden	7.0	7.4	6.0	6.8	9.9	9.8	10.3	11.4	10.0	7.2	13.7	12.1	8.6	9.0	8.0	7.4	4.2	4.2	5.8	6.4	10.5
Switzerland	3.6	6.6	6.7	8.7	9.8	6.7	1.7	1.3	1.0	3.6	4.1	6.5	5.6	3.0	3.0	3.4	0.7	1.5	1.8	3.2	5.4
Total of nine countries	5.0	6.3	6.7	8.2	11.4	10.7	8.6	7.7	5.6	5.5	8.7	9.0	7.4	5.5	5.4	4.3	2.1	2.5	2.9	3.7	4.7
Total western Europe	4.9	6.2	6.2	8.3	13.0	13.3	10.6	10.1	7.2	9.2	12.6	11.2	9.5	7.2	6.0	5.2	2.5	2.8	3.2	4.6	5.1
Greece	2.9	3.0	4.3	15.5	26.9	13.4	13.3	12.1	12.6	19.0	24.9	24.5	21.0	20.2	18.5	19.3	23.0	16.4	13.5	13.7	20.5
Portugal	6.4	11.9	10.7	12.9	25.1	15.3	21.0	27.4	22.0	24.2	16.6	20.0	22.4	25.5	29.3	19.2	11.8	10.2	9.6	12.7	13.5
Spain	5.6	8.3	8.3	11.4	15.7	16.9	14.9	24.5	19.8	15.7	15.5	14.5	14.4	12.2	11.3	8.8	8.7	5.3	4.8	6.8	6.7
Turkey	8.1	16.3	12.9	16.6	18.7	20.1	15.3	28.4	49.5	56.5	116.6	35.9	27.1	31.4	48.4	44.9	34.6	38.9	73.7	63.3	60.3
Yugoslavia	10.6	15.6	16.6	19.7	21.1	24.3	11.7	14.9	14.3	20.6	30.2	40.9	32.3	42.9	50.0	60.0	87.5	126.7	194.1	1252.0	580.0
Total southern Europe	5.8	9.7	9.0	13.1	18.4	17.1	15.3	24.1	25.4	25.4	38.3	20.7	18.5	18.3	21.5	18.6	16.2	14.2	20.9	20.1	20.3
Total Europe	5.0	6.6	6.5	8.8	13.5	13.6	11.0	11.5	9.1	10.8	15.3	12.2	10.4	8.3	7.5	6.6	3.9	4.0	5.0	6.2	6.6
United States	5.9	4.3	3.3	6.2	11.0	9.1	5.8	6.4	7.6	11.3	13.5	10.3	6.2	3.2	4.3	3.6	1.9	3.7	4.1	4.8	5.4
Canada	3.3	2.9	4.7	7.8	10.8	10.8	7.5	8.0	9.0	9.1	10.2	12.3	10.9	5.7	4.4	3.9	4.2	4.4	4.0	5.0	4.8
North America	5.7	4.2	3.4	6.3	11.0	9.3	5.9	6.6	7.7	11.2	13.3	10.5	6.5	3.4	4.3	3.6	2.0	3.7	4.1	4.8	5.4
Total	5.4	5.1	4.6	7.3	11.9	10.9	7.9	8.5	8.2	11.0	14.1	11.1	8.0	5.3	5.6	4.8	2.8	3.8	4.5	5.4	5.8

Source: Economic Commission for Europe, Economic Survey of Europe in 1990–1991, New York, 1991

Appendix Table 8A.6 Volume of exports of goods and services (annual percentage change)

	1970	1971	1972	1973	1974	1975	1976	1977	1978	1979	1980	1981	1982	1983	1984	1985	1986	1987	1988	1989	1990
France	16.1	9.2	12.0	10.8	8.8	-1.7	8.2	7.4	5.9	7.5	2.7	3.7	-1.7	3.7	7.0	1.9	-1.4	3.1	8.3	10.9	4.5
Germany, Federal Republic of	5.8	6.3	7.1	10.6	12.3	-6.8	9.7	3.9	3.2	4.3	5.1	7.7	3.4	-0.8	8.0	7.0	-0.5	0.4	5.5	9.9	8.6
Italy	-2.5	6.8	9.3	4.1	7.0	1.6	10.5	9.9	9.0	8.5	-8.7	7.6	-1.1	2.4	7.3	3.9	3.8	3.3	4.8	10.1	5.0
UK	5.2	7.0	1.1	11.9	7.3	-2.8	9.1	6.9	1.9	3.8	0.2	-0.8	0.8	2.0	6.6	5.9	4.6	5.7	0.2	4.4	4.4
Total of four countries	6.2	7.2	6.8	9.9	9.4	-3.3	9.3	6.4	4.4	5.6	0.8	4.6	0.8	1.4	7.3	5.0	1.2	2.8	4.6	8.8	6.0
Austria	16.4	5.9	9.2	2.2	10.7	-2.4	11.1	4.2	7.3	11.7	5.2	4.9	2.7	3.2	6.1	6.9	-2.7	2.4	9.5	10.5	9.9
Belgium	10.0	6.3	10.0	14.4	6.8	-8.9	11.7	12.7	3.4	7.1	3.3	3.1	2.1	3.2	5.7	1.3	5.4	7.1	9.0	7.6	7.0
Denmark	5.6	5.6	5.6	7.8	3.5	-1.8	4.1	4.1	1.2	8.4	5.2	8.2	2.5	4.9	3.5	5.0	0.0	5.1	7.3	6.0	4.6
Finland	8.7	-1.3	14.5	7.3	-0.6	-14.0	12.8	15.7	8.9	8.8	8.4	4.9	-1.1	2.5	5.4	1.2	1.3	2.6	3.7	1.6	2.2
Ireland	4.4	4.1	3.6	10.9	0.7	7.2	8.1	14.0	12.3	6.5	6.4	2.0	5.5	10.5	16.6	6.6	2.9	13.4	8.7	10.1	5.0
Netherlands	11.9	10.7	10.0	12.1	2.6	-3.1	9.9	-1.8	3.3	7.4	1.5	1.5	-	3.5	7.3	5.5	2.9	3.5	7.8	5.5	5.2
Norway	0.1	1.1	14.1	8.3	0.7	3.1	11.3	3.6	8.4	2.6	2.1	1.4	-0.1	7.6	8.2	10.7	1.6	1.2	5.4	10.3	7.2
Sweden	8.6	4.8	5.9	13.7	5.3	-9.3	4.3	1.5	7.8	6.1	-0.6	2.0	5.7	9.9	6.9	1.4	3.2	3.9	3.0	2.4	0.7
Switzerland	6.8	3.9	6.4	7.9	1.0	-6.6	9.3	9.7	3.7	2.5	5.1	4.6	-2.9	1.1	6.3	8.3	0.4	1.7	5.8	4.8	4.7
Total of nine countries	8.9	6.0	9.0	10.6	3.8	-5.1	9.3	5.1	5.0	6.6	3.1	3.2	1.2	4.4	6.7	4.8	2.2	4.2	7.0	6.3	5.4
Total western Europe	7.2	6.7	7.6	10.2	7.3	-4.0	9.3	6.0	4.6	6.0	1.7	4.1	0.9	2.5	7.1	5.0	1.6	3.3	5.5	7.9	5.8
Greece	12.4	11.9	22.9	23.4	0.1	10.6	16.4	1.8	16.4	6.7	6.9	-5.9	-7.2	8.0	16.9	1.3	14.0	16.0	9.1	2.0	4.4
Portugal	-1.6	9.9	18.5	4.2	-15.7	-15.6	0.0	5.9	9.1	33.0	2.2	-4.4	4.7	13.6	11.6	6.7	6.8	8.6	10.2	16.5	12.0
Spain	17.5	13.0	12.2	9.0	0.8	-1.4	10.1	8.5	10.7	6.4	0.6	8.4	4.8	10.1	11.7	2.7	1.3	5.9	7.5	5.2	3.8
Turkey	14.3	15.5	14.6	26.2	-11.0	-1.1	37.5	-21.8	12.9	-12.3	7.4	62.2	36.9	14.6	20.4	11.3	-0.6	26.0	16.5	7.5	-1.5
Yugoslavia	3.3	3.7	17.6	6.8	1.0	-1.3	9.3	-3.1	-2.4	14.9	7.5	12.0	-18.5	-4.4	6.4	7.9	-2.6	0.5	4.9	4.8	2.2
Total southern Europe	10.7	10.7	15.2	10.4	-2.4	-1.8	11.8	2.2	8.9	8.9	3.2	9.4	2.1	8.6	12.7	4.9	2.3	9.6	9.2	6.4	3.7
Total Europe	7.4	7.0	8.1	10.2	6.6	-3.8	9.5	5.7	4.9	6.2	1.8	4.4	1.0	2.9	7.5	5.0	1.6	3.8	5.8	7.7	5.6
United States	9.3	0.0	8.5	21.6	9.9	-0.7	5.0	1.5	9.3	8.3	10.1	-0.4	-8.8	-2.7	6.1	2.9	11.9	15.3	18.3	11.4	8.4
Canada	8.7	5.2	7.8	10.6	-2.0	-6.8	10.6	8.9	13.6	5.0	2.7	4.4	-2.2	6.4	17.7	6.0	4.5	3.0	8.9	0.7	4.3
North America	9.2	1.2	8.3	19.0	7.3	-1.9	6.0	3.0	10.2	7.6	8.5	0.6	-7.4	-0.7	8.8	3.7	10.0	12.3	16.1	9.1	7.6
Total	7.9	5.3	8.2	12.7	6.8	-3.2	8.4	4.9	6.5	6.6	3.9	3.2	-1.6	1.9	7.9	4.6	4.1	6.4	9.1	8.2	6.3

Source: Economic Commission for Europe, Economic Survey of Europe in 1990–1991, New York, 1991

Appendix Table 8A.7 Current account balances (billion US dollars)

	1970	1971	1972	1973	1974	1975	1976	1977	1978	1979	1980	1981	1982	1983	1984	1985	1986	1987	1988	1989	1990
France	-0.2	0.2	-0.1	1.4	-3.9	2.7	-3.4	-0.4	7.1	5.1	-4.2	-4.8	-12.1	-5.2	-0.9	—	2.4	-4.4	-3.5	-3.8	-7.7
Germany, Federal Republic of	0.8	1.0	1.2	5.2	10.6	4.4	3.7	4.0	9.1	-5.6	13.9	-3.3	5.0	5.4	9.8	17.0	40.1	46.1	50.5	55.4	44.0
Italy	0.8	1.6	2.1	-2.5	-8.0	-0.5	-2.8	2.5	6.3	5.5	-10.0	-9.7	-6.4	1.4	-2.5	-3.5	2.9	-1.7	-6.2	-10.6	-13.1
UK	2.0	2.7	0.5	-2.4	-7.5	-3.4	-1.7	-0.2	1.9	-0.9	7.5	14.5	8.0	5.8	2.6	4.8	0.2	-7.4	-27.3	-32.1	-28.7
Total of four countries	3.4	5.5	3.7	1.8	-8.7	3.2	-4.2	5.9	24.3	4.2	-20.6	-3.3	-5.4	7.4	9.0	18.2	45.6	32.6	13.5	8.8	-5.5
Austria	-0.1	-0.1	-0.2	-0.3	-0.2	-0.2	-1.1	-2.2	-0.7	-1.1	-1.7	-1.5	0.6	0.2	-0.3	-0.3	0.1	-0.4	-0.5	0.1	0.3
Belgium	0.7	0.6	1.3	1.4	0.8	0.2	0.4	-0.6	-0.8	-3.1	-4.9	-4.2	-2.6	-0.5	-0.1	0.7	3.1	2.8	3.6	3.2	4.3
Denmark	-0.5	-0.4	-0.1	-0.5	-1.0	-0.5	-1.9	-1.7	-1.5	-3.0	-2.5	-1.9	-2.3	-1.2	-1.6	-2.7	-4.5	-3.0	-1.8	-1.4	0.5
Finland	-0.2	-0.3	-0.1	-0.4	-1.2	-2.1	-1.1	-0.1	0.7	-0.2	-1.4	-0.4	-0.8	-0.9	—	-0.8	-0.7	-1.8	-2.8	-5.1	-6.7
Ireland	-0.2	-0.2	-0.1	-0.3	-0.7	-0.1	-0.4	-0.5	-0.8	-2.1	-2.1	-2.6	-1.9	-1.2	-1.0	-0.7	-0.7	0.4	0.7	0.5	0.4
Netherlands	-0.6	-0.2	1.2	2.4	3.0	2.4	3.4	1.2	-1.2	0.2	-1.0	3.7	4.5	5.0	6.6	4.0	3.6	3.7	5.4	8.0	9.3
Norway	-0.2	-0.5	-0.4	-0.4	-1.1	-2.5	-3.7	-5.0	-2.1	-1.0	1.1	2.2	0.7	-1.0	2.9	3.1	-4.5	-4.1	-3.7	0.2	3.2
Sweden	-0.3	0.4	0.6	1.4	-0.6	-0.3	-1.6	-2.2	-0.3	-2.4	-4.4	-2.8	-3.4	-1.0	0.2	-1.6	0.1	-1.2	-2.5	-5.2	-5.4
Switzerland	0.2	0.3	0.5	-0.9	-2.8	0.8	2.3	1.9	2.1	-0.2	-0.2	3.4	2.5	1.2	6.1	6.0	4.7	6.3	8.8	8.5	8.5
Total of nine countries	-1.3	-0.5	3.0	2.6	-3.6	-2.5	-3.7	-9.2	-4.7	-12.9	-17.2	-4.0	-2.7	3.6	12.9	7.7	1.0	2.5	7.2	8.7	14.4
Total western Europe	2.2	5.0	6.7	4.4	-12.3	0.7	-7.9	-3.3	19.6	-8.8	-37.8	-7.3	-8.1	11.0	21.9	25.9	46.6	35.2	20.7	17.6	8.9
Greece	-0.4	-0.3	-0.4	-1.2	-1.1	-0.9	-0.9	-1.1	-1.0	-1.9	-2.2	-2.4	-1.9	-1.9	-2.1	-3.3	-1.7	-1.2	-1.0	-2.6	-3.6
Portugal	0.1	0.3	0.4	0.3	-0.8	-0.8	-1.3	-1.0	-0.5	-0.1	-1.1	-2.6	-3.3	-0.5	-0.5	0.4	1.1	0.6	-0.6	-0.6	-1.2
Spain	0.1	0.9	0.6	0.6	-3.2	-3.5	-4.3	-2.1	1.6	1.1	-5.2	-5.0	-4.2	-2.7	2.0	2.9	4.0	-0.2	-3.8	-10.9	-15.7
Turkey	—	—	0.2	0.7	-0.6	-1.6	-2.0	-3.1	-1.3	-1.4	3.4	-1.9	-1.0	-1.9	-1.4	-1.0	-1.5	-0.8	1.6	1.0	-2.4
Yugoslavia	-0.4	-0.4	0.4	0.5	-1.0	-0.6	0.2	-1.3	-1.3	-3.7	-2.3	-1.0	-0.5	0.3	0.5	0.8	1.1	1.2	2.5	2.4	—
Total southern Europe	-0.7	0.4	1.2	0.9	-6.7	-7.4	-8.3	-8.6	-2.3	-5.9	-14.2	-12.9	-10.8	-7.3	-1.6	-0.2	3.1	-0.4	-1.3	-10.7	-22.9
Total Europe	1.5	5.4	7.9	5.3	-19.1	-6.7	-16.3	-11.9	17.3	-14.7	-51.9	-20.2	-18.9	3.7	20.3	25.7	49.7	34.8	19.4	6.9	-14.0
United States	2.3	-1.4	-5.8	7.1	1.9	18.1	4.2	-14.5	-15.4	0.2	1.2	7.3	-5.9	-40.2	-99.0	-122.3	-145.4	-162.2	-129.0	-110.0	-13.7
Canada	1.0	0.4	-0.3	0.3	-1.3	-4.6	-4.2	-4.1	-4.3	-4.1	-1.0	-5.1	2.2	2.5	2.0	-1.5	-7.3	-6.9	-8.2	-14.1	-95.0
North America	3.3	-1.1	-6.1	7.4	0.6	13.5	—	-18.6	-19.7	-3.9	0.2	2.1	-3.6	-37.7	-97.0	-123.7	-152.7	-169.1	-137.2	-124.1	-108.7
Total above	4.8	4.3	1.8	12.7	-18.5	6.8	-16.2	-30.5	-2.4	-18.6	-51.7	-18.1	-22.5	-34.0	-76.7	-98.0	-103.0	-134.4	-117.8	-117.2	-122.7
Japan	2.0	5.8	6.6	-0.1	-4.7	-0.7	3.7	10.9	16.5	-8.7	-10.8	4.8	6.8	20.8	35.0	49.2	85.8	87.0	79.6	57.0	35.8
Total	6.8	10.1	8.4	12.5	-23.2	6.1	-12.5	-19.6	14.2	-27.3	-62.5	-13.3	-15.7	-13.2	-41.7	-48.8	-17.2	-47.3	-38.2	-60.2	-86.9

Source: Economic Commission for Europe, *Economic Survey of Europe in 1990-1991*, New York, 1991

Appendix Table 8A.8 Annual unemployment rates (percentage of total labour force)

	1970	1971	1972	1973	1974	1975	1976	1977	1978	1979	1980	1981	1982	1983	1984	1985	1986	1987	1988	1989	1990
France	2.5	2.7	2.8	2.7	2.8	4.0	4.4	4.9	5.2	5.9	6.3	7.4	8.1	8.3	9.7	10.2	10.4	10.5	10.0	9.4	8.9
Germany, Federal Republic of	0.8	0.9	0.8	0.8	1.6	3.6	3.7	3.6	3.5	3.2	2.9	4.2	5.9	7.7	7.1	7.2	6.4	6.2	6.2	5.6	5.1
Italy	5.3	5.3	6.3	6.2	5.3	5.8	6.6	7.0	7.1	7.6	7.5	7.8	8.4	8.8	9.4	9.6	10.5	10.9	11.0	10.9	9.9
UK	3.0	3.6	4.0	3.0	2.9	4.3	5.6	6.0	5.9	5.0	6.4	9.8	11.3	12.4	11.7	11.2	11.2	10.3	8.5	6.9	6.4
Total of four countries	2.8	3.0	3.4	3.1	3.1	4.4	5.0	5.3	5.4	5.3	5.7	7.3	8.4	9.4	9.5	9.5	9.5	9.4	8.8	8.0	7.4
Austria	1.1	1.0	1.0	0.9	1.1	1.5	1.5	1.4	1.7	1.7	1.5	2.1	3.1	3.7	3.8	3.6	3.1	3.8	3.6	3.1	3.6
Belgium	2.1	2.1	2.7	2.7	3.0	5.0	6.4	7.4	7.9	8.2	8.8	10.8	12.6	12.1	12.1	11.3	11.2	11.0	9.7	8.1	7.9
Denmark	1.3	1.6	1.6	1.0	2.3	5.3	5.3	6.4	7.3	6.2	7.0	9.2	9.8	10.4	10.1	9.0	7.8	7.8	8.6	9.3	9.6
Finland	1.9	2.2	2.5	2.3	1.7	2.2	3.8	5.8	7.2	5.9	4.6	4.8	5.3	5.4	5.2	5.0	5.3	5.0	4.5	3.4	3.4
Ireland	5.8	5.5	6.2	5.7	5.3	8.3	9.2	9.0	8.2	7.3	8.1	10.0	12.1	13.7	15.4	16.8	17.1	16.9	16.3	15.0	14.6
Netherlands	1.0	1.3	2.2	2.2	2.7	5.2	5.5	5.3	5.3	5.4	6.0	8.5	11.4	12.0	11.8	10.6	9.9	9.6	9.2	8.3	7.3
Norway	1.6	1.5	1.6	1.5	1.5	2.3	1.7	1.4	1.8	2.0	1.6	2.0	2.6	3.4	3.1	2.6	2.0	2.1	3.2	4.9	5.2
Sweden	1.2	2.1	2.2	2.0	1.6	1.3	1.3	1.4	1.8	1.7	1.6	2.1	2.6	2.9	2.6	2.4	2.2	1.9	1.6	1.4	1.5
Switzerland	–	–	–	–	–	0.3	0.7	0.4	0.3	0.3	0.2	0.2	0.4	0.8	1.0	0.8	0.8	0.8	0.7	0.6	0.6
Total of nine countries	1.4	1.7	2.0	1.9	2.0	3.3	3.7	4.1	4.4	4.2	4.3	5.6	6.8	7.2	7.2	6.7	6.3	6.2	6.0	5.5	5.4
Total western Europe	2.5	2.7	3.1	2.8	2.8	4.1	4.7	5.0	5.1	5.1	5.4	6.9	8.1	8.9	9.0	8.9	8.8	8.7	8.2	7.5	7.0
Greece	4.2	3.1	2.1	2.0	2.1	2.3	1.9	1.7	1.8	1.9	2.8	4.0	5.8	7.8	8.1	7.8	7.4	7.4	7.7	7.9	8.3
Portugal	2.2	2.1	2.1	2.2	1.8	3.5	5.8	7.1	7.9	8.2	8.0	7.7	7.5	7.9	8.4	8.5	8.5	7.0	5.7	5.0	4.7
Spain	0.9	1.2	3.1	2.5	2.6	3.6	4.5	5.1	6.8	8.4	11.1	13.8	15.6	17.0	19.7	21.1	20.8	20.1	19.1	16.9	16.0
Turkey	7.8	7.8	7.6	7.9	8.4	8.7	7.9	7.5	7.8	9.7	11.6	11.6	12.3	12.1	11.8	11.3	10.5	9.5	9.8	10.2	10.2
Yugoslavia	7.7	6.7	7.0	8.1	9.0	10.2	11.4	11.9	12.0	11.9	11.9	11.9	12.4	12.8	13.3	13.8	14.1	13.6	14.1	14.9	15.9
Total southern Europe	4.5	4.5	5.0	4.9	5.2	5.9	6.0	6.2	7.0	8.5	10.4	11.4	12.5	13.1	14.0	14.3	13.7	12.9	12.5	11.9	11.6
Total Europe	3.0	3.1	3.5	3.3	3.4	4.5	5.0	5.3	5.6	5.8	6.5	7.9	9.1	9.8	10.1	10.1	9.9	9.6	9.1	8.5	8.0
United States	4.8	5.8	5.5	4.8	5.5	8.3	7.6	6.9	6.0	5.8	7.0	7.5	9.5	9.5	7.4	7.1	6.9	6.1	5.4	5.2	5.5
Canada	5.6	6.1	6.2	5.5	5.3	6.9	7.1	8.0	8.3	7.4	7.4	7.5	10.9	11.8	11.2	10.4	9.5	8.8	7.7	7.5	8.1
North America	4.9	5.8	5.6	4.9	5.5	8.2	7.6	7.0	6.2	6.0	7.0	7.5	9.6	9.7	7.8	7.4	7.2	6.4	5.6	5.4	5.8
Total	3.8	4.3	4.4	3.9	4.2	6.0	6.1	6.0	5.8	5.9	6.7	7.7	9.3	9.8	9.1	9.0	8.8	8.3	7.7	7.2	7.1

Source: Economic Commission for Europe, Economic Survey of Europe in 1990–1991, New York, 1991

9

EASTERN EUROPE IN TRANSITION, 1970–1990

If the period 1970–90 was a chequered one for western Europe, its problems paled into insignificance compared with the parallel traumas experienced by eastern Europe. Even the most pessimistic forecasters would have been hard pressed to predict the course of events. In the early 1970s there seemed every indication that the impressive growth rates of the 1960s would continue. The Soviet Union began the period confidently, expecting to sustain communist rule both within and outwith its borders. Yet by its end communism had withered and died in East Germany, Poland, Czechoslovakia, Bulgaria and Hungary, while it was also out of favour in countries which had pursued an independent line from Moscow – Romania and Yugoslavia. In Europe, outside the Soviet Union, communism held on by the skin of its teeth only in Albania. Moreover, the very survival of communism as the governing system of the Soviet Union was being seriously questioned, with several republics demanding their independence.

While the 1989 revolutions in eastern Europe matched the French revolution of two centuries earlier for drama, it would be a mistake simply to review immediate causes. Rather, their spring roots also demand consideration, not least the failure of socialist economies to provide tolerable living standards for the mass of the population. The question also needs to be asked: why did the Soviet Union, which entered the 1970s as a recognized super power, lose its grip? Then, too, there is the failure of the Soviet economy to respond to *perestroika*. Elsewhere, efforts to introduce economic and social reforms to uphold existing socialist systems proved equally unsuccessful.

BORROWING FOR GROWTH

At their start, the 1970s were mapped out to continue reforms dating from the mid to late 1960s. Outside the Soviet Union, their extent was limited by the so-called Brezhnev doctrine. Too radical reform on western lines, which was contrary to Moscow's political, strategic and economic interests, could activate Soviet military intervention and occupation as it did in Czechoslovakia in 1968, when the 'Prague spring' was snuffed out. The intention was thus to make existing centrally planned systems more efficient as a means of sustaining growth. Common threads linking the various five-year plans that unfolded in 1970 included the need to delegate greater power to factory managers, the need to increase incentives for them and their work-force, and a greater freedom for enterprises to trade in foreign markets without undue state interference.

Another common ingredient was the desire to raise living standards. The East German Five Year Plan, for instance, had as its 'primary task' the improvement of the 'material and cultural living standard' of the population. There was an acute housing shortage which needed to be tackled – 500,000 new apartment units were planned by 1975. That year, Romania's dictator Nicolae Ceausescu claimed, somewhat spuriously, that his reforms were 'creating a new type of life that guarantees its people well-being and happiness' (see below). In some countries, the emphasis on socialist consumerism was more evident than elsewhere. This reflected the varying stages of economic development and the amount of exposure to higher living standards in western Europe, as in East Germany, Yugoslavia, Hungary and Czechoslovakia. During the 1970s many East Europeans acquired their first televisions, washing machines, fridges and, to a lesser extent, cars. Foreign holidays became the norm in several countries. By the middle of the decade thirty-four times as many Hungarians were going abroad compared with 1960. Such was the demand for high quality consumer goods in Yugoslavia that regular shopping trips were made to proximate western countries.

The emphasis on better living standards was not surprising. Success in this crucial area held out the prospect of political stability and improved labour productivity, a necessary condition for further growth as the working population fell in size and the number of peasants shrank, draining the reservoir of land workers that industry had previously drawn on. In the Soviet Union, for example, by 1971 the proportion of the population engaged in agriculture had declined to 26 per cent and by 1980 it stood at 14 per cent. This compared with a western average of 6 per cent. In less developed Bulgaria and Romania the contraction was less pronounced.

Migration to the towns provided a means of upward mobility to former peasants. But by the 1970s, with the mass exodus nearing completion, the new urban dwellers expected to improve their quality of life. This, in turn, brought pressure on city jobs and accommodation. At the end of 1970 former Polish land workers provoked riots in Gdansk. The immediate cause was an increase in food prices (soon reversed), but there was also frustration at the lack of consumer goods. Such scarcity was endemic throughout the eastern bloc but again variations were evident – Romanians, for instance, were very much in the Polish boat whereas Hungarians had less cause for grievance.

The start of the 1970s saw the thawing of the Cold War through *détente*, opening up the prospect of more intimate east–west economic ties. Relations between the two Germanies improved, with their volume of trade more than doubling between 1974 and 1985, when it reached DM 16.5 billion a year. Over the period, although intra-German trade still remained only a tiny percentage of West Germany's total foreign transactions, for East Germany its neighbour had assumed the status of most important trading partner after the Soviet Union. The basis of the economic relationship was West Germany's provision of large quantities of semi-finished goods and production materials with East Germany supplying consumer goods, such as clothing, porcelain and electric motors. West Germany, with an eye to possible future reunification, gave generous loans and credits and had normal European Community tariffs waived.

It was generally recognized in eastern Europe that a high-tech phase of growth had dawned for which it was ill prepared. Large quantities of western technology were deemed essential to bridge the gap with the west. Hungary, Yugoslavia, Poland and Romania, in particular, embraced a strategy of import-led growth which found its most comprehensive form in Poland. The idea was to use western machinery and equipment to develop more sophisticated and competitive home industries. These would then export high quality goods to the west, correcting the temporary imbalance between exports and imports and providing hard currency to repay western credits. That, at least, was the theory, though in practice things were to turn out very differently (see below).

One impact of this policy was to reduce the volume of intra-CMEA trade as the more efficient sectors of each member economy diverted their best products to the west. The CMEA nonetheless continued to play an important role within the eastern bloc as Table 9.1 indicates. In 1971 the 'Complex Programme' was agreed, which called for greater regional integration and introduced joint investment projects, almost all of them in the Soviet Union. Many concerned raw materials, such as oil and iron ore, for which the contribution of other CMEA members towards extraction costs was to increase. By 1976 these investments in the Soviet Union involved 1.4 billion roubles.

With the exception of Romania, the CMEA was almost totally dependent on the Soviet Union for supplies of oil, natural gas and other raw materials. Fortunately, in return for machinery and equipment, the Soviet Union

Table 9.1 Inter-CMEA trade as a percentage of total trade, 1971–5

Bulgaria	70
Czechoslovakia	64
Poland	50
East Germany	65
Romania	39
Hungary	65
Soviet Union	46

Source: G. Graziani, 'Dependency structures in COMECON', *Review of Radical Political Economy* 13, 1981, p. 71

Table 9.2 Composition of Soviet foreign trade in 1976 (per cent)

	Global	CMEA
Total exports	100.0	100.0
Machines and equipment	18.7	22.5
Fuels and other basic products	57.8	61.6
Consumer goods	3.1	2.8
Foodstuffs and others	20.4	13.1
Total imports	100.0	100.0
Machines and equipment	33.9	45.4
Fuels and other basic products	24.8	14.7
Consumer goods	13.0	19.1
Foodstuffs and others	28.3	20.8

Source: Graziani, 'Dependency structures in COMECON', *Review of Radical Political Economy* 13, 1981, p. 71

adopted a special CMEA pricing formula, with charges much below world market prices. At the height of *détente*, in the mid-1970s (see Table 9.2) the Soviet Union continued to provide the CMEA with greater amounts of machines and equipment together with fuel and raw materials than the west did. The Soviet Union also imported more machines and equipment and consumer goods from CMEA sources, notwithstanding their inferior quality *vis-à-vis* western producers. Though not a member of the CMEA, Yugoslavia was compelled by European Community tariffs to redirect much of its exports to the organization, the proportion rising from 32.3 to 41.9 per cent over 1973–8. But it remained dangerously dependent on western Europe for industrial goods, thereby creating balance of payments difficulties.

As Table 9.3 demonstrates, until the mid-1970s most CMEA countries had at least respectable industrial growth rates as measured in net material product. Indeed, several exceeded plan targets. Poland's and Romania's spectacularly rising figures reflected their greater reliance on large doses of western credit while the less addicted Bulgarian, Czech, East German and Hungarian economies returned more even results. The Soviet Union's performance was sluggish, highlighting inefficiency and the fact that, for political reasons, it preferred to give priority to CMEA trade even though it could have obtained better prices from the west for its raw materials.

IMPACT OF THE OIL SHOCKS

The effect of OPEC's oil price hike of 1973 was not as great on eastern Europe as on the west. Where the European Community needed to import almost 60 per cent of its energy requirements from third countries by 1975, the CMEA was autarkic in energy provision. Indeed, that year the organization could

Table 9.3 Net material product in eastern Europe (annual percentage change)

	1970	1971	1972	1973	1974	1975	1976	1977	1978	1979	1980	1981	1982	1983	1984	1985	1986	1987	1988	1989	1990
Bulgaria	7.1	6.9	7.7	8.1	7.6	8.8	6.5	6.3	5.6	6.6	5.7	5.0	4.2	3.0	4.6	1.8	5.3	5.0	2.4	−0.4	−13.6
Czechoslovakia	5.7	5.5	5.7	5.2	5.9	6.2	4.1	4.2	4.1	3.1	2.9	−0.1	0.2	2.3	3.5	3.0	2.6	2.1	2.4	1.3	−3.1
German Democratic Republic	5.6	4.4	5.7	5.6	6.5	4.9	3.5	5.1	3.7	4.0	4.4	4.8	2.6	4.6	5.5	5.2	4.3	3.3	2.8	2.1	−19.5
Hungary	4.9	5.9	6.2	7.0	5.9	6.1	3.0	7.1	4.0	1.2	−0.9	2.5	2.6	0.3	2.5	−1.4	0.9	4.1	−0.5	−1.1	−5.5
Poland	5.2	8.1	10.6	10.8	10.5	9.0	6.8	5.0	3.0	−2.3	−6.0	−12.0	−5.5	6.0	5.6	3.4	4.9	1.9	4.9	−0.2	−13.0
Romania	6.8	13.5	9.8	10.7	12.3	9.8	11.3	8.7	7.2	6.5	4.2	−0.4	4.0	6.0	6.5	−1.1	3.0	0.7	−2.0	−7.9	−10.5
Eastern Europe	5.7	7.3	8.0	8.3	8.6	7.6	6.1	5.8	4.2	2.0	0.3	−2.3	0.3	4.3	5.1	2.7	3.7	3.2	3.1	0.5	−12.0
Soviet Union	9.0	5.6	3.9	8.9	5.5	4.4	5.9	4.5	5.1	2.2	3.9	3.3	3.9	4.2	2.9	1.6	2.3	1.6	4.4	2.4	−4.0
Eastern Europe and the Soviet Union	8.0	6.1	5.1	8.7	6.5	5.4	5.9	4.9	4.9	2.1	2.7	1.7	2.8	4.1	3.6	2.2	3.0	2.1	4.0	1.8	−6.3

Source: United Nations, *Economic Survey of Europe in 1990–1991*, 1991, Appendix afford the luxury of a net export of 100 million tons Standard Coal Equivalent (SCE) – about a third of West German consumption. Its relatively favourable position enabled eastern Europe to continue the movement from coal to oil burning without much hesitation. Yugoslavia was an exception. Much more exposed to the first oil shock, belatedly it began to develop indigenous coal and hydroelectric resources, though to little effect.

As net exporters of energy, the Soviet Union, Romania and Poland benefited, to differing degrees, from the global explosion in world energy prices. The Soviet Union, the world's largest producer and exporter of oil, did best. It registered an improvement in its overall net barter terms of trade which averaged over 30 per cent a year over 1971–85. The ratio of import to export volumes improved in equal measure without incurring trade deficits. Romania expanded its oil-refining capacity and failed to curb energy-guzzling industries, but with its oil reserves nearing exhaustion this was a misguided policy. By 1980 oil production was reduced to only 250,000 barrels per day compared with a daily refining capacity of 700,000 barrels. The difference had to be imported, exposing the economy to price rises in crude oil and oil products (see below). Coal being its principal export, Poland profited from the increased demand for this alternative energy source.

In 1975 the Soviet Union, taking advantage of its improved bargaining position, embarked on a policy of narrowing the gap between Soviet and world oil prices. Immediately, Soviet CMEA prices increased by 30 per cent. An important change in the new CMEA Five Year Plan (1976–80) was to allow for annual price changes rather than, as before, for them to be held for the duration. The effect was to reduce the time lag for price rises to make themselves felt. CMEA members therefore faced extra costs, a situation which worsened after the second oil price shock of 1979. Some were more affected than others. Romania, which became a net oil importer that same year, paid the highest price. Having lost favourable contracts with Iran after the Shah's fall, Romania was exposed through its hostility towards the Soviet Union. In 1980 the latter would only supply 1.4 million tons of crude oil, for which it charged world market prices. One estimate suggests that the cost of Romania's denial of substantial quantities of Soviet oil at normal CMEA prices was at least $1 billion (Drewnowki 1982: 117). East Germany, too, was hard hit, with the price of its imported Soviet oil rising by 17.6 per cent in 1979. Perhaps worst affected was Yugoslavia which bore the full brunt of the rise in world oil prices. The dictates of energy conservation prompted not only petrol rationing but also passing on the full cost to the consumer, fuelling inflation, which rose from around 20 per cent in mid-1979 to 45 per cent two years later.

The position of the Soviet Union was not as favourable as it appeared. After three decades of uninterrupted growth, energy production slowed in the 1970s. Oil output peaked at 600 million tons in 1980. With the drying up of older wells, extraction and distribution costs escalated as new wells were sunk in western Siberia. To some extent, there was compensation from the exploitation of the world's largest gas field in the same location. In 1981 a $15 billion agreement was concluded with a West German–East European consortium to bring cheap gas to western Europe by pipeline. Siberia was also being exploited for its coal deposits. But it was far from being an ideal site. Siberia's remoteness demanded the construction of major feeder railways and special high voltage power lines. The extreme climate (causing permafrost) required the use of specialist machinery, much of which was only obtainable from western sources. Reflecting these difficulties, marginal oil extraction costs increased tenfold over 1974–82. Several key industries, such as petrochemicals, located themselves in the region to compensate, only to find that the difficulty of recruiting and retaining labour compelled them to pay wages as much as 75 per cent above the Soviet norm.

The combination of relatively cheap Soviet raw materials and increased western credits deflected their recipients from addressing underlying economic problems, thereby exacerbating them. Insulated from the impact of the first oil shock, east European states, not least Poland and Romania, continued their import-led growth policies. Only with the second oil shock did it finally become apparent that this approach could not succeed. The resulting recession in western Europe reduced demand for imports from eastern Europe and by raising interest rates worsened the latter's mounting debt.

But even without the second oil shock, it is doubtful whether the import-led growth strategy could have succeeded. For example, western bankers considered that even if Poland had achieved its annual growth rate targets of 3–4 per cent, not until the mid-1990s could its external debt have been reduced to a manageable size. In the event, eastern Europe simply lacked the trained personnel and economic infrastructure to absorb western technology properly and thereby produce competitive products. A great amount of western loans was misspent and wasted. Most east European governments elected to invest in energy-intensive sectors. Consumption of energy per unit of GNP within CMEA was around twice that in the west. Worse still, while under the impact of the first oil shock western Europe reduced its unit of consumption, in eastern Europe this continued to rise. The latter was about to be brought to account for its erroneous ways.

SLOWDOWN AND THE NEED FOR REFORM

The ill-considered Soviet invasion of Afghanistan in December 1979 ended the cosy climate engendered by *détente*. By the early 1980s western economists were pin-pointing eastern Europe's mountain of debts as a major problem. It was feared that the east would be unable to repay its debt, or even to service it. Socialist governments stood accused of wasting the money. Western banks were also in the dock, their crime being to lend huge sums to totalitarian regimes which were deemed incapable of sound economic management.

Table 9.4 Eastern Europe and the Soviet Union: balance of payments in convertible currencies (billion US dollars)

	1970	1971	1972	1973	1974	1975	1976	1977	1978	1979	1980	1981	1982	1983	1984	1985	1986	1987	1988	1989	1990
Bulgaria																					
Merchandise export	0.5	0.5	0.5	0.7	0.9	1.0	1.1	1.2	1.5	2.4	3.3	3.4	3.1	2.7	3.3	3.3	2.7	3.3	3.5	3.1	2.5
Merchandise import	0.5	0.5	0.6	0.8	1.1	1.8	1.5	1.5	1.5	1.8	2.5	3.1	2.6	2.7	3.0	3.7	3.5	4.2	4.5	4.3	3.3
Balance	–	–	–	–0.1	–0.2	–0.8	–0.4	–0.3	0.1	0.5	0.8	0.3	0.5	0.1	0.3	–0.4	–0.8	–1.0	–1.0	–1.2	–0.8
Invisibles	–	–	–	–	–	–0.1	–	0.1	–	0.1	0.1	0.3	0.3	0.2	0.4	0.3	0.1	0.2	0.1	–0.1	–0.3
Current account	–	–0.1	–	–0.1	–0.2	–0.9	–0.4	–0.3	0.1	0.6	0.9	0.6	0.8	0.3	0.7	–0.1	–0.7	–0.8	–0.8	–1.3	–1.1
Czechoslovakia																					
Merchandise export	0.8	1.0	1.2	1.6	2.2	2.1	2.1	2.5	2.9	3.5	4.4	4.2	4.1	4.0	4.0	3.9	4.3	4.5	5.0	5.4	5.9
Merchandise import	0.9	1.0	1.2	1.7	2.4	2.5	2.8	3.1	3.3	4.1	4.4	3.9	3.4	3.2	3.1	3.2	4.1	4.7	5.1	5.0	6.1
Balance	–0.1	–0.1	–	–0.2	–0.2	–0.4	–0.7	–0.6	–0.4	–0.5	–	0.3	0.7	0.8	0.9	0.7	0.2	–0.1	–0.1	0.4	–0.2
Invisibles	0.1	0.1	0.1	0.2	0.1	0.1	0.2	–	–	–	–0.3	–0.3	–0.1	0.1	0.2	0.1	0.2	0.2	0.2	–0.1	–
Current account	–	–	0.1	–	–0.1	–0.3	–0.6	–0.6	–0.4	–0.6	–0.3	–	0.4	0.9	1.1	0.7	0.4	0.1	0.1	0.3	–0.2
German Democratic Republic																					
Merchandise export	1.3	1.4	1.6	2.2	3.0	2.9	3.5	3.4	3.7	4.3	5.7	7.1	8.3	9.0	9.1	10.6	9.0	8.8	8.9	9.6	–
Merchandise import	1.5	1.6	2.1	2.9	4.0	4.0	5.1	4.8	4.7	6.1	7.4	7.1	6.8	7.7	8.1	7.9	8.2	9.1	9.9	10.5	–
Balance	–0.3	–0.2	–0.4	–0.7	–1.0	–1.0	–1.5	–1.4	–1.0	–1.8	–1.7	–	1.5	1.3	1.0	2.7	0.8	–0.4	–1.1	–0.9	–
Invisibles	0.2	0.2	0.2	0.3	0.1	0.2	0.3	0.3	0.3	0.5	0.1	–0.4	–0.3	–0.1	–	–	0.3	0.6	0.5	0.2	–
Current account	–0.1	–	–0.2	–0.5	–0.9	–0.8	–1.3	–1.1	–0.7	–1.3	–1.6	–0.4	1.1	1.2	0.9	2.8	1.1	0.2	–0.6	–0.8	–
Hungary																					
Merchandise export	0.6	0.6	0.9	1.5	2.1	2.2	2.3	2.7	3.2	4.1	4.9	4.9	4.8	4.8	4.9	4.2	4.2	5.0	5.5	6.4	6.3
Merchandise import	0.7	0.8	0.9	1.4	2.5	2.5	2.5	3.0	4.0	4.2	4.6	4.4	4.2	4.1	4.0	4.1	4.7	5.0	5.0	5.9	6.0
Balance	–0.1	–0.2	–	0.1	–0.4	–0.3	–0.2	–0.4	–0.8	–0.2	0.3	0.4	0.7	0.8	0.9	0.1	–0.5	–	0.5	0.5	0.3
Invisibles	–	–	–	–0.1	–0.1	–0.2	–0.2	–0.4	–0.5	–0.7	–0.6	–1.2	–1.0	–0.7	–0.8	–1.0	–1.0	–0.9	–1.3	–2.0	–0.2
Current account	–0.1	–0.3	–0.1	–	–0.5	–0.5	–0.4	–0.8	–1.2	–0.8	–0.4	–0.7	–0.3	0.1	0.1	–0.8	–1.5	–0.9	–0.8	–1.4	0.1
Poland																					
Merchandise export	1.1	1.3	1.6	2.3	3.5	4.1	4.3	4.7	5.3	5.9	7.2	5.5	5.0	5.4	5.8	5.8	6.2	6.9	7.9	8.1	10.9
Merchandise import	1.0	1.1	1.8	3.6	5.6	6.9	7.0	6.6	7.4	8.0	8.1	6.2	4.6	4.3	4.4	4.6	5.1	5.9	7.0	8.0	8.6
Balance	0.1	0.2	–0.2	–1.3	–2.1	–2.8	–2.7	–1.9	–2.1	–2.1	–0.9	–0.8	0.4	1.1	1.5	1.2	1.1	1.0	0.9	0.1	2.2
Invisibles	0.1	0.1	0.2	0.2	–	–0.2	–0.1	–0.3	0.4	–1.0	–1.7	–2.4	–2.6	–2.3	–2.2	–1.7	–1.7	–1.4	–1.5	–2.0	–1.5
Current account	0.1	0.3	–	–1.1	–2.1	–3.0	–2.8	–2.1	–2.4	–3.1	–2.7	–3.1	–2.2	–1.2	–0.7	–0.5	–0.6	–0.4	–0.6	–1.9	0.7

Romania																					
Merchandise export	0.7	0.8	1.1	1.7	2.6	2.8	3.4	3.7	4.0	5.4	6.5	7.2	6.2	6.2	6.9	6.3	5.1	5.9	6.5	6.0	3.5
Merchandise import	0.8	0.9	1.1	1.7	2.9	2.9	3.3	3.8	4.6	6.5	8.0	7.0	4.7	4.6	4.7	4.8	3.2	3.4	2.9	3.5	5.1
Balance	-0.1	-0.1	-0.1	-0.1	-0.3	-0.1	0.1	-0.1	-0.6	-1.2	-1.5	0.2	1.5	1.7	2.2	1.4	1.9	2.4	3.6	2.6	-1.6
Invisibles	-0.1	-0.1	-0.1	-0.1	-0.2	-0.1	-0.1	-0.2	-0.2	-0.5	-0.9	-1.0	-0.9	-0.8	-0.6	-0.5	-0.4	-0.2	-	-0.3	0.1
Current account	-0.2	-0.1	-0.2	-0.2	-0.5	-0.3	-0.1	-0.3	-0.8	-1.7	-2.4	-0.8	0.7	0.9	1.5	0.9	1.5	2.2	3.6	2.9	-1.5
Eastern Europe																					
Merchandise export	5.0	5.6	7.0	9.8	14.2	15.2	16.7	18.2	20.6	25.6	31.9	32.3	31.5	32.2	34.0	34.0	31.5	34.4	37.3	38.7	29.1
Merchandise import	5.4	6.0	7.7	12.1	18.4	20.7	22.2	22.8	25.4	30.7	35.0	31.7	26.3	26.5	27.3	28.2	28.7	32.4	34.5	37.3	29.1
Balance	-0.4	-0.4	-0.8	-2.3	-4.2	-5.4	-5.5	-4.6	-4.8	-5.2	-3.1	0.5	5.1	5.7	6.7	5.8	2.7	2.1	2.9	1.5	-
Invisibles	0.1	0.3	0.4	0.5	-	-0.3	-	-0.5	-0.7	-1.7	-3.3	-5.0	-4.5	-3.5	-3.0	-2.8	-2.4	-1.6	-1.9	-3.7	-2.0
Current account	-0.3	-0.1	-0.3	-1.8	-4.2	-5.7	-5.5	-5.2	-5.5	-6.9	-6.4	-4.5	0.7	2.2	3.7	3.0	0.3	0.5	0.9	-2.2	-2.1
Soviet Union																					
Merchandise export	4.8	5.1	5.7	9.5	13.6	14.2	16.6	20.7	22.8	30.9	38.2	39.1	43.4	44.2	43.3	36.9	34.6	40.8	42.7	45.1	48.8
Merchandise import	4.3	4.6	6.2	9.0	12.0	18.7	19.3	18.8	21.8	26.7	34.8	39.9	39.1	38.0	36.6	36.2	33.3	32.7	39.2	47.4	50.2
Balance	0.4	0.5	-0.4	0.5	1.6	-4.5	-2.7	1.9	0.9	4.2	3.4	-0.7	4.3	6.2	6.7	0.7	1.4	8.1	3.5	-2.3	-1.4
Invisibles	0.5	0.3	0.3	0.6	0.7	0.3	0.1	-	-	0.1	-0.4	-0.9	-0.7	-0.4	-	-0.7	-0.9	-1.0	-1.2	-1.7	-3.1
Current account	0.9	0.8	-0.2	1.1	2.4	-4.2	-2.6	1.9	1.0	4.3	3.0	-1.6	3.6	5.8	6.7	0.1	0.4	7.1	2.3	-4.0	-4.3
Eastern Europe and the Soviet Union																					
Merchandise export	9.7	10.7	12.7	19.3	27.8	29.4	33.3	38.9	43.4	56.5	70.2	71.4	74.9	76.4	77.4	70.9	66.1	75.2	80.0	83.9	77.8
Merchandise import	9.8	10.6	13.9	21.0	30.4	39.3	41.4	41.7	47.3	57.5	69.8	71.6	65.4	64.5	64.0	64.4	62.0	65.0	73.7	84.7	79.3
Balance	-	0.1	-1.2	-1.8	-2.6	-9.9	-8.1	-2.8	-3.9	-0.9	-0.3	-0.2	9.4	11.9	13.4	6.5	4.1	10.2	6.3	-0.8	-1.5
Invisibles	0.6	0.6	0.7	1.1	0.7	-	0.1	-0.5	-0.6	-1.6	-3.7	-5.9	-5.2	-3.9	-3.0	-3.4	-3.4	-2.6	-3.2	-5.4	-5.1
Current account	0.6	0.7	-0.5	-0.7	-1.9	-9.9	-8.1	-3.3	-4.5	-2.6	-3.4	-6.1	4.2	8.0	10.4	3.1	0.8	7.6	3.2	-6.1	-6.6

Source: United Nations, *Economic Survey of Europe in 1990–1991*, 1991, Appendix

In fact, the total East European debt was dwarfed compared with Latin America's colossal bill, which was twelve times as great.

Nevertheless, the debt problem was serious and in the 1980s, to a greater or lesser degree, East European countries were to be afflicted by what became known as 'the Polish disease'. Briefly, this may be defined as an inability to bridge the technological gap with the west through imports. The result is a worsening balance of payments situation, with exports failing dismally to match imports. The scale of the accumulated foreign debt then acts as a decelerator and a drag on future growth. As Table 9.4 indicates, imports then have to be cut back in order to improve the balance of payments position. Over the period 1979–89 almost every east European country registered at least one year of negative growth (see Table 9.3). East Germany bucked the trend but 'only with a harsh austerity programme and significant economic assistance from West Germany' (Dawisha 1990: 170). So did the Soviet Union, but its industrial growth was considerably below target (see below).

By 1980–1 Poland was in crisis. An illegal trade union, Solidarity, sprang up, initially to protect living standards, though ultimately it would assume political ambitions. A cohesion of urban and rural workers, it soon boasted 10 million members and was a force to be reckoned with. After a wave of strikes in the summer of 1980, the government was forced to recognize Solidarity and to sack the Communist Party's leader since 1970, Edward Gierek, who was held responsible for the failed import-led growth strategy.

But the foreign debt legacy could not be removed so easily. In 1971 Poland's net external debt was a manageable $1.2 billion, but by 1979 it had risen to $20.5 billion (excluding short-term loans), reflecting the persistent inability of exports to overtake imports after 1972. Debt service (amortization and interest) rose twentyfold over the 1970s and by 1980 was absorbing 81.8 per cent of export earnings. Many investment projects, started in the early 1970s, had to be halted, either reducing export capacity or denying the population consumer goods. As economic growth slowed down from the mid-1970s (see Table 9.3), consumer demand could not be satisfied. In March 1979 the Ministry of Internal Trade admitted that this was the case with 280 products. Soon essential consumer articles were being rationed.

Open inflation infiltrated the system with even the official cost of living index admitting a rise from 3 to 8.5 per cent over 1975–80. Farmers, tired of being offered worthless money by state purchasing agencies, withheld food supplies. Poland stopped making scheduled payments on its debts at the end of 1980. One year later the import and export sectors collapsed as Poland struggled, in vain, to raise $500 million to cover interest due on its debts as the consequence of a rescheduling agreement (April 1981). With the economy flat on its back and chaos reigning in the streets the ruling Communist Party imposed martial law on 13 December 1981, when the ironically titled Military Council for National Salvation under a Polish general, Wojciech Jaruzelski, took over. This alternative was preferable to Soviet military intervention, but although Solidarity was temporarily curbed the price was the imposition of American-led western sanctions. They would not be lifted until 1983 after martial law ended.

The Polish experience was a portent of what was to come later in the decade. At the time, Solidarity's gallant revolt did no more than attract limited support from workers' groups in the Soviet Union. That it failed to set off widespread discontent in the eastern bloc was partly due to the belief that living standards generally had risen in the 1970s. Imports of high quality western consumer goods contributed to this illusion. So too did supplies of western grain which enhanced meat production.

The truth was that across eastern Europe agricultural productivity had failed miserably to rise to the needs of more advanced industrial development (Table 9.5). Although there was some bad luck – Poland, for one, suffered an unusual run of above-average frost, snow, floods and other natural disasters which impaired food supply – policy mistakes amplified the problems. Generally, there were too many inefficient state farms and not enough private farms or co-operatives. A key weakness was the failure to improve agricultural labour productivity. In East Germany, despite heavy investment, this factor improved by only 45 per cent between 1970 and 1984, whereas for West Germany it was as much as 98 per cent. At the start of the 1970s Erich Honecker, General Secretary of the ruling Socialist Unity Party, declared that his country must become self-sufficient in foodstuffs. As it turned out, this aim was not to be achieved. Across eastern Europe agricultural output trends were disastrous, often resulting in food shortages and necessitating rationing which inevitably engendered discontent. It was as if a stabilizing rug had been pulled from under the leaderships of eastern Europe. No matter how hard they tried, they could not find their feet again. Poland was a classic case. There per capita food consumption fell as much as 15 per cent over 1981–3, just at the time when the Jaruzelski regime was seeking legitimacy and support for economic reform. The knock-on effect of food shortages was to impair labour productivity and to undermine official blandishments seeking to portray an improving situation.

Lamentable agricultural output was a common East European problem, but in the Soviet Union it was, if anything, even more of an Achilles heel. It had been hoped to attain self-sufficiency in grain by 1980. But that year imports amounted to 27.8 million tonnes, and they would remain at that level or higher throughout the 1980s. Its import dependency would have been even costlier had it not coincided with a glutted world market. As it was, grain imports accounted for over one-fifth of the total Soviet import bill, proving a drain on hard currency reserves. This was a price that had to be paid in 1980–1, after the second poorest home harvest since the 1960s, when food shortages in Soviet cities precipitated several unofficial strikes.

By the early 1980s it was apparent that the Soviet economy was in deep water. Leonid Brezhnev's final years in office from the early 1970s to 1982

Table 9.5 Gross agricultural output in eastern Europe (annual percentage change)

	1970	1971	1972	1973	1974	1975	1976	1977	1978	1979	1980	1981	1982	1983	1984	1985	1986	1987	1988	1989	1990
Bulgaria																					
Total	3.9	1.9	5.6	1.3	-1.5	7.5	4.1	-4.7	4.3	6.1	-4.6	5.9	5.2	-7.2	7.0	-12.3	11.7	-5.1	-0.1	0.4	-8.8
Crop	2.3	-0.3	8.5	0.2	-7.5	7.8	5.6	-9.5	4.5	5.6	-8.7	10.2	7.9	-17.4	14.4	-22.5	22.7	-8.8	-0.3	4.1	-14.0
Animal	6.9	6.1	1.4	3.1	7.4	7.3	2.0	2.0	4.0	6.5	0.3	2.2	2.6	3.0	1.1	-2.9	3.7	-1.9	0.4	-2.6	-3.7
Czechoslovakia																					
Total	1.3	2.0	4.3	3.8	2.2	-1.0	-3.2	9.4	2.1	-3.3	4.8	-2.5	4.4	4.2	4.4	-1.6	0.6	0.9	2.9	1.8	-3.7
Crop	-4.5	0.4	4.5	4.0	1.5	-2.6	-8.2	16.8	1.7	-7.2	6.2	-5.3	13.9	2.8	6.1	-4.1	-2.5	1.8	4.0	1.7	-5.2
Animal	6.3	3.3	4.1	3.6	2.7	0.2	0.5	4.3	2.4	-0.3	3.9	-0.5	-2.0	5.4	3.1	0.4	2.9	0.3	2.1	2.0	-2.6
German Democratic Republic																					
Total	3.8	-0.3	9.3	-0.3	7.2	-2.0	-5.0	6.2	1.1	3.0	1.3	1.5	-4.1	3.9	6.6	3.9	–	-0.3	-2.1	1.6	–
Crop	10.8	-5.9	18.3	-7.8	8.8	-9.6	-12.5	20.9	–	5.3	-3.2	2.3	1.5	0.9	11.5	5.3	-3.7	-0.3	-6.6	1.4	–
Animal	–	4.0	4.4	5.3	6.1	2.2	-0.6	-0.1	1.7	1.8	3.8	1.5	-7.0	5.5	4.1	3.1	2.2	-0.3	0.3	1.7	–
Hungary																					
Total	-5.7	7.6	2.6	6.3	3.2	3.7	-2.7	10.9	1.1	-1.5	4.6	2.0	7.3	-2.7	2.9	-5.5	2.4	-2.0	4.3	-1.3	-6.5
Crop	-16.4	9.5	5.8	7.8	0.5	4.7	-7.1	12.3	-1.5	-3.2	7.6	1.6	9.4	-7.5	4.9	-5.4	3.7	-5.5	7.5	0.1	-10.5
Animal	10.4	5.5	-1.0	4.5	6.4	2.5	2.7	9.6	3.7	0.1	1.9	2.4	5.3	2.2	1.0	-5.6	1.1	1.5	1.5	-2.7	-2.0
Poland																					
Total	2.2	3.6	8.4	7.3	1.6	-2.1	-1.1	1.4	4.1	-1.5	-10.7	3.8	-2.8	3.3	5.7	0.7	5.0	-2.3	1.2	1.5	-1.4
Crop	4.3	1.1	7.8	6.5	-0.7	-3.0	5.0	-7.2	5.4	-3.7	-15.2	18.9	-2.5	5.9	7.4	-2.0	6.3	-2.0	-0.3	2.7	–
Animal	-1.1	6.6	9.0	8.2	4.2	-1.0	-8.7	13.7	2.6	1.3	-5.6	-8.9	-3.2	0.4	3.7	4.0	3.2	-2.7	3.2	-0.1	-3.2
Romania																					
Total	-4.9	18.9	9.7	1.0	1.1	2.9	17.3	-0.8	-1.2	5.7	-5.0	-0.4	6.9	–	13.3	0.7	-5.5	-8.9	5.7	-5.1	-3.0
Crop	-11.8	26.3	7.6	-3.2	0.6	0.6	21.5	-5.0	-4.3	6.5	-6.1	-1.0	15.2	-3.5	19.1	1.1	-8.8	-14.0	8.4	-1.7	–
Animal	5.4	8.9	12.5	7.7	1.5	6.7	11.5	5.6	2.7	3.7	-3.1	-0.6	-3.7	5.0	6.2	0.5	-1.4	-2.6	3.0	-8.9	–
Eastern Europe																					
Total	0.5	5.1	7.3	4.1	2.3	0.2	1.2	3.2	2.1	0.8	-3.7	1.9	1.5	1.2	6.8	-0.9	1.8	-2.9	1.9	–	–
Crop	-1.1	3.9	8.7	2.0	0.7	-1.8	1.8	1.4	1.5	-0.4	-5.9	6.5	5.3	-0.7	10.0	-2.5	1.4	-4.2	1.5	1.4	–
Animal	2.8	5.9	6.4	6.3	4.4	1.9	-0.8	7.4	2.7	1.9	-1.3	-2.3	-2.2	3.1	3.6	0.9	1.9	-1.4	2.1	-1.8	–

Soviet Union																					
Total	10.3	1.1	-4.1	16.1	-2.7	-5.3	6.5	4.0	2.7	-3.1	-1.9	-1.0	5.5	6.2	-0.1	0.1	5.3	-0.6	1.7	0.8	-2.3
Crop	11.8	-1.3	-7.7	27.1	-10.0	-10.5	18.4	-1.8	5.0	-5.9	-2.3	-2.4	9.2	6.0	-1.9	-1.0	6.1	-2.7	-1.4	1.0	-4.3
Animal	8.7	3.5	-0.6	6.1	5.2	-2.5	-2.4	9.4	0.8	-0.7	-1.6	0.1	2.6	6.3	1.4	1.0	4.7	1.2	4.1	1.6	-0.8
Eastern Europe and the Soviet Union																					
Total	7.0	2.4	-0.4	12.0	-1.1	-3.5	4.6	3.7	2.5	-1.8	-2.5	-0.1	4.1	4.5	2.1	-0.2	4.1	-1.4	1.8	0.5	—
Crop	7.6	0.3	-2.5	18.3	-6.7	-7.6	12.7	-0.8	3.9	-4.2	-3.5	0.4	7.9	3.8	1.8	-1.5	4.5	-3.2	-0.4	1.1	—
Animal	6.7	4.3	1.7	6.2	4.9	-0.9	-1.8	8.7	1.5	0.3	-1.5	-0.8	0.9	5.2	2.1	1.0	3.7	0.4	3.4	0.5	—

Source: United Nations, *Economic Survey of Europe in 1990–1991*, 1991, Appendix came to be called *zastoi* (stagnation) (Table 9.6). All major economic indicators turned downwards from the mid-1970s, creating increasing concern among the leadership. There was a recognition that economic weakness could mean losing the renewed arms race with the United States, begun in 1980 by the newly elected American president, former actor Ronald Reagan, who denigrated the Soviet Union as 'the evil empire'. Two years later the American leader considered the Soviet economy to be in a 'desperate situation'. One of his spokesmen went as far as to call it a 'basket case'.

Table 9.6 Soviet economic growth, 1966-85 (per cent per annum)

	1966-70	1971-5	1976-80	1981-5
National income	7.1	5.1	3.8	3.1
Industrial output	8.5	7.4	4.5	3.7
Agricultural output	3.9	2.4	1.7	1.1

Source: I. Derbyshire, *The Politics in the Soviet Union*, London: Chambers, 1987, p. 91

Certainly, there was no lack of Soviet commitment in the arms field. Indeed, western experts suspected that as much as 10-15 per cent of GNP was devoted to the military-industrial sector. But huge expenditure alone was not enough. There was also a technological dimension. Wherever Soviet weaponry came up against American (as in the Syrian-Israeli clashes) the former's inadequacies were exposed. In 1987 Mikhael Gorbachev bemoaned that 'the most worrying [feature] is that we have started lagging behind in scientific-technical development'. Another manifestation of this was in the field of microcomputers. By 1987 there were only around 200,000 of them in the whole Soviet Union against over 25 million in the United States which were of much greater sophistication. The military commitment helped depress production through siphoning off high quality resources (absorbing about a third of machinery output in the 1970s).

The enormous effort devoted to armaments, conventional and nuclear, helps to explain why the share of services actually fell from 29.5 to 20.3 per cent in 1950-80, the reverse expectation for an advanced industrialized nation. Again, while investment in industry rose from 58 to 72 per cent in 1970-80, it was not used effectively. For instance, a new blast furnace technique developed in the Soviet Union was employed by only 11 per cent of its steel industry compared with 75 per cent of Japan's. Nor was there sufficient replacement investment, with the result that up to 40 per cent of available machine tool capacity was engaged on equipment repair. Much Soviet investment focused on energy and agriculture, with housing and transportation systems badly neglected, laying the seeds for future unrest. Finally, management and organization left much to be desired. Neither managers nor workers were seen as being sufficiently motivated. A leaked government document dating from 1983 – the Novosibirsk Report – was scathing about the labour force. The Soviet worker's productivity was too low, he lacked discipline and motivation, often being involved in 'pilfering, various shady dealings at state expense, the development of illicit business, "backhander" payments and official remuneration irrespective of the results of work' (Aage 1984: 19). Here was an early recognition of the emergence across eastern Europe of the 'underground economy', which was to become ever more significant as living standards declined.

PERESTROIKA: IMPETUS FOR REFORM

It is little realized that one of Gorbachev's immediate predecessors as General Secretary of the Communist Party of the Soviet Union, Yuri Andropov (1982–4), initiated the process of reform. He began to address the perceived problems of labour discipline, low agricultural output and poor scientific diffusion in industry. But the so-called 'Andropov effect' was no more than a quickly dissolved ripple, aided by exceptionally mild winters, which reduced the strain on the creaking railway system and contained demand for fuel. Andropov confessed he 'felt the need to be very cautious in dealing with an economy on such a scale and of such complexity' as the Soviet Union's and in the final analysis was only tinkering with the system. Much bolder reform initiatives were needed.

They were provided by Gorbachev. Assuming office in March 1985, he was consumed by the need to cure the economy's ills. His policy of *uskorenie* (acceleration) similarly focused on the symptoms of deceleration – inefficiency, poor quality products and technological backwardness. Gorbachev appeared like a breath of fresh air in comparison with his recent predecessors. Comparatively young (he had not fought in the Second World War), vigorous and outspoken, he was even prepared to go on the streets and engage in dialogue with ordinary citizens. These characteristics, combined with his optimistic and idealistic oratory, were reminiscent of President Kennedy. Gorbachev's slogans, enunciated whenever he encountered criticism, were '*perestroika*' (restructuring) and '*glasnost*' (openness). Ultimately, Gorbachev failed to resurrect the economy, though his revisionism unleashed forces which brought down communism across eastern Europe.

Gorbachev embarked on a series of campaigns intended to revitalize the ailing Soviet economy. The twelfth Five Year Plan sought to increase the proportion of investment for the modernization and retooling of existing factories from 38.5 to 50.5 per cent over 1986–90. The underlying concept was the notion that such intensive re-equipment would raise the average level of technology, resulting in increased efficiency and quality. Success would wean the Soviet Union from its dependence on imported manufactures and provide the bedrock for the growth of the neglected consumer sector by the end of the century. A related campaign saw the establishment of a new independent agency, Gospriemka, in 1986, charged with enforcing new quality standards. The aim was for 95 per cent of Soviet machines to be compatible with the best world standards by 1991–3.

A further series of measures attacked the 'human factor'. *Glasnost* was initially directed against corrupt and inefficient state officials, from the Politburo to factory management. Meeting workers on factory visits, Gorbachev encountered heated resentment towards bureaucrats and their special privileges – shops stocking goods unavailable to the general population, dachas, hospitals, limousines with reserved lanes on highways. Where Stalin used terror to achieve his ends, Gorbachev sought to make officials more accountable and exposed them to public criticism. Most important, they no longer held their positions for life. By February 1986 a new generation of technocrat specialists had replaced state ministers in charge of such key industries as oil, petrochemicals, iron and steel and transport. To streamline planning, a number of super-ministries were created, through merging minor ministries. There was, too, an anti-alcohol campaign, which recalled American Prohibition. Vodka was one of the few commodities in plentiful supply, but its increased consumption fostered absenteeism from work and low industrial productivity. Alcohol production was cut, prices were raised to punitive levels, the number of selling outlets was reduced and their opening hours were restricted, the minimum drinking age went up, and fines were levied for drunkenness. Finally, there was an attempt to control the mushrooming underground economy. This campaign aimed to eradicate speculation, embezzlement, bribery and the employment of state facilities for private gain.

In none of these areas was success attained. Acute bottlenecks soon manifested themselves in machine-building and by 1989 production was way off target. Initially, Gospriemka's over-zealous pursuit of its mission saw around 6 billion roubles' worth of output rejected in 1987. This said much about the appalling quality of Soviet manufactures. It was also a level of rejection that could not be tolerated. Gospriemka accordingly lost its teeth and, once more, quantity, the god of centrally planned economies, ruled the roost. The anti-alcohol campaign became a victim of its own success. Restricting opening hours and officially available alcohol only created queues, which increased the time that addicted workers took off. The policy stimulated a vast moonshining industry, inflating the size of the black market. What the government failed to recognize was vodka's appeal as a means for the population to escape the drab reality of communism. Soft drinks, the officially preferred alternative, just did not compare in this crucial respect. Gorbachev, derided by drinkers as 'the Mineral Water Secretary', lost some of his initial popularity.

Other east European states either watched developments in the Soviet Union as interested and sympathetic onlookers or were determined not to be diverted from their own chosen paths. In the latter category fell East Germany and Romania. To the Honecker regime, any suggestion of 'market forces' was heresy. The industrial structure must be determined in advance. There could be nothing accidental about it. The East German government also wanted to see how *perestroika* worked itself out. This view from the sidelines approach reflected the official view that there was nothing fundamentally wrong with the economy. The Honecker regime was already well into an austerity programme and a campaign to improve labour productivity. New combines – Kombinates – incorporated research and development with production under one roof in an effort to reduce the time taken to introduce new technology into manufacturing processes. There were around 130 Kombinates at national level, with an average of 25,000 workers each. They produced components of a particular product and operated as a monopoly. A limited number of private and collective enterprises were also introduced into the service sector in an effort to satiate consumer demand. There was the recognition that *perestroika* carried with it dangerous political implications via its sister concept, *glasnost*. When a minister spoke in favour of *glasnost*, he was despatched to a mental clinic!

In Romania, Ceausescu's path to modernism involved Stalinist methods which were anathema to Gorbachev. In March 1988 the increasingly despised dictator began 'systemization'. Intended to achieve urbanization by the year 2000, the policy involved the destruction of half of the country's 13,000 villages. Its brutality was exemplified by the bulldozing of a cluster of villages around Bucharest with just 48 hours' notice. Ceausescu's attitude towards *perestroika* was also determined by his previous announcement, in December 1982, that Romania would pay off its foreign debt by 1990. This goal entailed cutting back drastically on western food imports, with the result that widespread rationing was in place from 1983. The authoritarian regime was totally insensitive towards even the most basic requirements of the population. In consequence, living standards were the lowest in Europe except for Albania, the continent's poorest country. Ceausescu's extensive family controlled all key positions – his brothers oversaw the armed forces, counterintelligence and agriculture, his wife Elena's brother managed the trade unions, and their son headed the Young Communist League. Together they enjoyed a lavish lifestyle reminiscent of the most decadent Roman emperors. In Romania the only concession to private enterprise was the tolerated existence of the black market, not least because it benefited corrupt government officials.

Bulgaria and Czechoslovakia were less overtly hostile to *perestroika*, but in practice only pursued superficial reforms. In July 1987 the Bulgarian leadership announced sweeping political and economic reforms, which seemingly went much deeper than the Soviet role model. Only subsequently did it emerge that there was little substance beneath the rhetoric, merely a desire to keep on good terms with Moscow. The Czech economy remained dominated by heavy industry, with the official private sector employing only 0.6 per cent of the working population as late as 1988. Hungary, too, pursued only minor reforms despite being afflicted by the lowest growth rate in eastern Europe when Gorbachev came to power and having failed to shake off its foreign debt which by 1989 was the highest both per capita and per unit of GNP. In Yugoslavia, *glasnost* struck a cord, symbolized by a growing public debate on the country's future. As for Poland, Jaruzelski's government was sympathetic towards Soviet reforms, not least because Solidarity remained a potent force. In 1987 it went as far as to hold a referendum on proposed political and economic reforms. Even so, the military dictator went ahead with a modified programme despite failing to win sufficient support.

THE SHORTAGE ECONOMY

By the late 1980s the 'shortage economy' had become the norm for eastern Europe, sowing the seeds for revolution. Shortage of revenue was endemic throughout the region. In 1988 the Soviet Union admitted that its internal budget had been in deficit since 1976. In 1985 the shortfall was about 2.5 per cent of GDP, by 1987 almost 8.5 per cent. Subsequently, Gorbachev conceded, 'We lost control over the financial situation. . . . This was our most serious mistake in the years of *perestroika*.'

Gorbachev called the deficit 'the worst heritage from the past', but in many ways the actions of his regime only served to worsen the shortfall in revenue. Most important of all, it failed to reverse the slowdown in economic growth. The anti-alcohol campaign (see above), an own goal if ever there was one, deprived the state of an estimated 6.2 billion roubles in turnover tax in 1985–6, aggravating the budget deficit. Although there was some cutback in military expenditure as relations with the west improved, the defence sector continued to absorb vast amounts which are impossible to quantify given the fact that only a small proportion was disclosed in published figures. The occupation of Afghanistan was believed to have cost five billion roubles annually. This Soviet 'Vietnam' was not finally unhitched until 1988 when the occupying troops at last began to be withdrawn. In seeking mitigating factors, Gorbachev was undoubtedly unlucky to have been burdened with the financial consequences of two major disasters. First, on 26 April 1986 the world's worst recorded nuclear accident occurred at the Chernobyl nuclear power complex in the Ukraine. The official death toll was put at 31 but was almost certainly much higher. A radioactive cloud, which was eventually to affect north western Europe, contaminated surrounding farmland. The loss of 4 million kilowatts of electricity necessitated power cuts in the winter of 1986–7. Second, Armenia suffered from an earthquake on 7 December 1988, necessitating an emergency aid programme.

The effort to keep the external Soviet account in balance took several forms. Exports, especially of fuels and raw materials, to the non-socialist countries were increased while imports were reduced. Gold exports were also raised substantially. But several forces conspired to defeat the objective. The cost of the campaigns including machinery imports, increased extraction costs for oil, the fall in world oil prices (the value of petroleum export sales fell from 30.9 to

20.7 billion roubles in 1984–8) and poor grain harvests in 1988 and 1989 ate into hard currency reserves.

Another price to pay was increasing discontent among the population. Imported consumer goods were cut back in 1986–9 (affecting sales tax revenue) because of the need for western machine tools to service heavy industry. As the size of the budget deficit increased, so money printing presses worked over-time. Only the control of basic goods prices in state shops suppressed inflation, but other prices began to rise. Gorbachev hoped for some relief from co-operatives and private farms, but they were so hidebound with regulations that they failed to increase the supply and range of goods available. By June 1989 there were only 133,000 co-operatives throughout the Soviet Union com-pared with 90 million in China. Again, the private farm initiative was no more than a laboratory experiment, with only 20,000 existing in April 1989. Both sectors responded to long queues by increasing their prices, bringing discredit on themselves (some farms fell victim to arsonists). Soviet television, no longer the propaganda vehicle of old, carried interviews with women angry with Gorbachev at the queues they faced. Driven by the twin fears of a future fall in the value of the rouble and no goods to buy, citizens resorted to hoarding. The buyers' panic ensured that Soviet stores, at various times, were emptied of such basic stocks as milk, sausage, meat and salt. A further impact of the lack of goods was to push up savings, with the growth rate of households' financial assets rising substantially from the mid-1980s, reaching 14.9 per cent in 1989.

It was a similar story in Poland. Too much money was chasing too few goods, leading to rationing and mass queuing on a first come, first served basis. In one instance, it took a fortnight for a family to take it in turns to queue for a washing machine. The housing situation was even more absurd. No one could join the Co-operative Housing Association accommodation list until they were 18. By 1987 the waiting list was 57 years which meant, given a life expectancy of 67 years, that applicants could expect to be eight years dead by the time they succeeded! For some, the answer to the shortages was the black market. Trading in American dollars gave the beleaguered Jaruzelski regime a means to reduce the mountain of money in circulation, not least because of the zloty's rapidly depreciating value.

It should be noted that budget deficits and inflation were symptoms of the efforts to reform centrally planned economies. Once this process got under way it became much more difficult to direct monetary flows so that govern-ment revenues matched expenditures. Printing money to finance the deficit was the line of least resistance, but was no panacea as it brought inflation. More open government in the Soviet Union forced the admission of a budget deficit. The public was no longer fooled by reassuring statistics which did not correspond to reality. As the head of the Soviet statistical office, *Goskomstat*, remarked, there was no longer any point to efforts 'to attempt to save the "honour of the uniform" by claiming that in spite of occasional shortcomings, which are being overcome, the situation on the whole and in general is not bad'. Elsewhere, socialist pride dictated that the figures were massaged to conceal the true picture. Not until 1989–90, after revolutions had swept away the old guard (see below), did revised figures become available. They revealed, for instance, that Bulgaria's fiscal deficit was as much as one-tenth of net material product by 1988, Hungary's budget deficit was 55 billion forints by 1989, while East Germany's domestic debt was put at 130 billion marks, almost half of national income.

The shortage economy was exemplified in Romania by energy. Epitomizing the waste and inefficiency was the aluminium plant at Slatinia which consumed as much electricity as the entire consumer sector. Electricity and gas tariffs were raised to damp down demand and restrictions on consumption were introduced. The average household was only allowed enough electricity to power one light bulb per room for two to three hours a day. There was, too, a shortage of light bulbs and lighting equipment. Further exacerbating the situation were periodic failures of the national grid. As for gas, apartments could only be heated to very low temperatures. The lack of electricity meant that around a quarter of the land area intended for irrigation was neglected. This contributed to food scarcity (see above).

In East Germany another variant of the shortage economy was on display: labour. In December 1979 Honecker alluded to 'the new situation' created by the retirement of a large percentage of the work-force. There were not enough foreign workers willing and able to fill the gaps. The shortfall was worsened by the tendency in centrally planned economies to hoard workers when target deadlines approached and through the use of antiquated machinery and equipment. By 1989 a staggering 17 per cent of employees in manufacturing and energy provision (280,000 workers) devoted their time to machine repair. The shortage of labour produced a statistical mirage: as there was no labour reserve, it appeared as if East German labour productivity was outpacing West German labour productivity. Pride and propaganda led the Honecker regime to insist that all was well. What it could not hide was the fact that on the other side of the Berlin Wall West Germans enjoyed a much more attractive lifestyle, romanticized in glossy television programmes which could be picked up in East Germany.

REVOLUTION IN EASTERN EUROPE

By 1989 the economies of eastern Europe were in a morass, sinking ever deeper into difficulties no matter what palliatives were tried. Sharply declining living standards and rising nationalism proved the death knell for the one-party communist state. It was no longer possible to shirk the fact that socialist economies could not compete with western technology or consumerism. But because most of the countries of eastern Europe had embarked on some form of market reform an inherent contradiction became apparent. The simple fact was that it was not possible to superimpose a free market economy onto a centrally planned one. The coexistence of the two systems meant that the market economy was continually held back and rendered ineffective. State controls, for instance, dictated that not all prices reflected scarcity (except on the black market). Suffocating restrictions ensured that no budding class of entrepreneurs emerged. The army of meddling bureaucrats created by central planning was naturally hostile to the birth pangs of private enterprise, which was seen as job threatening. Ultimately, only political revolution could resolve the contradiction.

The Soviet Union demonstrated all these shortcomings and more. The 1988 Enterprise Law had the intention of shifting decision-making gradually from the centre to the enterprises themselves. State orders were to decrease as a proportion of output each year (though they would remain by far the greater part). Managers could dispose of any target surplus at the best price they could negotiate. The theory was that the anticipated profits would replace state subsidies, thus easing the budget deficit.

The half-baked measure was doomed to failure. It patently failed to promote a move to the market system or reduce the role of planners and ministries. With no wholesalers to sell surplus to, most managers preferred, as before, to deal with the ministries. These, in turn, were pleased to accept, not least because the business justified their continued existence. In many ways, the Enterprise Law worsened the situation. Free to select product mix, managers increased the proportion of expensive goods, squeezing out cheaper items. Elected by the work-force, managers responded easily to demands for higher wages, thereby increasing overall demand. Only belatedly, in June 1990, did Gorbachev act to remove the workers' right to select their managers.

These examples could be multiplied. Suffice it to say that by 1989 *perestroika* had failed to produce a fundamental restructuring of the Soviet economy. In contrast, *glasnost* had taken much deeper root. Even though Gorbachev had not dared to expose himself to popular election, democratization at lower levels and the introduction of a parliament in June 1989 made him appear increasingly conservative compared with more radical reformers, such as Boris Yeltsin. *Glasnost*, with its open criticism of the Soviet past, had another unwanted ramification for Gorbachev: it encouraged the three Baltic states, Latvia, Lithuania and Estonia, incorporated into the Soviet Union by Stalin in 1940, to seek their independence. Nor were they the only trouble spots. In 1988 inter-ethnic conflict erupted between the republics of Azerbaijan and Armenia over the disputed enclave of Nagorno-Karabakh. The same year Georgians called for their independence. There were nationalist stirrings too in Russia, the Ukraine, Byelorussia and Moldavia.

The economic consequences of rising nationalism were profound. The Baltic states, better supplied than many other parts, attracted non-residents in search of provisions. The Baltic authorities responded by banning the sale of selected products to outsiders. Soon this phenomenon spread throughout the Soviet Union. After Moscow insisted that only residents could buy its produce, eight surrounding regions retaliated by banning deliveries of milk to the Soviet capital. The Azeri blockade of Armenia prevented goods from coming in or out. Central planners had boasted that they did not need to duplicate supplies. But the dispute cut off a Vladimir tractor factory from its only source of tyres, with the result that many machines were supplied to rural areas without tyres. Again, as most cigarette paper was produced in Armenia, national shortages resulted.

In the past, strikers were either imprisoned or committed to mental institutions. *Glasnost* changed all this and the strike became a weapon of ethnic and worker unrest. Heavy industry workers went on strike not for more wages but for more consumer goods on which to spend their money. During July 1989 over half a million workers in Siberia and the Ukraine came out over poor food supplies and provisions such as soap. Since these regions were vital to the economy, the government was forced to import more, adding to its debt problem. The first mass miners' strike took place a month after the Congress of the People's Deputies opening session, inspired by its unprecedented criticisms of the government.

Karl Marx had predicted that capitalism would explode. In the event, it was communism which imploded. The Soviet Union's internal problems placed it in no position, even if it had desired, to prevent other East European countries from renouncing communism. Gorbachev's wish to reduce the huge nuclear weapons stockpile through *détente* with the west evidenced his recognition that its technological and financial assistance was vital. By comparison, the Soviet Union's economic ties within the CMEA were increasingly seen as a burden. From 1986 the Soviet Union's exports to other CMEA members declined dramatically, reflecting a shift of trade towards the west and declining oil prices. Such was the turnaround that by 1989 both Hungary and Czechoslovakia had built up trade surpluses with the Soviet Union of the order of 1 billion transferable roubles. Envious of the European Community, in July 1988 Gorbachev tried, and failed, to convert the CMEA into a genuine common market. While Hungary and Poland supported the idea, Bulgaria and Czechoslovakia were lukewarm, East Germany had reservations, with Romania definitely opposed. A similar division was apparent over the proposed introduction of a convertible currency, the necessary precondition of a common market. In January 1989 the CMEA celebrated its fortieth anniversary, but by then it was looking increasingly like a spent force. A sharp fall in intra-CMEA trade started in 1989, accelerating in 1990 when it fell by as much as one-fifth in volume.

Events were now to move rapidly, as communism was swept away in eastern Europe in a domino-like way. The process was facilitated by instant communications via television and radio, with news of one revolution spreading quickly and causing another. The underlying reason was the pent-up frustration and resentment of populations at their governments' failure to provide them with decent living standards. Most important was the Soviet

Union's benevolent attitude to change. In March 1989 Gorbachev approved the new Hungarian multi-party system and accepted the round table negotiations between Solidarity and the Polish government, which produced free elections in which the Communist Party was roundly beaten. Increasingly, Soviet spokesmen suggested that the Brezhnev doctrine was no longer sacrosanct. In a famous remark, one said that it was now 'the Sinatra doctrine' – allowing other countries to 'do it their way'. Gorbachev himself reaffirmed this in speeches of June and July 1989 when he said that each state had the right to build socialism as it saw fit.

The new mood soon manifested itself in East Germany. Hungary was one of the few places where the population was allowed to travel abroad. Now that communism had collapsed there, it became a magnet for East Germans seeking a new life in the west. West German television reported that Hungary had opened its frontier with Austria, which became an escape route into West Germany. Hundreds, and then thousands made the bid for freedom. On 7 October 1989 East Germany celebrated its fortieth anniversary, with Gorbachev and Honecker standing side by side at the anniversary parade. A nearby demonstration rang out with the cry, 'Gorby, help us!' Soon mass protests had broken out in the major cities. Honecker was forced to resign on 18 October 1989, but this palliative was not enough. More demonstrations followed, with yet more people leaving when Czechoslovakia opened its frontier on 3 November. Conceding defeat, the ruling Politburo resigned and the opposition New Forum was legalized. By now the exodus totalled 200,000 – 1 per cent of the population. On 9 November the unthinkable happened – East Germany opened its frontiers, including the Berlin Wall, whose dismantlement was begun by jubilant citizens hacking at its hated concrete structure.

The next day the longest serving leader in eastern Europe, Todor Zhivkov, was toppled from power in Bulgaria by party colleagues. His misguided efforts to 'Bulgarianize' the country's Muslim community prompted a mass exodus into Turkey and severely damaged the economy. Attention then switched to Czechoslovakia, where demonstrations in Prague quickly spread and led the government to resign early in December. Finally, the hated Nicolae Ceausescu was removed from power in Romania. Increasingly, he and his extended family, which was prepared to let the population inhabit a Dark Ages environment while they wallowed in luxury, were regarded as an anachronism. With the armed forces refusing to act against demonstrators, Ceausescu and his wife attempted to flee. Caught, after a summary trial reminiscent of the French revolution, they were executed on Christmas Day.

Yugoslavia, the first communist regime established outside the Soviet Union following the Second World War, looked destined to survive the upheavals. In reality, the Balkan question, which had lain virtually undisturbed since 1918, was about to raise its ugly head again. Already, efforts towards further economic reform had foundered on differences between the republics of Croatia, Slovenia and Serbia on how they should be implemented. Politically, only Serbia wished to preserve the federation; the other republics wanted either a looser arrangement or outright independence. Increasingly, it looked as if only civil war could resolve the situation.

THE OUTLOOK FOR CHANGE

It is one thing to bring down a regime overnight, quite another to restructure and revitalize an economy. A number of common problems were faced by the new regimes: first, the need to convert the currency which required a price shock, or shocks, to adjust to world market prices; second, the abolition of central planning; last, the privatization of state enterprises and the creation of legal and financial infrastructures to stimulate private industry. There were also problems unique to a particular country, the most obvious being German reunification in the case of East Germany where the original owners of property confiscated by the state in 1949–89 were entitled to compensation. Nothing could be done with a commercial building until they were traced. Sometimes multiple owners appeared. Intending property developers had to compensate them before going ahead. In Romania, the new regime wisely reversed Ceausescu's barbaric policies – foodstuffs geared for export were redirected to the consumer market, 'systematization' was ended, large and expensive construction projects were halted, domestic restrictions on the use of electricity and gas were lifted, and energy and thermal-heat was redirected from industry to the municipal and private sectors. The result of this pro-consumer approach, predictably enough, was to place a severe strain on the balance of payments, with imports from the convertible currency area increasing by 54.3 per cent in the first three quarters of 1990.

As no country had yet successfully jumped across the enormous chasm separating communism from capitalism, there was no consensus on the correct sequencing. The danger with excessive devaluation, as adopted by Poland in January 1990, was that it brought cost-push inflation. On the other hand, it could be argued that such a move would encourage many firms to export. In 1990 Polish exports rose by 15 per cent in volume, while the rest of eastern Europe's (excluding those of Yugoslavia) contracted by some 10 per cent. Hungary and Romania preferred a more gradualist approach, but this assumed the continuance of a stable political base.

The signs were that the new regimes would find it difficult to create order from the chaos they inherited, not least because external conditions were not always favourable. The world economic slowdown, the collapse of CMEA trade, the brief, but stinging, oil price shock resulting from the Iraqi invasion of Kuwait, all these factors represented further hurdles over a long course. Gorbachev had once spoken of a 'Common European Home' and many east European governments cherished the hope that the two halves of Europe could converge and become one big happy family under the umbrella of the European Community.

That ambition could only be a distant dream, the immediate task being the modernization of the economies. As in the 1970s, western aid was sorely needed. The new Romanian regime went cap in hand to the IMF, coming away with credits of over $1 billion. Not a member of the IMF, the Soviet Union, now seen as a credit risk by western banks concerned at the uncertain political situation and what they considered wasted expenditure, could only obtain $17 billion of new credits in 1990 through them being underwritten by western governments.

The wheel had turned full circle, but unlike the 1970s the west was not prepared to lend without influence. There was no prospect of another Marshall Plan. In 1990 the Group of 24 (G24) advanced industrial nations agreed to back reforms in eastern Europe, providing greater access to their markets, technical assistance and limited financial support. The same year, the G24 and international financial institutions met the urgent balance of payments problems of Hungary and Poland with new credits. The latter country's payments were rescheduled to give its reforms greater time to work. The European Community also began negotiations with Czechoslovakia, Hungary and Poland with a view to creating an industrial free trade system.

While the west also looked to bolster Soviet reforms, close study suggested that the Soviet economy was so inefficiently run that any major aid would be wasted. In December 1990 the Houston Four Report recommended that assistance be restricted to three areas: food, technical aid and selected projects (especially energy). By that time, the big question was how much longer could Gorbachev survive. Public support for him had plunged to 20 per cent by July 1990 (from a high of 90 per cent in his early days). The economic revival he had promised now seemed a pipedream and he was blamed for bringing the Soviet Union to the brink of economic collapse. Even the official Soviet statistical agency conceded that GNP fell by 2 per cent in 1990, the first fall since 1945. Taking inflation into account, it was probably of the order of 8–10 per cent. By 1990 parliaments in all fifteen Soviet republics had passed resolutions demanding their own sovereignty. Some major cities began to take the initiative towards market reform without reference to the centre. His authority diminished, Gorbachev offered to change the country's name to the Union of Sovereign Soviet Republics. Cynics suggested that the UFFR was a better title – the Union of Fewer and Fewer Republics. Soon, the Goliath of communism was to be toppled from its pedestal by nationalist stones coming from all directions, along with innumerable statues of the once revered Lenin.

Eastern Europe's dramatic transformation from communist states to fledgling democracies over the period under review stemmed from the failure to match the growth levels achieved in the 1960s. Extensive western credits and, for most countries, insulation from the worst effects of the oil shocks provided the means to avoid addressing fundamental economic and social problems in the 1970s. But by the following decade less favourable circumstances compelled socialist governments to introduce limited reforms which invariably promised much but delivered little. The one reform which might have made all the difference – the introduction of a true free market economy – was consciously avoided, essentially because it would have turned communism on its head. Even as late as April 1990 Gorbachev bemoaned: 'They say, "Let's have free enterprise and give the green light to all forms of private ownership". . . . But I cannot accept such ideas. . . . They are impossible ideas.' The result of introducing only limited private ventures into the morasse of a centrally planned economy was inevitably that their green shoots failed to take root.

Eastern Europe's communist regimes, by and large, continued to structure their economies in favour of sector A (heavy, construction and defence industries) to the detriment of sector B (light, consumer industries). *Perestroika*, wherever it appeared, merely tinkered with the existing system; it patently failed to transform it. What had sustained growth in the 1960s – high inputs of capital investment, labour and raw materials – were no longer available in the required dosages. With these inputs becoming scarce, planners sought to increase productivity through imports of western technology, but the opportunity was wasted. By the late 1980s demonstrators were calling not just for political freedom but also for comprehensive market reforms. The revolutions of 1989 provided the platform for reforms on western lines, but also brought the prospect of high unemployment. It is yet to be seen whether the new governments can bridge the chasm between east and west and Europe can truly be integrated in economic terms. With members of the European Community falling out with each other over closer political and economic links that prospect must remain doubtful to say the least.

BIBLIOGRAPHY

GENERAL WORKS

Alpert, P. *Twentieth Century Economic History of Europe*, New York: Schuman, 1951.

Ashworth, W. *A Short History of the International Economy since 1850*, Harlow: Longman, 3rd edn, 1975.

Bairoch, P. 'Europe's gross national product: 1800–1975', *Journal of European Economic History* 5, Fall 1976.

Cipolla, C. M. (ed.) *The Fontana Economic History of Europe*, vol. 5, *The Twentieth Century* (Parts 1 and 2), and vol. 6, *Contemporary Economies* (Parts 1 and 2), London: Collins/Fontana, 1976.

Clough, S. B. *The Economic Development of Western Civilisation*, New York: McGraw-Hill, revised edn, 1968.

——, Moodie, T. and Moodie, C. (eds) *Economic History of Europe: Twentieth Century*, London: Macmillan, 1969.

Darby, H. C. and Fullard, H. (eds) *The New Cambridge Modern History*, vol. 14, *Atlas*, Cambridge: Cambridge University Press, 1970.

Landes, D. S. *The Unbound Prometheus: Technological Change and Industrial Development in Western Europe from 1750 to the Present*, Cambridge: Cambridge University Press, 1969.

Lundberg, E. *Instability and Economic Growth*, New Haven, CT: Yale University Press, 1968.

Maddison, A. 'Economic growth in western Europe, 1870–1957', *Banca Nazionale del Lavoro Quarterly Review* 15, 1962.

—— *Economic Policy and Performance in Europe 1913–1970*, London: Collins/Fontana, 1973.

Marwick, A. *Britain in the Century of Total War: War, Peace and Social Change, 1900–1967*, Harmondsworth: Penguin, 1968.

—— *War and Social Change in the Twentieth Century*, London: Macmillan, 1974.

OECD *Basic Statistics of Industrial Production, 1913–1960*, Paris: OECD, 1962.

Parker, R. A. C. *Europe 1914–45*, London: Weidenfeld & Nicolson, 1969.

Scoville, W. C. and La Force, J. C. (eds) *The Economic Development of Western Europe from 1914 to the Present*, Lexington, MA: D. C. Heath, 1969.

Spulber, N. *The State and Economic Development in Eastern Europe*, New York: Random House, 1966.

Svennilson, I. *Growth and Stagnation in the European Economy*, Geneva: United Nations, 1954.

Thomson, D. *Europe since Napoleon*, Harmondsworth: Penguin, 1966.

279

CHAPTER 1   THE END OF THE OLD REGIME, 1914–1921

Aldcroft, D. H. *From Versailles to Wall Street: The International Economy, 1919–1929*, London: Penguin, 1977.
Alpert, P. 'The impact of World War I on the European economy', in W. C. Scoville and C. J. La Force (eds) *The Economic Development of Western Europe from 1914 to the Present*, Lexington, MA: D. C. Heath, 1969.
Bowley, A. L. *Some Economic Consequences of the Great War*, London: Thornton Butterworth, 1930.
Hardach, G. *The First World War 1914–1918*, London: Penguin, 1977.
Keynes, J. M. *The Economic Consequences of the Peace*, London: Macmillan, revised edn, 1922.
League of Nations *Europe's Overseas Needs 1919–1920 and How They Were Met*, Geneva: League of Nations, 1943.
—— *Relief Deliveries and Relief Loans 1919–1923*, Geneva: League of Nations, 1943.
Mantoux, E. *The Carthaginian Peace or the Economic Consequences of Mr. Keynes*, London: Oxford University Press, 1946.
Marwick, A. *The Deluge*, London: Bodley Head, 1965.
Mendershausen, H. *The Economics of War*, New York: Prentice Hall, 1941.
Milward, A. S. *The Economic Effects of the World Wars on Britain*, London: Macmillan, 1970.
Mitrany, D. *The Effect of the War in South-Eastern Europe*, New Haven, CT: Yale University Press, 1936.
Notestein, F. W., Taeuber, I. B., Kirk, D., Coale, A. J. and Kiser, L. K. *The Future Population of Europe and the Soviet Union*, Geneva: League of Nations, 1944.
Stearns, P. N. *European Society in Upheaval*, London: Macmillan, 1967.

CHAPTER 2   RECOVERY AND INSTABILITY PROBLEMS IN THE 1920s

Aldcroft, D. H. *The Inter-war Economy: Britain 1919–1939*, London: Batsford, 1970.
—— *From Versailles to Wall Street, 1919–1929*, London: Penguin, 1977.
Angell, J. W. *The Recovery of Germany*, New Haven, CT: Yale University Press, revised edn, 1932.
Bandera, V. N. *Foreign Capital as an Instrument of National Economic Policy: a Study Based on the Experience of East European Countries Between the World Wars*, The Hague: Nijhoff, 1964.
Berand, I. T. and Ranki, G. *Economic Development in East Central Europe in the 19th and 20th Centuries*, New York: Columbia University Press, 1974.
Bresciani-Turroni, C. *The Economics of Inflation: a Study of Currency Depreciation in Post-War Germany*, London: Allen & Unwin, 1937.
Brown, W. A. Jr *The International Gold Standard Reinterpreted 1914–1934*, 2 vols, New York: National Bureau of Economic Research, 1940.
Cagan, P. 'The monetary dynamics of hyperinflation', in M. Friedman (ed.) *Studies in the Quantity Theory of Money*, Chicago, IL: University of Chicago Press, 1956.
Clough, S. B. *The Economic History of Modern Italy*, New York: Columbia University Press, 1964.
Dahmén, E. *Entrepreneurial Activity and the Development of Swedish Industry, 1919–1939*, trans. by A. Leijonhufvud, Homewood IL: Irwin, 1970.
Davis, J. S. *The World Between the Wars 1919–39: An Economist's View*, Baltimore, MD: Johns Hopkins University Press, 1969.

Dulles, E. L. *The French Franc 1914–1928: The Facts and Their Interpretation*, London: Macmillan, 1929.

Falkus, M. E. 'The German business cycle in the 1920s', *Economic History Review*, 28, 1975.

Graham, F. D. *Exchange, Prices and Production in Hyperinflation Germany, 1920–23*, Princeton, NJ: Princeton University Press, 1930.

Grossman, G. *The Industrialization of Russia and the Soviet Union*, London: Collins/ Fontana, 1971.

Harris, C. R. *Germany's Foreign Indebtedness*, London: Oxford University Press, 1935.

Jack, D. T. *The Restoration of European Currencies*, London: P.S. King, 1927.

Kemp, T. *The French Economy, 1919–1939: The History of a Decline*, Harlow: Longman, 1972.

Kirk, D. *Europe's Population in the Inter-War Years*, Geneva: League of Nations, 1946.

Laursen, K. and Pedersen, J. *The German Inflation, 1918–1923*, Amsterdam: North-Holland, 1964.

League of Nations *International Currency Experience: Lessons of the Interwar Period*, Geneva: League of Nations, 1944.

—— *The Course and Control of Inflation: a Review of Monetary Experience in Europe after World War I*, Geneva: League of Nations, 1946.

Lewis, W. A. *Economic Survey 1919–1939*, London: Allen & Unwin, 1949.

Meyer, R. H. *Bankers' Diplomacy: Monetary Stabilisation in the Twenties*, New York: Columbia University Press, 1970.

Moulton, H. G. and Pasvolsky, L. *War Debts and World Prosperity*, Washington, DC: Brookings Institution, 1932.

North, D. C. 'International capital movements in historical perspective', in R. F. Mikesell (ed.) *U.S. Private and Government Investment Abroad*, Eugene, OR: University of Oregon Books, 1962.

Nove, A. *An Economic History of the USSR*, London: Penguin, 1969.

Palyi, M. *The Twilight of Gold 1914–1936: Myths and Realities*, Chicago, IL: Henry Regnery, 1972.

Pasvolsky, L. *Economic Nationalism of the Danubian States*, London: Allen & Unwin, 1928.

—— *Bulgaria's Economic Position*, Washington, DC: Brookings Institution, 1930.

Pollard, S. and Holmes, C. (eds) *Documents of European Economic History*, vol. 3, *The End of Old Europe 1914–1939*, London: Edward Arnold, 1973.

Rogers, J. H. *The Process of Inflation in France, 1914–1927*, New York: Columbia University Press, 1929.

Royal Institute of International Affairs *The Balkan States: A Review of the Economic and Financial Developments of Albania, Bulgaria, Greece, Roumania and Yugoslavia since 1919*, London: Oxford University Press, 1936.

—— *The Problem of International Investment*, London: Oxford University Press, 1937.

Shepherd, H. L. *The Monetary Experience of Belgium 1914–1936*, Princeton, NJ: Princeton University Press, 1936.

Stearns, P. N. *European Society in Upheaval*, London: Macmillan, 1967.

Taylor, J. *The Economic Development of Poland, 1919–1950*, New York: Cornell University Press, 1952.

Tracy, M. *Agriculture in Western Europe: Crisis and Adaptation since 1880*, London: Cape, 1964.

CHAPTER 3   ECONOMIC CRISIS AND RECOVERY, 1929–1939

Aldcroft, D. H. 'The development of the managed economy before 1939', *Journal of Contemporary History* 4, 1969.

BIBLIOGRAPHY

Arndt, H. W. *The Economic Lessons of the Nineteen-Thirties*, London: Cass, reprinted 1963.

Basch, A. *The Danube Basin and the German Economic Sphere*, London: K. Paul, Trench, Trubner, 1944.

Berend, I. T. and Ranki, G. *Economic Development in East-Central Europe in the 19th and 20th Centuries*, New York: Columbia University Press, 1974.

—— and —— *Hungary: A Century of Economic Development*, Newton Abbott: David & Charles, 1974.

Carroll, B. A. *Design for Total War: Arms and Economics in the Third Reich*, Paris: Mouton, 1969.

Ellis, H. S. *Exchange Control in Central Europe*, Cambridge, MA: Harvard University Press, 1941.

Galbraith, J. K. *The Great Crash 1929*, Harmondsworth: Penguin, 1961.

Gilbert, M. *Currency Depreciation*, Philadelphia, PA: University of Pennsylvania Press, 1939.

Harris, S. E. *Exchange Depreciation: Its Theory and History with some Consideration of Related Domestic Policies*, Cambridge, MA: Harvard University Press, 1936.

Herty, F. *The Economic Problem of the Danubian States. A Study in Economic Nationalism*, London: Gollancz, 1947.

Hodson, H. V. *Slump and Recovery, 1929–37*, London: Oxford University Press, 1938.

Kindleberger, C. P. *The World in Depression, 1929–1939*, London: Penguin, 1973.

Klein, B. H. *Germany's Economic Preparations for War*, Cambridge, MA: Harvard University Press, 1959.

Knauerhase, R. *An Introduction to National Socialism 1920–1939*, Columbus, OH: C. E. Merrill, 1972.

League of Nations *The Course and Phases of the World Economic Depression*, Geneva: League of Nations, 1931.

Montgomery, G. A. *How Sweden Overcame the Depression, 1930–33*, Stockholm: Benniers, 1938.

Overy, R. J. 'Transportation and rearmament in the Third Reich', *Historical Journal* 16, 1973.

—— 'Cars, roads and economic recovery in Germany, 1932–8', *Economic History Review* 28, 1975.

Political and Economic Planning *Economic Development in South-East Europe*, London: PEP, 1945.

Polonsky, L. *The Little Dictators*, London: Routledge & Kegan Paul, 1975.

Rees, G. *The Great Slump: Capitalism in Crisis, 1929–33*, London: Weidenfeld & Nicolson, 1970.

Richardson, H. W. *Economic Recovery in Britain, 1932–9*, London: Weidenfeld & Nicolson, 1967.

Robbins, L. *The Great Depression*, London: Macmillan, 1934.

Rothschild, J. *East Central Europe Between the Two World Wars*, Washington, DC: American University Publishers Group, 1947.

Rothschild, K. W. *Austria's Economic Development Between the Two Wars*, London: Frederick Muller, 1974.

Royal Institute of International Affairs *The Baltic States*, London: Oxford University Press, 1938.

—— *South-Eastern Europe: a Political and Economic Survey*, London: Oxford University Press, 1939.

Sarti, R. *Fascism and the Industrial Leadership in Italy, 1919–1940*, Berkeley, CA: University of California Press, 1971.

Seton-Watson, H. *Eastern Europe Between the Wars 1918–1941*, Cambridge: Cambridge University Press, 1945.

Temin, P. 'The beginning of the depression in Germany', *Economic History Review*, 24, 1971.
—— *Did Monetary Forces Cause the Great Depression?*, New York: W. W. Norton, 1976.
Thomas, B. *Monetary Policy and Crisis: A Study of Swedish Experience*, London: Routledge, 1936.
Timoshenko, V. P. *World Agriculture and the Depression*, Ann Arbor, MI: University of Michigan Business Studies, vol. 5, 1933.
Warriner, D. *Economics of Peasant Farming*, London: Oxford University Press, 1939.
van der Wee, H. (ed.) *The Great Depression Revisited: Essays on the Economics of the Thirties*, The Hague: Nijhoff, 1972.
Welk, W. G. *Fascist Economic Policy*, Cambridge, MA: Harvard University Press, 1938.
Williams, D. 'The 1931 financial crisis', *Yorkshire Bulletin of Economic and Social Research* 15, 1963.
Yeager, L. B. *International Monetary Relations: Theory, History and Policy*, New York: Harper & Row, 1966.

CHAPTER 4   WAR AND RECONSTRUCTION, 1940–1950

Borrie, W. D. *The Growth and Control of World Population*, London: Weidenfeld & Nicolson, 1970.
Brown, A. J. *Applied Economics, Aspects of the World Economy in War and Peace*, London: Allen & Unwin, 1947.
Frumkin, G. *Population Changes in Europe since 1939*, London: Allen & Unwin, 1951.
Klein, B. H. *Germany's Economic Preparations for War*, Cambridge, MA: Harvard University Press, 1959.
Kulischer, E. M. *Europe on the Move: War and Population Changes, 1917–47*, New York: Columbia University Press, 1948.
Marwick, A. *War and Social Change in the Twentieth Century*, London: Macmillan, 1974.
Mayer, H. C. *German Recovery and the Marshall Plan, 1948–1952*, Bonn: Edition Atlantic Forum, 1969.
Meimberg, R. *The Economic Development in West Berlin and in the Soviet Union*, Berlin: Berliner Zentralbank, 1951.
Mendershausen, H. *Two Postwar Recoveries of the German Economy*, Amsterdam: North-Holland, 1955.
Milward, A. S. *The German Economy at War*, London: Athlone Press, 1965.
—— *The New Order and the French Economy*, London: Oxford University Press, 1970.
—— *The Fascist Economy in Norway*, London: Oxford University Press, 1972.
—— *War, Economy and Society, 1939–1945*, London: Penguin, 1977.
Roskamp, K. W. *Capital Formation in West Germany*, Detroit, MI: Wayne State University Press, 1965.
Royal Institute of International Affairs *Occupied Europe: German Exploitation and its Post-War Consequences*, London: RIIA, 1944.
Toynbee, A. and Toynbee, V. M. (eds) *Hitler's Europe: Survey of International Affairs 1939–1946*, London: Oxford University Press for Royal Institute of International Affairs, 1954.
United Nations (Department of Economic Affairs) *Economic Report: Salient Features of the World Economic Situation 1945–47*, New York, January 1948.
United Nations (Economic Commission for Europe) *Economic Surveys of Europe in 1948, 1949, 1950, 1951*, Geneva, 1949, 1950, 1951, 1952.

—— *Economic Survey of Europe Since the War: a Reappraisal of Problems and Prospects*, Geneva, 1953.

Wallich, H. C. *Mainsprings of the German Revival*, New Haven, CT: Yale University Press, 1955.

Wright, G. *The Ordeal of Total War 1939–1945*, New York: Harper & Row, 1968.

Zagoreff, S. D., Vegh, J. and Bilimovich, A. D. *The Agricultural Economy of the Danubian Countries 1935–45*, Stanford, CA: Stanford University Press, 1955.

CHAPTER 5   WESTERN EUROPE'S SUSTAINED EXPANSION, 1950–1970

Abert, J. G. *Economic Policy and Planning in the Netherlands, 1950–1965*, New Haven, CT: Yale University Press, 1969.

Bjerve, P. J. 'Trends in quantitative economic planning in Norway', *Economics of Planning* 8, 1968.

Bremer, J. and Bradford, M. R. 'Incomes and labour market policies in Sweden, 1945–70', *IMF Staff Papers* 31, 1974.

Bronfenbrenner, M. (ed.) *Is the Business Cycle Obsolete?*, Chichester: Wiley, 1969.

Carré, J. J., Dubois, P. and Malinvaud, E. *French Economic Growth*, London: Oxford University Press, 1975.

Cohen, C. D. *British Economic Policy, 1960–1969*, London: Butterworth, 1971.

Cohen, S. S. *Modern Capitalist Planning: The French Model*, London: Weidenfeld & Nicolson, 1969.

Denison, E. F. *Why Growth Rates Differ*, Washington, DC: Brookings Institution, 1967.

Denton, G. R., Forsyth, M. and Maclennan, M. *Economic Planning and Policies in Britain, France and Germany*, London: Allen & Unwin, 1968.

Dow, J. C. R. *The Management of the British Economy, 1945–1960*, Cambridge: Cambridge University Press, 1964.

Emery, R. F. 'The relation of exports and economic growth', *Kyklos* 20, 1967.

Hallett, G. *The Social Economy of West Germany*, London: Macmillan, 1973.

Hansen, B. *Fiscal Policy in Seven Countries, 1955–1965*, Paris: OECD, 1969.

Hennessey, J., Lutz, V. and Scimone, G. *Economic Miracles: Studies in the Resurgence of the French, German and Italian Economies since the Second World War*, London: Andre Deutsch, 1964.

Hough, J. R. 'French economic policy', *National Westminster Bank Quarterly Review* May 1976.

Jones, H. G. *Planning and Productivity in Sweden*, London: Croom Helm, 1977.

Keith, E. G. (ed.) *Foreign Tax Policies and Economic Growth*, New York: Columbia University Press, 1966.

Kiker, B. F. and Vasconcelles, A. S. 'The performance of the French economy, 1949–1964', *Economics of Planning* 8, 1968.

Kindleberger, C. P. *Europe's Postwar Growth: The Role of Labour Supply*, Cambridge, MA: Harvard University Press, 1967.

Krenzel, R. 'Some reasons for the rapid economic growth of the German Federal Republic', *Banca Nazionale del Lavoro Quarterly Review* 64, 1963.

Licari, J. A. and Gilbert, M. 'Is there a postwar growth cycle?', *Kyklos* 27, 1974.

Lindbeck, A. *Swedish Economic Policy*, London: Macmillan, 1975.

Lubitz, R. 'Export-led growth in industrial economies', *Kyklos* 27, 1973.

Lundberg, E. *Instability and Economic Growth*, New Haven, CT: Yale University Press, 1968.

Lutz, V. *Italy: A Study in Economic Development*, London: Oxford University Press, 1962.

Maddison, A. 'The postwar business cycle in Western Europe and the role of government policy', *Banca Nazionale del Lavoro Quarterly Review* 13, 1960.
—— *Economic Growth in the West*, London: Allen & Unwin, 1964.
—— 'Explaining economic growth', *Banca Nazionale del Lavoro Quarterly Review* 25, 1972.
Maynard, G. and van Ryckeghem, W. *A World of Inflation*, London: Batsford, 1976.
Michaely, M. *The Responsiveness of Demand Policies to Balance of Payments: Postwar Patterns*, New York: National Bureau of Economic Research, 1971.
OECD *The Growth of Output 1960–1980*, Paris: OECD, 1970.
Oulès, F. *Economic Planning and Democracy*, Harmondsworth: Penguin, 1966.
Podbielski, G. *Italy: Development and Crisis in the Post-War Economy*, London: Oxford University Press, 1974.
Postan, M. M. *An Economic History of Western Europe, 1945–1964*, London: Methuen, 1967.
Sandford, C. T., Bradbury, M. S. and associates *Economic Policy*, London: Macmillan, 1970.
Shonfield, A. *Modern Capitalism: The Changing Balance of Public and Private Power*, London: Oxford University Press, 1965.
—— 'Stabilisation policies in the West: from demand to supply management', *Journal of Political Economy* 75, 1967.
United Nations (Economic Commission for Europe) *Economic Survey of Europe in 1961*, Part 2, *Some Factors in Economic Growth in Europe During the 1950s*, Geneva, 1964.
—— *Economic Survey of Europe in 1971*, Part 1, *The European Economy from the 1950s to the 1970s*, New York, 1972.
Whiting, A. 'An international comparison of the instability of economic growth', *The Three Banks Review* March 1976.
Zweig, K. *Germany Through Inflation and Recession: An Object Lesson in Economic Management, 1973–1976*, London: Centre for Policy Studies, 1976.

CHAPTER 6 THE SOCIALIST ECONOMIES OF EASTERN EUROPE, 1950–1970

Alton, T. P. 'Economic structure and growth in Eastern Europe', in Joint Committee of US Congress, *Economic Developments in Countries of Eastern Europe*, Washington, DC: US Government Printing Office, 1970.
Balassa, B. and Bertrand, T. J. 'Growth performance of eastern European economies and comparable western European countries', *American Economic Review* May 1970.
Ernst, M. 'Postwar economic growth in eastern Europe (a comparison with western Europe)', in *New Directions in the Soviet Economy*, Part IV, *The World Outside*, Washington, DC: US Government Printing Office, 1966.
Goldman, J. 'Fluctuation and trend in the rate of economic growth in some socialist countries', *Economics of Planning* 8, 1968.
Lavigne, M. *The Socialist Economies of the Soviet Union and Europe*, trans. by T. G. Waywell, London: Martin Robertson, 1974.
Nove, A. *An Economic History of the USSR*, Harmondsworth: Penguin, 1972.
Spulber, N. *The State and Economic Development in Eastern Europe*, New York: Random House, 1966.
Staller, G. J. 'Fluctuations in economic activity: planned and free-market economies, 1950–60', *American Economic Review* 54, 1964.

United Nations (Economic Commission for Europe) *Economic Survey of Europe in 1961*, Part 2, *Some Factors in Economic Growth in Europe During the 1950s*, Geneva, 1964.
—— *Economic Survey of Europe in 1971*, Part 1, *The European Economy from the 1950s to the 1970s*, New York, 1972.
Wilczynski, J. *Socialist Economic Development and Reforms*, London: Macmillan, 1972.
Zaubermann, A. *Industrial Progress in Poland, Czechoslovakia and East Germany 1937–1962*, London: Oxford University Press, 1964.
—— 'Russia and Eastern Europe, 1920–1970', in C. M. Cipolla (ed.) *The Fontana Economic History of Europe*, vol. 6, *Contemporary Economies*, Part 2, London: Collins/Fontana, 1976.

CHAPTER 7   WESTERN CAPITALISM IN THE 1970s

Argy, V. 'Monetary stabilisation and the stabilisation of output in selected industrial countries', *Banca Nazionale del Lavoro Quarterly Review* 129, 1979.
Bacon, R. and Eltis, W. *Britain's Economic Problem: Too Few Producers*, London: Macmillan, 1976.
Bilson, J. F. O. 'The "vicious circle" hypothesis', *IMF Staff Papers* 26, 1979.
Capie, F. and Collins, M. 'The developed world in recession: an historical comparison', *The Banker* 127, 1977.
Cobham, D. 'The politics of the economics of inflation', *Lloyds Bank Review* 128, 1978.
Cornwall, J. *Modern Capitalism*, Oxford: Martin Robertson, 1977.
Cuthbertson, K. *Macroeconomic Policy: The New Cambridge, Keynesian and Monetarist Controversies*, London: Macmillan, 1979.
Eckstein, O. *The Great Recession*, Amsterdam: North-Holland, 1978.
Eltis, W. 'The failure of Keynesian conventional wisdom', *Lloyds Bank Review* 122, 1976.
Giarini, O. and Loubergé, H. *The Diminishing Returns of Technology: An Essay on the Crisis in Economic Growth*, London: Pergamon, 1978.
Haberler, G. *Economic Growth and Stability*, Los Angeles, CA: Nash, 1974.
Heller, H. R. 'International reserves and world-wide inflation', *IMF Staff Papers* 23, 1976.
Hill, T. P. *Profits and Rates of Return*, Paris: OECD, 1979.
Jones, D. 'Output, employment and labour productivity in Europe since 1955', *National Institute Economic Review* August 1976.
Klein, P. A. *Business Cycles in the Postwar World*, Washington, DC: American Enterprise Institute for Public Policy Research, 1976.
Knox, F. *Governments and Growth*, London: Saxon House, 1976.
—— *Labour Supply in Economic Development*, London: Saxon House, 1979.
McClam, W. D. 'Targets and techniques of monetary policy in western Europe', *Banca Nazionale del Lavoro Quarterly Review* 124, 1978.
Maddison, A. 'Phases of capitalist development', *Banca Nazionale del Lavoro Quarterly Review* 121, 1977.
—— 'Long run dynamics of productivity growth', *Banca Nazionale del Lavoro Quarterly Review* 128, 1979.
Mandel, E. *The Second Slump: A Marxist Analysis of Recession in the Seventies*, London: New Left Books, 1978.
Meiselman, D. I. and Laffer, A. B. (eds) *The Phenomenon of Worldwide Inflation*, Washington, DC: American Enterprise Institute for Public Policy Research, 1975.
Mensch, G. *Stalemate in Technology*, Cambridge, MA: Ballinger, 1979.
OECD *Towards Full Employment and Price Stability*, Paris: OECD, 1977.

—— *Public Expenditure Trends*, Paris: OECD, 1978.
—— *The Case for Positive Adjustment Policies*, Paris: OECD, 1979a.
—— *Facing the Future*, Paris: OECD, 1979b
—— *Monetary Targets and Inflation Control*, Paris: OECD, 1979c.
Oppenheimer, P. M. and Posner, M. V. 'World Economic expansion amidst monetary turbulence', *Midland Bank Review* Spring 1979.
Paldam, M. 'Towards the wage-earner state: a comparative study of wage shares 1948–75', *International Journal of Social Economics* 6, 1979.
Parkin, M. and Zis, G. (eds) *Inflation in the World Economy*, Manchester: Manchester University Press, 1976.
Peacock, A. T. and Shaw, G. K. 'Is fiscal policy dead?', *Banca Nazionale del Lavoro Quarterly Review* 125, 1978.
Perkins, J. O. N. *The Macroeconomic Mix to Stop Inflation*, London: Macmillan, 1980.
Rostow, W. W. *The World Economy: History and Prospect*, London: Macmillan, 1978.
—— *Getting from Here to There*, London: Macmillan, 1979.
Shadow European Economic Policy Committee 'Europe enters the eighties', *Banca Nazionale del Lavoro Quarterly Review* 129, 1979.
Thirlwall, A. P. 'The balance of payments constraint as an explanation of international growth rate differences', *Banca Nazionale del Lavoro Quarterly Review* 128, 1979.
Thornton, J. S. 'The wage/tax spiral in the UK', *The Business Economist* 11, 1979.
Vaciago, G. 'Fiscal versus monetary rules', *Banca Nazionale del Lavoro Quarterly Review* 124, 1978.
Worswick, G. D. N. 'The end of demand management', *Lloyds Bank Review* 123, 1977.

CHAPTER 8   WESTERN EUROPE IN THE 1980s: THE SEARCH FOR STABILITY

Abramovitz, M. *Thinking About Growth*, Cambridge: Cambridge University Press, 1989.
Adams, W. J. *Restructuring the French Economy: Government and the Rise of Market Competition since the War*, Washington, DC: Brookings Institution, 1989.
Atkinson, P. and Chouraqui, J. C. 'The origins of high real interest rates', *OECD Economic Studies* 5, 1985.
Baker, L., Brittan, A. and Major, R. 'Macroeconomic policy in France and Britain', *National Institute Economic Review* 110, 1984.
Barbone, L. and Poret, P. 'Structural conditions and macroeconomic responses to shocks: a sensitivity analysis for four European countries', *OECD Economic Studies* 12, 1989.
Boltho, A. (1984) 'Economic policy and performance in Europe since the second oil shock', in M. Emerson (ed.) *Europe's Stagflation*, Oxford: Oxford University Press, ch. 17.
Brett, E. A. *The World Economy since the War: The Politics of Uneven Development*, London: Macmillan, 1985.
Chan-Lee, J. H. and Sutch, H. 'Profits and rates of return', *OECD Economic Studies* 5, 1985.
——, Coe, D. T. and Prynes, M. 'Macroeconomic changes and macroeconomic wage disinflation in the 1980s', *OECD Economic Studies* 8, 1987.
Coe, D. T. 'Nominal wages, the NAIRU and wage flexibility', *OECD Economic Studies* 5, 1985.
—— and Holtham, G. 'Output responsiveness and inflation: an aggregate study', *OECD Economic Studies* 1, 1985.

Coe, D. T., Durand, M. and Stiehler, U. 'The disinflation of the 1980s', *OECD Economic Studies* 11, 1988.

Commission of the European Communities *European Economy* 42, 1989.

—— *European Economy*, 46, 1990.

Dean, A., Durand, M., Fallon, J. and Hoeller, P. 'Savings trends and behaviour in OECD countries', *OECD Economic Studies* 14, 1990.

Duchene, F. and Shepherd, G. (eds) *Managing Industrial Change in Western Europe*, London: Pinter, 1987.

Emerson, M. (ed.) *Europe's Stagflation*, Oxford: Oxford University Press, 1984.

Englander, A. S. and Mittelstadt, A. 'Total factor productivity and structural aspects of the slowdown', *OECD Economic Studies* 10, 1988.

Englander, A. S., Evenson, R. and Hanazaki, M. 'R&D, innovation and the total factor productivity slowdown', *OECD Economic Studies* 11, 1988.

Fitoussi, J. and Phelps, E. S. *Slump in Europe*, Oxford: Blackwell, 1988.

Friedlander, R. and Sanders, J. 'The public economy and economic growth in western market economies', *American Sociological Review* 50, 1985.

Graham, A. and Seldon, A. (eds) *Government and Economies in the Postwar World: Economic Policies and Comparative Performance 1945–85*, London: Routledge, 1990.

Haberler, G. 'The slowdown of the world economy and the problem of stagflation', in D. Lal and M. Wolf (eds) *Stagflation, Savings and the State*, New York: Oxford University Press, 1986.

Katz, C. J., Mahler, V. A. and Franz, M. G. 'The impact of taxes on growth and distribution in developed capitalist economies: a cross national study', *American Political Science Review* 77, 1983.

Lal, D. and Wolf, M. (eds) *Stagflation, Savings and the State: Perspectives on the Global Economy*, New York: Oxford University Press, 1986.

Lawrence, R. Z. and Schultz, C. L. (eds) *Barriers to European Growth: a Transatlantic View*. Washington, DC: Brookings Institution, 1987.

Layard, R., Nickell, S. and Jackman, R. *Unemployment: Macroeconomic Performance and the Labour Market*, Oxford: Oxford University Press, 1991.

Llewellyn, J. 'Resources, prices and macroeconomic policies: lessons from two oil price shocks', *OECD Economic Studies* 1, 1983.

McCormick, B. J. *The World Economy: Patterns of Growth and Change*, Oxford: Philip Allan, 1988.

Maddison, A. 'Growth and slowdown in advanced capitalist economies: techniques of quantitative assessment', *Journal of Economic Literature* 25, 1987.

—— *The World Economy in the Twentieth Century*, Paris: OECD, 1989.

Marglin, S. and Schor, J. *The Golden Age of Capitalism: Reinterpreting the Postwar Experience*, Oxford: Clarendon Press, 1990.

Marris, S. 'Why Europe's recovery is lagging behind, with an unconventional view of what should be done about it', *Europe* March–April 1984.

OECD *Structural Adjustment and Economic Performance*, Paris: OECD, 1987.

—— *Historical Statistics 1960-1989*, Paris: OECD, 1991.

Oxley, H. and Martin, J. P. 'Controlling government spending and deficits: trends in the 1980s and prospects for the 1990s', *OECD Economic Studies* 17, 1991.

Price, R. W. R. and Muller, P. 'Structural budget indicators and the interpretation of fiscal policy stance in OECD countries', *OECD Economic Studies* 5, 1985.

Sassoon, D., 'Italy', in Graham, A. and Seldon, A. (eds) *Government and Economies in the Postwar World: Economic Policies and Comparative Performance 1945–85*, London: Routledge, 1990.

Saunders, P. and Klau, F. 'The role of the public sector: causes and consequences of the growth of government', *OECD Economic Studies* 4, 1985.

Schafer, J. R. 'What the U.S. current account deficit of the 1980s has meant for other OECD countries', *OECD Economic Studies* 10, 1988.

Somers, F. (ed.) *European Economies: a Comparative Study*, London: Pitman, 1991.

Tsoukalis, L. *The New European Economy: the Politics and Economics of Integration*, Oxford: Oxford University Press, 1991.

United Nations *World Economic Survey 1990*, New York: United Nations, 1990.

—— *Economic Survey of Europe 1990–1991*, New York: United Nations, 1991.

Urwin, D. *Western Europe since the War*, London: Longman, 1989.

CHAPTER 9 EASTERN EUROPE IN TRANSITION, 1970–1990

Aage, H. 'Economic problems and reforms: Andropov's 15 months', *Nordic Journal of Soviet and East European Studies (Sweden)* 1 (2), 1984.

Almond, M. *The Rise and Fall of Nicolae and Elena Ceausescu*, London: Chapman and Hall, 1991.

Aslund, A. *Gorbachev's Struggle for Economic Reform*, London: Pinter, 1989.

Borend, I. *The Hungarian Economic Reforms 1953–1988*, Cambridge: Cambridge University Press, 1990.

Bryson, P. J. and Melzer, M. *The End of the East German Economy*, London: Macmillan, 1991.

Carter, B. and Singleton, F. *The Economy of Yugoslavia*, London: Croom Helm, 1982.

Childs, D. *The GDR: Moscow's German Ally*, London: Allen & Unwin, 1983.

Commission of the European Communities *European Economies Special Edition No. 2: The Path of Reform in Central and Eastern Europe*, Brussels: European Community, 1991.

Dawiska, K. *Eastern Europe, Gorbachev and Reform*, Cambridge: Cambridge University Press, 2nd edn, 1990.

De Nevers, R. *The Soviet Union and Eastern Europe: The End of an Era*, London: Brasseys, 1990.

Derbyshire, I. *The Politics in the Soviet Union*, London: Chambers, 1987.

Dowson, A. H. *Planning in Eastern Europe*, London: Croom Helm, 1986.

Drewnowski, J. (ed.) *Crisis in the East European Economy*, London: Croom Helm, 1982.

Federal Institute for Soviet and International Studies *The Soviet Union, 1987–1989: Perestroika in Crisis?*, London: Longman, 1990.

Gilberg, T. *Nationalism and Communism in Romania*, Oxford: Westview Press, 1990.

Gomulka, S. *Growth, Innovation and Reform in Eastern Europe*, Madison, WI: University of Wisconsin Press, 1986.

Goodman, M. I. *What Went Wrong With Perestroika*, New York: Norton, 1991.

Graziani, G. 'Dependency structures in Comecon', *Review of Radical Political Economy* 13, 1981.

International Monetary Fund and others *A Study of the Soviet Economy*, 3 vols, Paris: OECD, 1991.

Johnson, P. M. *Redesigning the Communist Economy*, New York: Boulder, 1981.

Kennedy, P. *The Rise and Fall of the Great Powers*, London: Unwin Hyman, 1988.

Korbonski, A. 'CMEA, economic integration and perestroika: 1949–1989', *Studies in Comparative Communism* 23, 1990.

Lane, D. *Soviet Society under Perestroika*, London: Routledge, 2nd edn, 1992.

McAuley, A. (ed.) *Soviet Federalism: Nationalism and Economic Decentralisation*, Leicester: Leicester University Press, 1991.

Narkiewicz, O. A. *Eastern Europe 1968–1984*, London: Croom Helm, 1986.

Nello, S. S. *The New Europe: Changing Economic Relations between East and West*, London: Harvester Wheatsheaf, 1991.

Nove, A., Hohmann, H. H. and Seidenstecher, G. *The East European Economies in the 1970s*, London: Butterworth, 1982.

Okey, R. *Crisis in Eastern Europe: Roots and Prospects*, London: Social Market Foundation, 1990.

Pockney, B. P. *Soviet Statistics since 1950*, Aldershot: Gower, 1991.

Schopflin, G. 'The end of communism in eastern Europe', *International Affairs* 66, 1990.

Selbourne, D. *Death of the Dark Hero: Eastern Europe, 1987–90*, London: Cape, 1990.

Spulber, N. *Restructuring the Soviet Economy*, Ann Arbor, MI: University of Michigan Press, 1991.

Summerscale, P. *The East European Predicament*, Aldershot: Gower, 1982.

Sword, K. (ed.) *The Times Guide to Eastern Europe*, London: Times Books, 1990.

United Nations, *Economic Survey of Europe in 1981*, New York: United Nations, 1982.

—— *Economic Survey of Europe in 1989–1990*, New York: United Nations, 1990.

—— *Economic Survey of Europe in 1990–1991*, New York: United Nations, 1991.

Van Brabant, J. M. *Remaking Eastern Europe – On the Political Economy of Transition*, London: Kluwer, 1990.

Wadekin, K. E. (ed.) *Communist Agriculture: Farming in the Soviet Union and Eastern Europe*, London: Routledge, 1990.

Winiecki, J. *The Distorted World of Soviet-type Economies*, London: Routledge, 1988.

Zwass, A. *The Economies of Eastern Europe in a Time of Change*, London: Macmillan, 1984.

INDEX

Africa 13
agriculture 13, 32, 37, 38, 44, 147, 173,
  263; collectivization of 170, 189;
  decline in share of 135, 175, 176,
  177; importance of in eastern Europe
  37–8, 44–6, 88–9, 93–4, 175–6, 177;
  in wartime 13, 112–13; recovery of
  after Second World War 122, 130
Albania 128, 129, 253
Allied Supreme Council 23
Alsace-Lorraine 19, 20, 97
American Relief Administration 23
Andropov, Yuri 267
Asia 14
Australia 15, 69, 211
Austria 4, 17, 19, 26, 30, 31, 41, 44,
  45, 91, 137, 209, 234, 236, 239;
  agricultural production 122;
  depression in 1930s 63, 64; financial
  crisis in 1931 72–3; growth post-1950
  133, 134, 139, 140, 141; industrial
  production 12, 37, 64, 122, 198;
  inflation 11, 33, 36, 50, 52–3, 201;
  output 64, 133–4, 197–8; physical
  destruction after First World War
  8–9; recession in 1970s 197–9;
  Second World War, impact of 109
  passim, and recovery from 122;
  stagnation in 1930s 64, 77, 86–7;
  territorial losses 20–1
Austria-Hungary 13–14; break-up of
  Empire 15, 20–1; inflation 11;
  population losses after First World
  War 6–8; war expenditure 16

balance of payments 124–6, 149, 222
Balkans 8, 9
Baltic countries 15, 44, 45

Bank of England 56
Bank of France 55
Bank for International Economic
  Cooperation 193
Belgium 4, 23, 32, 33, 41, 43, 46, 50,
  75, 137, 237; agriculture 122;
  currency stabilization 53; depression
  early 1930s 64; First World War
  impact 9–10, 33, 38; government
  policies 157; growth post-1950 134,
  136, 139 *passim*, 197–9; industrial
  production 12–13, 38, 122, 198;
  inflation 11, 52, 201; output 64, 134,
  197; recession in early 1970s 197–8;
  Second World War impact 107, 108,
  109 *passim*, and recovery from 123–6;
  war debts 49; war expenditure 10
Berlin 2; blockade of 117, 126–7; slow
  post-war recovery 127, 128; war
  damage 127
Bessarabia 20, 115
Bohemia 21
boom (1919–20) 6, 24, 25–9; causes of
  25–6; consequences of 28–9; reasons
  for collapse of 27–8
boom (later 1920s) 40–6; collapse of 63
  passim
Brezhnev, Leonid 263; doctrine of 253,
  275
budget deficits 219, 221, 224, 231–3,
  243
Bukovina 115
Bulgaria 4, 9, 17, 20, 30, 31, 35, 50,
  64, 90, 106, 253, 269, 275;
  agriculture 88, 170, 177; consumption
  178; economic reforms 187–90;
  growth post-1950 174–7, 179–83;
  incomes 88, 93, 96; industrial